Perspectives on Poverty and Income Distribution

by James G. Scoville
UNIVERSITY OF ILLINOIS

D. C. HEATH AND COMPANY
Lexington, Massachusetts • Toronto • London

Preface

The format of this book and the Editor's critical analyses have evolved from attempts to teach courses on income distribution, poverty and social welfare at Harvard and the University of Illinois and is gratefully dedicated to those students who have endured and illuminated its development.

The readings progress from a general theory of income distribution with particular emphasis on those factors which affect the level of distribution of wage-earners' incomes, in Part 1, to an examination of some of the determinants of income distribution, such as capital ownership and education, in Part 2.

Defining "the problem of poverty" as the existence of unusually low incomes, Part 3 discusses the lower range of income distribution in the United States as well as the incidence of poverty on various social groups and classes. Part 4 takes a lengthy look at the relationship between race and poverty and summarizes two very different theories of racial discrimination.

Since this book accepts the premise that society must increase the incomes of the poor, the remaining three chapters center on actual or alternative approaches. Part 5 focuses on current redistribution of income through the tax system and presents proposals for new programs, particularly the "negative income tax." Part 6 assesses the prospects for the poor through the jobs they can find and the wages they can earn in the labor market. Part 7 is concerned with the growth, level and deficiencies of current public assistance programs and with an alternative proposal for children's allowances. The book ends with President Nixon's message on welfare reform, which embodies the practical results of nearly a decade of debate on the ideas contained in the two previous parts. The language of some of the readings has been altered for matters of consistency.

J.G.S.

Contents

362.5
S43p

Introduction

The framework adopted in this volume differs from the standard, generally descriptive approach to discussing the problem of poverty, social welfare, and economic policy. By and large, presentation of the life-styles and sufferings of the poor will be left to the sociologists and journalists who earn their keep by writing about real life. This book attempts to view the problem of poverty as one aspect of the whole process of income distribution, and then to identify and explore the points in that process where economic policies can be applied to generate a different distribution of income. The schematic presentation shown below will perhaps add clarity.

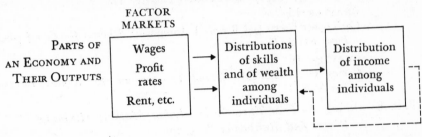

The personal distribution of income is the final output of the system at a particular time. This distribution flows from the two other parts of the economic system. In the first place, we see the factor markets in which the rates of wages, profit, rents and other incomes to the factors of production are determined. These rates of return are then applied to the distribution among individuals of the society's stock of physical and human capital. It is in this simple framework that the personal distribution of income will be analyzed.

Moreover, it is clear that the three pieces of the chain are related in other, more dynamic ways. The personal distribution of income through "feedback" affects the future distribution of the human and physical wealth of the society. The rich will save, and will thus control capital assets in the future; the poor will not save, and they and their offspring will have little chance of increasing future incomes through capital ownership. Analogous feedback and inheritance influences apply to some kinds of education. Thus vicious circles of poverty are born.

One further virtue of the above diagram is that it focuses our attention on the various places in the system where policies can be implemented to alter the final distribution of income among individuals. One possibility is to straightforwardly attack the final outcome, and to take from the rich and give to the poor. Schemes of taxation, most particularly the "negative income tax," are designed to do this.

Yet this is not the only possible approach to the problem of redistributing the final output of the economic system. We could, for example, consider programs to redistribute the ownership of the means of production — the human and physical capital of the society. Socialism is one means of doing this; taxes on the ownership of capital (though rare) are another means. In long-range terms, free education to a high level may reduce existing inequalities in the opportunity to obtain human capital, while death duties and estate taxes may be used to break up concentrations of ownership of physical capital.

One final range of programs which will change the distribution of personal incomes focuses its attack on the factor markets themselves. Minimum wage legislation may serve to raise the bottom end of the income distribution. Other programs — hiring the disadvantaged, creation of new jobs, elimination of discriminatory practices — may raise the incomes of certain groups who were previously unemployed or underpaid.

Part 1

Historical Perspective on Income Distribution

Editor's Survey

Wages are the principal source of individuals' incomes in a modern economy. The average level of wage incomes and the dispersion of these incomes around their average are significant determinants of the degrees of poverty and inequality which characterize a society. Practical considerations, as well as the dictates of economic theory, lead to concern with the distribution of some 70 percent of the GNP of the U.S. and other industrialized countries. This introductory chapter attempts to synthesize the historical development of economists' thinking about labor incomes. The readings which follow this chapter will deal with modifications of the wage theory we have, with the influence of unequal distributions of property and education on the distribution of income, and with programs designed to alter the income distributions which flow from the operations of a market economy.

In the following, it will be useful to distinguish at the outset between factors influencing the wages paid to differing occupations (or bundles of skills and abilities) and the factors affecting the level of the whole wage structure. It should be clear that the forces determining whether a carpenter earns 25 percent more than a laborer, rather than 24 percent more, are different conceptually from those which yield as their result a carpenter's wage of $7.00 per hour in 1970.

Moreover, in analyzing the way incomes are distributed, it is customary to distinguish between *personal* income distribution and *functional* income distribution. By this distinction, we separate the components of personal income according to the service rendered for which they were paid. Thus, of a family's total income of $8,000, some $7,500 might be wages for labor services in the nearby steel plant; $500 might be interest (income for the services of capital) from a savings bank. This distinction is sometimes rather difficult to make in practice (to separate the labor and capital incomes of the owner-operator of a pizza joint, for example), but may be helpful in organizing our thinking.

With these two brief observations in mind, let us survey the development of economists' hypotheses about the forces and factors behind the process of income distribution. Because the emphasis of modern economists is on moving from the moral imperatives of "what ought to be" to the analysis of "what is," we shall begin with Adam Smith, whose *The Wealth of Nations* (1776) is considered the first conventional landmark in economic analysis, and omit any detailed discussion of the medieval writers whose analysis of incomes was firmly rooted in notions of social justice. Their concept of the "just price" for labor was part of a larger social philosophy involving the arrangements for a hierarchial society, where almost everyone has his proper place. Moreover, for some medieval writers, there were forms of income which were morally intolerable — usury foremost among them — and were therefore theoretically unacceptable for Christians. In this particular area, modern students might receive a refresher course in the historical divergence between theory and practice in earthly affairs.

Turning first to the question of why some wages are higher than others, consider the influences Adam Smith described in *The Wealth of Nations:*

> The whole of the advantages and disadvantages of the different employments of labour must, in the same neighbourhood, be either perfectly equal or continually tending to equality.

> If in the same neighbourhood, there was any employment evidently either more or less advantageous than the rest, so many people would crowd into it in the one case, and so many would desert it in the other, that its advantages would soon return to the level of other employments. This at least would be the case in a society where things were left to follow their natural course, where there was perfect liberty, and where every man was perfectly free both to *chuse* what occupation he thought proper, and to change it as often as he thought proper. Every man's interest would prompt him to seek the advantageous, and to shun the disadvantageous employment.

> The five following are the principal circumstances which, so far as I have been able to observe, make up for a small pecuniary gain in some employments, and counter-balance a great one in others:

> First, the wages of labour vary with the ease or hardship, the cleanliness or dirtiness, the honourableness or dishonourableness of the employment. Thus in most places, take the year round, a journeyman taylor earns less than a journeyman weaver. His work is much easier. A journeyman weaver earns less than a journeyman smith. His work is not always easier, but it is much cleaner. A journeyman blacksmith, though an artificer, seldom earns so much in twelve hours as a collier, who is only a labourer, does in eight. His work is not quite so dirty, is less dangerous, and is carried on in day-light and above ground.

> Secondly, the wages of labour vary with the easiness and cheapness, or the difficulty and expence of learning the business. . . . The difference between the wages of skilled labour and those of common labour, is founded upon this principle.

> Thirdly, the wages of labour in different occupations vary with the constancy or inconstancy of employment. Employment is much more constant in some trades than in others. In the greater part of manufactures, a journeyman may be pretty

sure of employment almost every day in the year that he is able to work. A mason or bricklayer, on the contrary, can work neither in hard frost nor in foul weather, and his employment at all other times depends upon the occasional calls of his customers. He is liable, in consequence, to be frequently without any. What he earns, therefore, while he is employed, must not only maintain him while he is idle, but make him some compensation for those anxious and desponding moments which the thought of so precarious a situation must sometimes occasion. Where the computed earnings of the greater part of manufacturers, accordingly, are nearly upon a level with the day wages of common labourers, those of masons and bricklayers are generally from one half more to double those wages .... The high wages of those workmen are not so much the recompence of their skill, as the compensation for the inconstancy of their employment.

Fourthly, the wages of labour vary according to the small or great trust which must be reposed in the workmen. The wages of goldsmiths and jewellers are everywhere superior to those of many other workmen, not only of equal, but of much superior ingenuity; on account of the precious materials with which they are intrusted. We trust our health to the physician; our fortune and sometimes our life and reputation to the lawyer and attorney. Such confidence could not safely be reposed in people of a very mean or low condition. Their reward must be such, therefore, as may give them that rank in the society which so important a trust requires. The long time and the great expence which must be laid out in their education, when combined with this circumstance, necessarily enhance still further the price of their labour.

Fifthly, the wages of labour in different employments vary according to the probability or improbability of success in them. The probability that any particular person shall ever be qualified for the employment to which he is educated, is very different in different occupations. In the greater part of mechanic trades, success is almost certain; but very uncertain in the liberal professions. Put your son apprentice to a shoemaker, there is little doubt of his learning to make a pair of shoes: But send him to study the law, it is at least twenty to one if ever he makes such proficiency as will enable him to live by the business. In a perfectly fair lottery, those who draw the prizes ought to gain all that is lost by those who draw the blanks. In a profession where twenty fail for one that succeeds, that one ought to gain all that should have been gained by the unsuccessful twenty.[1]

In the two centuries since Smith wrote, the analysis of relative earnings for various skills and occupations has become more detailed and sophisticated. Yet for all of the advances, our conception of the influences upon wage differentials remains much as Smith described. As an example, the point about the relative costliness of education and training required has been rediscovered in the 1960's, given a new name — "The Theory of Human Capital" — and blossomed with a substantial literature. Perhaps the only two significant amendments or additions to the Smithian scheme involve the question of relative productivities and the problem of discrimination. As the reader will perceive, most of the influences summarized in *The Wealth of Nations* are those which affect the cost of producing a certain type of worker, which costs determine the position of the supply curve for the various occupations. If one were to assume (in the tradition of the classical economists of Smith's time

[1] (New York: Modern Library, 1937), pp. 100-106.

and after) that the cost of producing a trained worker (or a commodity) is independent of the number or quantity produced, then cost conditions become sufficient to determine the long-run relative wages or prices.[2] If these conditions of constant cost do not hold, then we must know something about the shape of the demand curve for labor in order to find out what the earnings of different trades will be. In brief, the demand curve depends upon the productivity of the workers involved. This amendment to the Smithian argument is discussed more fully below, when the average level of wages is considered.

The second modification to the theory — discrimination — is of much more recent origin. One of the results of discrimination may be variations in the rates of pay within an occupation, so that (for example) a Negro carpenter is paid less than his equally competent white associate, or that a woman receives a lower rate of pay than a man for performing the identical duties. Alternatively, discrimination may show up in the form of restricting employment in certain groups to members of one or another race or sex. Thus, certain construction occupations (the lower paid) are open to and perhaps dominated by Negro workers; others have been historically closed to them. Sleeping car porters are black (however many that may be) while locomotive engineers are white. The same type of job demarcation applies to sex: nurses and grade school teachers are women; doctors and college teachers are men. We shall discuss two models of discrimination and some of their implications particularly as they apply to race in Part IV.

So much for differences in wages among persons. As we consider the proportion of the population below a poverty standard, it is clear that one major determinant is the average level of wages. What have economists had to say about the forces behind average wages?

Considering workers as a more or less homogeneous group, undifferentiated by skills or other inherent or acquired abilities, let us first look at Smith's analysis of the determinants of "the" wage rate for this work force. This line of analysis not only survived in principle as economic doctrine for nearly a century, but can still be found in an occasional conservative economic column or public service message. This analysis, for reasons that will be obvious, went by the title of "The Doctrine of the Wages Fund." It was asserted (and assumed) by Smith and his successors that there existed a "fund destined for the payment of wages," which was the result of society's accumulated savings out of all its past income less that part of those savings which had been tied up in physical capital — machinery, buildings, etc. Individual employers who held portions of this Wages Fund would use it (by definition) for the employment of labor. At any point in time, there is a fixed number of laborers competing for the employment which this fund would support, and it is simply

[2] You may visualize this in terms of the standard supply and demand diagram found in your textbook; if the supply curve is horizontal (perfectly elastic in the long run), then the positioning of the demand curve is irrelevant to the answer you will get regarding long-run relative prices.

the ratio between the size of the fund (WF) and the number of laborers (L) that determines the wage rate (w). The greater the Wages Fund or the less the number of workers seeking to share in that fund, the higher would be the short-run level of wages. In the longer run of history, it was expected that the population (and hence the number of competing laborers) would adjust in response to high or low wages, so that long-run equilibrium wages would approximate those required for subsistence (note again the interactions of assumptions and analysis, and particularly the crucial importance of the meaning of "subsistence").

The foregoing is a crude, and to some extent unfair summary of the first scientific attempt at an economic theory of the average level of wages. Most writers would have been dismayed at our simplistic treatment as they dealt with complexities which we do not have time for in this essay. For example, Ricardo was aware that "subsistence income" could be culturally determined, and hence was susceptible to change over time.[3] But for our purposes, let us note some of the principal results and conclusions which can be drawn from it:

1. It is not a rich country, but rather one that is rapidly growing, that will have high wages. Rapid growth will mean that the Wages Fund is "leading" the number of laborers with consequent upward pressure on wages. Countries which are not growing, whatever their richness, will find population adjusting to the "funds destined for its support" through the pseudo-mechanism of the subsistence wage.

2. It can be established that a trade union can have no direct beneficial effect on the laboring populace. The Wages Fund is fixed, hence if wages are raised, it follows directly that some workers must be thrown out of jobs. If allowed to do so, those disemployed would compete the wage rate back to its original level. If not allowed to compete with the union members, they would compete with other nonunion workers, driving their wage rate down. Either way, the average of all wages in the society would remain the same. A similar analysis can be applied to enactment of a minimum wage.[4]

3. It is possible, with rather rigid assumptions, to establish that increased use of machinery is deleterious to the welfare of the workers. David Ricardo, a most ingenious economist, turned this trick by observing that — by definition — the source of capital for investing in more machinery had to be the Wages Fund. Thus, increased mechanization reduced the size of the fund, while the number of laborers remained unchanged — wages or employment must therefore go down.

We should note that these three problems are still matters of concern to economists and laymen alike. Moreover, with particular regard to Propositions

---

[3] Note that the long-run Wage-Fund, Population, and Wage-Level analysis becomes even fuzzier with this admission.

[4] To any charge of over-simplification of the analysis, one can point to the treatment by Robert Torrens; a political economist and member of Parliament in the early 1800's, which is not significantly more sophisticated.

1 and 3, the conclusions of later economic theory are particularly in disagreement. Proposition 3 was hardly even accepted at the time Ricardo enunciated it.

Moving forward in time with the question of the average level of wages, we shall consider the two traditions evolving from the classical approach which seem to have most claim for our attention. The first of these streams of thought is associated with Karl Marx and his intellectual descendants, whose approaches to the problem of wages and income distribution are quite clearly in the classical spirit.

The Marxian Approach

Karl Marx maintained the classical distinction between fixed capital (machinery, etc.) and circulating capital (which we have called the Wages Fund). Capitalists pay out circulating capital (or variable capital, in Marx's terminology) to workers in the form of wages, and receive in return the output of the worker's labor. In this regard, the theory differs little from that of Smith and Ricardo; in fact, much of our discussion will involve putting different name-tags on many of the same classical concepts.

At the risk of offending Marxists and/or scholars in Marxist theory, the exposition of Marxian wage theory and its translation into current English will be brief and incomplete with a simple goal in mind — to present an example of a wage theory based on "exploitation" of labor.

By Marx's analysis, the value[5] of the commodities which the capitalist receives from his work force far exceeds the wages paid to them. In part, this difference arises from the wear and tear (depreciation) of any capital goods associated with labor in the process of production. Such depreciation charges are a legitimate part of the cost of any good. But even when depreciation is allowed for, wages are still below the value added to the commodity through the worker's efforts. This difference Marx calls surplus value, and it, in relation to the wage actually paid the worker, is a measure of the intensity with which labor is being exploited. Note that, in contrast with the customary loose usage of the pejorative term, exploitation, we see here a definition which may have some empirical meaning.

There is, according to Marx, a variety of reasons why workers are subjected to exploitation. Their wages may be held down because there are relatively too many of them, due in part to the rapidity of technological change and consequent rates of worker displacement which occur under capitalism. Yet behind all the reasons lies a common cause: capitalists own capital and hence

---

[5] It is not the purpose of this book to cover all aspects of historical economic theorizing, so I beg forgiveness for omitting a lengthy discussion of just what "value" might mean. Let us only draw attention to the fact that value for Marx means something rather different than it does in common dollars-and-cents terms. This it tied up with Marx's interpretation of something called "The Labor Theory of Value."

the absolute power over workers' fates; the worker, destitute of capital as he is, has no choice but to submit to the employers' terms.

Behind this line of reasoning stands a point which is of particular concern to students of the economics of income distribution. This problem centers on the role and function of profit in a market economy. You will notice above that, in determining the degree of worker exploitation, we subtracted from the value of output only the workers' wages and the wear and tear on capital goods. The question: is the role of capital in production limited to passing on its value in the form of depreciation?[6] More specifically, does capital not have a productivity of its own, which makes a contribution to the total output above and beyond the value of the equipment involved? If the answer to this question is yes — to which most modern economists would agree — then the owners of capital goods, like the owners of skills and effort, will receive from the market economy a reward (profit) for their possessions' contribution to output. The next section deals with the other side of this case.

One reason for this brief excursion into Marxism is to be found in a recent resuscitation of classical notions by Baran and Sweezey. Their 1966 volume, *Monopoly Capital,* has been enjoying considerable vogue among the Student Left and New Left. Its intellectual ancestry is unclear to some students, as it represents an attempt to translate the classical Marxian hypotheses for the most part into modern English. However, much of the analysis is closer to Smith in its emphasis on society's economic surplus than to Marx and a focus on exploitation. Most modern economists are not concerned that their basic format for analysis is between one and two centuries old, but would point out that like Marx, they have endorsed the position that capital is a passive and non-productive part of the process of production.

Neoclassical Economics and the Marginal Revolution

By the 1870's, the classical theory of wage determination was in serious difficulty. On the one hand, the doctrine of the Wages Fund possessed deficiencies that could not be remedied; in particular, the fact that the size of the fund itself could not be satisfactorily determined by existing theory. If the fund destined for the maintenance of labor was indeterminate, so then was the level of the average wage rate. On the other hand, the role of profits along with much of the theoretical apparatus of economics was confronted by the Marxian challenge. The marginalist approach was successful inasmuch as it countered both of these difficulties.

One feature of this marginalist approach was an updated (if rather more removed from real life) theoretical conception of the employment relation-

---

[6] Visualize this as follows: You buy or build an oven to bake bread, and know that it will wear out after 1 million loaves have been produced. Thus, one one-millionth of the price of the oven is entered into the cost of producing each loaf of bread. By Marxian accounting, the contribution of capital to output is limited to this transference.

ship between employer and worker. The classicists and Marx had viewed the employer as possessing a fund which he expended on the hiring of workers or the "purchase of labor-power." The employer advanced the wages to the worker, who then performed labor and gave over the output to the employer. This conception rather clearly embodies elements of the employment relationship of an earlier day. Consider a farmer who employs hands throughout the season, in principle paying them wages by which they are supported, and finally recouping the Wages Fund, plus profits, at the harvest. The marginalists substituted shorter time lags between effort and output, with a greater emphasis on the simultaneity of workers' efforts and their wage reward.

Here we conceive of an employer, who possesses (for example) a machine which needs the assistance of labor in the process of production. This case might be reflected by data such as those in Table 1. Here the owner of the machine has asked his engineers for technical data on production and his economic seer for an estimate of the price for which it will sell. He has then obtained the following information:

TABLE 1. *Output and Revenue per Day from Employing Labor with a Hypothetical Machine*

Number of Men Employed	Number of Doofers	Price of Doofers	Total Revenue	Marginal (Incremental) Revenue
0	0	$2	0	—
1	20	2	$ 40	$40
2	35	2	70	30
3	45	2	90	20
4	50	2	100	10
5	50	2	100	0

In this very simplified example, all that the manufacturer now needs to know is the price for which he can hire labor, namely the going wage rate, and he will then know how many he should hire. If it costs $25 per day to hire a worker, he will gladly hire the first man, thereby adding $40 to his revenue but only $25 to his costs, and he will also hire the second man. A third man would add only $20 to his income, while costing him $25; he will not be hired. This, in barest outline, is the working of the marginal theory at the enterprise level.

By extension of this line of reasoning, it can be shown that a competitive market economy will produce a set of wage rates and prices for other productive factors which correspond exactly to their marginal contributions to output. Moreover, under certain conditions, it can be established that the factor prices so determined will achieve the pleasing result of allocating the whole of GNP among the various claimants. In other words, if each worker is paid his marginal product, each landowner receives the mp of his land, and each owner of machines and equipment the mp of those capital goods, when we add up the incomes that result, precisely 100 percent — no more, no less — of GNP will have been distributed between labor, capital, and landholders. Not only does this present us with some theoretical justification for confidence in the workability of a competitive market system, it has also disposed of the Marxian "bugbear" — exploitation. Where can we find exploitation if each worker, like each unit of capital or land, is being compensated for its independent marginal contribution to output? In his euphoria at demolishing the Marxian challenge, one could go even further as did J. B. Clark — observing the theoretical niceties of the marginal model, he exclaimed "Truly the laborer is worthy of his hire!"

Insofar as economists possess a decent theory of wages, the marginal productivity approach still holds the place of honor. But matters are clearly not so simple. We must recognize a variety of theoretical and practical considerations which may weaken or invalidate conclusions derived from the marginal model. The first of these is purely theoretical — the assumptions needed to generate the results above are quite restrictive. For instance, the outcome is not so satisfying if some industries in our economy are characterized by economies of scale. Secondly, we must take cognizance of the sheer fact that our economy has never been (and never will be) composed of atomistic firms freely competing for both the consumer's dollar and for the services of the factors of production. Industrial giants dot the landscape, possessing some monopoly power in the sale of their products along with considerable power to influence the prices they pay for factors of production. The labor market contains powerful institutions — unions — whose express purpose is to thwart the forces of competition. Laws and social customs further interfere with the operations of markets. Finally, once "capital" has taken form in specific kinds of machines and "labor" has become a concrete set of skills, the factors of production lose the short-run flexibility which we assumed in Table 1.

For these reasons among many others, it is clear that the marginal theory is likely to reveal relatively few insights about the short-run operations of the labor market. Let us, for example, consider the 1970 request by the Teamsters Union for a 75 percent increase in wages over the coming three years. Ignoring inflation for the moment, are we to interpret this as meaning that they think their marginal productivity has gone up by that percentage? Would a knowledge of the marginal theory have allowed us to predict an increase of that size? Rather clearly, the answers to those questions must be no. An analysis of the case would stress the bargaining power of the Teamsters in comparison to the truck owners, the rate of expansion of the industry, the level of profits, and so on.

Such would be the case with most questions of day-to-day wage determination, or with the levels of other factor prices as well. Yet there may be a role for the marginal theory in analyzing long-term changes. Returning to Table 1, suppose the manufacturer of doofers has made his decision, and set up his plant with one machine manned by two workers. Should a strong labor union or minimum wage law appear on the scene, raising the wage to $35 a day, our manufacturer would perhaps like to lay off the second man. In this regard, in the short run, the design of his machine and the layout of his plant are likely to have him "locked in" to a 1 machine: 2 men circumstance that he cannot evade. In the long run, however, when the machine wears out, he will redesign the work to employ only one man. These sorts of adjustments can be predicted by the marginal theory. John L. Lewis was well aware that higher wages would stimulate mechanization of the mines, resulting in fewer jobs for coal miners. The long-term disappearance of the soda jerk is probably not due to changes in Americans' desire for sundaes, but rather to the widespread introduction of minimum wages in excess of their productivity.

Even if we grant the theory some power of long-term prediction, most of the interesting short-term cases remain exceptions to the rule. Much of the reading that follows involves situations where the mechanism has clearly broken down, and where the breakdown may tend toward self-perpetuation. Other readings focus on the social welfare policy measures undertaken as possible correctives. The utility of the above brief refresher course on wage theory lies mainly in reminding us of the long-term adjustments which may take place in response to a change in one of the solutions coming out of the system.

Part 2

The Distributions of Income, Wealth, and Education

Editor's Survey

This part has a dual purpose: to look at the structure and evolution of income distribution in the United States, and to examine the underlying distributions of wealth ownership and education. It is perhaps unfortunate that the three major selections are rather "dated," but we are restricted to working with such data as are available. As the results of the 1970 Census emerge, new studies should appear, which will bring the record up to date.

The selection by Haley is largely self-explanatory, as he surveys the numerous factors which could have an impact on the personal and functional distributions of income. The data reveal that income distribution in the U.S. became more equal between 1929 and the end of World War II, while the degree of inequality has remained remarkably stable since then. Haley takes us behind this statistical record to focus upon the changes which have occurred in the forces which shape income distributions. The Lampman and Miller articles deal in more depth with two of the most important underlying factors.

To assist in our evaluation of the American record on income equality, some United Nations data pertaining to income distribution in Europe have been included. These findings may not strike the student as being particularly relevant to a pressing American problem. They do, however, provide a yardstick by which we may judge whether income inequality or poverty is a peculiarly American problem. The United States does not seem to fall near either extreme of the equality scale, while the level of income per capita in the U.S. is certainly greater than in many of the countries for which data are presented.

Beyond comparisons with other countries, there are more difficult questions that the student should raise in the process of evaluating America's income distribution. In a market economy, there are a number of functions which dispersions in income are supposed to perform — to what extent do the personal and functional distributions here surveyed seem to be doing the job?

15

Where (as in the case of race) do they seem aberrant? What impacts will future changes that you might foresee in the level and distribution of education, the regional residential patterns, or type of industry have on income inequality in the United States?

Finally, a technical point on the measurement of income inequality needs to be cleared up. At a number of points, reference is made to "concentration ratios" or "Gini coefficients." By either name, this is a very simple measure of inequality of distribution, which is easily explained by reference to the diagram below. Suppose that you had income data for all the households in the United States; you could then arrange this information to rank households from bottom to top in size of income. You would then be able to find out what percentage of the total income of all households was received by various fractions of the number of households. Thus, the bottom 10% might receive 2% of the income, while the top 5% receive 20%. This distribution would be shown by the curved line in the diagram below. If all households had equal

DISTRIBUTION OF INCOME

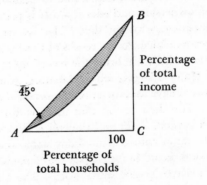

Percentage of total households

income, the cumulative distribution would coincide with the 45° line: 10% of the households would have 10% of the total income, etc. The further away from the diagonal, the more unequal is the distribution of income.

The Gini ratio is calculated from this type of data in the following way. Since the 45° line represents perfect equality, the deviation of the actual distribution from it will measure inequality. The Gini ratio is simply the value of the shaded area divided by the whole area of the triangle ABC. For perfect equality, its value would be zero; for perfect inequality (100% of the income in the hands of one household), it would have value of one.

CHAPTER 1

Changes in the Distribution of Income in the United States

Bernard F. Haley

The purpose of the present paper is to present a selection from the wealth of data bearing on changes in the distribution of income in the United States, and to indicate some of the more important structural changes in the U.S. economy that have had an impact on the distribution.* Although data available would permit a consideration of income distribution by occupation, by race, by age-groups, by regions, by education, and other variables, attention will be mainly focused on: (1) the changes in the size distribution of income for the United States as a whole since 1929, and (2) changes in the distribution between property and labour in the United States since 1850.

I. The Size Distribution of Income

Estimates of the size distribution of personal incomes of families and unattached individuals in the United States are given, in 1963 dollars, in Table 1.[1] The pattern of the distribution is the typical one: strongly skewed, a modal income well below the mean income per family, and a long tail stretching over the upper-income range. Since 1929 the whole distribution has moved upward in real terms, although it was lower than in 1929 during a substantial part of the 1930's. For the entire period 1929-63 the average rate of growth in the mean income (in 1963 prices) was 1.6 percent.

As the income distribution has moved upwards, it has also flattened somewhat, the percentage of consumer units in the lower-income classes decreasing, that in the upper-income classes increasing, and the percentage in the modal

Reprinted from Jean Marchal and Bernard Ducros, editors, *The Distribution of National Income* (New York: Saint Martin's Press, 1968), by permission of the publisher. © 1968 The International Economic Association. Also reprinted by permission of Macmillan and Company, Ltd.
* The author is heavily indebted to M. W. Reder for helpful comments on an earlier draft.

class decreasing. This tendency for the distribution to flatten is not necessarily accompanied by a reduction in the degree of inequality of the distribution.[2] The latter is more clearly revealed in Table 2, which shows the distribution among quintiles and the top 5 percent of consumer units for selected years.

TABLE 1. *Size Distribution of Personal Income of Consumer Units 1929, 1941, 1947, 1963 (Dollars of 1963)*

Income	Percent Distribution			
	1929	1941	1947	1963
Under $2,000	30	27	16	11
$2,000-$3,999	38	28	28	18
$4,000-$5,999	16	22	26	20
$6,000-$7,999	7	12	14	18
$8,000-$9,999	3	5	7	12
$10,000-$14,999 }	6	6	{ 6	13
$15,000 and over }			{ 3	8
Average (Mean) Income Per Consumer Unit	$4,300	$4,599*	$5,520	$7,510

*1962 dollars.
SOURCES: U.S. Department of Commerce.
Note—*Consumer units consist of families and unattached individuals. Families are units of two or more persons related by blood, marriage, or adoption and residing together. Unattached individuals are persons not living with relatives. Family personal income include wage and salary receipts, other labour income, proprietors' and rental income, dividends, personal interest income, and transfer payments. Certain imputed items are included, such as non-monetary wages, net value of food and fuel consumed by farm-operated families, net rental value of owner-occupied homes, and imputed interest.*

TABLE 2. *Distribution of Family Personal Income among Quintiles and Top 5 Percent of Consumer Units in Various Years*

Quintiles	Percent Distribution					
	1929	1935-36	1941	1947	1955	1962
Lowest }	13	{ 4	4	5	5	5
Second }		{ 9	10	11	11	11
Third	14	14	15	16	16	16
Fourth	19	21	22	22	22	23
Highest	54	52	49	46	45	45
Top 5 percent	30.0	26.5	24.0	20.9	20.3	19.6

SOURCES: For the 1929 figures, U.S. Bureau of the Census, 1960, *Historical Statistics of the United States, Colonial Times to 1957;* 1935-36 and 1941, *Rev. Econ. Stat.,* February, 1954; 1947, 1955, and 1962, *Surv. Curr. Bus.,* April 1958 and *Surv. Curr. Bus.,* April 1964.

It is clear that in the period 1929-47 a significant reduction in the inequality of the distribution occurred.[3] This is shown by both an increase in the share of the lowest two quintiles and a decrease in the share of the highest quintile and, even more, in the share of the top 5 percent of consumer units. The Gini concentration ratio* decreased from .47 for the income of consumer units in 1935-36 to .41 in 1946.[4]

Since 1947 the inequality of the distribution has not changed significantly. This is brought out more clearly in Table 3 in which changes in the respective shares of the top and lowest income groups, as estimated by three different

TABLE 3. *The Share of the Top and the Lowest Income Group as Estimated by the Department of Commerce, the Bureau of the Census, and the Survey Research Center*

	Family Personal Income (Commerce)		Family Income (Census)		Income of Spending Units (Survey Research Center)	
	Lowest Quintile	Top 5 Percent	Lowest Quintile	Top 5 Percent	Lowest Quintile	Top 5 Percent
1947	5.0	20.9	5	18	4	33
1948	n.a.	n.a.	5	17	4	31
1949	n.a.	n.a.	5	17	4	30
1950	4.8	20.4	4	17	4	29
1951	5.0	21.0	5	17	4	31
1952	4.9	21.0	5	18	4	30
1953	4.9	20.0	5	16	4	31
1954	4.8	20.0	4	16	4	29
1955	4.8	20.3	5	17	4	30
1956	4.8	20.2	5	16	4	31
1957	4.7	20.2	5	16	4	29
1958	4.7	20.0	5	16	4	27
1959	4.6	20.0	5	16	4	29
1960	4.6	19.6	5	17	4	28
1961	4.6	19.6	5	18	4	30
1962	4.6	19.6	5	16	n.a.	n.a.

SOURCES: Department of Commerce, *Surv. Curr. Bus.*, April 1958; *Surv. Curr. Bus.*, April 1964. Census, *Current Population Reports*, Series P-60, No. 33, January 1960; No. 41, October 1963. Survey Research Center *Federal Reserve Bulletin*, July 1954, August 1957, July 1959; *1962 Survey of Consumer Finances*, p. 12.

Note—The Department of Commerce figures are for consumer units (families and unattached individuals). The Census figures are for families only. The Survey Research Center figures are for spending units (a spending unit consists of persons living in the same dwelling and belonging to the same family who pool their incomes to meet major expenses).

* The Gini concentration ratio is the ratio of the area between the diagonal line of complete equality and the Lorenz curve of income distribution to the entire triangular area under the diagonal.

agencies, can be compared. The Dept. of Commerce figures, carried to one decimal place, appear to show a slight decrease in the relative share of both the lowest quintile and the top 5 percent of consumer units. But the Bureau of Census and the Survey Research Center series, available only as rounded off, show no such tendencies. The concentration ratio,[5] which was .41 for 1944, 1946, and 1950, was .39 for 1952, .4 for 1956, and .4 for 1958, the last year for which it was computed.[6]

Various hypotheses have been advanced to explain the reduction in inequality in the period 1929-47 and the absence of any significant change in inequality in the period since 1947.

(1) Changes in the Relative Importance of the Various Types of Income

As Table 4 shows, the percentage share of wages and salaries increased sharply between 1929 and 1939. It increased again between 1950 and 1953, but has been relatively stable since 1953. Transfer payments also increased during the 1930's and again in the period since 1953.

TABLE 4. *Percent Distribution of Family Personal Income by Major Types of Income, in Various Years (Billion dollars)*

Type of Income	1929	1939	1947	Average 1950-55	Average 1956-62	1962
Wages and salaries	59.6	63.3	63.5	66.6	67.1	66.8
Transfer payments	1.7	4.0	6.3	5.7	7.4	8.1
	61.3	67.3	69.8	72.3	74.5	74.9
Self-employment income	17.6	16.3	19.1	15.6	12.5	11.6
Property income	21.1	16.4	11.1	12.1	12.9	13.5

SOURCES: 1929 and 1939 *Am. Econ. Rev.*, Proc., May 1957, 47; other years *Surv. Curr. Bus.*, April 1963.

Self-employment income, which increased in relative importance during the war, has shown a declining percentage share since 1947. Both the increase during the war and the decline since the war are due in considerable part to underlying changes in the relative importance of farm-operator income. In 1947, the mean income of farm-operator families was nearly four times as high as it was in 1936, while the mean income of non-farm families was only a little more than twice as high.[7] On the other hand, since 1947 the mean income of farm-operator families has risen only 40 percent, while the mean income of all consumer units has risen about 70 percent;[8] and the number of farm-operator families has declined while the total of consumer units has been increasing. At the same time there has occurred a slight decrease in the percentage share of business and professional income in the aggregate of personal income for non-farm families, while the share of wages and salaries in this aggregate has moderately increased.[9] These latter two changes no doubt have reflected a shift from self-employment to employee status in the non-farm sector.

Property income (interest, rent, dividends) as a percentage of family personal income declined sharply between 1929 and 1947, and has increased slightly since the latter year. Also, both interest and dividends, but particularly the latter, have been included in the incomes of an increasing proportion of consumer units during the past decade.[10] Among the circumstances responsible for the decline in the relative share of property income in 1929-47 were: the decline in interest rates, low corporate profits during the 'thirties, and the high corporate income taxes imposed during the war and after.

An increase in the share of wages and salaries, such as occurred particularly in the period 1929-39 and since 1953, would tend to reduce the share of the upper-income groups even if the increase were distributed proportionately to all of the recipients of this type of income; for wages and salaries constitute a much smaller share of the incomes of those in upper-income groups than of those in lower-income groups. Also, the concentration ratio for wages and salaries is typically lower than for self-employment income or for property income.[11] Since transfer payments go mainly to lower-income groups, the increase in this type of payment has also tended to reduce the inequality of the distribution, although its impact has been relatively small.[12]

The decline in the relative importance of property income between 1929 and 1947 tended also to reduce the inequality of the distribution. There is some basis for believing that this tendency was supplemented by a tendency for property income to become somewhat less concentrated.[13]

The lack of significant change in the inequality of the income distribution since 1947, in contrast to the period 1929-47, is in part related to the mixed impact of changes in the relative importance of different income types.[14] On the one hand the decline in the relative importance of property income ended about 1947, and thereafter the share of property income tended upward. Furthermore, in spite of the tendency toward a diffusion of stock ownership mentioned earlier, there appears to have been no significant change in the concentration of net worth of spending units in the period since 1947.[15]

On the other hand the decline in the relative share of self-employment income since 1947 has tended, along with the increase in the share of wages and salaries (particularly in 1950-53) and the increase in transfer payments, to favour a continuation in the tendency toward reduced inequality. There has at the same time been some reduction in the concentration ratios for two of the important components of self-employment income, families headed by 'managers, officials, and proprietors, excluding farm — self-employed', for whom the concentration ratio in 1948 was .444 and in 1960 was .399; and families headed by 'farmers and farm managers', for whom the concentration ratio decreased from .550 in 1948 to .461 in 1960.[16]

Changes have also occurred in the concentration ratios for wages and salaries income, and the impact of these changes is considered in the immediately following subsection.

TABLE 5. *Percent of Aggregate Wage or Salary Income Received by Each Fifth of Wage or Salary Recipients Ranked by Income in Various Years*

	Income Received Percent of Wage or Salary		
Quintiles	1939	1949	1951
Lowest	3.4	2.6	3.0
Second	8.4	10.1	10.6
Third	15.0	18.7	18.9
Fourth	23.9	26.2	25.9
Highest	49.3	42.4	41.6

SOURCES: H. P. Miller, *Income of the American People,* New York, 1955, p. 104.

(2) Changes in Income Differentials within the Wages and Salaries Sector

Particularly between 1939 and 1949 important changes occurred in income differentials within the wages and salaries sector. The net effect in that period was to reduce the inequality of distribution of wages and salaries. Table 5 shows the outcome in terms of the quintiles of wage or salary recipients. Since 1949, however, it is doubtful whether any reduction in inequality of distribution of wages and salaries has occurred; and in fact the circumstances tending to increase inequality appear to have been strong.

The underlying changes are examined at four levels: (a) changes in the relative importance of different industries; (b) changes within individual industries; (c) changes in the relative importance of major occupation groups; and (d) changes in skill differentials and in sex ratios within individual occupations.

(a) The major changes that have occurred in the relative importance of different industries since 1939 have been the relative decline of employment in agriculture and the relative increase of employment in manufacturing; construction; retail trade; finance, insurance, and real estate; business and repair services; personal services; professional services; and public administration. The proportion of persons employed in agriculture dropped from 19 percent of the total employed in 1940 to 6 percent in 1963.[17] Since the coefficient of concentration has been higher for wage and salary recipients in agriculture than in other industries[18] and since the median income of the former group has been persistently much lower than that of wage and salary recipients in other industries, the shift of labour out of agriculture has contributed to the reduction in the inequality of distribution of wages and salaries that occurred between 1939 and 1949; and it has tended to offset the counter-effect of an increase in the concentration ratio for wages and salaries in industries generally that has occurred since 1949.[19]

Second only in importance to the reduced percentage of agricultural employment has been the increased importance of employment in government.[20] The dispersion of wage and salary income is less in government than in other sectors, and earnings per employee are very close to the national average. The share of government employment has increased from about 9 percent of total employment in 1929 to about 15 percent in 1950 and has continued at about the latter percentage.

(b) Although the changes in the industrial distribution of the labour force contributed to the reduction in inequality of the distribution of wages and salaries between 1939 and 1949, more important, according to Miller[21] were the changes in the dispersion of wage income within individual industries. He found that there was a narrowing of wage differentials for men in all but 5 of 117 industries examined. And Kravis has discerned "a tendency for earnings in particular industries to 'regress' toward the mean for all industries."[22] for example, the finance, insurance, and real estate sector had annual earnings per employee 47 percent above the national average in 1929, but only 8 percent above in 1950.

Between 1949 and 1960, however, as has already been noted, concentration ratios for wages and salaries income in each of the census industrial categories increased respectively for male and female workers. At the same time the proportion of female workers increased, particularly in retail trade; finance, insurance, and real estate; services; and public administration; but in only the first two of these categories was the concentration ratio for women workers lower than for men in 1960.[23]

(c) With regard to the distributional impact of changes in occupational structure, it has been estimated that:[24]

Between 1910 and 1955 the percentage of workers in unskilled employment was cut in half, the percentage in semi-skilled work rose by 50 percent, the percentage in white-collar work doubled, as did the percentage in the 'professional, technical and kindred workers' classification. This change is clearly such as to encourage a narrowing of income inequality.

The change in occupational structure was in the direction of an increase in the proportion of workers in occupations having higher incomes and/or less unequal distributions of income.[25] The proportion of service workers and labourers, occupations characterized by relatively high income dispersion and median earnings well below the average, decreased, while the proportion of craftsmen, for whom the income dispersion was somewhat less and median earnings near the average, increased by about one-third between 1940 and 1952. There also occurred a decrease in the income differential between high-paid and low-paid occupations.

Between 1952 and 1960, however, the number of craftsmen, operatives and labourers decreased, while salaried professional workers and salaried managers (other than farm) increased about one-half, household workers about one-third, clerical workers and sales workers about one-quarter, and service workers about one-fifth.[26] Although the median income of salaried professional workers is relatively high, their concentration ratio is relatively low, and the sex ratio did not change significantly in the period 1952-60. On the other hand, the concentration ratio and median income are both high for salaried managers. In the case of clerical workers, nearly all of the increase was in female workers for whom the concentration ratio is low and the median income higher than for female workers in general. Practically all of the increase in household workers was in female workers also, but in this case the concentration ratio is high and median income low. For sales workers the sex ratio did not change significantly; median income for men is relatively high, for women about average; concentration ratios are high. In the case of service workers nearly all of the increase was in female workers for whom median income is low and concentration ratio is a little higher than average.

Of those occupational categories that decreased in relative importance after 1952, concentration ratios are relatively low for craftsmen, operatives, and labourers other than farm labourers; relatively high for farm labourers. On the whole, the decrease in these categories probably tended to be accompanied by an increase in the inequality of distribution of wages and salaries. The same tendency was probably strengthened by the increase in relative importance of salaried managers, household, service, and sales workers. On the other hand, the increase in the proportion of salaried professional workers and clerical workers may have worked the other way. The net effect of these changes upon the distribution of wages and salaries is uncertain; but it is clear that in the period since 1952, in contrast to 1939-51, no strong tendency towards a decline in inequality accompanied the shifts in occupational structure that occurred.

(d) Within occupations, there occurred a narrowing of inequality of the wage and salary income distribution during and after the war. An important reason for this was the reduction in unemployment that occurred during that period.[27] There has also been a significant reduction in skill differentials within occupations, possibly due to the broadening of education, the reduction in the proportion of foreign-born in the labour force, the imposition and raising of a minimum wage (or a rise in the 'social minimum'), trade-union pressure as well as reduced unemployment.[28] However, there is evidence[29] that the narrowing of differentials among major occupations may have halted, and that it may even have been reversed.

That such a reversal may have occurred is borne out by changes in occupational concentration ratios between 1952 and 1960.[30] In the case of the following occupational categories, all of which increased in relative importance during the period, concentration ratios increased: professional (male), clerical (female), sales (male and female), household (female), services (male and female). Concentration ratios also increased for the following occupational categories whose relative importance decreased during the period: craftsmen (male), operatives (male), and labourers (male). Of the remaining occupational categories, the concentration ratio decreased only for professional workers (female), a category whose relative importance increased; and the concentration ratio remained about the same for salaried managers (male) and operatives (female), the former increasing and the latter decreasing in relative importance.

This rather strong tendency for concentration ratios to increase rather than decrease for different occupational categories since 1952 matched the increase in concentration ratios for wages and salaries that occurred in the different industry categories during the same period. Furthermore, as was pointed out in connection with changes in occupational structure during this period, the increase in the female-male sex ratio, while tending to reduce inequality in the case of clerical workers, worked the other way in the cases of household, sales, and service workers.

Altogether the strong circumstances tending to reduce inequality of the wage and salary distribution for individuals in the period 1939 to about 1950 have been weakened or reversed in the period since 1950.

(3) Movement of Population from Rural to Metropolitan Areas

The shift of families and employed labour out of agriculture has of course been accompanied by an increase in the proportion of families living in urban areas and a decrease in the proportion living in rural farm areas. But as Table 6 shows, there also has occurred an increase in the proportion of families living in rural non-farm (e.g., suburban) areas. The concentration ratio for all families and that for unrelated individuals both declined between 1947 and 1959 — the former moderately and the latter considerably. Underlying the moderate decline in the concentration ratio for families is the considerable decline in ratio for rural farm family incomes and the decline in the relative importance of this sector which has the highest concentration ratio of the three. But the decline in inequality for all families would have been greater during this period if it had not been for the increase in relative importance of the rural non-farm sector of family incomes coupled with the increase in the concentration ratio for this sector. The very fact that the decline in inequality of family incomes in the aggregate since 1947 was so moderate is no doubt related to this circumstance.

The more considerable decline in the concentration ratio in the case of unrelated individuals than in the case of families is the outcome of a decline in the ratio for both urban and rural non-farm individuals, and it occurs in spite of an increase in the ratio for rural farm individuals. Note that these ratios behaved quite differently for unrelated individuals than for families; but the outcome, a decline in concentration ratios for both families and unrelated individuals is the same.[31]

We need to explore the possibility that the changes in concentration ratios between 1947 and 1959 shown in Table 6 for different groups of families might have been related to changes during the same period in the average age of

TABLE 6. *Number of Families and Unrelated Individuals, Median Incomes, Concentration Ratios, and Shares of Top 5 Percent, Classified by Urban, Rural Non-farm, and Rural Farm, 1947 and 1959*

	Total (Millions)		Median Income (1959 Dollars)		Concentration Ratio		Share Top 5 Percent	
	1947	1959	1947	1959	1947	1959	1947	1959
All Families	37.3	45.1	3,957	5,417	.378	.369	17.5	16.3
Urban	22.5	27.6	4,383	5,754	.344	.344	16.4	16.1
Rural Non-farm	8.3	13.6	3,688	5,360	.348	.356	16.2	15.8
Rural Farm	6.5	3.8	2,585	2,801	.493	.456	24.8	20.5
Unrelated Individuals	8.1	10.7	1,325	1,557	.568	.512	33.3	23.2
Urban	5.8	8.2	1,568	1,801	.548	.495	31.6	22.9
Rural Non-farm	1.3	2.0	927	1,126	.531	.518	25.7	22.3
Rural Farm	.9	.5	877	625	.560	.609	32.7	36.1

SOURCE: U.S. Bureau of the Census, Technical Paper No. 8, Washington, 1963, Table 1, pp. 36-45.
Note—These are Census figures; incomes do not include income in kind or imputed income items. Unrelated individuals are persons (other than inmates of institutions) not living with any relatives.

the family head or in the number of earners per family. Similarly there is the possibility that changes in concentration ratios in this period for the different groups of unrelated individuals might have been related to changes in average age or in the percentage of non-earners. These possibilities will be considered in succeeding sections.

(4) Age

Since 1947 both the percentage of families having heads aged 65 or over and the corresponding percentage for unrelated individuals have increased. However, in both cases the increase has been particularly marked in the lower-income brackets, under $5,000 in the case of family heads and under $3,000 in the case of unrelated individuals (see Table 7). The concentration ratio for this age-group is higher than for any other,[32] in part because of the prevalence of part-time employment or no employment at all for heads of families and individuals 65 years of age or more. Hence this change in the age pattern of the population since 1947 might have been expected to be accompanied by an increase of the inequality of the income distribution for all families and unrelated individuals.[33]

The tendency towards an increase in the age of family heads was particularly marked, between 1947 and 1959, in the case of the rural farm group. For these families, the percentage of family heads aged 55 and over increased from 32 to 36 percent. The corresponding percentage for heads of urban families increased only from 29 to 30; and that for heads of rural non-farm families remained unchanged at 25.[34] Yet in spite of the high concentration ratio consistently found for age-groups 55 and above, the concentration ratio for the rural farm group decreased during the period, and that for urban families remained unchanged. Although the concentration ratio for rural non-farm families increased, this increase was not related to a corresponding change in the average age of the family head.

TABLE 7. *Percentage of Heads of Families and Unrelated Individuals Aged 65 or Over, by Income Groups, 1947 and 1960*

Family Income	Heads of Families (percent)		Income	Unrelated Individuals (percent)	
	1947	*1960*		*1947*	*1960*
Under $3,000	20	31	Under $1,000	43	48
$3,000 to $4,999	6	13	$1,000 to $2,999	26	41
$5,000 to $9,999	7	6	$3,000 to $4,999	10	12
$10,000 and over	11	7	$5,000 and over	19	10
All Families	*11*	*13*	*All Individuals*	*30*	*34*

SOURCE: U.S. Bureau of the Census, Technical Paper No. 8, Washington, 1963, Tables A and B, pp. 6-13.

The fact that concentration ratios for all families and for unrelated individuals decreased in spite of the increase in the percentage of family heads and unrelated individuals in the older age-group may be related to the increase that occurred in the percentage of individuals over 65 receiving social security and other transfer payments during the period. Thus the concentration ratios both for families whose heads were aged 65 or over and for unrelated individuals in the same age-group decreased between 1947 and 1959 relatively more than the average for other age-groups.[35]

(5) Increase in Number of Earners per Family

An increase in the number of earners per family would have no effect upon the inequality of the income distribution if the increases in earnings were to be distributed among the families in proportion to previous income levels. However, as Table 8 shows, the proportion of families with two or more earners has increased relatively more in the lower-income groups (below $5,000) than

in the middle- and upper-income groups in the period 1947 to 1960. This does
not prove that the increase in the number of earners per family has tended to
reduce the inequality of the distribution; but it does suggest that this tendency
may well have been operative.

TABLE 8. *Percentage of Families with Two Earners or More, Classified by
Family Income Groups, 1947 and 1960*

Family Income	1947	1960	Percent Increase in Proportion
Under $3,000	20	27	42
$3,000 to $4,999	29	39	34
$5,000 to $9,999	56	54	—*
$10,000 and over	54	67	24
All Families	35	46	31

* Decrease.
SOURCE: See Source Table 7.

The increase in the number of families with two or more earners was greatest in the rural farm group, next greatest in the rural non-farm, and least in
the urban.[36] The decrease in the concentration ratio for rural farm families
(Table 6) as compared with the other two groups may be partly attributable
to the fact that the proportion of families with two or more earners increased
from 27 to 46 percent between 1947 and 1959. The corresponding percentages for rural non-farm families were 31 and 43; for urban families, 39 and 46.
The slightly lower percentage in the case of rural non-farm families in 1959
may be attributable to a somewhat lower average age of head than in the
case of the other two groups, which likely meant more younger children whose
age made it less easy for the wife to work. In 1959, 51 percent of heads of
families in the rural non-farm group were in the 25 to 44 age bracket; the
corresponding percentages for urban and rural farm family heads were
respectively 43 and 35.[37]

In the case of unrelated individuals, the urban group is by far the most
important (Table 6). The concentration ratio for non-earners is typically
higher than for earners.[38] Between 1947 and 1959 the percentage of non-
earners increased from 31 to 38, and a particularly marked decline occurred
in their concentration ratio. It is possible therefore that the decline in the
concentration ratio for urban unrelated individuals was connected with the
increase in the number of retired persons (in turn related to the aging of the
population) and to the decline in inequality of income distribution among
them.

The rural non-farm group of unrelated individuals is numerically much less important than the urban, but is growing as rapidly. Between 1947 and 1959 the percentage of non-earners remained about the same (about 45 percent), but the concentration ratio for non-earners declined much more than in the case of earners. Again, the increase in the number of retired persons seems to have been accompanied by a decline in the inequality of income distribution among them.

The rural farm group of unrelated individuals is unimportant in size and is declining. The concentration ratio is much higher for earners than for non-earners, but the increase in the concentration ratio between 1947 and 1959 was particularly marked for non-earners who remained, however, about the same proportion of the group (about 34 percent).

(6) Education

Those family heads with relatively less education are particularly vulnerable to unemployment.[39] Furthermore, lack of education constitutes a barrier to income increases for family heads; while those heads with more education receive more income increases than decreases over time.[40] The dispersion of secondary and advanced education among the population, such as has been occurring in the United States, should be accompanied by a reduction in income inequality. It has been shown that this has indeed been the tendency,[41] but that the effect of the dispersion of education has been quite small as compared, for example, with the effect of the shifts that have occurred in occupations. As Morgan points out:[42]

It seems clear that more jobs for women, less unemployment for men, and fewer farmers have had more effect on income inequality than changing age or educational distribution of the population, or even the income tax.

(7) Regional Shifts: Racial Differences

Between 1929 and 1946 there occurred a significant narrowing in the relative difference in average-income levels among states and regions in the United States. The coefficient of variation declined from 32 in 1929 to 18 in 1946.[43] A slight further narrowing has recently occurred, bringing the coefficient of variation to 16 for 1963.

During the Second World War, when most of the reduction occurred, there was a sharp increase in industrialization and improved utilization of existing labour resources in the Southeast and Southwest. At the same time, because of high prices and full utilization of resources, income from agriculture was at a high level in the Rocky Mountain and Plains regions as well as in the South. These changes in the efficiency of resource utilization occurred without corresponding shifts in population. Consequently, *per capita* personal income fell, relative to the national average, in the Mideast, Far West, New England, and Great Lakes states, and rose in the regions previously mentioned.

Since the war, while these same tendencies toward increased efficiency in resource utilization have been operative, there also has occurred a differential population growth by regions to match the increases in state and regional incomes. White population has shifted from the Northeast and Central Plains to the Southwest and West. There has been a substantial out-migration of Negroes from the South to the North and West. But since growth in personal income by regions has about matched growth of population by regions, *per capita* incomes by regions have changed little, relative to the national average, since 1948.

The migration of Negroes must have tended to reduce inequality of income distribution nationally, since in general the movement carried with it an increase in incomes for the migrants to a level closer to the median. The median income of nonwhite families in the South in 1960 was $2,735 as compared with the national median for nonwhite families of $3,190.[44]

The migration of white population from the Northeast and North Central regions to the Southwest and West no doubt tended also to affect the national income distribution for families, but the direction of the effect cannot be determined. Median income for families was higher than the national median in the case of the two regions from which the out-migration mainly came; it was lower than the national median in the Southwest and higher than the national median (and higher than in the Northeast and North Central regions) in the West.[45]

At the national level, the concentration ratio for the income distribution of nonwhite families decreased insignificantly from .363 to .357 between 1947 and 1960, while that for Negroes increased insignificantly from .406 to .414.[46]

(8) Conclusions

Needless to say, the various hypotheses that have been reviewed overlap one another. For example, regional changes, the relative decline of employment in agriculture, and the shift of population from rural to urban areas are all related to the relative decline of agriculture as an industry. The influence of diffusion of education is no doubt related to the reduction in unemployment. However, without regard to implicit duplication of this sort, the preceding analysis can now be summarized.

The decline in the inequality of the income distribution that occurred between 1929 and 1947 appears to have been due mainly to: (1) the increase in the percentage share of wages and salaries in family personal income; (2) the decrease in the percentage share of property income; (3) the relative decline of employment in agriculture; (4) the relative increase of employment in government; (5) a shift in the occupational structure resulting in a higher proportion of workers in occupations having higher incomes and/or less unequal distributions of income; (6) a reduction of income and wage-rate differentials within occupations; and (7) the narrowing in relative differences in average-income levels among states and regions. A minor role has been played by increased dispersion of education. The change in the age pattern of the population has also played a minor part, but in the direction of increasing inequality.*

Of these circumstances, the first, the fourth, the fifth, and the seventh have exerted little influence in reducing inequality in the period since 1947. The second has clearly operated in the opposite way, and probably also the sixth. In addition the increase in the proportion of families in rural non-farm areas has also tended to increase the concentration ratio of the income distribution — although this tendency was not necessarily additive with the tendency for the relative share of property income to increase. In general the relative stability of the income distribution since 1947 has been due to an approximate balance in the relative strength of these various tendencies — with a slight downward drift, perhaps, to be explained by the continuing movement out of agriculture.

II.   The Functional Distribution of Income

The national accounting data that come nearest to showing income 'earned' by the factors of production are those for the allocation of national income. However, the breakdown of the accounting data into wages, interest, rent, and profit does not provide counterpart data to the economic theorist's concepts that go by those names. To give only one example, national-accounting rent is limited to 'rental income of persons' and has little relation to the economist's notion of rent as a return to those resources the supply of which is unresponsive to variations in the returns to them.[47]

Some of these difficulties are alleviated if the accounting figures for interest, profits, and rent are aggregated and treated as a 'property' share to be considered over against a labour share. However, there still remains the essentially insoluble problem that accounting data for the return to unincorporated business enterprise (hereafter called entrepreneurial income) is a joint return to the entrepreneur's capital invested and to his labour expended in the enterprise. Although numerous and ingenious bases for separating the two elements have been suggested, all such devices must necessarily be in some degree arbitrary. But unless one of these devices is adopted, the accounting data leave us with three 'shares'— wages, entrepreneurial income, and property income from incorporated business — that have no counterpart in the theoretical analysis of factor distribution. Since a decline in the proportion of the gainfully employed who are individual proprietors has been fairly steady since at least the middle of the nineteenth century the accompanying upward trend in

---

* Since the analysis has been limited to the distribution of family income before taxes, the effect of the highly progressive federal income tax has not directly been involved. Indirectly, no doubt, the tax has had some impact on property income through its effect on the distribution of property.

wages is difficult to interpret. Whether it represents an increase in the share of labour as a factor and a decrease in that of property as the other factor cannot be determined because of the impossibility of separating out the wages and property-income constituents of the declining joint income of individual proprietors.

There have been a few pioneer attempts to discover what happened to the relative shares of labour and property in the latter half of the nineteenth century in the United States. A recent study which was revised and combined some of these early results[48] provides us with estimates of the labour and property shares by census years from 1849-50 to 1909-10. This study attempted to separate out an imputed return to labour from entrepreneurial income by assuming that individual proprietors earned for their labour the equivalent of the average annual earnings of hired labour. The residual was attributed to the proprietors' invested capital. (This method of imputation will hereafter be referred to as the labour basis, in contrast to the asset basis which attributes to the proprietors' invested capital the rate of return earned by other property in the form of interest, rent, and corporate profits.[49] Use of the asset basis makes the return to entrepreneurial labour a residual.)

According to Budd's estimates, the share of employed plus self-employed labour decreased from 68.3 percent of total private income in 1849-50 to 62.4 percent in 1909-10.[50] In contrast, the share of wages of employed labour alone showed an upward trend (from 41.4 percent of total private income in 1849-50 to 46.0 percent in 1909-10) in spite of a steady decline in the wages share in the agricultural sector.[51] Between 1850 and 1910 the importance of the agricultural sector, whether measured by income or employment, was reduced about one-half, and mainly because of this reduction the proportion of hired labour to the total gainfully employed in the private sector steadily increased. It was principally the relative decline of agriculture (in which the share of wages was low and declining) and the relative advance of industry (in which the share of wages was high) that resulted in a net increase in the wages share during the period.

The downward trend in the share of employed plus self-employed labour, in spite of the upward trend in the wages share alone, was also due to the relative decline of agriculture. In the case of the share of employed plus self-employed labour, the weight of this share in agriculture was relatively high (though declining) for the period as a whole, as compared with its weight in industry; consequently the strong downward trend of this share in agriculture more than offset the effect of a moderate upward trend of the share in industry. On the other hand, in the case of the wages share alone, the weight of this share in agriculture was relatively low as compared with its weight in industry and consequently the upward trend in industry overbalanced the downward trend in agriculture.

For the period since 1900 the data are both more adequate and more reliable. Table 9, in the first three columns, provides the basic data by decade-average percentages.[52] The advance in the wages share (as a proportion of private income) that Budd found in the period 1850-1910 has a counterpart in the steady increase in the share of employee compensation (as a proportion of national income) in the period since 1900 (see column 1). In our earlier

TABLE 9. *Functional Shares in National Income, Averages of Percentage Shares by Decades, 1900-1963*

	Distributive Shares			Property Share, Various Concepts			
Period	Employee Compensa-tion (1)	Entre-pre-neurial Income (2)	Interest, Rent, and Corporate Profit (3)	Asset Basis (4)	Labour Basis (5)	Propor-tional Basis (6)	Econ-omy-wide Basis (7)
1900-09	55.0	23.6	21.4	36.8	23.0	30.6	28.0
1905-14	55.2	22.9	21.8	38.0	24.4	30.7	28.3
1910-19	53.2	24.2	22.6	38.0	30.6	31.9	29.8
1915-24	57.2	21.0	21.8	34.6	23.9	29.8	27.6
1920-29	60.5	17.6	22.0	32.3	21.9	28.4	28.6
1925-34	63.0	15.8	21.1	27.9	17.2	26.8	25.1
1930-39	66.8	15.0	18.1	23.9	12.7	23.4	21.3
1929-38	66.6	15.5	17.8	23.5	11.2	23.2	21.1
1934-43	65.1	16.5	18.4	24.3	17.0	24.2	22.0
1939-48	64.6	17.2	18.3	25.8	21.5	24.3	22.1
1944-53	65.6	16.4	18.1	24.7	21.5	23.8	21.6
1949-58	67.4	13.6	19.0	26.0*	21.9	23.8	22.0
1954-63	69.9	11.8	18.3	—†	19.9‡	22.4	20.7

* 1949-57.   † Not available.   ‡ 1954-63.
SOURCE: I. B. Kravis, *The Structure of Income*, Philadelphia, 1962, p. 124. Column 6 (up to 1930-39) from *Rev. Econ. Stat.*, May 1954, *36*, p. 178. Figures for 1949-58 and 1954-63 computed by author.

discussion of the size-distribution of family income a similar upward trend in the percentage share of wages and salaries in family income was found for the period 1929-53. As in the earlier period, the upward trend in the wages share of national income since 1900 reflects, at least in substantial degree, the relative decline in agriculture and the shift out of self-employment into wage and salary employment. Both of the latter two changes are also reflected in column 2 of Table 9, showing the decline in the share of entrepreneurial income since 1900 — a downward trend which was also characteristic of the period 1850-1910 for entrepreneurial income as a percentage of private income, and characteristic of the period since 1929 for self-employment income as a percentage of family personal income (Table 4).

Another reason that has been suggested to explain, in part, the rise in the share of employee compensation is the increase in the importance of the government sector. Since our national accounting procedures do not attribute any return to capital employed in government, the expansion of the government sector automatically carries with it a corresponding expansion in the proportion of wages to national income. The importance of this circumstance can, however, easily be exaggerated. Between 1929 and 1963 compensation of employees of government (including military personnel) as a percentage of national income increased from 5.6 to 12.4 percent.

Three recent studies have examined the behaviour of employee compensation as a proportion of *private* national income or product. One of these,[53] for the period 1899 to 1929, shows that compensation of employees as a percentage of the business sector's gross product had no trend, upward or downward, in contrast to the upward trend of employee compensation as a percentage of national income (see column 1 of Table 9). Two studies of the period since 1929[54] show respectively (1) that employed labour's share of business gross product rose from 46.2 percent in 1929 to 53.6 percent in 1957, and (2) that employed labour's share of privately produced income rose from 55.6 percent in 1929 to 64.7 percent in 1955. A comparison of these two sets of results with those for employee compensation as a percentage of national income (Table 9, column 1) suggests that the growth of the government sector has not been a major factor affecting the accounting estimates for the shares of labour and property since 1929.

When, however, national-income-originating sectors are more narrowly defined, employee compensation becomes a much more stable percentage. Thus Denison has shown that, for 1929-52, employee compensation originating in each of three sectors — non-farm corporations, non-farm proprietors and partnerships, and farms — as a percentage of income originating in the respective sectors showed no significant trend.[55] A more recent study by Phillips[56] uses the device of expressing the share of employee compensation as a percentage of the proportion of employees in the labour force as a means of allowing for structural changes in the economy bearing upon labour's share. These 'wage-parity ratios' showed the same upward trend for employee compensation as a whole as was exhibited in Table 9, column 1. However, when the computation was made for the private sector and for the private non-agricultural sector, in both cases the wage-parity ratio, after increasing during the great depression, showed no significant trend thereafter.[57] Hence it can be argued that, when the sector is defined so as to make it reasonably homogeneous, there has been a tendency towards stability of labour's share.

The share of interest, rent, and corporate profit — column 3 of Table 9 — in national income has been more nearly stable than the other two shares as presented in that Table, although it has shown a moderate decline in the period 1930 to the present taken as a whole. A comparable decline in the case of the corresponding share of interest, rent, and dividends in family personal income (Table 4) for the period 1929-47 was attributable to the decline in interest rates, low corporate profits during the 1930's, and the high corporate income taxes imposed during the war and after. The same reasons no doubt contribute to the explanation of the lower level of interest, rent, and corporate profits as a share in national income for the period since 1929. But in the latter case, no return to a somewhat higher level after 1947 (such as we found in the case of this share of family income) has appeared. A possible reason for this difference may be that accelerated depreciation allowances (particularly since 1954) have affected total corporate profits more than dividends. Indeed, total corporate profits in 1963 were 67 percent above the 1948 level, while dividends as a constituent of personal income were 147 percent above the 1948 level.

Table 9 also shows, in columns 4 to 7, for four different ways of separating out an imputed property share from entrepreneurial income, four corresponding estimates of the total property share for the period 1900-9 to 1954-63. The asset basis (column 4) yields a higher property share than the labour basis (column 5), since in the former case the return to entrepreneurial labour, while in the latter case the return to entrepreneurial investment, is treated as the residual. (Entrepreneurial income does not run at a high enough level to provide *both* a return to entrepreneurial labour equal to employed labour's average compensation and a return to entrepreneurial investment equal to the rate of return on other property.) Neither of these bases for separating out an imputed property share from entrepreneurial income carries much conviction.

Column 6 (the proportional basis) shows estimates for the property share when the return imputed to entrepreneurial property is determined by the application of a constant percentage division. The particular percentage employed here was 35 percent.[58] The outcome is a percentage share for property which lies between those derived respectively on the asset and the labour bases. But as Kravis points out, the application of such a constant division not only is arbitrary but also impairs the usefulness of the results for a study of whether relative shares have in fact varied, and if so in what way.

Finally, in column 7 the proportion of entrepreneurial income included in the property share is determined by the current relationship, for each year, between labour and property income in the rest of the economy excluding the entrepreneurial sector. This appears to be as reasonable a basis as any.

The interesting fact, however, is that, for all our ways of computing the property share so as to include an imputed return to entrepreneurs' investment, the share shows a downward trend (and the share of labour shows an upward trend) for the period since 1900-9. The downward trend in the property share is steepest when the asset basis is used, and is least steep when the labour basis is used. If, in fact, the whole of entrepreneurial income were to be attributed to entrepreneurial labour, labour's share in national income would have even then shown a moderate increase during the period since 1900-9.

Conclusions

National accounting data do not provide figures that can be used satisfactorily to throw light on the applicability of theories of functional distribution. However, on any basis on which entrepreneurial income may be split between labour and property shares, the share of national income attributable to labour has increased during the period since 1900. This outcome is in contrast to the declining relative share of labour (when entrepreneurial income is divided on the labour basis) that was found for the period 1849-50 to 1909-10.

These two opposed tendencies respectively evident in the earlier and the later period of economic development of the U.S. economy are both in considerable part traceable to the same underlying causes — the relative decline of agriculture and the shift out of self-employment into wage and salary employment. But in the earlier period, since for the period as a whole the average share of employed and self-employed labour in agriculture had a relatively heavy weight, the net effect was a decline in the share of employed and self-employed labour. On the other hand, in the period since 1900, agriculture was no longer as important a sector relative to industry, the share of employed and self-employed labour in industry was higher than in agriculture (on the labour basis at least) and rising, and the outcome for the total share was a rising rather than a falling trend.

Another structural change which may have played some part during the later period has been the increasing importance of the government sector for which accounting procedures allow a disproportionate share to employed labour.

The decline in the share of interest, rent, and corporate profits has been moderate. It has continued from 1929 to the present, in contrast to the behaviour of interest, rent, and dividends as a share in family personal income, which has increased moderately since 1947.

When labour's share of national income originates in a sector so defined as to be homogeneous, such as private non-farm business for example, something approximating stability of the share has been characteristic of the last twenty years. But there is still room for considerable skepticism as to how persistent or how general any such tendency may be.

REFERENCES

1. Estimates of the whole distribution are not available for years prior to 1929; and the reliability of the 1929 and 1941 sets of figures is probably considerably less than those of 1944 and subsequent years.

    In addition to estimates made by the Department of Commerce, which are available for most years since 1944, there are also annual estimates by the U.S.

Bureau of the Census for the income distribution of both families and persons 14 years of age and over, available for years since 1944, and annual estimates by the University of Michigan Survey Research Center for the income distribution of "spending units," available for years since 1946. There have been a number of surveys of family income by the U.S. Bureau of Labor Statistics for individual years, the most recent of which, for 1950, is reviewed by I. B. KRAVIS *(The Structure of Income,* Philadelphia, 1962). The relations between these various sets of data are reviewed by SELMA F. GOLDSMITH ("The Relation of Census Income Distribution Statistics to Other Income Data," *An Appraisal of the 1960 Census Income Data,* Studies in Income and Wealth, vol. 23, pp. 65-107, Princeton, 1958).

2. JEANNETTE M. FITZWILLIAM, "Size Distribution of Income in 1962," *Surv. Curr. Bus.,* April 1963, p. 18.

3. SIMON KUZNETS *(Shares of the Upper Income Groups in Income and Savings,* New York, 1953, pp. 585, 635), has provided estimates of the share of the top 5 percent of income recipients, on a *per capita* basis, for the period 1917-48. The tendency revealed by his figures for 1929-48 corresponds with that shown by Table 2. In the period 1917-28, on the other hand, the inequality of the distribution appears on the whole to have increased moderately. Kuznets' "basic" variant income share (employee compensation, entrepreneurial income rent, interest, and dividends) for the top 5 percent increased from 24.6 to 26.78 percent. The subsequent decline brought the figure down to 17.41 percent in 1947. The share for the top 5 percent for his "economic income" variant (the basic variant corrected for non-reporting of state and local government salaries before 1938, omission of imputed rent, and use of an inappropriate income base in classifying tax data) increased from 26.1 percent in 1919 to 32.06 percent in 1928 and 32.12 percent in 1932. It decreased to a low point of 18.68 percent in 1944.

4. I. B. KRAVIS, *The Structure of Income,* Philadelphia, 1962, p. 204.

5. *Ibid.,* p. 204.

6. However, as J. A. PECHMAN (Comment on "The Relation of Census Income Distribution Statistics to Other Income Data," *An Appraisal of the 1950 Census Income Data,* Studies in Income and Wealth, vol, 23, pp. 107-115, Princeton, 1958) *Ibid.* has pointed out, the stability shown by the figures may be illusory. It is likely that changes in the tax laws and in tax practices have considerably altered the content of family personal income. Methods of compensating employees designed to avoid high tax rates, use of the preferential capital gains rates, the practice of splitting incomes among family members are illustrations.

7. H. P. MILLER, *Income of the American People,* New York, 1955, p. 123.

8. JEANNETTE M. FITZWILLIAM, "Size Distribution of Income in 1962," *Surv. Curr. Bus.,* April 1963, p. 16.

9. LEE SOLTOW, "Shifts in Factor Payments and Income Distribution," *Am. Econ. Rev.,* June 1959, 49, p .397.

10. MAURICE LIEBENBERG and JEANNETTE M. FITZWILLIAM, "Size Distribution of Income in 1961," *Surv. Curr. Bus.,* April 1962, pp. 13-14.

11. For the present it is assumed that the concentration ratios for these differing types of income were unchanged during the period under consideration. In 1950 the concentration ratio for wages and salaries was between .31 and .35 for urban

consumer units as compared with .62 and .68 for self-employed income, and .50 to .60 for property income (I. B. KRAVIS, *The Structure of Income,* Philadelphia, 1962, p. 193). These coefficients were derived from the BLS survey of 1950 income; and they refer to the inequality of distribution of *after*-tax income of each type.

12. The Survey Research Center study of 1961 income shows that the lowest quintile of spending units received 29 percent of aggregate transfer income, the next highest quintile 35 percent (GEORGE KATONA, C. A. LININGER, and R. F. KOSOBUD, *1962 Survey of Consumer Finances,* Survey Research Center, University of Michigan, Ann Arbor, 1963, p. 23).

13. I. B. KRAVIS, *The Structure of Income,* Philadelphia, 1962, p. 224.

14. LEE SOLTOW ("Shifts in Factor Payments and Income Distribution," *Am. Econ. Rev.* June 1959, *49,* pp 395-398) shows, for the personal income distribution of non-farm multi-person families, that the decline in inequality between 1929 and 1947 was related significantly to the increase in the percentage shares of wages and salaries and of transfer payments, and the decrease in the relative importance of dividends and interest. The lack of significant change in inequality since 1947 he attributes to the relative stability of the percentage shares of the different types of income, except for a moderate increase in the share of wages and salaries at the expense of the share of business and professional income.

15. Net worth of spending units, the Survey Research Center finds, is much more unequally distributed than is income. No large shift occurred in the concentration from 1953 to 1962 (GEORGE KATONA, C. A. LININGER, and R. F. KOSOBUD, *1962 Survey of Consumer Finances,* Survey Research Center, University of Michigan, Ann Arbor, 1963, pp. 118, 121).

16. H. P. MILLER, *Trends in the Income of Families and Persons in the United States: 1947 to 1960,* U.S. Bureau of the Census, Technical Paper No. 8, Washington, 1963, pp. 152-160.

17. Actually the decline in the proportion of persons engaged in agriculture began much earlier — from more than half the work force in 1870 to less than 40 percent in 1900 (I. B. KRAVIS, *The Structure of Income,* Philadelphia, 1962, p. 125).

18. In 1960 the concentration ratio for wage and salary income of males in agriculture, forestry, and fisheries was .474 compared with .355 for professional services: .368 for finance, insurance and real estate; .357 for business and repair services; .451 for personal services; .296 for manufacturing; .331 for construction; and .244 for public administration — the industries which expanded most between 1949 and 1960 (H. P. MILLER, *Trends in the Income of Families and Persons in the United States: 1947 to 1960,* U.S. Bureau of the Census, Technical Paper No. 8, Washington, 1963, Table 17, p. 326).

19. *Ibid.,* p. 336.

20. R. J. LAMPMAN, "The Effectiveness of Some Institutions in Changing the Distribution of Income," *Am. Econ. Rev. Proc.,* May 1957, *47,* p. 521; and I. B. KRAVIS, *The Structure of Income,* Philadelphia, 1962, p. 218.

21. "Changes in the Industrial Distribution of Wages in the United States, 1939-49," *An Appraisal of the 1950 Census Income Data,* Studies in Income and Wealth, vol. 23, Princeton, 1958, pp. 358-359.

22. I. B. KRAVIS, *The Structure of Income,* Philadelphia, 1962, p. 217.

23. See footnote 18.
24. R. J. LAMPMAN, "The Effectiveness of Some Institutions in Changing the Distribution of Income," *Am. Econ. Rev.*, Proc., May 1957, *47*, p. 521.
25. H. P. MILLER, *The Income of the American People*, New York, 1955, Chapters 8, 9, and LEE SOLTOW, "The Distribution of Income Related to Change in the Distribution of Education, Age, and Occupations," *Rev. Econ. Stat.*, November 1960, *42*.
26. H. P. MILLER, *Trends in the Income of Families and Persons in the United States: 1947 to 1960*, U.S. Bureau of the Census, Technical Paper No. 8, Washington, 1963, Table 14, pp. 276, 284.
27. H. P. MILLER, *Income of the American People*, New York, 1955, p. 116.
28. M. W. REDER, "The Theory of Occupational Wage Differentials," *Am. Econ. Rev.*, December 1955, *45*, pp. 833-845.
29. U.S. Bureau of the Census, *Current Population Reports*, Series P-60, No. 33, January 15, p. 6.
30. See footnote 18.
31. The behavior of the concentration ratios for unrelated individuals does not correspond with that for *all* individuals above the age of 14 and having money incomes. The concentration ratios were higher in 1959 than in 1947 for all individuals in the urban and rural non-farm groups, and for rural farm females; but slightly lower for rural farm males. (H. P. MILLER, *Trends in the Income of Families and Persons in the United States, 1947 to 1960*, U.S. Bureau of the Census, Technical Paper No. 8 Washington, 1963, Table 12, pp. 212-251.) An interesting model illustrating the complicated way in which the shift from agricultural to non-agricultural sectors may affect the income distribution is developed by KUZNETS.
32. JAMES MORGAN, "The Anatomy of Income Distribution," *Rev. Econ. Stat.*, August 1962, *44*, p. 273.
33. LEE SOLTOW ("The Distribution of Income Related to Changes in the Distribution of Education, Age, and Occupations," *Rev. Econ. Stat.*, November 1960, *42*, p. 452), demonstrates statistically that this has been the tendency, but that the effect on the income distribution has been quite small. See JAMES MORGAN ("The Anatomy of Income Distribution," *Rev. Econ. Stat.*, August 1962, *44*, pp. 273-274).
34. H. P. MILLER, *Trends in the Income of Families and Persons in the United States: 1947 to 1960*, U.S. Bureau of the Census, Technical Paper No. 8, Washington, 1963, Table 3, pp. 76, 98.
35. *Ibid.*
36. *Ibid.*, Table 6, pp. 130, 150.
37. *Ibid.*, Table 3, pp. 76, 98.
38. *Ibid.*, Table 6, pp. 132, 150.
39. JAMES MORGAN, "The Anatomy of Income Distribution," *Rev. Econ. Stat.*, August 1962, *44*, p. 277.
40. *Ibid.*
41. LEE SOLTOW, "The Distribution of Income Related to Changes in the Distribution of Education, Age and Occupations," *Rev. Econ. Stat.*, November 1960, *42*, pp. 450-452.
42. See footnote 39; page 279.

43. R. E. GRAHAM, JR., "Factors Underlying Changes in the Geographical Distribution of Income," *Surv. Curr. Bus.*, April 1964, p. 30.

44. H. P. MILLER, *Trends in the Income of Families and Persons in the United States: 1947 to 1960*, U.S. Bureau of the Census, Technical Paper No. 8, Washington, 1963.

45. *Ibid.*, Table 9, p. 168.

46. *Ibid.*, Table 9, pp. 168, 188.

47. This and other differences have been frequently pointed out; for example (Arthur Grant, "Issues in Distribution Theory: The Measurement of Labour's Relative Share, 1899-1929," *Rev. Econ. Stat.*, August 1963, *45*, pp. 273-275).

48. E. C. BUDD, "Factor Shares, 1850-1910," *Trends in the American Economy in the Nineteenth Century*, Studies in Income and Wealth, vol. 24, Princeton, 1960, pp. 365-398.

49. I. B. KRAVIS, *The Structure of Income*, Philadelphia, 1962. The author is heavily indebted to Kravis for the presentation of this section.

50. BUDD's results, based on W. I. KING's figures, are supported by other estimates of Labor's share which BUDD derived from KUZNETS' figures. These showed a decline in the share of employed plus self-employed labor from 73.4 percent of net private product in 1869-78 to 62.9 percent in 1904-13. (E. C. BUDD, "Factor Shares, 1850-1910," *Trends in the American Economy in the Nineteenth Century*, Studies in Income and Wealth, vol. 24, Princeton, 1960, pp. 385, 387).

51. *Ibid.*, p. 373.

52. Note that these figures are not comparable with BUDD's figures for the earlier period. The latter are based on "total private income" (which excludes income received from government employment), and are adjusted to the labor basis — the basis which is also employed in column 5 of Table 9. But Table 9 throughout is based on national income, not private income.

53. ARTHUR GRANT, "Issues in Distribution Theory: The Measurement of Labour's Relative Share, 1899-1929," *Rev. Econ. Stat.*, August 1963, *45*, pp. 273-279.

54. SIDNEY WEINTRAUB, *Forecasting the Price Level, Income Distribution, and Economic Growth*, Philadelphia, 1959, p. 14 and R. M. SOLOW, "The Constancy of Relative Shares," *Am. Econ. Rev.*, September 1958, *48*, p. 620.

55. E. F. DENISON, "Income Types and the Size Distribution," *Am. Econ. Rev.*, Proc., May 1954, *44*, pp. 256-257.

56. "Labor's Share and 'Wage Parity,'" *Rev. Econ. Stat.*, May 1960, *42*, pp. 164-174.

57. *Ibid.*, pp. 171-172.

58. I. B. KRAVIS, *The Structure of Income*, Philadelphia, 1962, pp. 129-130. Actually for the period 1900-1909 and 1930-1939, the percentage employed was not constant but varied somewhat from 35. The figures in column 6 for this period are Johnson's ("The Functional Distribution of Income in the United States, 1850-1952," *Rev. Econ. Stat.*, May 1954, *316*, pp. 176-177). He estimated that the share of farm operators' income attributable to property varied from about 43 percent in 1900-1914 to about 36 percent in the 1940's, while the share of non-farm entrepreneurial income attributable to property was about 35 percent throughout the period.

CHAPTER 2

Income Distribution in Europe

United Nations

An earlier secretariat study examined the major changes in income distributions between the prewar and postwar periods for a number of western European countries.[1] It was shown there that there had been a general (though not very strong) tendency towards a reduction in inequality; of the five countries examined, the movement was more evident in West Germany, Sweden, and Denmark than in the Netherlands or the United Kingdom. It was also shown that the tendency towards more equality continued in the later nineteen forties and early nineteen fifties, largely through a deterioration in the relative position of people in the top decile group.

The size distribution of before-tax incomes for the early or mid-1950's and for the latest year available is shown in Table 1 and in the figure, for eight western European countries.[2] The changes over the last decade or so are less uniform than those which took place between 1939 and the early 1950's. Over more recent years income dispersion for the household sector as a whole has widened in some countries and narrowed in others, while in a third group such (small) changes as have occurred among the various income groups have tended to offset each other. The first group of countries (experiencing a widening income dispersion) includes Finland, Sweden, and France.[3] In all three countries the share of total income received by persons in higher income groups rose while the share of those in lower income groups declined. In Sweden the watershed falls between the fifth and sixth decile. groups, in Finland between the sixth and seventh, while in France it is in the seventh decile. Finland shows the most marked widening in income dispersion. All three countries show a notable fall in the relative incomes of the poorest groups.

Reprinted with omissions from *Incomes in Postwar Europe: A Study of Policies, Growth, and Distribution (Economic Survey of Europe in 1965)* (Geneva: United Nations Economic Commission for Europe, 1967).

TABLE 1. *Percentage Distribution of Personal Income Before Tax[a] by Decile[b] and Percentile Groups*

	United Kingdom		West Germany			Netherlands		Denmark		Norway		Sweden		France		Finland	
	1954	1964	1955	1960	1964	1952	1962	1953	1963	1957	1963	1954	1963	1956	1962	1952	1962
Decile groups																	
1	5.5	2.0	1.7	2.0	2.1	1.3	1.3	1.4	1.7	1.1	1.0	2.0	1.6	0.7	0.5	1.0	0.5
2	}	3.1	2.9	3.0	3.2	2.9	2.7	3.2	3.3	3.4	3.5	3.6	2.8	2.2	1.4	3.1	1.9
3	4.5	4.2	3.9	4.4	4.7	4.1	4.2	4.4	4.7	4.6	5.3	5.0	4.1	3.3	2.9	4.8	3.5
4	5.8	6.0	5.0	5.6	5.4	5.7	5.8	5.8	6.1	6.3	6.8	6.2	5.5	5.4	4.7	5.9	5.2
5	7.3	7.5	5.9	5.9	6.5	7.0	7.4	7.8	7.7	7.9	8.5	7.8	7.7	6.8	6.4	7.2	6.8
6	8.6	9.1	7.1	7.1	7.2	8.4	8.6	9.1	9.1	9.7	10.0	9.3	9.7	7.8	7.6	9.0	8.6
7	10.4	11.0	8.3	8.0	8.4	10.6	10.0	10.8	10.9	11.0	11.3	11.0	11.3	10.3	10.3	10.7	11.1
8	12.7	12.9	9.2	9.5	9.6	11.7	11.6	13.3	13.3	13.0	13.1	12.7	13.2	12.4	12.5	13.0	13.1
9	14.8	14.9	12.0	11.5	11.5	14.3	14.6	16.2	16.1	15.4	15.6	15.5	16.1	17.0	16.9	16.4	16.8
10	30.4	29.3	44.0	43.5	41.4	35.0	33.8	28.0	27.1	27.6	49.9	27.6	29.9	34.1	36.8	28.9	32.5
Total	100	100	100	100	100	100	100	100	100	100	100	100	100	100	100	100	100
Percentile groups																	
90-92.5	4.4	4.7	3.6	3.7	3.7	4.2	4.8	5.0	4.9	4.7	4.9	5.0	4.9	5.2	5.6	5.2	5.5
92.5-95	5.0	5.4	4.2	4.1	4.0	5.8	5.4	5.0	5.3	5.0	4.6	5.3	5.4	6.5	6.2	5.7	6.0
95-97.5	6.1	6.2	5.6	5.4	5.7	7.0	6.6	6.3	5.9	6.1	6.1	6.1	6.5	7.5	8.0	6.1	7.1
97.5-98.75	4.4	4.0	4.2	4.2	4.8	5.0	5.0	3.6	4.0	3.8	3.3	4.1	4.1	4.9	6.0	3.9	4.7
98.75-100	10.5	9.0	26.4	26.1	23.2	13.0	12.0	8.1	7.0	8.0	6.0	6.8	7.0	10.0	11.0	8.0	9.2
Total	30.4	29.3	44.0	43.5	41.4	35.0	33.0	28.0	27.1	27.6	24.9	27.3	27.9	34.1	36.8	28.9	32.5
Inequality coefficient	0.40	0.40	0.51	0.49	0.47	0.45	0.44	0.40	0.39	0.40	0.36	0.38	0.40	0.48	0.52	0.41	0.47
Maximum equalization percentage[c]	29	28	36	35	33	31	30	28	27	27	25	26	29	34	37	29	33

A clear tendency towards a reduction in income inequality, displayed at both ends of the scale, appears only in Norway. Data for West Germany are difficult to interpret since undistributed profits of private companies are included,[4] and the reduction in inequality shown in Table 6.1 between 1960 and 1964 may largely reflect the reduced margin of profits of corporations between the two years. The change in income dispersion among wage- and salary-earners . . . suggests that the tendency towards a reduction in income inequality — well-pronounced between pre-war and the early 1950's — became weaker in the later 1950's and practically ceased in the early 1960's. West Germany is thus no exception to the prevailing tendency: the forces narrowing the income dispersion appear to be weakening.

The reduction in income dispersion has been very modest in the United Kingdom, the Netherlands and Denmark (after tax). These countries, like West Germany and Norway, show one common feature: all fall in the income share of the top decile group mainly borne by the top percentile groups. At the other end of the scale, experience has varied. In the United Kingdom, the share of income absorbed by the three lowest decile groups has declined, the middle decile groups being the net decliners. In the Netherlands, the lowest decile group kept its relative position but there was a worsening in the second lowest group. In Norway, there was no significant change. But in West Germany and Denmark (after tax) the relative income share of the lowest groups was somewhat improved.

Though not much can be read into small changes over a relatively short period, the impression remains that the income gap between people in low income groups (where non-active persons such as pensioners account for a high share of total numbers and total income) and people in middle income groups has increased in several countries; the poor have become poorer in relation to the middle groups, whether the rich have become, by the same measure, richer or not.

It may be of some interest to measure income dispersion also on a quartile basis (Table 2). The quartile ratios for the total household sector (part A of Table 2 supplement the indications given by the "Gini coefficients" and by the

---

[a] *Total personal income for the United Kingdom, West Germany, Netherlands and France. Assessed income for the Scandinavian countries. Data for West Germany provided, before publication, by Professor G. Göscke. Deutsches Institut für Wirtschaftsforschung, Berlin. The figures include undistributed profits of corporations. Data for Denmark refer to "after-tax" income.*

[b] *Calculated by reference to the number of taxpayers, except for France where the unit is the household.*

[c] *The maximum equalization percentage shows the share of income to be transferred from high to low income ranges in order to obtain equal distribution. It corresponds to the maximum vertical distance between the Lorenz curve and the diagonal representing equal distribution.*

EDITOR'S NOTE — Comparable inequality coefficients may be of interest for some socialist countries of Eastern Europe. For all households, Yugoslavia in 1963 had a Gini Coefficient of .32, while Hungary in 1962 showed one of .27 (Ch. 12, p. 20 and Ch. 9, p. 26, respectively, of this source).

TABLE 2. *Indicators of Income Dispersion in Some Western European Countries*

A. Total household sector

	United Kingdom		West Germany			Netherlands		Sweden		France		Denmark		Norway		Finland	
	1954	1964	1955	1960	1964	1952	1962	1954	1963	1956	1962	1953	1963	1957	1963	1952	1962
Quartile ratio Q_3/Q_1	2.93	3.06	2.41	2.13	2.12	2.54	2.62	2.87	3.31	3.43	3.65	3.05	2.80	2.73	2.51	2.91	3.84
Interquartile deviation $(Q_3-Q_1) M$	1.02	1.06	0.84	0.73	0.73	0.88	0.88	0.96	1.09	1.20	1.24	1.06	0.99	0.94	0.86	1.08	1.27
Skewness: $(Q_3-M)/(M-Q_1)$	1.16	1.18	1.08	1.10	1.11	1.03	0.91	0.97	1.07	1.39	1.34	1.21	1.21	1.05	1.01	1.49	1.29
$(Q_3-M)/M$	0.55	0.57	0.44	0.39	0.38	0.45	0.42	0.47	0.57	0.70	0.71	0.58	0.54	0.48	0.43	0.65	0.71
$(M-Q_1)/M$	0.47	0.48	0.40	0.35	0.35	0.43	0.46	0.49	0.53	0.50	0.53	0.48	0.45	0.46	0.43	0.43	0.55

B. Wage- and salary-earners

	United Kingdom		West Germany			Netherlands		Sweden		France		
	1954	1964	1955	1960	1964	1952	1962	1954	1963	1952	1956	1962
Quartile ratio Q_3/Q_1	1.96	2.04	1.94	1.79	1.76	2.54	2.62	2.52	2.62	1.81	1.89	1.97
Interquartile deviation $(Q_3-Q_1) M$	0.67	0.70	0.64	0.58	0.55	0.86	0.84	0.84	0.88	0.63	0.65	0.69
Skewness: $(Q_3-M)/(M-Q_1)$	1.19	1.16	0.99	1.09	1.03	0.96	0.73	0.86	0.90	1.81	1.33	1.44
$(Q_3-M)/M$	0.36	0.38	0.32	0.30	0.28	0.42	0.35	0.39	0.42	0.40	0.37	0.41
$(M-Q_1)/M$	0.31	0.32	0.32	0.28	0.27	0.44	0.48	0.45	0.46	0.22	0.28	0.28

"maximum equalization percentages" reported in Table 1. Both types of measure indicate a widening of income dispersion in Finland, France and Sweden, and a narrowing in Denmark, Norway and West Germany. However, in the United Kingdom and the Netherlands the quartile ratio shows a

DISTRIBUTION OF HOUSEHOLD INCOME BEFORE TAX

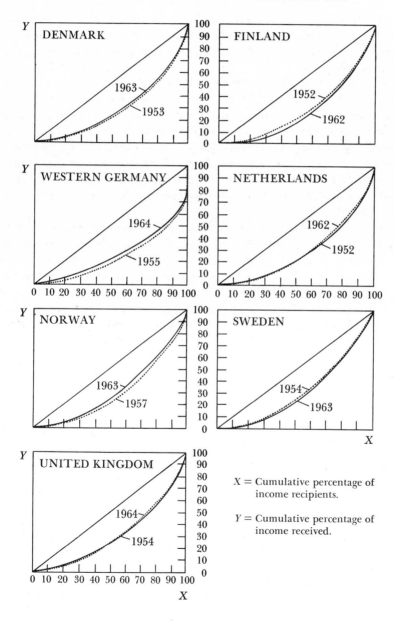

X = Cumulative percentage of income recipients.

Y = Cumulative percentage of income received.

widening in income dispersion (and not a narrowing, as shown by the coefficients of Table 1), reflecting the relatively improved position of the income groups standing between the quartiles. On the other hand, skewness increased slightly in the United Kingdom and western Germany and rather markedly in Sweden, while the distribution became more symmetrical in the other countries. The last two lines of Table 2 show whether and to what extent changes in the skewness are due to incomes standing above or below the median. In Finland, for instance, the distribution became more symmetrical, as well as more unequal, because the distance between the lower quartile and the median increased much more than the distance between the upper quartile and the median.

The changes in income dispersion in the household sector as a whole may result from several causes: a fall in the level of pensions, etc., relatively to average incomes, or a relative increase in the number of pensioners; a widening gap between the lowest and average pay level; or an increase in the proportion of young earners or unmarried women earners (who would count as separate incomes for tax purposes). These distinctions are extremely important for any analysis of the problem of low-income families, but the relative importance of all these different factors cannot easily be discovered from the data available.

From these different measures, and taking into account the statistical factors that may impair comparability of the income data, it is impossible to rank the countries according to the degree of inequality in income distribution with any certainty. Broadly, however, it appears that, whichever measure is adopted, Norway can be described as a country with relative equality in the distribution of household income, while France and to a lesser extent Finland show relative inequality. The other five countries stand in various intermediate positions according to the method of measurement used.

REFERENCES

1. See "The Distribution of Personal Income by Size" in an *Economic Survey of Europe in 1956,* Chapter IX, Geneva.
   The study also included a discussion of various methodological and statistical points.
2. Table 1 brings up to date the data contained (for those countries) in Table 3 of Chapter IX of the 1956 Survey (*op. cit.*). The data, when not otherwise specified, refer to yearly income and include male and female, part-time and full-time workers. The statistical unit, as mentioned in the text, is the taxpayer and not the family (which may include more than one taxpayer) except in France. In all countries except Sweden, the incomes of husband and wife are considered as one income. The figures for Denmark refer to incomes *after tax* (no pre-tax figures being available). They are included here for information, but are not to be regarded as comparable with the figures for other countries.
3. Data for France are less significant as an indication of trends because of the short

span between the two years shown; cyclical and random factors may have influenced the results to a considerable extent.

4. In the German data, undistributed profits of companies are not imputed to individuals (on the basis of the number of shares or some other method), but companies are combined with individuals.

CHAPTER 3

Changes in the Share of Wealth
Held by Top Wealth-Holders, 1922-1956

Robert J. Lampman

This paper presents estimates derived from federal estate tax data of the numbers of top wealth-holders* and of the aggregate amounts of wealth held by them for selected years between 1922 and 1956. Changes in the concentration of wealth during that period are delineated by relating the numbers of top wealth-holders to the population and the amount of wealth held by the top group to independent estimates of the amount of wealth held by all persons.

*   *   *

Sources of Data and Methods of Estimation

The principal source of data upon which this study is based is tabulations of federal estate tax returns. The federal estate tax has been in existence since 1916 and some information on returns filed has been published for most years. The minimum filing requirement, which is currently $60,000, has varied from $40,000 to $100,000 over the period. However, the necessary information concerning age and sex of decedents, cross-classified by type of property, is presented in such a way as to enable the derivation of a detailed representation of the distribution of wealth among living persons for relatively few years. For 1953 the Internal Revenue Service made available to the National Bureau of Economic Research the most complete tabulation of estate tax returns which has ever been prepared. In this tabulation the variables of gross estate

Reprinted with omissions from *Review of Economics and Statistics,* vol. XLI, no. 4 (November 1959), (Cambridge: Harvard University Press, 1959), by permission of the publisher.
* The term "top wealth-holder" is here defined to mean a living person having wealth in an amount above the estate tax exemption.

size, age, sex, and residence (by community-property state or non-community-property state) of decedents were cross-classified by type of property. For the year 1944 a similar breakdown, but without sex or residence information, had been prepared by the Internal Revenue Service and was the basis for the intensive study by Horst Mendershausen.* For 1948, 1949 and 1950 there is information by age and gross estate size which makes possible an estimate of aggregate gross estate without a breakdown by type of property. Similar but unpublished data for 1941 and 1946 were made available to Mendershausen. Data on economic estate by net estate size and age are available for 1922, 1924, 1941, 1944 and 1946. Finally, data on the sex of decedents by age and size of estate are available only for the years 1922, 1923, 1948, 1949, 1950 and 1953.

The method which was followed in dealing with estate tax returns is known as the estate multiplier method. This method calls for multiplying both the number of, and the property of, decedents in each age-sex group by the inverse of the mortality rate experienced by that age-sex group. This process yields an estimate of the number of living persons and the amount of estate in each age-sex group and in each estate size class. A simple hypothetical example will illustrate what is involved. Suppose that out of a population of 1,000 men aged 40 to 50, 2 men died in the year with estates of between $100,000 and $200,000. Suppose further that it is known that 5 percent of all the 1,000 men aged 40 to 50 died in the year. Then it may be assumed that the 2 men who died with $100,000-$200,000 estates were 5 percent of all the living men in the group with estates of this size. Hence, to estimate the number of living men in this estate size class we should multiply 2 by 20 (the inverse of 5 percent) to get the answer of 40 living men having $100,000-$200,000 estates.

The leading disadvantage of thus deriving wealth estimates from estate tax returns arises from the fact that the "sampling" is done by death rather than by a random draw of living persons. This means that a connection can be established between decedent wealth-holders and living wealth-holders only by use of a set of mortality rates which are assumed to reflect the mortality experience of the upper wealth-holding groups. The selection of mortality rates presents an opportunity for considerable error in the estimation of the number of living persons in each estate size and, similarly, in the aggregate of wealth held by such persons. Other problems arise to the extent that decedents' reported estates may differ from the "actual" estates of non-decedents in the same age-sex groups.

Space here does not allow a full exploration of these two difficulties. However, we have attempted to find the most appropriate set of multipliers for this purpose, and have examined in detail the peculiarities of the method of sampling by estate tax returns. We have estimated quantitative corrections in

* Raymond T. Goldsmith, *A Study of Saving in the United States,* vol. III, part III (Princeton: Princeton University Press), pp. 277–381.

those instances in which by law or practice individual wealth items are included, excluded, or differently valued than an ideal definition of personal wealth would require. In the course of the inquiry two ideal definitions were improvised. "Prime wealth" is used to connote the wealth to which a person has full title and over which he has power of disposal. "Total wealth" is a broader concept; it includes prime wealth and also wealth in which a person may have an income interest but over which he may not have any present power of disposal. Examples of the latter are rights to personal trust funds or to equities in pension and retirement funds. Our rough estimates indicate that basic variant aggregate estimates (which are the blown-up estate tax data with only one correction, namely that for reduction of insurance face value to equity amounts) are not substantially different from an ideally arrived at estimate of prime wealth, but are considerably lower than the aggregate of total wealth.

Share of Top Wealth-Holders in 1953

In 1953 there were 36,699 decedents for whom estate tax returns were filed. The aggregate gross estate reported on those returns was $7.4 billion. By use of the estate multiplier method it is estimated that the number of living persons in that year with $60,000 or more of gross estate was 1,658,795 and that their gross estates aggregated $309.2 billion. This number of persons comprised 1.04 percent of the total population and 1.6 percent of the adult population. They held about 30 percent of the total of personal wealth on the basis of either the prime wealth or total wealth variant of personal wealth (see the figure).

SHARE OF PERSONAL SECTOR EQUITY (PRIME WEALTH VARIANT) HELD BY TOP WEALTH-HOLDERS, 1953.

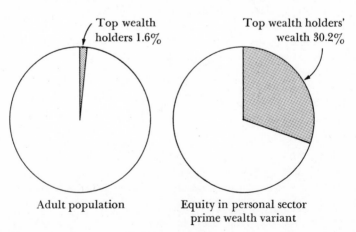

Top wealth holders 1.6%

Top wealth holders' wealth 30.2%

Adult population

Equity in personal sector prime wealth variant

The top wealth-holders, i.e., those with estates of $60,000 or more, in 1953 held 30.2 percent of the prime wealth in the personal sector, and 32.0 percent of the total wealth. These columns also show estimates of the share of each of several types of property held by top wealth-holders. These range from over 100 percent for state and local bonds down to 9 percent for life insurance reserves. Particular interest attaches to the corporate stock figure. Our estimate for 1953 is that the top wealth group held 82 percent of all the stock in the personal sector. This matter is discussed in more detail . . . in the section on type of property.

Top Wealth-Holders and the Adult Population in Selected Years, 1922-1953 (As it is defined in the text, a "top wealth-holder" is a living person having wealth in an amount above estate tax exemption level. The sharp drop in number of top wealth-holders in 1929 was due to the extraordinary high estate tax exemption of $100,000 effective in that year.)

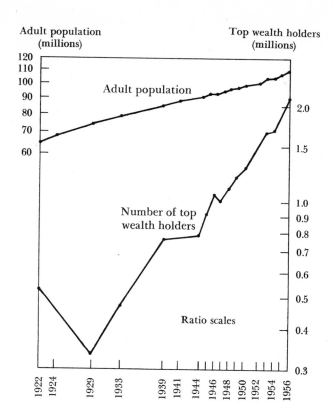

Historical Changes in Inequality

[Detailed tables which have been omitted from this selection] enable a comparison of top wealth-holders and the personal sector for the years 1953, 1949, 1945, 1939, 1929, and 1922. In looking for trends over the decades the reader should remember that varying numbers of wealth-holders are involved in each year. These changes are due to changing exemption limits, changing prices and incomes, and changing population numbers. The second figure records the changing number of top wealth-holders and the changing population between 1922 and 1953.

Comparison over the years, at least as regards aggregate economic estate, is facilitated by Table 1.

It shows the same top percent of population in 1953 as the total group of estate tax wealth-holders were in some earlier years. Thus, in 1922 the estate tax wealth-holders comprised 0.47 percent of the total population and held 29.2 percent of the wealth. In 1953 the top 0.47 percent held 22.0 percent of the wealth. . . . The easiest way to see what changes are involved is to hold the percent of population constant, which can be done with minimum guessing only for the top one-half percent of the population for the series of years. (See bottom row in Table 1.) This shows quite clearly that there were three periods with inequality declining in jumps from the 1920's to the 1930's, and then to the war and postwar periods.

TABLE 1. *Share of Top Groups of Wealth-Holders Shown as Percent of Total Population in Personal Sector Total Equity Selected Years, 1922-1953*

Percent of Population	1922	1929	1933	1939	1945	1949	1953	1954	1956
				Percent of Wealth					
Top 0.27	..	29.0	..	..	16.9	..	18.0		
0.37	..	..	23.3	..	18.6	..	20.2		
0.47	29.2	..	..	..	20.2	..	22.0		
0.58	..	..	..	29.1	21.8	..	23.8		
0.65	..	..	..	..	23.2	..	24.8		
0.80	..	..	..	..	..	22.7	26.6		
1.04	..	..	..	..	..	..	28.5	28.0	
1.26	..	..	..	..	..	..	..	..	33.0
Top 0.50	29.8	32.4	25.2	28.0	20.9	19.3	22.7	22.5	25.0

The change in inequality over time is modified somewhat by considering the percent that estate tax wealth-holders are of adults rather than of the total population. In 1920 persons over 20 years were 57.9 percent of the total population; in 1930, 61.1; in 1940, 65.9; in 1950, 65.7 percent; and in 1955, 63.8. While the share of wealth held by the top 0.5 percent of all persons fell from 32.4 in 1929 to 22.7 percent in 1953 (Table 1), the share held by the top 0.44 percent of adults had a slightly larger percentage fall from 29.0 to 18.7 percent (Table 2). The fact that there were more children, most of whom held zero wealth, per 100 of population in the 1920's than in 1953 means that the top one percent of adults were a larger part of the total population in 1953 than in 1922. Further, it means that to include the top one percent of adults in 1953 one has to count down to smaller estate sizes than in 1922. Presumably it is because of this that we find a greater loss of share on an adult than on an all-person basis. The share of the top one percent of adults shows a greater fall over the years than does the share of wealth of the top one-half percent of all persons. The top one percent of adults held 31.6 percent of wealth in 1922 and 23.6 percent in 1953.

TABLE 2. *Share of Top Groups of Wealth-Holders (Shown as Percent of Total Adult Population) in Personal Sector Total Equity Selected Years, 1922-1953*

Percent of Population Aged 20 Years and Over	1922	1929	1933	1939	1945	1949	1953	1954	1956
Top 0.44		29.0	23.3				18.7		
0.79	29.2						22.0		
0.89				29.1			22.9		
0.98					22.9		23.5		
1.26						22.7	25.9		
1.57							28.0		
1.60							28.5		
1.90									33.0
Top 1.00	31.6	36.3	28.3	30.6	22.8	20.8	23.6	23.6	26.0

CHAPTER 4

Annual and Lifetime Income
in Relation to Education: 1939-1959

Herman P. Miller

Numerous studies, conducted under varying economic conditions, have shown that persons with more schooling tend to earn more money. This relationship seems reasonable if it is assumed that the attainment of more schooling, particularly at the secondary school and college level, in some measure improves the productivity of the individual and thereby compensates for the investment of time, effort, and money. On the other hand, it is by no means inevitable that money invested in education will necessarily pay dividends or that the rate of return will be constant over time. There is always the possibility, indeed the probability, that the higher incomes of those with more years of schooling are due in part to differences in intelligence, home environment, family connections, and other factors which result from individual differences in ability and opportunity. Therefore, to some extent, the observed relationship between schooling and earnings may be a spurious one. It is, of course, difficult if at all possible to measure the extent to which these extraneous factors enter this relationship. There is, however, some evidence that "ability" as measured by scholastic achievement is highly correlated with earnings.

Economists have also long argued that earnings differentials could be reduced by an increase in education. Von Thünen was one of the earliest proponents of the use of educational policy as a means of reducing income differentials. In 1826 he asked "why in a competitive organization the incomes of manual workers remained persistently so far below the incomes of manufacturers and farmers." His explanation was that "manual workers were lacking in the elements of school knowledge without which, in spite of any other

Reprinted with omissions from *American Economic Review*, December 1960, by permission of the publisher.

qualifications, it was impossible to be an entrepreneur." In 1887, Marshall also saw in education the beneficent possibility for narrowing wage differentials.[1] More recently, Seymour Harris, noting the rapid rise in the extension of higher education, has expressed concern about the possibility that the persistent increase in the supply of college-trained workers will so flood the market that "college students within the next twenty years are doomed to disappointment after graduation, as the number of coveted openings will be substantially less than the numbers seeking them."[2] The same concern has been expressed by several noted educators including James B. Conant.[3]

During a relatively short period, such as that considered in the present report, the tendency for education to result in a reduction of income differentials could be more than offset by an increase in the demand for the services of skilled workers due to technologicacl changes in the economy. Since the supply of skilled workers, particularly those with college training, has increased considerably during the past generation, we shall attempt to determine to what extent the increase in the demand for their services has offset the tendency for their incomes to increase proportionately less than other workers.

Some of the basic statistics pertaining to the relationship between annual income and educational attainment are presented in Table 1, which shows the variations in average (mean) annual income over the past generation for men with different amounts of schooling.* Women have been excluded from the analysis; since a large proportion of them do not enter the labor market and many of those who do are employed on a part-time basis only, the relationship between their income and education may be distorted. In contrast, practically all adult men are full-time workers and it can therefore be assumed that any advantages which may accrue from more schooling are reflected in their incomes.

Table 1 shows that in every year for which data are presented the completion of an additional level of schooling was associated with higher average incomes for men. This finding parallels that obtained in numerous other studies of the relationship between education and income dating back to the early part of this century.[4] Although the income levels have changed considerably during the past 20 years, the basic relationship between the extent of schooling and income appears to have remained much the same. Contrary to the expectations of some analysts, the economic advantages accruing from the completion of additional years of schooling have not diminished in recent years.

Although income generally tends to increase with education, Table 1 shows that a year spent in completing a given level of schooling (e.g., the fourth year in high school) yields a greater return than any of the years lead-

---

* EDITOR'S NOTE. The original source should be consulted for additional data showing the education-income relationship for various age groups. Notes on the sources and limitations of these figures will also be found in the original.

TABLE 1.   *Mean Income (or Earnings) for Male 25 Years of Age and Over, by Years of School Completed and Age:* 1939, 1946, 1949, 1956, *and* 1958

Years of School Completed & Age	1939	1946	1949	1956	1958
Total: 25 Years Old and Over:					
Elementary: Total	$1,036	$2,041	$2,394	$3,107	$3,096
Less than 8 years	(e)	1,738	2,062	2,613	2,551
8 years	(e)	2,327	2,829	3,732	3,769
High School: 1 to 3 years	1,379	2,449	3,226	4,480	4,618
4 years	1,661	2,939	3,784	5,439	5,567
College: 1 to 3 years	1,931	3,654	4,423	6,363	6,966
4 years or more	2,607	4,527	6,179	8,490	9,206

ing up to graduation. This difference may reflect a selection in terms of ability between those who do and those who do not complete their schooling. Thus in 1958, men who started high school but did not graduate, received on the average an annual income of about $400 more per year of schooling than men who completed their schooling with graduation from elementary school. High school graduates, however, received about $500 more of annual income per year of schooling than men who started high school but never graduated. Similarly, men who attended college but did not graduate had, on the average, about $700 more per year of schooling than high school graduates. The comparable differential for college graduates was about $900 per year of schooling.

*   *   *

Estimates of lifetime income provide summary measures of the financial returns associated with education which cannot be readily obtained from the annual data presented obove. The estimates of lifetime income presented here are derived figures — one might say synthetic figures — based on variations in the payments to individuals in different age and education groups at a given time, specifically the calendar years for which data are presented. The figures are, therefore, based on a cross-section of the population in 1939, 1946, 1949, 1956, and 1958, and not on life-cycle data which would trace a man's income from the time he starts to work until he retires. Actually there is some question whether life-cycle data would be more suitable for the present analysis; cross-section data have the advantage that "they are free from the influence of variants such as periods of industrial depression or unsual activity with their changes in opportunities for employment, in wage rates, and in the cost of living."[5]

Standard life-table techniques were used in computing the figures shown in Table 2. First, an estimate was made of the number of 100,000 children born in 1939, 1946, 1949, 1956, and 1958 who would survive to each given year of age. These estimates were made from the appropriate life tables.[6] By way of illustration, it was estimated that out of 100,000 infants born alive in 1956, about 96,000 would survive to age 18, at which time they would enter the labor market. The basic problem consisted of estimating the life span of these 96,000 survivors and the amount of income they would receive during their lifetime. For this purpose, it was assumed that survival rates for men in

TABLE 2. *Lifetime Income (Earnings) Based on Arithmetic Means for Males in Selected Age Groups, by Years of School Completed, for the United States*

Years of School Completed & Age	1939[a]	1946[b]	1949[c]	1956[d]	1958[c]
Income from Age 18 to Death:					
Elementary: Total	(e)	(e)	$113,330	$154,593	$154,114
Less than 8 years[d]	(e)	(e)	98,222	132,736	129,764
8 years	(e)	(e)	132,683	180,857	181,695
High School: 1 to 3 years	(e)	(e)	152,068	205,277	211,193
4 years	(e)	(e)	185,279	253,631	257,557
College: 1 to 3 years	(e)	(e)	209,282	291,581	315,504
4 years or more	(e)	(e)	296,377	405,698	435,242
Income from Age 25 to Death:					
Elementary: Total	(e)	$ 87,004	104,998	143,712	143,808
Less than 8 years[d]	(e)	74,369	91,095	123,295	120,965
8 years	(e)	98,702	122,787	168,004	169,976
High School: 1 to 3 years	(e)	107,940	141,870	192,254	198,881
4 years	(e)	135,852	174,740	237,776	241,844
College: 1 to 3 years	(e)	161,699	201,938	281,553	305,395
4 years or more	(e)	201,731	286,833	391,992	419,871
Income from Age 18 to 64:					
Elementary: Total	$ 40,005	(e)	100,413	138,127	137,786
Less than 8 years[d]	**(e)**	(e)	86,912	117,930	115,418
8 years	(e)	(e)	116,968	161,124	161,643
High School: 1 to 3 years	56,653	(e)	132,371	182,795	188,362
4 years	71,453	(e)	159,487	224,529	231.509
College: 1 to 3 years	77,775	(e)	180,841	254,092	279,640
4 years or more	109,961	(e)	251,493	354,457	382,982
Income from Age 25 to 64:					
Elementary: Total	37,172	74,071	91,932	127,047	127,286
Less than 8 years[d]	(e)	62,334	79,654	108,310	106,449
8 years	(e)	84,687	106,889	148,033	149,687
High School: 1 to 3 years	53,011	92,044	121,943	169,501	175,779
4 years	67,383	114,023	148,649	208,322	215,487
College: 1 to 3 years	73,655	138,871	173,166	243,611	269,105
4 years or more	104,608	168,983	241,427	340,131	366,990

[a] *Retricted to persons reporting $1 or more of wage or salary income and less than $50 of other income for native whites and Negroes.*
[b] *Total money earnings.*
[c] *Total money income.*
[d] *Includes persons reporting no years of school completed, not shown separately.*
[e] *Not available.*

each education group would be the same as for all white males in 1956. On this basis, it was estimated that these 96,000 men would live a total of nearly 5,000,000 man-years between age 18 and the time the last one died. It was further assumed that during each year of life, these men would receive an average income corresponding to that received by men in the same age group with the same amount of education. The averages used for this purpose are those shown above in Table 1 plus estimates for age groups under 25 based on published and unpublished data of the Census Bureau. The averages (means) are based on persons reporting $1 or more of income, excluding the relatively small number of men in most age groups without income.

There are several cautions that should be considered before discussing the figures in Table 2. First, the figures are not exactly comparable from year to year due to changes in the income concept. The data for 1939 are for wages and salaries, 1946 are for earnings, and 1949, 1956, and 1958 are for total income. These variations in concept may have some impact on changes over time. A more general consideration is the fact that the estimates reflect the economic conditions and other circumstances which existed in each of the years for which data are shown. Some of the differences from year to year may reflect changes in these circumstances. The increase, for example, in the value of a college education by about $140,000 between 1949 and 1958 reflects the increase in prices as well as changes in the underlying relationships. These factors demonstrate an important advantage of the cross-sectional approach used in preparing the estimates. Since the averages used for each year are based on the experience for that year, they implicitly provide estimates in dollars of constant purchasing power for persons in all age groups in that year.

A final caution relates to the possible intrusion of extraneous factors in the relationship between lifetime earnings and education. Family influence in the form of financial help while at college and assistance in obtaining relatively high-paying jobs cannot be ignored; but, at the same time, should not be exaggerated. In 1950, about one-third of the college students away from home came from families with less than average incomes. Few of these students could expect much financial help from their families, or assistance in locating lucrative job opportunities.

In every year for which data are presented, additional schooling is associated with a very substantial increase in lifetime income. On the basis of conditions in 1958, an elementary school graduate could expect to receive during his lifetime about $52,000 (or two-fifths) more income, on the average, than the person who had no schooling or who terminated his formal education before completing the eighth grade. The difference between the expected lifetime income of the average elementary school and high school graduate was equally striking. In 1958, the average elementary school graduate could expect a lifetime income of about $182,000 as compared with about $258,000 for the average high school graduate. The expected income differential associated with the four years of high school education therefore amounted to about $76,000 or 42 percent.

Since a college degree is the "open sesame" to many, if not most, high-paying jobs, it should come as no surprise that the greatest income gains associated with additional schooling appear at the college level. On the basis of 1958 data, a college graduate could expect to receive about $435,000 income during his lifetime as compared with $258,000 for the average high school graduate. It can, therefore, be estimated that the approximately 4½ years of schooling beyond the high school level were associated with an increase of about $177,000 in lifetime income or about $40,000 per year of schooling.

EDITOR'S NOTE. The previous selection has summarized the relationship between education and income. Thus, the final step in assessing the impact of education on the distribution of income should be a survey of the distribution of education itself. This would form a clear parallel with the earlier discussion of the distribution of real wealth. Unfortunately, the connection between educational distributions and income distribution patterns is not so simple. For various reasons, a given quantity of education (unlike a quantity of real wealth) may be worth more or less in the market, for reasons not related to the education itself but to the nature of the person in whom it is embodied (for example, race and sex characteristics). Again, a certain lump of education may be worth more in some industries or regions than in others.

Despite these caveats, some indicators of education's probable influence on income distribution and the incidence of poverty should be offered. The figures below show the median years of school completed by all persons 25 years old or above, broken down by race, sex, and residence. Interested students can find more detailed presentations in periodic Census reports on population characteristics.

Median Schooling, March 1967

	White	Negro
Males	12.1	8.7
Central city residents	12.1	9.7
Metropolitan suburb residents	12.3	8.9
Residents outside metropolitan areas	11.0	6.7*
Females	12.1	9.6
Central city residents	12.1	10.5
Metropolitan suburb residents	12.3	10.7
Residents outside metropolitan areas	11.8	8.0*

*These two figures are for "nonwhite;" hence, they are not strictly comparable with figures for Negroes alone.

REFERENCES

1. "The normal earnings of a carpenter and a surveyor might be brought much nearer together than they are, by even so slight and easy an improvement on our present social arrangements as the extending to all persons of adequate natural ability the opportunity of receiving the training required for the higher ranks of industry." (A. C. PIGOU, editor, *Memorials of Alfred Marshall*, New York, 1956, p. 214).

2. S. E. HARRIS, *The Market for College Graduates,* Cambridge, Mass., 1949, p. 64.

3. J. B. CONANT, *Education in a Divided World,* Cambridge, Mass., 1948, p. 198.

4. Educational Policies Commission, *Education and Economic Well-Being in American Democracy,* National Education Association and American Association of School Administrators, Washington, D.C., 1940, p. 115.

5. W. S. WOYTINSKY, "Income Cycle in the Life of Families and Individuals," *Soc. Sec. Bull.,* June 1943, p. 9.

6. The following life tables were used: 1939, Life Table for White Males from *U.S. Life Tables and Actuarial Tables,* 1939-1941, Bureau of the Census, 1946; 1946, Abridged Life Table for White Males, 1946, *Vital Statistics of the United States,* 1946, Pt. I; 1949, Abridged Life Table for White Males, 1949, *Vital Statistics of the United States,* 1949, Pt. I; 1956, Abridged Life Table for White Males, 1956, *Vital Statistics — Special Reports,* Vol. 48, No. 6, June 19, 1958; 1958, Abridged Life Table for White Males, 1957, *Vital Statistics — Special Reports,* Vol. 50, No. 2, July 28, 1959.

Part 3

The Incidence and
Causes of Poverty

Editor's Survey

This is a book about poverty, among other things. Yet when we attempt to forge a rigorous definition of poverty, which might give us a yardstick to test whether someone is poor, we find that we are dealing with a rather loose concept. Indeed, the search for an absolute level of living standards which can be identified with poverty in every place and at all times must end in failure. This is not to say that such efforts have not been made. The idea of "subsistence wages" which we encountered in Part I reflects one such fruitless attempt by an early generation of economists. Other attempts have been made to measure the bare minimum of calories, other nutritional needs, clothing and shelter which will allow a man to survive. Even here, the relative nature of poverty or subsistence must already be obvious — it will take more of almost everything to survive in New England than in Pago Pago.

Speaking more generally, it should be obvious that it is not only the absolute level of one's living standard that determines his poorness. To be poor in India or Egypt is hardly the same as to be poor in the United States. Less sophisticated conservative writers have often used this undeniable fact to establish (to their satisfaction) that America's "poor" are hardly poor at all. But this is not the lesson which we should draw from a world-wide survey of the varying amounts of material comforts associated with being poor. Instead, we should recognize that a measure of deprivation must be an integral part of any definition of poverty. Indeed, the amount by which one falls short of society's average level of well-being may be a more important determinant of poverty than the standard of living which the poor individual endures.

The definition of any level of income below which we wish to consider poverty to lie must reflect or incorporate some judgment about the degree of deprivation which makes one poor in a given society. One poverty line used in the United States was derived in a way which makes this clear: Department of Agriculture estimates of costs of basic food needs were used as a basis, which were then multiplied by three (low-income families in this country typically spend one-third of their income on food). It is clear that the building blocks for the estimate — estimated "needs" — are conditioned by the surrounding society with regard to their level and particularly their composition.

Once a working definition of poverty has been developed, one can proceed to analyze patterns and movements in the poor population. The rough criterion used in the 1964 *Economic Report* served as the basis for the call to arms of the war on poverty. The articles by Orshansky and Jackson and Velten use more elaborate and sensitive poverty lines to depict the impacts of poverty in the United States. The reader should bear in mind, however, that the cold, hard data which we see are dependent on the numerical definition of poverty which has been adopted. It is for this reason that some writers have used a number of different lines to measure the "poor" or the "near-poor."

The figures here presented show progress in the reduction of poverty over the last decade. According to more recent revised data, this trend continued beyond the 1966 cutoff date of Orshansky. From 1966 to 1968, with continuation of low levels of unemployment and rising wages, the percentage of Americans living below the poverty level fell from 15 to 13. Of this decline, the largest relative impact was on the incidence of poverty among nonwhites where the proportion of poor fell from 40 to 33 percent. The comparable reduction for whites was from 11 to 10 percent. Despite these improvements, the incidence of poverty is still three times greater for nonwhites than for the white population.

Part of the reduction in measured incidence of poverty over the last decade is due to an apparent increase in the degree of deprivation (shortfall from society's average) required to be counted as poor. Thus, in 1959 the poverty line for a non-farm family of four ($2,973) was 46 percent of the median income of all families in the United States. Although the dollar value of that poverty line had increased by 1968 (to $3,553), its standing relative to all family incomes had fallen to 41 percent. It is easy to see how this happened: The poverty lines were adjusted upward for increases in the consumer price index, while other incomes were increasing faster than the rate of price inflation. The poverty line was frozen at a fixed level of real income, but other real incomes were increasing. There is thus no mystery about what *did* happen over this decade.

The real issue is: What *should* happen to the relative standing of the poverty level as a rich nation becomes richer? If we were correct in our earlier observations that poverty is as much relative deprivation as absolute level of material comforts, then today's measured poor must be considered to be somewhat worse off than the poor of 1959. They have lost ground with respect to the living standards of other Americans. When we turn to the area of public policy, this finding takes on additional significance. Many welfare reform or negative income tax proposals would use "the" poverty line as part of income maintenance techniques. Here the student should consider what relationship the poverty line should bear to average levels of income. Should the real value of the poverty line be shifted upward, so that the poor share in the increasing real income of our society? If so, should the real poverty line rise faster or slower than increases in our productivity? What information would we need to fairly and thoroughly examine the issues involved?

CHAPTER 5

The Problem of Poverty in America

Council of Economic Advisers (1964)

Eliminating Poverty — A National Goal

There will always be some Americans who are better off than others. But it need not follow that "the poor are always with us." In the United States today we can see on the horizon a society of abundance, free of much of the misery and degradation that have been the age-old fate of man. Steadily rising productivity, together with an improving network of private and social insurance and assistance, has been eroding mass poverty in America. But the process is far too slow. It is high time to redouble and to concentrate our efforts to eliminate poverty.

Poverty is costly not only to the poor but to the whole society. Its ugly by-products include ignorance, disease, delinquency, crime, irresponsibility, immorality, indifference. None of these social evils and hazards will, of course, wholly disappear with the elimination of poverty. But their severity will be markedly reduced. Poverty is no purely private or local concern. It is a social and national problem.

But the overriding objective is to improve the quality of life of individual human beings. For poverty deprives the individual not only of material comforts but of human dignity and fulfillment. Poverty is rarely a builder of character.

The poor inhabit a world scarcely recognizable, and rarely recognized, by the majority of their fellow Americans. It is a world apart, whose inhabitants are isolated from the mainstream of American life and alienated from its values. It is a world where Americans are literally concerned with day-to-day survival — a roof over their heads, where the next meal is coming from. It is a world where a minor illness is a major tragedy, where pride and privacy

Reprinted with omissions from *The Annual Report of the Council of Economic Advisers,* 1964.

must be sacrificed to get help, where honesty can become a luxury and ambition a myth. Worst of all, the poverty of the fathers is visited upon the children.

Equality of opportunity is the American dream, and universal education our noblest pledge to realize it. But, for the children of the poor, education is a handicap race; many are too ill-prepared and ill-motivated at home to learn at school. And many communities lengthen the handicap by providing the worst schooling for those who need the best.

Although poverty remains a bitter reality for too many Americans, its incidence has been steadily shrinking. The fruits of general economic growth have been widely shared; individuals and families have responded to incentives and opportunities for improvement; government and private programs have raised the educational attainments, housing standards, health, and productivity of the population; private and social insurance has increasingly protected families against loss of earnings due to death, disability, illness, old age, and unemployment. Future headway against poverty will likewise require attacks on many fronts: the active promotion of a full-employment, rapid-growth economy; a continuing assault on discrimination; and a wide range of other measures to strike at specific roots of low income. As in the past, progress will require the combined efforts of all levels of government and of private individuals and groups.

All Americans will benefit from this progress. Our Nation's most precious resource is its people. We pay twice for poverty: once in the production lost in wasted human potential, again in the resources diverted to coping with poverty's social by-products. Humanity compels our action, but it is sound economics as well.

The sections below will chart the topography of poverty.* A few significant features of this bleak landscape deserve emphasis in advance. Poverty occurs in many places and is endured by people in many situations; but its occurrence is nonetheless highly concentrated among those with certain characteristics. The scars of discrimination, lack of education, and broken families show up clearly from almost any viewpoint. Here are some landmarks:

— One-fifth of our families and nearly one-fifth of our total population are poor.

— Of the poor, 22 percent are nonwhite; and nearly one-half of all non-whites live in poverty.

— The heads of over 60 percent of all poor families have only grade school educations.

— Even for those denied opportunity by discrimination, education significantly raises the chance to escape from poverty. Of all nonwhite families

*EDITOR'S NOTE. The tentative poverty benchmark employed by the Council in this path-breaking report was a family income of $3,000/yr. or less.

headed by a person with 8 years or less of schooling, 57 percent are poor. This percentage falls to 30 for high school graduates and to 18 percent for those with some college education.

— But education does not remove the effects of discrimination: when non-whites are compared with whites at the same level of education, the nonwhites are poor about twice as often.

— One-third of all poor families are headed by a person over 65, and almost one-half of families headed by such a person are poor.

— Of the poor, 54 percent live in cities, 16 percent on farms, 30 percent as rural nonfarm residents.

— Over 40 percent of all farm families are poor. More than 80 percent of nonwhite farmers live in poverty.

— Less than half of the poor are in the South; yet a southerner's chance of being poor is roughly twice that of a person living in the rest of the country.

— One-quarter of poor families are headed by a woman; but nearly one-half of all families headed by a woman are poor.

— When a family and its head have several characteristics frequently associated with poverty, the chances of being poor are particularly high: a family headed by a young woman who is nonwhite and has less than an eighth grade education is poor in 94 out of 100 cases. Even if she is white, the chances are 85 out of 100 that she and her children will be poor.

Strategy Against Poverty

Public concern for the poor is not new. Measures to prevent, and particularly to relieve, poverty have an ancient origin in every civilization. Each generation in America has forged new weapons in the public and private fight against this perennial enemy. Until recent decades the focus was primarily on the alleviation of distress, rather than on prevention or rehabilitation. Yet all the while, the sources of poverty have been eroded as a by-product of a general advance in economic well-being and of measures designed to achieve other social goals. Universal education has been perhaps the greatest single force, contributing both to social mobility and to general economic growth.

The social legislation of the New Deal, strengthened and expanded in every subsequent national administration, marked a turning point by recognizing a *national* interest in the economic well-being and security of individuals and families. The social insurance programs established in the 1930's were designed principally to alleviate poverty in old age and to shield families from the loss of all income during periods of unemployment. The tasks for our generation are to focus and coordinate our older programs and some new ones into a comprehensive long-range attack on the poverty that remains. A new federally led effort is needed, with special emphasis on prevention and rehabilitation.

Maintaining High Employment

The maintenance of high employment — a labor market in which the demand for workers is strong relative to the supply — is a powerful force for the reduction of poverty. In a strong labor market there are new and better opportunities for the unemployed, the partially employed, and the low paid. Employers have greater incentive to seek and to train workers when their own markets are large and growing. To fight poverty in a slack economy with excess unemployment is to tie one hand behind our backs. We need not do so.

Accelerating economic growth. In the longer run the advance of standards of living depends on the rate of growth of productivity per capita, and this in turn depends on science and technology, capital accumulation, and investments in human resources. Growth also expands the resources available to governments and private organizations to finance specific programs against poverty.

Fighting discrimination. A program to end racial discrimination in America will open additional exits from poverty, and for a group with an incidence of poverty at least twice that for the Nation as a whole. Discrimination against Negroes, Indians, Spanish-Americans, Puerto Ricans and other minorities reduces their employment opportunities, wastes their talents, inhibits their motivation, limits their educational achievement and restricts their choice of residence and neighborhood. Almost half of nonwhite Americans are poor. For nonwhites infant mortality is twice as high as for whites; maternal deaths are four times as frequent; expectation of life for males at age 20 is almost five years less.

Discriminatory barriers have been erected and maintained by many groups. Business and labor, other private organizations and individuals, and all levels of government must share in their removal.

The economic costs of discrimination to the total society are also large. By discrimination in employment, the Nation denies itself the output of which the talents and training of the nonwhite population are already capable. By discrimination in education and environment, the Nation denies itself the potential talents of one-ninth of its citizens. But the basic case against discrimination is not economic. It is that discrimination affronts human dignity.

The Executive Branch is vigorously pursuing nondiscriminatory policies and practices. It has proposed comprehensive Civil Rights legislation that would help make it possible for all Americans to develop and use their capabilities. But it will have its full effect only when all Americans join in dedicating themselves to the justice of this cause.

Improving regional economies. In a dynamic economy, whole regions lose their economic base when their natural resources are depleted or changes in taste and technology pass them by. Appalachia and the cutover areas of the Northern Lakes States are contemporary examples. State and regional programs, assisted by the Federal Government through the Area Redevelopment Administration, seek to restore in such regions a viable economic base suitable to their physical and human resources.

Rehabilitating urban and rural communities. Overcrowded, unsanitary, and unsafe neighborhoods are a drag on the economic progress of a whole city. Eradication of slums can provide improved opportunities for their residents and enable them to contribute more to the community. Improved relocation programs are essential to avoid pushing the poor from an old slum to a new one. Improved community facilities and services, including day care centers for children of working mothers, are needed in low-income urban areas. (Nine million children under 12 have mothers who work outside the home. Of these, fully 400,000 are now expected to care for themselves while their mothers work full time.) Among facilities that are critically needed for slum families are adequate housing, hospitals, parks, libraries, schools, and community centers. Improvement of the physical environment, however, is not enough. Especially when newcomers to urban areas are involved, there need to be programs to facilitate adaptation to the new environments. The Administration's proposed National Service Corps could aid and supplement local efforts to provide these and other urgently needed services.

Parallel programs for rehabilitation are needed in depressed rural areas. In some rural communities, even in whole counties, almost every family is at the poverty level. In such situations local resources cannot possibly provide adequate schools, libraries, and health and community centers. A healthy farm economy is basic to the strength of farm communities; and the Rural Area Development program and the ARA are also of assistance in improving income and employment opportunities on and off the farm. Particular attention must be paid to the special problems of depressed nonfarm rural areas — such as the Ozarks or the larger part of rural Appalachia; of Indians on reservations; and of migrant workers.

Improving labor markets. Improved employment information can help potential workers learn about and take advantage of new job opportunities, sometimes in different industries, occupations, and locations. A strengthened Federal-State Employment Service, better guidance and counseling services, development of a system for early warning of labor displacement resulting from technological change, assistance in worker relocation (as provided by the Trade Expansion Act and in the recent amendments to the Manpower Development and Training Act), increased amounts and duration of unemployment insurance benefits and extension of its coverage — all these will enable more persons to maintain or increase their earnings.

Expanding educational opportunities. If children of poor families can be given skills and motivation, they will not become poor adults. Too many young people are today condemned to grossly inadequate schools and instruction. Many communities lack resources for developing adequate schools or attracting teachers of high quality. Other communities concentrate their resources in the higher income areas, providing inadequate educational opportunities to those at the bottom of the economic ladder. Effective education for children of poor families must be tailored to their special needs; and such education is more costly and surely more difficult than for children from homes that are economically and socially more secure. The school must play a larger role in the development of poor youngsters if they are to have, in fact, "equal opportunity." This often means that schooling must start on a pre-school basis and include a broad range of more intensive services. The President's program against poverty will propose project grants to strengthen educational services to children of the poor.

Where such special efforts have been made, it has become clear that few children are unable to benefit from good education. Only a small percentage of those born each year are incapable of acquiring the skills, motivation, and attitudes necessary for productive lives. The idea that the bulk of the poor are condemned to that condition because of innate deficiencies of character or intelligence has not withstood intensive analysis.

Enlarging job opportunities for youth. Recent legislation for Vocational Education will help to improve the preparation of teen-agers for productive employment. Improved counseling and employment services are needed for those leaving school. The Administration's proposed Youth Employment Act will strengthen on-the-job training and public service employment programs, and will establish a Youth Conservation Corps.

Improving the nation's health. The poor receive inadequate medical care, from before birth to old age. And poverty is perpetuated by poor health, malnutrition, and chronic disabilities. New and expanded school health and school lunch programs will improve both health and education. The recent Report of the President's Task Force on Manpower Conservation, based on a survey of Selective Service rejectees, lends particular emphasis to the importance of improving our health programs, especially those aimed at children and young people. That Report also underlines the need to cope with educational deficiencies by expanded vocational and literacy training and improved counseling.

Legislation has recently been enacted to increase the supply of physicians and dentists, and to expand mental health services. The poor have a special stake in our ongoing programs of medical research. Many aged persons are confronted by medical needs beyond their financial means. Passage of the program to provide hospital insurance for the aged under the social security system is an urgent immediate step.

Promoting adult education and training. In an economy characterized by continual technological advance, many adults will not be able to earn incomes above the poverty line without new skills and training. The Manpower

Training and Development Act and the training programs under the Area Redevelopment Act represent public recognition of this need. These and other programs to train and retrain workers must be expanded and strengthened, placing more emphasis on those with the greatest educational deficiencies. In particular, our relatively modest efforts to provide basic literacy have proved the value of such training. Many who have been regarded (and have often regarded themselves) as uneducable can and do learn the basic skills, and these in turn equip them for training programs supplying the specific skills sought by employers. Such basic education is now being made available to many more adults.

Assisting the aged and disabled. Continued long-run improvement of social insurance benefits, along with expanded programs to cover hospital-related costs for the aged, and augmented construction of housing to meet the particular needs of the aged, are necessary steps in a continuing campaign against poverty.

Organizing the Attack on Poverty

In this latest phase of the Nation's effort to conquer poverty, we must marshal already developed resources, focus already expressed concerns, and back them with the full strength of an aroused public conscience.

Poverty, as has been shown, has many faces. It is found in the North and in the South; in the East and in the West; on the farm and in the city. It is found among the young and among the old, among the employed and the unemployed. Its roots are many and its causes complex. To defeat it requires a coordinated and comprehensive attack. No single program can embrace all who are poor, and no single program can strike at all the sources of today's and tomorrow's poverty.

Diverse attacks are needed, but we must not lose sight of their common target — poverty. Many programs are directed against social problems which the poor share with the non-poor — insecurity of income, depressed regional economies, inefficient and unattractive rural and urban environments, disabilities of health and age, inadequate educational opportunities, racial discrimination. These are all to the good. But we must not let poor individuals and families get lost between these programs. Programs must be sufficiently coordinated that, whatever else they individually accomplish, they act together to lift the economic and social status of America's poor. And soon. For war has now been declared on poverty as such.

This coordinated attack must be adapted to local circumstances. The needs of the poor are not the same in East Kentucky and in West Harlem. Coordinated programs of community action will play a critical role in the assault on poverty. Communities will be encouraged and helped to develop individual programs aimed at the special problems of their own poor families. Individual communities thus can participate in a nationwide action, research and demonstration program, backed by the interest and resources of State and local governments and private organizations, and the coordinated efforts of Federal agencies working in such fields as education, health, housing, welfare, and agriculture.

Conquest of poverty is well within our power. About $11 billion a year would bring all poor families up to the $3,000 income level we have taken to be the minimum for a decent life. The majority of the Nation could simply tax themselves enough to provide the necessary income supplements to their less fortunate citizens. The burden — one-fifth of the annual defense budget, less than 2 percent of GNP — would certainly not be intolerable. But this "solution" would leave untouched most of the roots of poverty. Americans want to *earn* the American standard of living by their own efforts and contributions. It will be far better, even if more difficult, to equip and to permit the poor of the Nation to produce and to earn the additional $11 billion, and more. We can surely afford greater generosity in relief of distress. But the major thrust of our campaign must be against causes rather than symptoms. We can afford the cost of that campaign too.

The Nation's attack on poverty must be based on a change in national attitude. We must open our eyes and minds to the poverty in our midst. Poverty is not the inevitable fate of any man. The condition can be eradicated; and since it can be, it must be. It is time to renew our faith in the worth and capacity of all human beings; to recognize that, whatever their past history or present condition, all kinds of Americans can contribute to their country; and to allow Government to assume its responsibility for action and leadership in promoting the general welfare.

CHAPTER 6

The Shape of Poverty in 1966

Mollie Orshansky

At the end of 1959, a total of 38.9 million Americans in 13.4 million households were classified as poor. Four years later the number with inadequate income had declined by about 3½ million. By the end of 1966, the same income standard — considered by some almost too niggardly to be American — counted 9¼ million fewer persons as living in poverty than were so designated in 1959.

The number not sharing fully in the Nation's prosperity thus was growing smaller, but the fact that it is mainly certain groups who are bypassed is more obvious and hence more disturbing. It becomes then even more challenging to ensure for all Americans the good living long taken for granted by the majority.

The fact that there now exists, if only until a better measure is developed, an official working definition of poverty, makes it possible to evaluate progress and pinpoint specific areas of concern in a way not feasible before.

In 1965 the Social Security Administration developed two criteria to assay the relative economic well-being of different types of households in this country, and the lower of these two dollar measures is being used as the current delineator of poverty for program planning.[1] The implied level of living is that afforded by an income in 1966 of about $65 weekly for an average family of four not living on a farm (and correspondingly more for larger households and less for smaller). The slightly less stringent measure, labeled "near poor," requires about a third more in income, or about $20 more for a four-person family, than the amount of income at the poverty threshold.*

Reprinted with omissions from the *Social Security Bulletin,* March 1968.
*EDITOR'S NOTE. Numerous very detailed tables on poverty incidence are to be found in the original.

The poverty and low-income criteria, adjusted for price changes, have been carried back as far as 1959, so that it is possible to see the changes in both the number and the kinds of households identified as poor or near poor during the seven successive years of plenty.

The Poverty Roster, 1966

By 1966, the income of the United States population had climbed to a new high. Even after allowance for higher prices, families averaged $5 in real income for every $4 available to them in 1959. But though a majority in the country were enjoying record-high incomes, a total of 29.7 million persons, or 1 out of every 7 noninstitutionalized Americans, were in households with money incomes for the year below the poverty line. The poor were distributed throughout 11 million households, which contained one sixth of all the Nation's children under age 18. Indeed, in 1966 as in 1959, such youngsters made up half of all the persons in poor families.

The total for the poverty roster in 1966 denoted a drop of 9.2 million from the number counted poor in 1959, a year when nearly every fourth person was living in a household with income insufficient to cover even the barest necessities. The number called near poor — those with incomes barely above the poverty threshold yet still in what might be termed the low-income range — is now, however, 15.2 million, very little different from the 15.8 million so characterized 7 years before. Another 5 million would be added to the ranks of the economically deprived were we to include the 2 million persons in institutions — not now in the count but ranking among the poorest of the poor — as well as the many aged persons and parent-child groups not now on the poverty roll but who would be there if they had to rely on their own resources instead of on those of the more fortunate relatives whose homes they share.

Included among the 45 million Americans designated poor or near poor in 1966 were 18-28 percent of the Nation's children and from 30 to 43 percent of the aged — groups whose members could do little on their own to improve their income. Minorities, however defined, were less favored than the rest. Counted poor were nearly 1 in 4 of those living on farms, compared with 1 in 7 of the nonfarm population, but most of the poor were not on a farm. The total with low incomes included from 12 to 19 percent of the white population and from 41 to 54 percent of the nonwhite. Of the total in poverty, however, 2 out of 3 were white, and among the near poor 4 out of 5 were white.

As might be expected, the family with the head currently employed was only one-fourth as likely to be poor as one with the head unemployed or out of the labor force altogether. Yet every sixth poor family of two or more persons was that of a white man under age 65 who had worked every week in the year — the kind of family that has the best chance to escape poverty in our society.

Because income of families generally rose more than enough to offset rising prices between 1959 and 1966 while the poverty line was adjusted only by the amount of such price rise, those counted poor at the end of the period were even less well off, compared with the nonpoor population, than those counted poor at the beginning. But beyond this, the profile of poverty had changed, leaving more difficult problems to solve. The decline in the number considered poor was largely a result of increased job opportunities and higher earnings. Those equipped to make the most of such possibilities fared best. By 1966, families of a woman with children, the aged, and the households of the disabled accounted for about 3 million of the 6 million families counted poor.

For the aged as for the disabled, changes in social security benefits and other existing public programs to provide income when earnings are lacking could serve to improve economic status and thus alleviate poverty.[2] But for families with young children, in straitened circumstances because there is no father in the home or because his earnings are too low to support the number dependent on him, other remedies have yet to be devised. One type of proposal currently under discussion is to make money grants for children in families during their minority.

The final section of this article reports on the number of households who received payments from existing public income-support programs in 1965 and suggests how many households not poor as we now count them were removed from poverty only by such payments, and how many payees who were poor before the payments remained poor even after they got them.

The Poverty Index

The index of poverty used as a reference criterion is a far from generous measure. It is the minimum income per household of a given size, composition, and farm-nonfarm status, as set by the Social Security Administration. In 1966 the Agriculture Department economy food plan, which is the core of the poverty index, provided for total food expenditures of only 75 cents a day per person (in an average four-person family). The index adds only twice this amount to cover all family living items other than food. It has not been adjusted for changes since 1959, except to allow for rising prices.*

Between 1959 and 1966 both the income received by consumers and the prices of what they bought continued to climb but income went up faster. Inevitably then, the poverty thresholds, adjusted only for price changes, were farther below general levels of income at the end of the period than at the outset. Median income of four-person families in 1966 was $8,340, according

---

* The measure of near poverty — about one-third higher in cost — centers about the low-cost food plan.

to the Bureau of the Census — just two and one-half times the nonfarm poverty threshold of $3,335. In 1959, by contrast, median income for four-person families was $6,070, about twice the poverty index cut-off line. In other words, the average income of four-person families had increased by 37 percent but the poverty line by only 9 percent, or one-fourth as much.[3]

Changes in Poverty, 1959–66

In 1959, 24 percent of the Nation's households — counting as households both one-person units and families of two or more persons — had so little income as to be counted poor. Seven years later only 17.7 percent had too little money income to support the number dependent on them. What is perhaps of greater significance than the general improvement is that, as already indicated, more of the poor in 1966 were persons of limited earning capacity or those whom age, home responsibilities, race discrimination, or other factors kept out of the labor force altogether.

Children — particularly if they live in a home without a father — and old people are at a disadvantage, compared with persons aged 18-64, when it comes to earning. The number of children under age 18 being reared in poverty went down from 16.6 million in 1959 to 12.5 million in 1966, but the number near poor dipped by only 0.4 million to reach 6.6 million. All told, even in 1966, after a continued run of prosperity and steadily rising family income, one-fourth of the Nation's children were in families living in poverty or hovering just above the poverty line.

Though the poverty rate among all persons aged 18-64 or older declined by more than one-third in the 7-year period, for the aged as a group it dropped only 20 percent. Children in a family with a woman at the head were only 17 percent less likely to be poor in 1966 than in 1959; for children in a home headed by a man the risk of poverty was 40 percent lower in 1966 than it had been earlier.

As a group, persons aged 65 or older were even worse off than the youngsters. Those counted poor in 1966 numbered 5.4 million, the same number as the count of aged poor 2 years earlier, and only half a million less than the count in 1959. In that year, one-third of all aged couples were poor, and in 1966 only one-fourth were so situated. But in 1966 the 1.2 million aged couples in poverty represented 1 in 5 of all families counted poor; in 1959 these couples had accounted for only 1 in 6 of the total. In similar fashion, the financial fate of the aged living alone was better than it once had been, but it still spelled poverty for the majority (55 percent). Moreover, compared with the situation in 1959 when aged unrelated individuals accounted for fewer than one-fifth of all households tagged poor, in 1966 every fourth household in poverty was that of an aged person living alone. Indeed, despite the overall drop in the number of poor of all ages, the number of elderly women living in solitary poverty was now 2.1 million, though it was only 1.8 million in the earlier year.

Such findings did not signify that these elderly persons as a group had less income than they used to have. It was rather that, thanks to Social Security and related programs, more of them had enough income to try going it alone — choosing privacy, albeit the privacy of poverty, rather than being an "other relative" in the home of their children. But despite spectacular improvement aided in large measure by increases in the number drawing OASDI benefits, and in the size of the checks, persons aged 65 or older remained the most poverty-stricken age group in the Nation.

Though the odds that households headed by women would have insufficient income were less than they used to be, the improvement was less marked than for units headed by men. In 1959, of all households counted poor, 5.4 million had a woman at the head and 8 million were headed by a man. By 1966 the number poor with a man at the head dropped 2.4 million, but the number poor and headed by a woman remained unchanged. (There was, to be sure, no telling how many were families who had been in poverty throughout the period and how many were replacing units elevated to better status or disbanded as families.) Accordingly, in 1966 households headed by a woman accounted for nearly one-half of all units tagged poor rather than the two-fifths they represented in 1959. And if there were children in the home making it difficult for the mother to work, the disadvantage was especially striking.

The number of poor families with a man at the head and children under age 18 went from 3.8 million to 2.4 million in 1966. But the 1½ million poor families headed by a woman with children numbered almost as many as those poor in 1959. Thus, though the total count of children in poverty was one-fourth less than it had been 7 years earlier, the number poor in families with a woman at the head was actually one-tenth higher.

The peril of poverty for the child with several brothers and sisters remained high: The family with five or more children was still three and one-half times as likely to be poor as the family raising only one or two and, just as in earlier years, almost one-half the poor children were in families with five or more children. The number of poor families with five or more children remained almost unchanged — 0.9 million in 1966, compared with 1.1 million in 1959 — with the added disadvantage that 29 percent of them now were headed by a woman, instead of 18 percent as in 1959. What is more, the economic deprivation associated with a father's absence was more common than it used to be: from 1959 to 1966 the proportion of all children under age 18 who were in a family headed by a woman rose from 9 to 11 percent; and in parallel fashion it was 1 in 3 of all poor children in 1966 who were minus a father, not 1 in 4 as in 1959. To make matters worse, the poverty rate among children in families headed by a woman was now four and one-half times as high as in families headed by a man; in 1959 it was only three and one-third times as high.

There was other evidence that economic growth had not helped all population groups in equal measure. The nonwhite population generally had not fared as well as the white during the 1959-66 upswing, though by the end of the period it was making greater strides than at the beginning. To be sure, in 1966 it was 1 in 3 nonwhite families who were poor compared with 1 in 10 white families, and back in 1959 it was 1 in 2 nonwhite families and 1 in 7 white families who were poor. It is also a fact that the nonwhite made up about one-third of the Nation's poor in 1966, compared with just over one-fourth in 1959 — a widening disadvantage explained only in small part by the greater population growth among the nonwhite.

The farm population, though still poorer than the nonfarm, had reduced the incidence of poverty by nearly one-half, a rate of improvement twice that registered by the nonfarm population. But with the nonfarm population growing while the farm population steadily declined, it was likely that many families had merely exchanged a farm address for a city one at which they might be even worse off than before.

Though in comparison with the situation in 1959 the poverty roster now included fewer poor families headed by a regularly employed man and more headed by men who encountered trouble finding and holding a job or by those out of the labor force altogether, the difficulty of the low-paid worker with a large family to support was growing more striking. In 1959, among families of a fully employed worker in poverty, one-half included one to three children under age 18 and 30 percent had more than three; 19 percent had none. Among the corresponding group in poverty in 1965, 37 percent had at least four children, 46 percent had from one to three, and only 16 percent had none.

It is clear that in the period since 1959, poverty, which never was a random affliction, has become even more selective, and some groups initially vulnerable are now even more so. There is still no all-embracing characterization that can encompass all the poor. Some are poor because they cannot work; others are poor even though they do. Most of the poor receive no assistance from public programs; others remain poor because they have no resources but the limited payments provided under such programs. And public programs to help the poor are in the main geared to serve those who cannot work at all or are temporarily out of a job. The man who works for a living but is not making it will normally find no avenue of aid.

The Geography of Poverty

About half of all the Nation's poor families — one-seventh of the white poor and two-thirds of the nonwhite poor — lived in the South in 1966. Incomes in that area continue to be lower than elsewhere, by more than could possibly be compensated for by any price differential. Despite the exodus of many nonwhite persons from the South in recent years, the South still spells home for about half of all nonwhite families in the country. It is thus the nonwhite population that is most immediately affected by the region's economic disadvantage. In 1966, white families in the South on an average had only $5 in income for every $6 enjoyed by white families elsewhere; Southern nonwhite families averaged less than $3 for every $5 of income of nonwhite families outside the South. A fifth of all nonwhite families not in the South and a third of the white families had at least $10,000 in income in 1966. Within the South, almost none of the nonwhite families and only a fourth of the white families had this much income.

The Southern States today support a larger proportion of their population on public assistance than is true of the rest of the country. Indeed, of the 10 States with the highest OAA recipient rate per 1,000 aged persons in December 1966, eight were Southern States, although eligibility requirements are at least as restrictive in the South as anywhere else.

Much of the burden of poverty among the fully employed — that is, in terms of weeks worked — rested on nonwhite men, and particularly so in the South. There, more than one-third of the nonwhite men who worked full time throughout 1965 had been poor, as were 7 percent of the white men. Elsewhere in the country the corresponding rates were 10 percent and 4 percent.[4]

About one-fourth of the white poor and two-fifths of the nonwhite poor resided in central cities of metropolitan areas. Yet, for the Nation as a whole, the white poor outnumbered the nonwhite even in the central cities. There were about 5½ million white persons counted poor in central cities and 4 million nonwhite. Because of the well-established difficulties of Negroes — whatever their income — in finding housing, a larger proportion of them, both poor and nonpoor, are clustered in what may be termed poverty areas of large cities than is true for the white population.[5]

The Working Poor

In our society it is a truism that work is the key to economc security. Yet though a job is usually necessary if one is to keep out of poverty, having one does not guarantee it.

With all the interest in more jobs for the poor, the statistics reveal that for many it is not more jobs that are needed but better ones. In 1966, 1 in 4 of all poor families was headed by a man who had worked throughout the year. The families of these working men included 8 million persons, or one-third of all the poor who were not keeping house by themselves. To put it more directly, of the 3 million families headed by a man under age 65 — leaving out families headed by an aged person or by a woman, persons who might have difficulty getting any work at all — half were "fully employed" in terms of time spent on the job. Seven out of 10 of these men were white and so presumably not subjected to discrimination in the hiring hall. Though a number of these men had large families, many had earnings so low they would have been poor with only two or three children to support. Overall, there was an average of 2.8 children under age 18 per family. Indeed, in 1965 — the latest year for which such details are available — of the men under age 65 heading a family in poverty despite their "full employment," three-fifths had no more than three children to support.

For many of the poor, particularly in households headed by women, it was the inability of the family breadwinner to find a job or keep one that accounted for their plight. When the family head did not work at all in 1966, 1 out of 3 families was counted poor, compared with only 1 in 17 when the family head was on a job every week in the year. But 9½ million persons were poor though they were in the family of a breadwinner who did have a job throughout 1966. To be sure, many families were poor because the head was unemployed part of the year. Families in poverty included 1 out of 4 of all those with the head looking for a job in March 1967, and 1 out of 5 of those whose family head had lost some weeks' pay in 1966 because of unemployment. Among men who were family heads and in the labor force in 1966, one-sixth of the poor had been out of work and actively seeking a job sometime during the year — an unemployment rate nearly three times that for the heads of nonpoor families. In families headed by women, the unemployment rate reported by the poor was about 12 percent, or twice that in nonpoor families.

All told among poor families headed by men under age 65, 5 out of 6 of the heads worked some time in 1966, and the majority of those who didn't were disabled.

As one would expect, the kind of job held was intimately related to the risk of poverty. The most poverty-prone calling for men was farming or unskilled labor; for women workers it was domestic service. Indeed, among women family heads employed as household workers in March 1967, nearly 3 in 5 reported family income for 1966 below the poverty line. Most of these women were nonwhite. Some women who go out to work achieve a better standard of living for their own family, but the families of some of the women who keep house for them are likely to remain on a substandard one.

Age and Poverty

A majority of the aged live alone or with just one other person. In 1966, 2 out of 5 households consisting of one aged person or an elderly couple fell below the poverty line, compared with but 1 in 7 of all other households. Families headed by aged persons generally have lower incomes than younger households of the same size because they are less likely to include a steady earner, and because the public programs that help many of the aged almost always pay less than the earnings they are intended to replace.

On the average, aged couples or persons living alone must get along on less than half the money income available to a young couple or single person — a difference greater than any possible differential in living requirements. The fact that for a variety of reasons, more and more aged persons are spending their last years living by themselves or just with a spouse rather than as part of a larger family group emphasizes the significance of the income disadvantage of such elderly households. Between 1959 and 1966 the number of non-aged one-person households rose by only 6 percent, but the number of elderly men and women living alone — or with nonrelatives only — was a third greater in 1966 than in 1959. In parallel fashion, with youngsters marrying and starting their families at an earlier age than they formerly did, the number of childless couples under age 65 rose only 2 percent in this 7-year period. At the same time, the number of aged couples increased by a fifth. There are thus relatively more elderly persons who must manage by themselves on their own meager resources.

The fact that aged men and women are less likely to work regularly than younger persons and that they earn less when they do work is the main reason why poverty is so much more prevalent among the aged. When families are matched by work experience and by sex of the head, aged families are not so much worse off than others. For example, the poverty rate for families of all aged men is nearly triple that of younger ones, but when the family head works the year round the rate of poverty among the aged is only twice that of the others. And, indeed, when the family head does not work at all, the average aged family will do better than a corresponding younger family because social security and other public support programs are more readily available to older people. Among the families headed by men who did not work at all in 1966, 28 percent of the aged were in poverty, compared with 37 percent when the head was aged 55-64 and 40 percent if he was under age 55.

Women in Poverty

Among the poor, women outnumbered the men, 8 to 5. In the age group 65 or older, there were nearly 2 women living in poverty for every man. Aged women living alone were particularly ill-favored, with more than 3 out of 5 purchasing their privacy only at the price of poverty, but whatever their age or family status the woman was poorer than the man. Those who had to double as family head and homemaker were three and one-half times as likely to be poor as men heading a family, and they were even more disadvantaged if they had children under age 6 to look after.

Of the 5.2 million women heading a family, 35 percent were counted poor and 2 out of 3 of those heading a family with children under age 6 were raising their youngsters on incomes too low to provide for them properly. Because their home responsibilities were greater than in nonpoor families, women in poor families would find it more difficult to hold down a full-time job and some could take no job at all. The woman in a poor family — whether wife or family head — had more children and younger children to care for. It is not surprising then to find that among poor families with a husband present, only 1 in 6 of the wives was in the paid labor force, but that in non-poor families, 2 in 5 were either working or looking for work.

Poor families generally were larger than those better off, mainly because they included more children, not because they had more adults. And every disadvantage of the poor family was greater if the head was a woman. As one instance in the women's families just about one-fifth of all family members were preschoolers under age 6, and 6 out of 10 members were not yet aged 18. In families of men in poverty, one-half the members were not yet aged 18, and about one-sixth were not yet 6 years of age.

The role of social security and other public programs in ameliorating poverty is quite evident in the situation of families headed by a woman. Because a woman responsible for a family cannot work as readily as a man and will earn less when she does, the families of women are generally much poorer than men's families. But by age 65 when most men heading a family are not working regularly either, the economic gap between the man's and woman's family lessens. With a head under age 55, a woman's family is nearly six times as likely to be poor as a man's between ages 55 and 64, the woman's family is two and one-third times as likely to be poor as the man's; at age 65 or older, the risk of poverty for a woman's family is about the same as for a man's and, if both are not working at all, the risk for the woman's family is about one-fourth less than the man's.

Children of the Poor

Children generally do not contribute income of their own to a family but must rely instead on the support of others. As a result, after the aged — whose earning capacity is also likely to be limited if not lacking altogether — children are the poorest age group, particularly if the father is absent. Three out of 5 youngsters in families headed by women were being raised in poverty — a total of 4½ million poor children — but there were also 8 million other children who were poor in unbroken families. The mother of young children, whether she herself is the family head or shares the responsibility with a husband, finds it hard to take a job, but many families can escape poverty only if both parents work and some not even then. Twelve percent of the husband-wife families were poor when the wife did not work and 5 percent even when she did. Perhaps more to the point in assessing remedial action against poverty is the fact that 4½ million children were counted poor though they were in the home of a man who had worked throughout 1966 and nearly 1 million more were in the family of a woman who held a job all year. Children with a working mother but minus a father receive little help from existing public programs unless they are the orphans of veterans or workers who were covered under OASDHI, but the children with a father present and working receive almost no help at all. Youngsters in large families were particularly bad off, and if the large family had a woman at its head, the odds were better than 4 out of 5 that it was poor.

All told, close to half the Nation's poor children were in families with at least five youngsters present, but the size and current living arrangements of families, as the Census normally counts them, are sometimes the result of poverty; they are not always the cause. Family groups with insufficient income, particularly if there is no man at the head, may share living quarters with relatives to help meet living expenses. Thus in nonpoor families in 1966, only 1 in 25 of the children under age 18 were not the children of the head or wife but children of other relatives. In poor families as a group, 1 in 10 children were related rather than own children, and in poor families headed by a woman, the proportion was 1 in 8.

Many families with four or five youngsters had insufficient income to support even two or three, though all would be less poor if they spread their limited resources among fewer members. For example, of the families poor in 1966 with a woman at the head and four children, one-half had less than $2,300 income for the year. Even on the assumption that there was no one else in the family, this median was 40 percent less than the minimum of $3,900 required to enable a nonfarm family of this size to stay above the poverty line and was not even enough for a mother and two children.

The Poverty Gap in 1965

The latest statistics on the aggregate dollar amount by which poor households fell short of their estimated income need are for 1965 when the total poverty roster numbered 31.9 million persons, of whom 14 million were under age 18. At that time the total dollar poverty gap — the aggregate difference between required and actual income — stood at $11 billion. This figure represented an overall reduction of 20 percent since 1959, but now one-fifth of the gap represented unmet need of families with children and headed by a woman, compared with one-sixth then. In contrast, the share of the total gap accounted for by families with children and a man at the head dropped from 37 percent in 1959 to 34 percent in 1965.

It must be remembered that aggregate deficits as computed represent a needs-resources gap, still remaining after payments of public assistance, OASDHI benefits, and any other public programs aiming to help families with insufficient income of their own. Many receive no such help. It has been estimated that only about a fourth of all persons counted poor receive any public asistance, and the proportion of poor households who receive assistance is even less. In 1965, as shown later in this article, only a fourth of all households whose income for the year was below the poverty line had received any public assistance payments.

Because, as a rule, women's families have fewer persons than men's families, the income needed for the women's families to stay above poverty is lower. But even allowing for this lesser need the families headed by women had incomes proportionately less in relation to estimated requirements than was true of families headed by a man.

For example, the median income deficit for poor families with children — that is, the difference between the family's actual money income and the minimum amount appropriate for a household of that size and composition — was $1,150 for the families headed by a man and $1,380 where the head was a woman. As a parallel to the fact that the larger the family the more likely it was to be poor, it was also true that irrespective of the sex of the head, the more children in the poor family the greater the dollar gap between the income it had to live on and what it should have had.

*   *   *

Public Income-Support Programs and Poverty

The Economic Opportunity Act authorized a number of new mechanisms to combat poverty, aimed for the most part at increasing earning power. The main task of providing income to those who are out of the labor force remains, as before, the function of income-maintenance programs already in operation for a number of years. Among the most prominent are social security, public assistance, veterans' pensions and compensation, unemployment insurance, and workmen's compensation. In the main, these programs make payments only when earnings are interrupted or stopped altogether, and almost always the payments are less than the earnings for which they can substitute.

Information on the amount of payments under these separate programs and the persons to whom they go are available on a regular basis in the operating statistics of the various administering agencies, but it is only infrequently and through special studies that it is possible to learn much about the other resources of recipients and to determine how the individual programs complement each other. For the year 1965, such an opportunity is provided in the data collected by the Bureau of the Census in the Current Population Survey for 1966.

From this source, information for 1965 is available separately on the amount of family income received from OASDHI benefits or public assistance payments and on the amount from all other public programs as a group.

The data have obvious limitations. In the brief interview, one cannot always be sure that the respondent identifies accurately the particular program of which he is a beneficiary. Moreover, in preparing income statistics, the Bureau of the Census uses a definition of a family — all related persons sharing a household at the time of the interview — that may not jibe with the definition of recipient unit used by the agency administering the program. An elderly woman or a mother-child unit may be eligible to receive public assistance or payments from a veterans' program because their own resources are very low, yet the relatives whose home they share may be better off financially.

It must be remembered also that the family characteristics relate to the situation at time of interview — that is, March 1966 — and the income data refer only to receipts in the calendar year 1965. Changes occurring either in living arrangements or income sources would not be identifiable. Thus, an aged person or a family group might in March 1966 be part of a family unit reporting a financial situation considerably different in both amount and source of income from what it had been when they were deemed eligible for public assistance — an elderly woman who received old-age assistance when she was living alone but who now lives with her son, for example, or perhaps a family group who were receiving aid to families with dependent children until the mother could arrange to take a job. And, finally, some persons supported in whole or in part by public programs during part of 1965 would not be alive in March 1966, and thus no income report would be available for them.

Within the limitations outlined, it is possible, however, to estimate how many households in 1965 were receiving some income from transfer payments and how many not now counted poor would have been poor without such payments.

Of the 60½ million households in the United States in March 1966 — counting as a household an unrelated individual as well as a family of two or more — 19.5 million or just under 1 in 3 reported that someone in the household received payment from a public income-maintenance program sometime during 1965. For two-thirds of these households, social security benefits made up at least part of the public income payment.

As expected, households with an aged head were much more likely to receive support from a public program than households with a head under 65 — 6 in 7 of the older households, compared with only 1 in 5 of the younger ones. Even among young families of a woman with children under age 18, only half received any help from a public program, and the program involved was more often public assistance than social security.

Among the households with payment from public assistance, which makes payments only to those considered in need by the standard of the State in which they live, 81 percent of the recipient households in 1965 had so little income otherwise that they would be below the poverty line in the absence of any assistance payments. But the amounts of assistance were so small that even with the payments counted in, two-thirds of all households receiving assistance were found among the 11.2 million households designated poor in 1965 — as the poor are counted in terms of money income including public transfer payments. In other words, of the households poor before receiving any public assistance, 5 out of 6 were still poor after they got it.

In contrast, among households with a payment from the social security program, which does not limit its payments with a means test, only about half of those poor before they drew their OASDHI checks were still poor afterwards: Before OASDHI benefits were added, for about 6 out of 10 households receiving benefit checks income was below the poverty line; after OASDHI benefits were added to income, only 3 in 10 were still below the poverty line.

For reasons already stated the estimates of households receiving transfers who are or were poor are understatements, but this is particularly true in the case of assistance: by definition; public assistance payments will not be made unless income from all other sources is below State standards. Some households whose income for the year is above the standard would nevertheless have needed assistance at some point to tide them over until entitlement under other public programs is in effect or until income from employment or other relatives is assured.

Thirty-seven percent of the households currently defined as poor in 1965, in terms of money income including any transfer payments, received OASDHI benefits, and a total of 54 percent received payments under some public program. A number of households classed as nonpoor achieved such status only because of these payments. If it had not been for the public programs, the number of households poor in 1965 would have been 15.9 million instead of the 11.2 million now shown in the poverty series. The social security program itself was responsible for keeping at least 3½ million households off the poverty roster: If there had been no OASDHI payments but only payments under other public programs the number of poor households would have been 14.8 million.

Obviously, OASDHI benefits would be a better protector against poverty for the aged than for those under age 65. The number of households with an aged head counted poor would have been two-thirds higher — 7.1 million rather than the 4.1 million now shown as poor — were it not for OASDHI benefits. Of the 9 million aged households enjoying these benefits in 1965, 67 percent were poor in terms of money income before adding in the benefits, but only 35 percent of all aged beneficiary households were still in poverty after counting in their benefits with other money income.

Even for households headed by a person under age 65, OASDHI benefits played a sizable role in correcting poverty. (In some of the young households, it was undoubtedly an aged "other relative" who was the actual beneficiary.) Instead of the 7.1 million households with a nonaged head counted poor in 1965 — in terms of money income, including public transfer payments —

there would have been 7.7 million households poor if there were no OASDHI benefits, or 8 percent more in poverty.

Among families with children under age 18 and a woman younger than age 65 at the head, the number below the poverty line would be 14 percent greater than at present, but for the existence of the social security program. About 0.6 million of these 2.7 million families reported drawing OASDHI benefits in 1965. For two-thirds of these beneficiary families, their income with the benefits excluded was below the poverty line. When the OASDHI benefits were added, only a third of these young beneficiary families were left with money income below the poverty line.

Additional analyses now under way will explore the relation of transfer payments to other sources of income and to the amounts by which income falls below the estimate of minimum requirements. It is already clear that for many already receiving help from public programs, it is the degree of help that must be increased if they are to escape poverty but that new programs or extensions of existing ones are required for those now in poverty and receiving no help at all. A majority of aged persons today already receive income from one public program, or another. As a group then, aged households now poor or near poor will benefit more from increasing amounts payable under such programs than from changed eligibility requirements. But both types of improvements will be needed for poor or near poor households headed by persons younger than age 65.

REFERENCES

1. For a description and discussion of both the Social Security Administration indexes, see the *Social Security Bulletin* for January and July 1965 and April, May, and December 1966.
2. See IDA C. MERRIAM, "Social Security Benefits and Poverty" (Social Security Administration, Research and Statistics Note No. 6), 1967.
3. Bureau of the Census, *Current Population Reports*, Series P-60, No. 53, "Income in 1966 of Families and Persons in the United States," and No. 35, "Income of Families and Persons in the United States in 1959." See also the *Social Security Bulletin*, April 1966.
4. *Economic Report of the President* (with *The Annual Report of the Council of Economic Advisers*), January 1967, page 139.
5. ARNO I. WINARD, "Characteristics of Families Residing in Poverty Areas Within Large Metropolitan Areas," paper presented at the annual meeting of the Population Association of America, April 1967.

CHAPTER 7

Residence, Race, and Age of Poor Families in 1966

Carolyn Jackson and Terri Velten

In recent years much research in the United States has been devoted to the study of poverty. Certain broad characteristics have emerged from the aggregate poverty data.[1] These generalities are well-known to the reader: Disproportionate numbers of the poor are elderly, beyond their working years. Although most poor people are white, nonwhite families are far more likely to be poor than are white families. About half the families counted poor in 1966 were headed by women with children, by the aged, or by the disabled.[2]

This article seeks other insights on poverty. Specifically, analysis is made of data on race and economic status in conjunction with the residential locale of families. What do the data tell us about where nonwhite families and white families live? Does the evidence on residence confirm or contradict common assumptions about poverty based on such factors as age, work experience, and family income? What relevance do these findings have for planners and administrators of antipoverty programs?

The limited information available on residence of families in 1967, by economic status, reveals that nonwhite families are divided between metropolitan and nonmetropolitan areas in a different manner than white families (table 1).[3] The nonpoor families, unlike the poor, are more concentrated inside metropolitan areas than outside. And it continues to be more likely that the nonwhite rather than the white family will be poor. The following figures show, for families in the United States in 1967, the proportions that were poor, classified by race and by area of residence.

Because detailed data for 1967 are not yet available, most of the discussion in this article refers to data for the income year 1966 collected by the Bureau of the Census in the Current Population Survey for March 1967. The stan-

Reprinted with omissions from the *Social Security Bulletin,* June 1969.

dard metropolitan statistical areas[4] have been subdivided into "central city" and "fringe" areas. The largest city (or cities) in the SMSA is the central city, and the areas not included in the central city are the fringe areas. The term fringe is often used interchangeably with the term suburb. Residents of SMSA's are considered the metropolitan population. Most metropolitan residents are urban dwellers, but some of them live on farms and in other rural places inside SMSA's. For this report, however, farm residents within the SMSA's have been excluded from the count of the metropolitan population and are counted with the nonmetropolitan farm population.

People living outside SMSA's have been classified as urban, rural nonfarm, or farm residents. Together they comprise the nonmetropolitan population. An urban area is a village, town, or city of at least 2,500 inhabitants. The rural nonfarm population includes those persons who live outside SMSA's, are not in urban areas, and do not maintain farm residence. Farm residence is determined by the land area on which farm products are produced for sale and by the yearly income from these sales.

For the purpose of this discussion, rural nonfarm and farm data have been combined to form a rural category where the farm population is too small to constitute a meaningful unit. With Negroes constituting more than 90 percent of the nonwhite poor and at least 80 percent of the nonwhite population above the poverty level in 1967, the terms Negro and nonwhite are used interchangeably here.

Incidence of Poverty

Age of Family Head

The age of the family head is an important factor in any analysis concerned with the poor and in policy decisions determining antipoverty strategies. If the head of a poor household is young, educable, and with many remaining years of earnings potential, solutions to the family's poverty will be different than if the "head of the house" is a senior citizen whose income is limited by retirement from the labor force or derives in whole or in part from public income-maintenance programs.

In 1966 approximately 12 percent of all families in the United States were poor. Among families headed by a person aged 65 or older, the percentage poor was double that for younger families. This disparity was more pronounced among white families than among nonwhite families and larger in rural areas than in central cities. The greater incidence of poverty among the aged was most marked in the suburbs, reflecting the large proportion of white families living there.

Race

Differences between white families and nonwhite families in poverty rates were more pronounced for those under age 65 than for the older groups.[5] In

TABLE 1. *Number and Percentage Distribution of Families by Income Below and Above the SSA Poverty Level, Race, and Residence in 1967*

Residence	All families			White families			Nonwhite families		
	Total	Poor	Nonpoor	Total	Poor	Nonpoor	Total	Poor	Nonpoor
	Number (in thousands)								
United States	49,834	5,309	44,525	44,814	3,766	41,048	5,020	1,543	3,477
Metropolitan	32,226	2,609	29,617	28,646	1,763	26,884	3,579	845	2,734
In central cities	14,629	1,597	13,032	11,844	920	10,924	2,784	675	2,109
Outside central cities	17,597	1,013	16,584	16,802	843	15,959	796	170	626
Nonmetropolitan	17,608	2,701	14,907	16,168	2,003	14,165	1,440	698	742
Nonfarm	15,165	2,297	12,868	13,933	1,706	12,227	1,232	591	641
Farm	2,443	404	2,039	2,235	297	1,938	208	107	101
	Percentage distribution								
United States	100.0	100.0	100.0	100.0	100.0	100.0	100.0	100.0	100.0
Metropolitan	64.7	49.1	66.5	63.9	46.8	65.5	71.3	54.8	78.6
In central cities	29.4	30.1	29.3	26.4	24.4	26.6	55.5	43.7	60.7
Outside central cities	35.3	19.1	37.2	37.5	22.4	38.9	15.9	11.0	18.0
Nonmetropolitan	35.3	50.9	33.5	36.1	53.2	34.5	28.7	45.2	21.3
Nonfarm	30.4	43.3	28.9	31.1	45.3	29.8	24.5	38.3	18.4
Farm	4.9	7.6	4.6	5.0	7.9	4.7	4.1	6.9	2.9

SOURCE: Derived from special tabulations of the Current Population Survey, March 1968, prepared by the Bureau of the Census.

the United States as a whole, only 8 percent of the white families headed by a person under age 65, compared with 33 percent of the nonwhite families, were poor. Where the family head was aged 65 or older, 20 percent of the white families and 47 percent of the nonwhite families were poor. The reliance on retirement income by families past their working years undoubtedly reduces — but does not eliminate — the economic advantage of the white over the nonwhite.

Racial differences were sharpest among the younger families living outside SMSA's, particularly in urban areas, where the poverty rate for nonwhite families was six times greater than that for white families.

Residence

In considering the prevalence of poverty in relation to residence, it should be pointed out that, though money income tends to be lower in small towns and rural areas, the Social Security Administration poverty index assumes the same minimum cash requirement except on farms. If the poverty index were adapted to reflect greater cost-of-living differences between large and small places, some nonmetropolitan residents might no longer be classed as poor.

On the other hand, the income of some poor families is so low that a modest reduction in the poverty standard would not lift them into the nonpoor classification, and there is very little information about the geographic differences in costs at a level of living as low as that presumed by the poverty index.

NUMBER AND PERCENTAGE DISTRIBUTION OF POOR FAMILIES BY AREA OF RESIDENCE, 1966

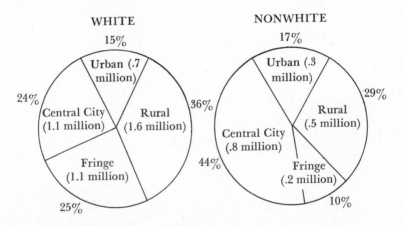

In any case, under the existing definitions, poverty rates reflect the combination of demographic factors such as age and race in the different areas.

For example, the poverty rate for all families does not show a sharp urban-rural contrast. [If we look at more detailed information,] a contrast is presented [original article] on race and age, however.

Residential Patterns Among the Poor and the Nonpoor

The primary concern throughout this analysis is with three broad age groups of family heads: aged 22-54, aged 55-64, and aged 65 and over. The fact that residence patterns differ markedly among families with the head in these age groups can materially affect the utility of specific anti-poverty measures.

Patterns Among the Poor

Residential patterns among poor white families did not vary greatly in 1966 with age of the head. Approximately 50 percent of all such families lived inside metropolitan areas, equally divided between central cities and suburbs. The proportion living outside nonmetropolitan areas was about the same for each age group. The principal distinction in the general pattern for these families was that for families headed by a person aged 55-64 the proportion living in rural areas was much greater than it was for families older or younger.

Poor nonwhite families displayed a sharply contrasting pattern. Close to 60 percent of the younger Negro families lived inside metropolitan areas, mostly in central cities. But where the nonwhite family head was over age 54, 60 percent of them lived outside metropolitan areas and the majority were rural dwellers.

The most striking feature about the residential location of poor Negro families — young and old — was that only 10 percent lived in the suburbs.

Patterns Among the Nonpoor

Other insights into the nature of poverty may be gained by looking beyond the poor to the other side of the poverty line. Families above the poverty line display many differences, both from one another and from the poor.

Among these nonpoor families, white families were spread in a completely different manner from the nonwhite. Two-thirds of the white families lived within the metropolitan areas, with a majority in the suburbs; only 20 percent were in rural areas — 5 percent on farms. Within metropolitan areas, white families with a head under age 55 were more likely to be in suburbs than older families were, particularly if the head was aged 65 or over. Moreover, a higher than average percentage of the family heads aged 55 or older were farmers.

Contrast this pattern of residential location to that for the nonwhite above the poverty level. Eighty percent of these families were inside SMSA's, predominantly in central cities. Only 2 percent were on farms. Among the younger, nonpoor Negro families — those with a head aged 22-54 — barely 10 percent lived in rural areas, farm or nonfarm. But almost 20 percent of the older Negro family heads were rural residents.

Another aspect of residential dispersion of these young, better-off nonwhite families was the relatively small number in towns outside SMSA's, a fact that probably reflects lack of job opportunities or suitable housing and little or no personal or family experience with such communities.

Comparison of Patterns for Poor and Nonpoor Families

About 63 percent of the nonwhite families above poverty lived in central cities, and just 18 percent were in suburbs. By contrast, among the white nonpoor 27 percent lived in central cities and 38 percent resided in the suburbs.

Among nonpoor families with an aged head there was more similarity in area of residence. For white and nonwhite aged families the proportions inside metropolitan areas were 61 percent and 66 percent, respectively.

In general, outside metropolitan areas poor families, regardless of race, tended to have a common pattern of residence. That is, nonmetropolitan poor families who were white were distributed in cities, small towns, and farms in a pattern more like that for poor Negro families of the same age than that for white families above the poverty line. The relationship between economic status and residence was also strong among nonwhite families. For corresponding groups of Negro families, the residential pattern for the nonpoor differed from that for the poor. The basic difference between families above and below the poverty line was that a much larger proportion of those above the line — particularly among the nonwhite — lived inside metropolitan areas and a much smaller proportion were rural residents.

Comparison of Areas by Age of Family Head

In 1966 little over two-thirds of all family heads were aged 22-54. The locale with the greatest proportion of these younger families was the suburbs, and the farming area had the largest share of families with an aged head.

Heads of Poor Families

Inside SMSA's. — Of the 6 million poor families, half lived inside metropolitan areas. Central cities were the home of more than 1.8 million of these families — 1.1 million of whom were white and 0.7 million nonwhite.

A closer look at the poor families within central cities shows that about 55 percent of the white families had a head aged 22-54 and 30 percent had an aged head. The Negro poor in central cities were younger than their white counterparts. Almost 75 percent of these Negro families were headed by a person aged 22-54, and barely 12 percent had a head aged 65 or older. The age of the head has direct bearing on family economic status because many old people no longer work regularly. Poor families that include potential earners, for example, may be able to escape from poverty as a result of industrial development within the central cities or their suburbs.

Outside SMSA's. — There were 3 million poor families in areas outside SMSA's: 1 million living in urban places, more than 1½ million living in rural nonfarm areas, and almost one-half million on farms.

Rural nonfarm areas were the locale with the largest number of poor white families and the second largest number of poor Negro families. Half the white and 58 percent of the Negro families were headed by a person aged 22-54. Half a million poor families lived on farms — 350,000 of them white, 140,000 nonwhite. And regardless of race, about 45 percent of these farm families had a person aged 55 or older as its head.

Thus, when nonfarm and farm areas are considered as a whole the economic health of rural communities may require about as much emphasis on income support for the aged and "nearly aged" as it does on education or training of potentially fully employed family heads.

Work as an Escape from Poverty

It is often asserted that a sure avenue for rising above poverty is through income from employment. The data indicate, however, that for many this route is not at all certain.

Work Experience

Among younger families with a male head, most of the men worked. The poor were no exception. In all residential areas at least 80 percent of the poor male family heads worked some time during the survey year. Inside SMSA's, 90 percent of the men heading white families worked and 95 percent of the nonwhite men.

Most of these men worked at least 40 weeks out of the year.* Of all families in poverty that were headed by an employed man aged 22-54, close to 70 percent of the white men and 75 percent of the nonwhite men worked at least 40 weeks. Among these family heads, considerable racial difference is found in central cities, where about 60 percent of the white men and 75 percent of the nonwhite worked for 40 or more weeks. . . .

The heads of nonpoor families had different work experience. About 90 percent of the Negro men and 95 percent of the white men who headed these families worked 40-52 weeks during the year. The disparity in the work experience of poor and nonpoor white family heads was greater than it was among corresponding groups of nonwhite families.

* In this report, a person working 40 weeks or more, at least 35 hours a week, is considered to be working full time.

In each type of area a larger proportion of the younger men heading non-poor families worked for 40-52 weeks than did poor family heads. Under-employment in terms of weeks worked was thus a serious handicap to the poor. It was more of a problem among white families than it was among the nonwhite.

One-third of the poor white men who had employment worked less than 40 weeks, but only about one-fourth of the poor nonwhite men had that little work. For many of the poor, the problem was low earnings coupled with a large family to support, as well as the inability to find work.

Earnings of Family Head

The earnings of young family heads who worked for 40 weeks or more differed with respect to area of residence and race (table 2). The earnings pat-

TABLE 2. *Average Earnings of Head, Average Family Income, and Percent of Income Earned by a Male Head Aged 22-54 Who Worked 40-52 Weeks Full Time in 1966, by Economic Status, Race of Head, and Nonfarm Residence.*

	Nonpoor		Poor	
Area of Residence	*White*	*Non-white*	*White*	*Non-white*
	Earnings of head			
Inside SMSA	$8,829	$6,081	$2,188	$2,699
Central city	8,327	5,996	2,451	2,782
Fringe	9,128	6,407	1,962	(1)
Outside SMSA	7,299	4,525	2,394	2,438
Urban	7,590	4,668	2,440	(1)
Nonfarm	7,062	4,410	2,372	2,441
	Family income			
Inside SMSA	$10,910	$8,407	$2,667	$3,150
Central city	10,497	8,361	2,975	3,207
Fringe	11,157	8,582	2,403	(1)
Outside SMSA	9,142	6,767	2,760	2,871
Urban	9,593	6,868	2,750	(1)
Nonfarm	8,775	6,685	2,765	2,863
	Percent of family income earned by head			
Inside SMSA	80.9	72.3	82.0	85.7
Central city	79.3	71.7	82.4	86.7
Fringe	81.8	74.7	81.6	(1)
Outside SMSA	79.8	66.9	86.7	84.9
Urban	79.1	68.0	88.7	(1)
Nonfarm	80.5	66.0	85.8	85.3

1 *Not shown for base less than 100,000.*

tern of the poor also differed from that of the nonpoor in these respects. The earnings of the poor were highest in the central cities, lowest in the suburbs. Regardless of race, the nonpoor workers who lived in the suburbs earned the most; those living in rural nonfarm areas earned least.

Among families above the poverty level, white men "outearned" Negro men, no matter where they lived. The disparity was greater outside metropolitan areas. There, Negro men earned little better than 60 percent of what their white counterparts earned. Inside SMSA's the ratio was about 70 percent.

Both white and nonwhite men who headed nonpoor families in the suburbs earned about $2,000 a year more than those whose families were in rural nonfarm areas, though the level of average earnings for the nonwhite was much lower. Thus the Negro male family head in the suburbs earned 45 percent more than his counterpart in rural nonfarm areas, but the comparable difference for white men was less than 30 percent. On the other hand, difference in earnings between residents of central cities and those in suburbs was greater for white families than for nonwhite families. For nonmetropolitan residents the same situation existed: White men living in small cities earned proportionately more, compared with those in rural nonfarm areas, than was true for the corresponding groups of nonwhite men.

Family Income

Relation to Earnings of Head

The poor man aged 22-54 with a family, like the nonpoor family head, earned most of the family income (table 2). Except for those living in the suburbs, men who headed a poor family earned a larger percentage of the family income than did men with a family above the poverty line.

The nonpoor were more apt to have, in addition to the earnings of a full-time male worker, other sources of income. In young families, most of the family income not earned by the man at the head was probably earned by the wife.[6]

Negro families above the poverty level, to a greater extent than white families, have had more than one earner. The Negro man heading a nonpoor family no matter where he lived earned a smaller proportion of the family income than the men heading other families. Only those who lived in the suburbs earned as much as three-fourths of the family income; outside metropolitan areas, the proportion was about two-thirds. By contrast, the earnings of white men heading nonpoor families constituted about 80 percent of the family income in all areas.

Except in central cities, the family income of Negroes above the poverty level — even with more than one earner — fell short, on the average, of the earnings of the white man heading a family above the poverty level.

Income Other than Earnings of Head

Among the poor, "other" income for families headed by nonaged men would, of course, be small. On the other hand, among the nonpoor, the amount of income other than earnings of the family head was considerable. On the average, this additional income almost equaled the average earnings of the head in poor families.

Income other than earnings of the man heading the family was greatest for those in central cities. White families in rural nonfarm areas had the least income from other sources. For Negro families, it was those in the suburbs who had the least.

Conclusion

Poverty among white families merits concern because of the large number involved — 3.7 million families in 1967. Poverty among nonwhite families is of even greater concern in that it affects 1 family in 3 in this group.

Poverty is a widely dispersed problem afflicting both cities and rural areas. In 1966, as in earlier years, nonwhite families below the poverty level were concentrated in the central cities and to a lesser degree in rural areas. Poor white families, on the other hand, lived primarily in the rural areas but also in the central cities and in the suburbs.

All the information on families indicates that, both for the central cities and the rural areas, concentrated efforts to find solutions to the poverty problems are urgently needed. The improvement of employment possibilities for those of working age and provisions for adequate retirement income would have an important impact.

The employment data for metropolitan and nonmetropolitan areas support the view currently gaining wider recognition that underemployment in addition to unemployment is a factor in the persistence of poverty for men heading poor families.[7] Although the majority of male family heads among the poor work all year, they do not earn enough to bring the family income above the poverty level.

Programs aimed at alleviating poverty for the aged will contribute to the well-being of a greater percentage of the white poor than of the nonwhite poor, since for white families poverty is more concentrated among the aged. The nonwhite poor will benefit proportionately more than the white poor from programs that improve employment opportunities.

Poverty is not restricted to any particular age, race, or type of community. Opportunities for an adequate income are often limited by obstacles over which individuals have no control. Anti-poverty efforts must therefore be directed toward providing the means by which anyone can surmount these obstacles and join the more fortunate majority of Americans.

REFERENCES

1. The concept of poverty used throughout the article is based on the Social Security Administration definition of a minimum income required for families of specified sizes. For detailed description of these measures of poverty, see the *Social Security Bulletin,* January 1965, pages 5-11, and July 1965, pages 3-10.
2. See MOLLIE ORSHANSKY, "The Shape of Poverty in 1966," *Social Security Bulletin,* March 1968, page 4.
3. See also Bureau of the Census, "Trends in Social and Economic Conditions in Metropolitan Areas," *Current Population Reports: Special Studies* (P-23, No. 27), February 7, 1969.
4. The Bureau of the Census defines a standard metropolitan statistical area (SMSA) as a county or group of counties that contains at least one city of 50,000 inhabitants or more or twin cities with a combined population of at least 50,000. See Bureau of the Census, "Income in 1964 of Families and Unrelated Individuals by Metropolitan-Nonmetropolitan Residence," *Current Population Reports: Consumer Income* (Series P-60, No. 48), pages 7-8.
5. See MOLLIE ORSHANSKY, "The Aged Negro and His Income," *Social Security Bulletin,* February 1964.
6. For husband-wife families in 1966, 14 percent of the wives in poor white families and 33 percent in poor non-white families worked. Comparable percentages for the nonpoor were 36 percent in white families and 53 percent in Negro families. See MOLLIE ORSHANSKY, op. cit., *Social Security Bulletin,* March 1968, pages 12-13.
7. For discussion on this subject, see Department of Labor, *A Sharper look at Unemployment in U.S. Cities and Slums;* Bureau of the Census, "The Extent of Poverty in the United States," *Current Population Reports* (Series P-60, No. 34), May 31, 1968, pages 3, 6-7; and the *Social Security Bulletin,* March 1968, page 15.

CHAPTER 8

Facts and Fictions About the Poor

Elizabeth Herzog

Anyone who tries to ferret out and report facts about the poor — to tell it like it is — encounters some statements that are simply not true and some that are true and not true at the same time. They may be true as far as they go but misleading if viewed out of context, or partly true but distorted into falsehood by oversimplification.

This article is limited to two examples, one concerning the need to view statistical data in context and the other concerning oversimplification and misapplication of a convenient concept.

Births Out of Wedlock

We constantly see references to "the alarming rise" in illegitimate births. Alarm could be directed to the sheer increase in numbers, or the assumed causes of the increase, or to the consequences and implications — actual or potential. And the word "alarming" could reflect either unadulterated fear, or fear compounded by hostility and resentment.

Because hostility and fear are so often associated with the crisis view, it is useful to consider the difference between seeing illegitimacy figures in and out of context (see figure). The trend line for births out of wedlock from 1940 to 1965 shows that during those years the numbers more than tripled to about 291,000 in 1965 from about 89,000 in 1940. This tremendous number and increase is the picture most often impressed upon the public. When this same trend line is shown as part of all live births, the rise is still clear, but it can be seen as part of a rise in the total number of births (see second figure).

Reprinted from *Monthly Labor Review*, February 1969.

BIRTHS OUT OF WEDLOCK IN THE UNITED STATES, 1940-1965 (Beginning 1959, includes Alaska; beginning 1960, includes Hawaii. From *Vital Statistics of the United States: 1964, Vol. I—Natality,* table 1-26 (1966) and *1965, Vol. I—Natality.* U.S. Public Health Service, National Center for Health Statistics.)

Thousands of births out of wedlock

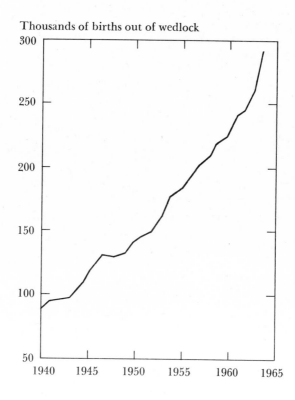

There is some question about the extent to which the greater rise in illegitimacy before 1961 was real and to what extent it resulted from improved reporting and better estimates — for all our national illegitimacy figures are estimates, based on reports from about 35 States. However, the main point is that even if births out of wedlock had not increased faster than births in wedlock, the bulk of the problem would still be with us. The problem is not in the increase but in a situation that has been with us for many years. We are faced not with a crisis but with the current phase of a long term situation. This, of course, does not reduce the number of unmarried mothers or the number of children to be served. It does, however, make a difference in our view of the problem which, in turn, conditions what we are willing and able to do about it. Panic and rage are not conducive to constructive problem-solving, and the crisis view breeds panic and rage.

One more brief exercise in perspective concerns unmarried mothers under twenty. Teenage girls, age 15 to 19, have the largest number of illegitimate births in any age group. This event often leads to the statement that "most unmarried mothers are under twenty," which is not true. The majority of unmarried mothers are not under twenty. More important, however, is the fact that, although teenagers are a large proportion of unmarried mothers, they are a much larger proportion of the principal population for whom unmarried motherhood is a risk — unmarried, widowed, divorced, and separated women. Among the Nation's unmarried mothers, teenagers are a smaller proportion of the total than they are of the total unmarried female population.

With the generation gap yawning before us, it is well to remember that 20 years ago teenagers produced a larger proportion of nonwedlock births than today, and that the illegitimacy rate among teenagers is lower and has risen less than among women in their twenties and thirties.

That word "rate" demands a passing bow, for clarity about the difference between illegitimacy rate and illegitimacy ratio is as necessary as it is rare. The ratio is the number of illegitimate babies per 1,000 live births. The rate is the number of births per 1,000 unmarried women of childbearing age. The ratio talks about babies, the rate talks about mothers. The ratio is useful for planning services, but worse than useless for considering trends, since it depends on the age and marital composition of the population, illegitimacy rate, and the fertility of married women. For example, the ratio among girls under 18 is bound to be high in comparison with older women, since few are married mothers. However, the illegitimacy rate is relatively low.[1]

There are two reasons for dwelling on this point. One is that ratios are surprisingly often published under the name of rates. The other is that the overall illegitimacy rate, after increasing substantially from 1940 to 1957, has more or less leveled off during the years 1957-66, oscillating within one or two points.[2] What it may do next remains to be seen. But, on the whole, the main reason for the increase in numbers of illegitimate births since 1957 is that there are more women. Since numbers, rates, and ratios are estimates, and since there is reason to suspect overreporting in others, yearly oscillations of one or two points are best disregarded.

The "Culture of Poverty"

A prime example of what is partly true and partly not true is the "culture of poverty." It is also an example of the dangers inherent in setting up a half-true label and then mistaking it for an explanation or using it as a substitute for thought.

The culture-of-poverty concept provides a reminder that, in some ways, different groups live in different worlds and respond to different imperatives.

Perhaps this should not have been necessary, but it was. Disraeli thrust such a reminder upon the attention of his fellow countrymen when a character in his novel, *Sybil,* declared that Queen Victoria was reigning over not one Nation, but two: ". . . two nations between whom there is no intercourse and no sympathy; who are as ignorant of each other's habits, thoughts, and feelings as if they were dwellers in different zones or inhabitants of different planets; who are formed by a different breeding, are fed by a different food, are ordered by different manners, and are not governed by the same law—

TOTAL LIVE BIRTHS AND ESTIMATED LIVE BIRTHS OUT OF WEDLOCK IN THE UNITED STATES, 1940-1955. (Beginning 1959, includes Alaska; beginning 1960, includes Hawaii. From *Vital Statistics of the United States: 1964, Vol. I — Natality,* tables 1-1 and 1-26 (1966) and *1965, Vol I — Natality.* U.S. Public Health Service, National Center for Health Statistics.)

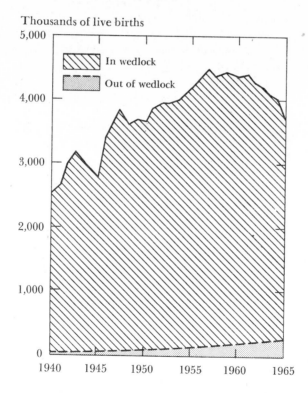

The Rich and The Poor."[3] Michael Harrington, more than a century later, was referring to that conversation when he called his book *The Other America,* and called the last chapter "The Two Nations." And Oscar Lewis, at about the same time, expressed a similar, though by no means identical, idea in referring to the culture of poverty.

The culture-of-poverty idea, for the short time in which it was being looked at with new eyes, did set up a ripple of fresh comprehension, and this is a contribution to be respected. What is to be deplored about the concept lies less in its original thoughtful formulation than in the way is has been applied by others.

Lewis pointed out that in some ways the poor of any industrialized country resemble each other more than they resemble the prosperous in their own society. He mentioned, for example, a number of economic traits, including "the constant struggle for survival, unemployment and underemployment, low wages, a miscellany of unskilled occupations, . . . the absence of savings, a chronic shortage of cash, the absence of food reserves in the home, the pattern of frequent buying or small quantities of food as needed arises, the pawning of personal goods, borrowing from local money lenders at usurious rates of interest, spontaneous informal credit devices . . . organized by neighbors, and the use of second-hand clothing and furniture."[4]

He also mentioned a number of social and psychological characteristics, including: ". . . living in crowded quarters, a lack of privacy, gregariousness, a high incidence of acoholism, frequent use of physical violence in the training of children, wife beating, early initiation into sex, free unions or consensual marriages, a relatively high incidence of the abandonment of mothers and children, a trend toward mother-centered families and a much greater knowledge of maternal relatives, the predominance of the nuclear family, a strong predisposition to authoritarianism, and a great emphasis on family solidarity — an ideal only rarely achieved. Other traits include . . . a sense of resignation and fatalism based upon the realities of their difficult life situation, a belief in male superiority which reaches its crystallization in *machismo* or the cult of masculinity, a corresponding martyr complex among women, and finally, a high tolerance for psychological pathology of all sorts."[5]

Much of what he said has been documented as a description of traits commonly found among the poor in any industrialized society. A few points have been sharply challenged. But the basic question is whether this much similarity of traits does indeed constitute a culture; and the basic problem lies in the applications and implications that others have derived from assuming that it does. Before grappling with the concept in general, a few examples are in order of the specifics that make the idea of a culture of poverty difficult either to accept or to reject without reservation.

With regard to economic patterns and the social habits derived from them, one may question whether these patterns and habits are culture traits or merely pragmatic responses to real life exigencies. If the latter, then they are not necessarily culture traits — that is, learned ways of life, transmitted from generation to generation — but rather responses of each generation to the circumstances in which it grows up. Some psychosocial characteristics often attributed to the culture of poverty can also be viewed as a response to reality, ready to change if reality fosters or at least permits change. It can be argued further that certain psychological attitudes commonly attributed to the poor are in fact the products of physical reality; and that some ascribed attitudes and values are erroneously ascribed.

For example, some psychological attributes often attributed to the culture of poverty are intertwined with the effects of hunger and malnutrition in such a way that they operate both as cause and as effect. The most familiar effects of extreme malnutrition are loss of weight, weakness, and anemia. In addition, according to one authority, various functional changes occur that are often mistaken for neurasthenic manifestations, including "excessive fatigueability, disturbances in sleep, inability to concentrate."[6] Other symptoms cited in connection with prolonged malnutrition are "depression, loss of ambition, apathy, lethargy, impotence, and a sensation of being old."[7] Obviously, some characteristics that nutritional experts attribute to diet deficiency are the same ones often ascribed to the culture of poverty.

School Achievement

Poor school performance by children of the slums is often attributed to the low esteem in which book learning is held by the culture of poverty, and the consequent lack of interest by parents in the schooling of their children. That inadequate diet can contribute to poor school performance has been established by systematic studies as well as by unsystematic observation.

Poor school performance is also promoted by lack of sleep, a deficiency which is caused in some instances by staying up late to watch television, but often is the result of overcrowded housing. To raise the subject of housing leads into an array of traits often associated with the culture of poverty, yet often produced by physical condition. Among those that have been described are pessimism and passivity, stress to which the individual cannot adapt, a state of dissatisfaction, pleasure in company but not in solitude, difficulty in household management and child rearing, and relationships that tend to spread out in the neighborhood rather than deeply into the family.[8] The effects of poor housing on physical health have been widely discussed, including safety, respiratory and skin diseases, lead poisoning, and rat bites.[9]

Because school achievement has been so important a focus of poverty problems and of efforts to solve them, it is especially appropriate for illustrating the possibility that features often ascribed to the culture of poverty may in fact be reflections of middle class behavior and attitudes. One such attitude, namely, the expectation of the teacher with regard to the child's ability to learn, has had some attention and is likely to receive more.

Scattered evidence is piling up in support of Kenneth Clark's thesis that ghetto children do poorly in school because the teachers expect them to do poorly.[10] In Washington, D.C., for example, the academic average in the public schools has been reported as far below the national norm. However, one school in a very poor neighborhood stood out far above the average for the city. According to newspaper accounts, the difference was that the school principal would not accept the proposition that ghetto children could not learn, and would not allow the teachers in her school to accept it. And the children did learn, as attested by the academic scores.[11] This kind of evidence was reinforced by an experiment in another city, where teachers in a very poor neighborhood were told that — on the basis of psychological tests — certain children in their classes were likely to show remarkable intellectual gains. The children, in fact, had been selected at random. Nevertheless, during the year those particular children did make gains significantly greater than those of their classmates. Apparently, because the teachers expected them to learn, they did learn.[12]

Another characteristic often attributed to the culture of poverty is lack of motivation. But motivation is a product of multiple ingredients and not a unitary trait. Moreover, it is a response as well as an attribute and is affected, as we have just seen, by nutrition, general health level, and other life circumstances that influence energy and ability to concentrate. It includes, also, aspiration and expectation, and the stronger of these is expectation. If expectation is very low, aspiration can be crippled. At one time, it was assumed that ghetto parents had very low educational aspirations for their children. A number of studies have made it clear, however, that the educational aspirations of very low-income parents for their children are often as high as, or higher than, those of the affluent.[13] Their expectations, on the other hand, had not been high. Nor have they seen themselves as playing any role in helping their children to actual educational achievement. A great deal of the effort to involve parents in school and pre-school activities has been directed toward convincing them that home and parents play a vital part in a child's school performance, and in demonstrating to them ways of making their part constructive.

Family Norms and Forms

Of all the features ascribed to the culture of poverty, perhaps the most deplored is family instability with all its concomitants — including female-headed families, illegitimacy, and dependence on public assistance, especially Aid to Families of Dependent Children (AFDC). Our census data assure us that family instability does characterize the poor in this country: Divorce and separation are on the whole inversely correlated with income.[14] Yet there is abundant evidence that the norms of stable family life are preferred by the poor as well as by the prosperous.

This point embodies and illustrates one of the chief problems about the culture of poverty concept. To be acceptable at all, the culture of poverty must be viewed, not as a culture but as a "subculture," a culture within a culture, existing within and as part of our prevailing culture of the middle class. With regard to family norms and forms especially, there is ample and increasing evidence that stable marriage and family life are accepted as a preferred ideal by most poor people, white and nonwhite. Such evidence was offered by Hylan Lewis's study of childrearing practices among low-income families,[15] has been supported by the investigations of Hyman Rodman,[16] by numerous reports and studies of AFDC clients — including that conducted by Greenleigh Associates,[17] and has recently been reinforced in a number of research and demonstration projects conducted under grants from the Department of Health, Education, and Welfare.

According to these and other reports, middle class standards of sex and family life do not rank as high on the value pyramid of the poor as on that of the prosperous. But they are preferred as luxuries one would gladly be able to afford — just as certain businessmen prefer certain forms of honesty, while considering them unrealistic for practice in daily life. This ability to believe in one set of values while practicing a different set is by no means unique to the poor. Many of us experience something like it occasionally or frequently. However, like the mote in the eye, or the spot in the middle of the forehead, it's easier to see on the other fellow.

The exigencies that prompt the poor to depart from preferred norms of family life and sex behavior include, among many things, early marriage, lack of education, employment problems, and welfare regulations. The man who is not a provider loses status in the eyes of the community, his family, and himself. He may leave because of this or because his family cannot obtain public assistance while he is present.

The vicious cycle is aggravated by the fact that the poor have larger families than the nonpoor. Not because large families are their choice. Overall, the preferred American family size is about the same at all economic levels, about three children.[18] However, the nonpoor have greater access to means of limiting the family and of averting extramarital pregnancy. It is by now a familiar fact that large families are more likely to be poor than small families, and that families which are both large and nonwhite run double risk of poverty.[19]

Illegitimacy is more frequent among the poor than the nonpoor. But the preferred norms include birth in wedlock for poor and nonpoor, white and nonwhite. On this point also, evidence piles up from many sources, and sometimes it is very poignant evidence. We hear of a child taunted by classmates for not knowing who his father is, punished by a teacher for reporting as reality his fantasies about a nonexistent father, sidling up to a strange man on the street in the hope of being called "Son."[20] The evidence also indicates, however, that at different economic levels, birth status occupies a different rank in the value hierarchy.

The different ranking of values is illustrated by Hylan Lewis' study, which was conducted in the District of Columbia. The mothers in his sample, white and nonwhite, dreaded unmarried motherhood for their daughters, prayed that it might not happen, and were devastated if it did. Yet they were equally emphatic, all of them, that if it did happen they would not try to persuade the young couple to marry — not unless they really loved each other.[21] A good marriage they viewed as one of life's chief blessings and certainly one of its rarest blessings; but a bad marriage, in their eyes, was worse than none. A study of the Detroit area reports greater readiness of white girls than of Negro girls to marry because of pregnancy.[22] It does not, however, report the economic status of the girls who were pregnant before marriage. Therefore, once again, a question remains, whether differences in illegitimacy rates are associated primarily with socioeconomic status or with color.

It is unfortunate that the white-nonwhite category is so much easier to apply than a socioeconomic classification, since it has led to reporting some figures (such as illegitimacy) only in terms of age and color. This habit of reporting, in turn, leads to overrating of ethnic factors and underrating other factors. It has been estimated that if illegitimacy statistics could be controlled for income, the difference between white and nonwhite illegitimacy rates would dwindle dramatically.[23]

The Slavery Heritage

In other respects also, the habit of reporting by color rather than by income fosters the habit of attributing to ethnic background differences that may in fact derive chiefly from socioeconomic status. For example, the differences in family life patterns between nonwhites and whites in poverty are dwarfed by the resemblances, if comparisons are made within specified income levels. Myron Lefcowitz, among others, has shown[24] that differences by income are more striking than differences by color, when controlled even very roughly by income; and that when Negro and white children with similar family incomes are compared, differences between them in educational achievement diminish and differences by class appear more striking than differences by color. Description of families in northern white slums could easily be mistaken for descriptions of families in the Harlem ghetto, whether one reads Lloyd Warner (1941) Hollingshead (1949) or Walter Miller (1959).[25]

This leads to a paradox: The culture of poverty concept bumps against the thesis that low-income Negro patterns of family life and sex behavior are primarily the heritage of the slavery years. The patterns so often described as a cultural legacy of slavery are to a large extent the patterns ascribed to the culture of poverty among people who have never been slaves. Yet those who invoke the slavery-specific thesis use it to document differences between Negroes and whites, and offer it as *the* explanation of behavior patterns among low-income Negroes.

With regard to the features ascribed — for example, family instability, woman-based households, overt sex antagonism, illegitimacy, large families, interpersonal violence, depression, apathy, sense of lacking control over one's own fate — no inconsistency is involved. Slavery, in fact, can be viewed — for some slaves and to some extent — as an extreme version of poverty with a few repulsive additions. The inconsistency lies in attributing to the heritage of slavery the same behavior patterns that, for other groups, are attributed to poverty, and then assuming that the slavery heritage, in itself, accounts for those behavior patterns when they occur among Negroes.

The point has been made that the differences between very low-income whites and Negroes are dwarfed by the similarities, with regard to characteristics so far investigated. This is not to argue against the existence of differences. It is also arguable, however, that such differences could be attributable to a century of prejudice, discrimination, and persecution as much as or more than to the preceding years of slavery.

The argument is complicated by the fact that, in our society, economic status to a large extent determines culture, so that it is very difficult to disentangle what we mean by culture and what we mean by class. This intertwining is, of course, built into the culture-of-poverty concept.

Subculture or Culture

The various specifics mentioned illustrate considerations that point to two conclusions concerning "the culture of poverty": If the concept is to be useful at all, it must be explicitly recognized as a subculture rather than a culture; but under any name, poverty lacks the essential elements of a culture.

With regard to the first point, the poor, like the nonpoor, on the whole accept the norms and standards of what has come to be called the mainstream culture. Any subculture coexists and competes with a number of other subcultures. Most citizens of the United States are members of a good many subcultures: Family, peers, colleagues, organizations, and so forth, each with its own norms and imperatives. Which set wins out at any given moment depends on the personal makeup and history of the individual, on the nature of the situation and on coincidental circumstances. The complexity of this mixture makes doubly inappropriate what I have called the "cookie-cutter concept of culture"— the idea that a culture produces individuals as identical as cookies cut from the same mold.[26]

A subculture of poverty, to the extent that it exists, can explain relatively little about a specific individual at a specific moment. It can, however, offer a pat phrase: "It's the culture," as a substitute for thought and for action.

To the extent that this substitute is accepted, the concept jeopardizes both thought and action. "It's the culture," can mean "they don't mind, that's the way they like it and anyway it's built-in, so you can't do anything about it." The second point is that, under any name, poverty lacks some essential elements of a culture. The chief one is a matter of identification. Members of a culture, or a subculture, have a sense of belonging to a culture entity with institutions, patterns, and shared beliefs. Committed members have a sense of allegiance as well as of identity. Even those who want to break away have the feeling that they are separating themselves from an entity that exists and claims them as members. Corollary to this is the sense of participating in the life of a broad group, sharing in a system of beliefs and practices. This positive aspect of culture, the sense of belonging, with its corollary elements of sharing and of participating, has not characterized the people who served as models for the culture of poverty concept.

On the contrary, some of the closest students of slum life emphasize the unincorporated quality of life in the slums. There are gangs and cliques, but their subculture is the gang or the clique. The neighborhoods consist of people who happen to live near each other. A salient characteristic of AFDC mothers and of many other slum dwellers is their social isolation. The lack of worldly goods, according to these observers of large city slums, does not create a sense of community, of common institutions and customs, practices and beliefs. The life-ways of the slum dwellers represent, not a system of culturally evolved patterns, but rather a series of adjustments to exigencies perceived as unpredictable and uncontrollable.

It may be asked, is a culture of poverty evolving from the civil rights movement and the Poor People's Campaign? If so, it is by no means what has been meant hitherto by the culture of poverty. Some salient traits of the movements now on the march represent the most conspicuous lacks in the so-called culture of poverty: Commitment, energetic motivation, hope. It may well be that these movements will shoulder aside preoccupation with and arguments about the culture of poverty. What they produce to supersede it remains to be seen. But no development will free us of the need to subject simple and easy generalizations to cautious and continuous checking against available evidence.

REFERENCES

1. Arthur A. Campbell, "Illegitimacy," in Clyde V. Kiser, et al., *Trends and Variations in Fertility in the United States* (Cambridge, Mass., Harvard University Press, 1967).
2. *Monthly Vital Statistics Report: Highlights, June 14, 1969* (U.S. Public Health Service, National Center for Health Statistics).
3. Benjamin Disraeli, *Sybil: or The Two Nations* (London, H. Colburn, 1845).
4. Oscar Lewis, *The Children of Sanchez: An Autobiography of a Mexican Family* (New York, Random House, Inc., 1961), p. xxvi.

5. *Ibid.*, pp. xxvi-xxvii.
6. NORMAN JOLLIFFE, "The Pathogenesis of Deficiency Disease," in NORMAN JOLLIFFE, F. F. TISDELL, PAUL R. CANNON, eds., *Clinical Nutrition* (New York, Harper & Brothers, 1950), p. 33.
7. ALVIN L. SCHORR, "The Nonculture of Poverty," *American Journal of Orthopsychiatry*, October 1964, p. 909.
8. ALVIN L. SCHORR, *Slums and Social Insecurity* (U.S. Social Security Administration, 1963), Research Report 1.
9. R. C. GRIGGS, et al., "Environmental Factors in Childhood Lead Poisoning," *Journal of the American Medical Association*, March 1964.
10. KENNETH B. CLARK, *Dark Ghetto* (New York, Harper & Row, 1965).
11. *Washington Post*, April 16, 1967, and April 26, 1967.
12. ROBERT ROSENTHAL and LENORE JACOBSON, "Self-Fulfilling Prophecies in the Classroom: Teachers' Expectations as Unintended Determinants." (Paper presented at the Annual Meeting of the American Psychological Association, Washington, D.C., September 1967.) 14 pp. Mimeographed.
13. MELVIN H. KOHN, "Social Class and Exercise of Parental Authority," *American Sociological Review*, June 1959, pp. 352-366. HYLAN LEWIS, "Child-Rearing Practices Among Low-Income Families," in *Casework Papers, 1961* (New York, Family Service Association of America, 1961).
14. ARTHUR A. CAMPBELL, "The Role of Family Planning in the Reduction of Poverty," *Journal of Marriage and the Family*, Vol. 30, No. 2, 1968, pp. 236-245.
15. HYLAN LEWIS, op. cit.
16. HYMAN RODMAN, "On Understanding Lower-Class Behavior," *Social and Economic Studies*, December 1959, Vol. 8, pp. 441-450.
17. *Facts, Fallacies and Future — A Study of the Aid to Dependent Children Program of Cook County, Ill.* (New York, Greenleigh Associates, Inc., 1960).
18. ARTHUR A. CAMPBELL, op. cit.
19. MOLLIE ORSHANSKY, "Recounting the Poor: A Five-Year Review," *Social Security Bulletin*, April 1966, pp. 20-37.
20. DICK GREGORY, *Nigger* (New York, E. P. Dutton & Co., Inc., 1964; JOHN H. ROHER and MUNRO S. EDMONSON, *The Eighth Generation* (New York, Harper & Brothers, 1960).
21. HYLAN LEWIS, "Culture, Class and Family Life Among Low-Income Urban Negroes," in ARTHUR ROSS, ed., *Employment, Race and Poverty* (New York, Harcourt, Brace & World, Inc., 1967).
22. WILLIAM F. PRATT, *"Premarital Pregnancies and Illegitimate Births in a Metropolitan Community — An Analysis of Age and Color Differentials."* Unpublished manuscript cited in STEPHANIE J. VENTURA, *Recent Trends and Differentials in Illegitimacy* (U.S. Department of Health, Education, and Welfare, Natality Statistics Branch, April 1968).
23. ARTHUR A. CAMPBELL, "Illegitimacy," op. cit., and ELIZABETH HERZOG, "Unmarried Mothers: Some Questions to be Answered and Some Answers to the Questioned," in *About the Poor: Some Facts and Some Fictions* (U.S. Department of Health, Education, and Welfare, 1968), Children's Bureau Publication No. 451, pp. 55-57.
24. MYRON LEFCOWITZ, *Poverty and Negro-White Family Structures.* (Background paper for White House Conference, "To Fulfill These Rights," Washington, November 1965.)

25. LLOYD W. WARNER and PAUL S. LUNT, *The Social Life of a Modern Community* (New Haven, Conn., Yale University Press, 1941); AUGUST B. HOLLINGSHEAD, *Elmstown's Youth — The Impact of Social Classes on Adolescents* (New York, John Wiley & Sons, Inc., 1949); WALTER B. MILLER, "Implications of Urban Lower-Class Culture for Social Work," *Social Service Review*, September 1959, pp. 219-236.

26. ELIZABETH HERZOG, "Some Assumptions About the Poor," *About the Poor: Some Facts and Some Fictions,* op. cit., pp. 35-51.

Part 4

Race, Discrimination, and Poverty

Editor's Survey

As with economic growth, the balance of payments, or consumer behavior, economists are concerned to build models of the economic relationships between different social or racial groups. Due in part to the loose definition of the word, economists have not concentrated their attention on producing a theory of "racism," but have focused on constructing economic models of discrimination. The two basic references on the topic are Gary Becker's *The Economics of Discrimination* (University of Chicago Press, 1957) and Lester Thurow's *Poverty and Discrimination* (Brookings, 1969).* The models of discrimination employed are quite different, as are their results. The reader should keep these two theories in mind while reading the selections in this chapter. What pieces of evidence appear to support one or the other?

Let us turn first to Becker's model, as it was developed earlier. This model assumes that individuals have "tastes for discrimination" in their relationships with members of other social or ethnic groups. The effect of these tastes appears in the form of additional costs required to compensate the individual for dealing with persons who are objects of discrimination. Thus, for example, I might be willing to perform a certain job for $3.00 per hour if my co-worker is a fellow white, while I would only perform the job for $4.00 if I am assigned a black associate. An analogy with the tariffs imposed in international trade is frequently drawn to illustrate the nature and economic impact of Becker's type of discrimination. As Becker points out, the more appropriate analogy is with transport costs, which have the similar effect of driving a wedge between the costs of producing some item and the price to the consumer, while avoiding the connotation of manipulation by the society which is associated with

* The reader must bear with the editor's prose in place of selections from the originals. Becker was preparing a revised edition, while Thurow's book was not (at the time of writing) generally available. The apparent importance of surveying these two theories thus necessitated a summary of the present kind.

tariffs. For the purposes of the present exercise, it makes little difference how the reader chooses to envision the manner in which Becker's tastes for discrimination are incorporated in the individual's preference functions.

If one views our society as composed of two sub-societies (white and black) engaged in inter-society trade in goods, services, and factors of production, then tastes for discrimination will have much the same effects on that trade as do transport costs or tariff barriers in trade between nations. Some of the more important conclusions may be summarized:

1. As a matter of pure fact, the white sub-society is much more wealthy per capita than the black. With perfect competition and no discrimination, the white society should export capital to the black, while the black sub-society should export labor. The end result would be an equalization of capital-labor ratios throughout the whole economy. When tastes for discrimination intervene, however, and additional "costs" are placed on the market prices of these exports and imports, then the standard result of international trade theory occurs. In short, the non-discrimination equilibrium amounts of capital and labor are not exported by the white and black sub-societies.

2. The result of this hindrance on exports implies that the capital-labor ratio in the white sub-society remains above that in the black. This affects the owners of factors of production in the two sub-societies in different ways. The discrimination-induced higher capital-labor ratio in the white sub-society benefits white labor, as it has more abundant capital to work with, which increases its marginal productivity and wages. The same higher capital-labor ratio works to the disadvantage of white-owned capital, as its abnormal abundance drives down the rate of return. The opposite result occurs in the black sub-society, where the capital-labor ratio is lowered by discrimination (which hinders the importation of capital and the exportation of labor). Black labor loses from having less capital to work with, while black capital gains from its artificial scarcity.

3. Perhaps the most important conclusion to follow from an analysis based on the transport cost analogy is that not one, but *both* sub-societies lose from discrimination. The levels of output and income in both white and black America are reduced through the impact of tastes for discrimination. Restrictions on free trade between the sub-societies operate to exactly the same end as restrictions on trade between nations. For purposes of public policy, it should be noted that this conclusion is of some importance. It is possible that a consumption-oriented society could be educated to change its preferences for discrimination, if it could be taught that individuals' tastes for discrimination resulted in lower levels of welfare for the discriminators.

The core of the Becker model centers upon the impact of individuals' tastes and preferences upon the operations of typical neoclassical markets. When we turn our attention to the later model of Thurow, we find that this is no longer the case. Instead of markets operating under the impediment of discrimination, Thurow develops a theory which is more openly exploitative and more institutionally oriented. Thurow views white society as operating in the fashion of a "de facto cartel." Its hand is further strengthened in these machinations through control over the major social institutions, particularly government.

In theory, a cartel exercises economic power through control of markets. The markets which the white de facto cartel controls are numerous indeed, according to Thurow. White society is able to act like a *monopsonist* (a single buyer for a given good or service) in the market for the services of black labor. The result: Lower wages for blacks and fewer employed than would occur in a competitive market for their labor. Furthermore, white society can act as *monopolist* (single seller) in the sale of goods and services to the black population. It is thus able to charge higher prices, provide goods of lower quality and poorer services than would result from more perfectly competitive markets. Beyond this, the white cartel can use its control of the government to increase and perpetuate discrimination against the black minority. One example would be found in the allocation of funds and facilities for education, to the end that the quality of black labor is kept low in comparison with white.

A standard textbook will tell you the result of operating a successful cartel — to transfer income from the rest of the society to the operators of the cartel. In just this fashion, Thurow concludes that the monopolistic control of factor and product markets by the white society results in a transfer of income from blacks to whites. His estimate of the amount of income above the competitive level which the white cartel is able to extract from the black population can run as high as $15 billion per year. You should note that this conclusion is exactly opposite to that of Becker. In Thurow's view, elimination of the discriminatory power of the de facto cartel would not result in economic gains for both groups, but for one at the expense of the other. In such a case, the political difficulties of removing discrimination may be a great deal more onerous.

Not only should the reader examine the following selections for data supporting the two different models, but he should try to answer questions of the following sort. Which of these models (if either) represents *the* theory of discrimination? Is it possible that both kinds of influence — tastes and cartel — could operate simultaneously? (If so, can we say anything about the gains and losses of the two sub-societies from discrimination?) We know something about controlling real cartels: How does one go about controlling de facto cartels? What factors shape individual's tastes for discrimination, and what policies could be pursued to counteract or reduce them?

CHAPTER 9

Poverty: The Special Case of The Negro

Alan Batchelder

Presumably, a Negro family receiving $2,400 annually would experience, because of such low income, discomfort identical with that experienced by a white family in exactly the same circumstances. Why then a special paper on Negro poverty? Because, in America, the white and Negro situations are never identical. Surely, because of discrimination, poor Negroes are psychologically more discomfited than poor whites. But economists do not investigate such discomfiture. Why, then, a special economics paper on Negro poverty?

Because at least five economic considerations distinguish Negro from white poverty. As Wordsworth observed of the echo, "Like, — but oh how different."

First, $1,000 buys less for a poor Negro than for a poor white.

Second, the demographic cross-section of the Negro poor is unlike that of the white poor.

Third, poor Negroes suffer though the general weal benefits from secular changes in urban renewal, education medians, agriculture, manufacturing location, technology, and social minimum wages.

Fourth, the effect of government transfer payments is different for poor Negroes than for poor whites.

Fifth, discrimination operates against Negroes to restrict access to education and to the jobs that can provide an escape from poverty.

These considerations will be discussed in turn.

Some Historical Perspective

When considering American Negro affairs, one must remember that social and economic conditions of Negroes are most responsive to unemployment rates. In 1900, 90 percent of American Negroes lived in the South, most on

Reprinted from the *American Economic Review*, May 1965, by permission of the publisher.

farms. The few urban Negroes were totally excluded from manufacturing and from all but menial and laborious jobs. The situation changed to the Negro's advantage only during German nationalism's wars. Wartime labor shortages induced managers of large manufacturing corporations to admit Negroes to the production jobs that permitted Negroes to make relative income gains.

During peacetime, the Negro position remained the same or deteriorated. When labor markets softened between 1949 and 1959, the income position of Negro men relative to that of white men fell in every section of the country.[1] Rising productivity cut the number of whites and Negroes living in poverty, but the incidence of poverty among Negroes rose between 1950 and 1962 from 2 to 2½ times the white rate.[2]

The past decade's many admonitions and laws opposing discrimination could not raise the Negro's relative economic position in the face of rising unemployment. If Negroes are to approach economic and civil equality in the future, unemployment rates must fall.

Full employment affects all Negroes. Attention now turns to the characteristics distinguishing poor Negro from poor White Americans.

The Negro Dollar: Second-class Money

When citing statistics of poverty, the portion of Negro families receiving incomes below a particular figure, e.g., $3,000, is often compared with the portion of white families receiving incomes below $3,000. Such comparisons implicitly assume the Negro's $3,000 buys as much as the white's $3,000. It does not.

American cities have two housing markets: the city-wide white market and the circumscribed Negro market. Because supply is restricted, Negroes[3] "received less housing value for their dollars spent than do whites. . . . Census statistics indicate that . . . non-white renters and home owners obtain fewer standard quality dwellings and frequently less space than do whites paying the same amounts." A Chicago welfare department study found[4] "housing defects significantly greater for Negro than for white families, despite the fact that rents for Negro families are 28% a month higher than for whites in private dwellings."

Landlords are sometimes judged greedy extortionists for charging Negro tenants higher rents than whites. But they are operating in a market of restricted supply; high Negro rents reflect supply and demand relationships, not conspiratorial landlord greed. Since 15 percent of the consumption expenditures of urban Negro families is for shelter,[5] real income is significantly reduced by relatively high rents.

Poor urban Negroes also pay more than whites for identical consumer durables bought on credit.[6] (Negroes pay more than whites for residential financing, too.[7]) The difference may be due to white reluctance to sell to Negroes (Becker's discrimination[8]), to Negro immobility, or to the sellers' assumption that poor Negroes are poorer risks than poor whites. Whatever the cause, real income suffers.

Poor Negro families average a half-person larger than poor white families.[9] Consequently, per capita real income of poor Negroes is even farther below per capita real income of poor whites.

If, then, $3,000 in Negro money buys only as much as $2,800 or even $2,500 in white money and is distributed over more people, one should keep in mind appropriate reservations when comparing percentage of whites with percentage of Negroes below some income level.

Differences in Demographic Characteristics

The Negro poor differ from the white poor in demographic characteristics. Remembering that Negro numbers will be understated, uniform dollar incomes can be used to identify nonwhite (not Negro) and white poor. Defining as poor, families with incomes under $3,000 and individuals living independently with incomes under $1,500 in 1959, four social-economic variables distinguish the nonwhite from the white poor.

First, the nonwhite poor are concentrated in the South. In 1960, 72 percent (52 percent)* of poor nonwhite families; only four of ten (27 percent) poor white families lived in the South (unless otherwise noted, all statistics in this section are from reference.[10]) The 32 point difference in southern concentration resulted because, in 1960, the proportion of nonwhites was double the proportion of whites living in the South.

Second, low income is more of a rural phenomenon for whites than for nonwhites; 18 of every 100 (4 percent) poor white families, 12 of every 100 (3 percent) poor nonwhite families lived on farms in 1960. Fully 84 percent (79 percent) of nonwhite, only 44 percent (63 percent) of white farm families were poor in 1959, but nonwhites have withdrawn from farming more completely than have whites.

Third, the aging of husbands is a much more important cause of white than of nonwhite poverty. Other forces are important in causing nonwhite poverty. In 1959, 29 percent of poor white families but only 13 percent of poor nonwhite families were headed by a man older than sixty-four years. Among unrelated individuals, 40 percent of the white poor, only 26 percent of the nonwhite poor were past sixty-four.

Fourth, nonwhite poverty, far more than white, is associated with families headed by women. American Negro women have always borne exceptionally heavy family responsibility. In 1910 there were 20 gainfully employed white women for every 100 employed white men; there were 67 employed Negro women for every 100 employed Negro men.[11] Even in 1959, only 8 percent of

---

* The figures in parentheses refer to individuals living independently.

white families but 21 percent of nonwhite families were headed by women. Three-fourths of these nonwhite families were poor in 1959. Consequently, 32 percent of all poor nonwhite families, only 19 percent of all poor white families, were headed by women in 1959.

Urban Renewal, Shrinking the Supply of Dwellings

A lilting song of World War I charged

> *It's the same the whole world over,*
> *It's the poor wot gets the blame,*
> *It's the rich wot gets the pleasure,*
> *Ain't it all a blooming shame.*

Forces afoot today give the affluent society and even poor whites the pleasure while injuring poor Negroes. One of these forces is urban renewal. It replaces slums with aesthetically attractive, commercially profitable structures, some of which provide low-income housing superior to that which the private market could provide.

Yet urban renewal seems to effect a net reduction in housing supply for poor Negroes. L. K. Northwood found[12] "the supply of housing has been reduced in areas formerly occupied by Negro families. . . . 115,000 housing units were . . . planned to replace 190,500 . . . *a net loss of 75,000.*" Because many urban Negroes live in slums, 60 percent of the persons dispossessed by urban renewal demolition have been Negroes.[13]

The long-run tendency to reduce the supply of low-cost housing is aggravated in the short run because time must elapse between demolition of old and dedication of new buildings. During short runs as long as five years[14] urban renewal reduces housing supply by demolition uncompensated by new construction.

Poor whites may move elsewhere; poor Negroes must face reduced supply. Reduced supply should raise prices, and there is evidence that Negroes displaced by urban renewal pay rent 10 percent higher after relocation than before.[15]

Until President Kennedy's November 1962 executive order, the supply-restriction effect was even greater, for no federal rule prohibited urban redevelopers from practicing racial discrimination.[16] The 1962 order alleviated the problem but could not end the irony that poor Negroes suffer from programs designed to promote urban welfare.

Education: The Illiterate Fall Farther Behind

E. F. Denison estimates[17] that from 1929 to 1957 improved education "contributed 42 percent of the 1.60 percentage point growth rate in product per person employed." Improved education is manifested in rising median school years completed. The 1950 Negro medians for men and for women, past age twenty-four, lagged white medians by 2.8 years. By 1960, Negro medians had pushed up a year and a third. So had white medians.[18] Average Negroes remained in the same relative position, but rising educational medians increased the comparative disadvantage of the 2,265,000 nonwhite functional illiterates (less than five years of school) making up 23.5 percent of the 1960 nonwhite population past age twenty-four.[19]

Many poor whites are illiterate, but figures on school years completed understate the number of illiterate Negroes and the size of their educational disadvantage. Understatements result for Negroes because so many attended inefficient segregated southern schools. Testing poor Negro literacy, Illinois departments of public aid recently sampled able-bodied Negroes aged 16-64 receiving public assistance (not a random sample of all Negroes). Each person was asked his school attainment; each took the *New Stanford Reading Test*. Of persons educated in Illinois, 3 percent were functionally illiterate; 35 percent tested as illiterate. Of persons educated in Mississippi 23 percent were functionally illiterate; 81 percent, four of five adults, tested as illiterate.[20]

Of nonwhites living North or West in 1960, 41 percent had been born in the South.[21] These educationally deprived poor southern Negroes are increasingly disadvantaged in regions where the median education of the local labor force and the quality of local schools rise each year.

Poor Negro boys are especially disadvantaged because of parental limitations and because their homes and the larger society offer so few successful men inspiring academic emulation. Special counseling and educational arrangements can offset those conditions and send slum boys to college,[22] but society devotes few resources to such arrangements.

Left ever farther behind rising national educational norms, poor Negro families are ever less qualified to compete for jobs or to help their children acquire the education required to escape poverty.

Agriculture: End of an Exodus

Since 1945, the mechanization of cotton culture has revolutionized southern agriculture.[23] There has also been persistent change in crops grown and livestock raised.[24] These changes raised agricultural productivity and expelled hand labor from southern farms. In 1930, there were 882,000 Negro farms (with 4,680,500 residents). In 1950, there were 559,000 (with 3,167,000 residents); in 1959 only 265,000 (with 1,482,000 residents).[25]

The economy benefits as productivity rises. The effect on Negroes is less favorable. As whites left, the white farms that averaged 130 acres in 1930 grew to average 249 acres in 1959. But Negro farms showed little growth. They averaged 43 acres in 1930 and 52 acres in 1960.[26]

Change has not resulted in larger, more prosperous Negro farms. Change has expelled from southern farms the most ill-educated Americans.

Looking ahead, the Negro reservoir is nearly exhausted. The number of rural farm Negroes in 1960 was only 47 percent the number in 1950.[27] The Negro exodus can never again approach the scale reached during the 1950's. Poor Negroes are already committed to the city.

Manufacturing Migration: Jobs Out of Reach

Since 1950, southern manufacturing has expanded more rapidly than northern. From 1950 to 1960, the number of manufacturing jobs grew 28 percent in the South, only 12 percent in the North.[28] Because most poor Negroes live in the South and because Negroes' wartime income gains were based on accession of Negroes to production jobs in manufacturing, Negroes are particularly affected by shifts in manufacturing employment.

Manufacturing's southern migration to new markets and new sources of raw material[29] has distributed American resources more efficiently. It has taken jobs to poor whites but not to poor Negro men. Between 1950 and 1960, the number of jobs in southern manufacturing rose by 944,000. Of these 944,000 jobs, 12,000 went to Negro women (proportionately fewer to white women) ; none went to Negro men.[30]

Manufacturing: Technological Change Blocks the Exits

During wartime, rural southern Negroes proved themselves in manufacturing and developed vested interests in the growth of unskilled and semiskilled manufacturing jobs.

Today, technological change benefits all by raising productivity. It also changes America's occupational cross-section. In 1880 textile mechanization replaced skilled workers with unskilled rural immigrants.[31] Negroes would prefer such changes today, but in 1964 skilled workers replaced unskilled.

In recent years, the occupations that during war gave Negroes a chance to get ahead have not grown as rapidly as the number of Negroes seeking work. Between 1947 and 1964, as male employment rose 10 percent, the number of manufacturing production jobs rose only 5½ percent.[32] Between 1950 and 1960, male employment rose 6.9 percent; the number of semiskilled jobs in manufacturing rose only 4.1 percent.[33]

Most unfavorable for aspiring unskilled poor Negroes, the number of men's laboring jobs in manufacturing fell 20 percent (by 200,000) between 1950 and 1960.[34]

These changes in America's occupational cross-section result from technological developments that raise society's affluence; but, as present trends continue, manufacturing will offer fewer exits from poverty for Negroes handicapped by rural southern origins.

The Rising Social Minimum Wage and the
Able-Bodied Unemployed

Two centuries ago, when sheep began gobbling up the people of England's countryside, the victims were deposited in cities in much the same condition as the untrained Negro migrants of today. The bold English peasantry, dispossessed from Sweet Auburn, could say of the city, "Thou found'st me poor at first and keep'st me so," but they were employed — though oppressively and irregularly.

Many Negroes transplanted to cities are unable to obtain steady work. Long's argument that America's social minimum wage rises above the marginal revenue product of society's least productive members[35] applies especially to urban Negroes with rural southern antecedents. Law and respectable custom press upward on the social minimum wage. The general welfare benefits as many low-income persons receive more money and employers increase efficiency to offset higher costs.[36] But the first increase in the minimum causes the discharge of the least able persons employed. Successive increases cause the discharge of successively more able persons among the less able employed.[37]

It is the function of the market to choose technology appropriate to available resources as reflected in flexible resource prices. But the market does not operate below the social minimum. Weighed down with their heritage from the Southern Way of Life, able-bodied Negroes with marginal revenue products below the social minimum wage must either find employers paying below the minimum or depend on transfers.

So much for forces benefiting the general public but hurting poor Negroes.

Transfer Payments: Paternal Substitute
and Golden Age Equalizer

For fifteen years, Negro unemployment rates have been double white rates.[38] This distinguishes Negro from white need for transfers, but does not distinguish poor Negroes from poor whites.

Respecting government transfers, poor Negroes do differ from poor whites because proportionately more Negro households have feminine heads and proportionately fewer Negroes are past sixty-four.

Relatively few Negroes receive OASDI (old age, survivors, and disability insurance). In 1962, 6.7 percent of the 12,500,000 recipients were nonwhite. This low figure was due to the nonwhite's shorter age span and the dissimilar work histories that led 73 percent of elderly whites but only 58 percent of elderly nonwhites to qualify.[39] In contrast, old age assistance goes to 38 percent of elderly nonwhites, 12 percent of elderly whites.[40]

OASDI brings elderly Negroes and whites close to income equality. For all persons, Negro income averages half of white income.[41] Yet the average income of nonwhites runs 80 percent the average total income of whites receiving OASDI.[42] This happens because many Negroes continue in poverty while many whites sink into poverty after retiring.

Because Negro fathers so often decamp, Negro children receive a disproportionate share of ADC (aid to families with dependent children). Of 900,000 families (with 2,800,000 children) receiving ADC in 1963, 44 percent were Negro.[43]

Per capita, ADC pays much less than retirement programs. Old age assistance meets 94 percent of the needs of the elderly; ADC supplies 58 percent of children's needs.[44] Playing surrogate to absent fathers of poor Negro families, ADC never raises incomes or aspirations above levels at which the mothers' and absent fathers' "only legacy to their children is the same one of poverty and deprivation that they received from their own parents."[45]

"The legacy of poverty" is a foreboding term. Seeking auspicious signs, at what points is Negro poverty most vulnerable to forces of improvement?

Prospects

Since poor Negroes pay more than poor whites for housing, any laws, changes of white hearts, or construction serving to increase the supply of housing open to Negroes will especially benefit the Negro poor.

Lengthening Negro men's lives, strengthening wedding bonds, and, most important, improving job opportunities for Negro men will strengthen the poor Negro family. This will immediately add a male income earner to the family and will eventually induce male youth to look more ambitiously toward futures in the market economy.

During the 1950's, the numbers of men and of women of working age grew equally, but the number of jobs for women grew 34.5 percent, the number for men only 7.3 percent.[46] This was especially important for Negro women whose income rose relative to that of white women and Negro men.[47] The trend continues; between 1960 and 1964, the number of jobs for women grew fourteen times as fast as the number of jobs for men.[48]

Because half of southern Negro mothers of preschool children work,[49] mothers and children would benefit from preschool nurseries freeing the mothers for work and preparing the children for school. Because many receive ADC, higher payments or training schools for ADC mothers would particularly benefit poor Negroes.

Since poor Negro mothers are least informed regarding birth control,[50] their education in this regard would permit great improvements in Negro health, real per capita incomes, and family manageableness.

Each year Negroes have less interest in programs aiding poor farmers, for farmers become more nearly all white each year. Contemplating old age, poor Negroes will benefit as urban migration and extension of coverage bring more under OASDI.

As social minimum wages rise, perhaps engineers will be able to provide employers with machinery that will combine profitably with the unskills of rurally educated southern Negroes. If not, they must depend upon transfers.

Finally, since southern segregated Negro schools have placed poor Negroes at a greater disadvantage than poor whites, since racial discrimination keeps qualified Negroes from demanding jobs, since weak labor markets remove the inducement that historically has been most important in helping Negroes score economic gains, the position of poor Negroes will improve dramatically in response to appropriate pressures at these three points.

Peroration

Because of discrimination in education and employment, there is one last important difference between the Negro and white poor. Logic rather than statistics suggests its existence. To begin, assume the innate ability distribution of Negroes is identical with that of whites. Next assume the inexorable winnowing out of those least able to earn is the dominant cause of white poverty, but is only a partial cause of Negro poverty. It follows that poor whites are the least able whites, but that poor Negroes include those least able as well as many of middling to superior ability. These able Negroes are poor because of racial discrimination; society denied them access to the channels in which their earning ability could be developed and used.

The economist then concludes that the marginal efficiency of social capital invested in educating and finding work for the Negro poor could be much higher than the marginal efficiency of social capital similarly invested in the white poor. However, we know that the conversion of the poor Negro's potential into dollar product is very difficult in American society. The potential return is latent in the Negro poor. Able innovators are required if that potential is to be realized.

REFERENCES

1. A. B. BATCHELDER, "Decline in the Relative Income of Negro Men," *Q.J.E.*, November 1964, pp. 525-548.
2. U.S. Bureau of the Census, *Statistical Abstract of the United States: 1964* (Washington, 1964), p. 339.
3. U.S. Commission on Race and Housing, *Where Shall We Live?* (Berkeley, 1958), p. 36.
4. Greenleigh Associates, Inc., *Facts, Fallacies and Future* (New York, 1960), p. 13.
5. U.S. Bureau of Labor Statistics, *Consumer Expenditures and Income, Urban United States, 1960-1961*, Supplement 1 to BLS Report 237-38 (Washington, 1964).

6. DAVID CAPLOVITZ, *The Poor Pay More* (Glencoe, Ill., 1963), pp. 12-20.
7. U.S. Commission on Civil Rights, *Report: 1959* (Washington, 1959), p. 344.
8. G. S. BECKER, *The Economics of Discrimination* (Chicago, 1957).
9. MOLLIE ORSHANSKY, "Children of the Poor," *Soc. Sec. Bull,* July 1963, p. 10.
10. U.S. Bureau of the Census, *U.S. Census of Population: 1960,* Supplementary Reports, *Low Income Families: 1960* PC(S1)-43, 24 February 1964.
11. U.S. Bureau of the Census, *U.S. Census of Population: 1910,* Vol. IV. *Occupational Statistics* (Washington, 1914), pp. 66-67.
12. U.S. Commission on Civil Rights, *1961 Report,* Book 4, *Housing* (Washington, 1961), pp. 107-108.
13. U.S. Commission on Civil Rights, *Report 1959* (Washington, 1959), p. 348.
14. EDGAR MAY, *The Wasted Americans* (New York, 1964), pp. 132-133.
15. H. W. REYNOLDS, JR., *"The Human Element in Urban Renewal," Public Welfare,* April 1961, pp. 72, 82.
16. U.S. Commission on Civil Rights, *The 50 States Report* (Washington, 1961), p. 441.
17. *The Sources of Economic Growth in the United States* (New York, 1962), p. 73.
18. U.S. Bureau of the Census, *Statistical Abstract of the United States: 1964* (Washington, 1964), p. 113.
19. U.S. Bureau of the Census, *U.S. Census of Population: 1960. Detailed Characteristics, U.S. Summary* (Washington, 1963), p. 420-421.
20. Cook County Department of Public Aid, *First They Must Read* (Chicago, 1964), p. 118.
21. U.S. Bureau of the Census, *U.S. Census of Population, 1960. Subject Reports. State of Birth* (Washington, 1964), p. 2.
22. R. L. PLAUT, "Increasing the Quantity and Quality of Negro Enrollment in College," *Harvard Educ. Rev.,* Summer, 1960, pp. 275-276.
23. J. H. STREET, *The New Revolution in the Cotton Economy* (Chapel Hill, 1957).
24. J. J. SPENGLER, "Demographic and Economic Change in the South, 1940-1960," *Change in the Contemporary South,* A. SINDLER, ed. (Durham, 1963).
25. U.S. Bureau of the Census, *Statistical Abstract of the United States: 1964* (Washington, 1964), p. 618; *U.S. Census of Population: 1930,* Vol. II: *General Report* (Washington, 1933), p. 599; *U.S. Census of Population: 1960. Detailed Characteristics, U.S. Summary* (Washington, 1963), pp. 239-360.
26. U.S. Department of Agriculture, *U.S. Census of Agriculture: 1959,* Vol. II, *General Report* (Washington, 1962), p. 1035.
27. U.S. Bureau of the Census, *U.S. Census of Population: 1960. Detailed Characteristics, U.S. Summary* (Washington, 1963), pp. 359-360.
28. *Ibid.,* pp. 730-732; *U.S. Census of Population: 1950.* Vol. II, *Characteristics of the Population, U.S. Summary* (Washington, 1953), pp. 407-411.
29. J. J. SPENGLER, "Demographic and Economic Change in the South, 1940-1960." *Change in the Contemporary South,* A. SPINDLER, ed. (Durham, 1963), pp. 46-47.
30. U.S. Bureau of the Census, *U.S. Census of Population: 1950,* Vol. II, *Characteristics of the Population, U.S. Summary* (Washington, 1953), p. 410; *U.S. Census of the Population: 1960. Detailed Characteristics, U.S. Summary* (Washington, 1963), pp. 728-729.
31. CHARLOTTE ERICKSON, *American Industry and the European Immigrant, 1860-1885* (Cambridge, Mass., 1957), p. 63.

32. U.S. Bureau of the Census, *U.S. Census of Manufactures: 1958,* Vol. II, *Industry Statistics,* Part 1 (Washington, 1961), p. 3; U.S. Bureau of Labor Statistics, *Employment and Earnings,* September 1964, II, p. 14.

33. U.S. Bureau of the Census, *U.S. Census of Population: 1960. Detailed Characteristics, U.S. Summary* (Washington, 1963), pp. 528-531.

34. *Ibid.,* p. 533.

35. C. D. LONG, "An Overview of Postwar Labor Market Developments" in *Proceedings of the 4th Annual Social Security Conference* (Kalamazoo, 1962), p. 16.

36. U.S. Bureau of Labor Statistics, "Plant Adjustments to the $1 Minimum Wage," *Monthly Labor Rev.,* October 1958, pp. 1139-1140.

37. *Ibid.,* p. 1141.

38. U.S. Bureau of the Census. *Statistical Abstract of the United States: 1964* (Washington, 1964), pp. 216-218.

39. MOLLIE ORSHANSKY, "The Aged Negro and His Income," *Soc. Sec. Bull.,* February, pp. 5, 9.

40. *Ibid.,* p. 11.

41. *Ibid.,* p. 5.

42. A. B. BATCHELDER, "Decline in the Relative Income of Negro Men," *Q.J.E.,* November 1964, pp. 525-48.

43. R. F. MUGGE, "Aid to Families with Dependent Children," *Soc. Sec. Bull.,* March 1963, pp. 3-4.

44. E. J. PERKINS, "Unmet Needs in Public Assistance," *Soc. Sec. Bull.,* April 1960, p. 7.

45. MOLLIE ORSHANSKY, "Children of the Poor," *Soc. Sec. Bull.,* July 1963, p. 12.

46. U.S. Bureau of the Census, *U.S. Census of Population: 1960. Detailed Characteristics, U.S. Summary* (Washington, 1963), pp. 528-531.

47. A. B. BATCHELDER, "Decline in the Relative Income of Negro Men," *Q.J.E.,* November 1964, pp. 531-533.

48. U.S. Bureau of the Census, *Statistical Abstract of the United States: 1964* (Washington, 1964), p. 216.

49. L. A. EPSTEIN, "Unmet Needs in a Land of Abundance," *Soc. Sec. Bull.,* May 1963, p. 9.

50. EDGAR MAY, *The Wasted Americans* (New York, 1964), pp. 153-166.

CHAPTER 10

I. The Negro Worker in Early America

Ray Marshall

The racial attitudes engendered by the American slave system have had a deep and continuing impact on labor race relations. In the antebellum South, and to a lesser extent in other areas of the country, direct and indirect competition between slaves and free workers created animosities between black and white workers which lasted long after emancipation. But the mutual antipathy between Negroes and whites was not due entirely to competition for jobs. It was based also on the fact that "The poor white envied the slave's security and hated him for his material advantages, while the slave envied the white man's freedom and hated him for the advantages of his whiteness."[1] Slavery also created the image of the Negro as an "inferior" person and therefore influenced white attitudes about his social, political, and economic acceptability. Although most slaves and free Negroes lived in the South, the "race problem" created by the attitudes toward them has not been restricted to that region. Indeed, as the following discussion will show, the migration of Negroes out of the rural South has created many problems elsewhere.

Population Movements

In 1790, when the population of the United States was 3,172,006, the Negro population was 757,208. All but 59,527 of these Negroes were slaves; the rest were classified as "free colored persons." In 1840, when slaves constituted 15 percent of the population of the United States, the Southern states had the following proportions:

Reprinted from Ray Marshall, *The Negro Worker* (New York: Random House, 1967) by permission of the publisher. © 1967 by Random House, Inc.

Virginia	36%	Tennessee	22%
North Carolina	33	Alabama	43
South Carolina	55	Mississippi	52
Georgia	41	Arkansas	20
Kentucky	23	Louisiana	48

SOURCE: *Compendium of the Enumeration of the Inhabitants and Statistics of the United States as Obtained at the Department of State from the Returns of the Sixth Census.* "Tables of Apportionment," p. 364.

Outside the South, no state had a slave population large enough to be recorded in the 1840 census except Delaware (3 percent), Maryland (19 percent), and Missouri (15 percent).

Table 1 shows, by region, the population distribution in 1860. The nearly 4 million slaves in the South in 1860 were owned by families that represented only 1.75 million of the region's more than 7 million whites.

TABLE 1

Region	White	Free Negro	Slave
South	7,033,973	258,000	3,838,765
Northeast	10,438,028	155,983	18
North Central	8,899,969	69,291	114,948
West	550,567	4,450	29

SOURCE: *Department of Commerce, Bureau of the Census. Historical Statistics of the United States, 1789–1945,* 1949, p. 25.

Although most Negroes remained in the South until the 1960's, the tendency for them to migrate to other areas started immediately after the Civil War and was stimulated by World War II. Of 7,450,589 nonwhites in the United States in 1890, 6,915,715 were born in the South, and of that number only 526,612, or 7.6 percent, lived outside that region. The proportion of nonwhites born in the South and living in other regions was only 4.2 percent in 1900, but jumped to 8.1 percent in 1920, when 9,676,149 of the nation's 10,623,838 nonwhites were born in the South. In 1860, 5.1 percent of all Negroes lived outside the South, where they constituted 1.2 percent of the total population, but by 1910 10.4 percent of the Negroes lived outside the South, where they made up 1.6 percent of the population. The census figures for the proportion of nonwhites in the South after 1910 were:

1920	85%
1930	74
1940	74
1950	64
1960	57

The 1960 figure of 57 percent really overstates the proportion of nonwhites in the South because it is based on the census definition of the South, which includes Maryland, the District of Columbia, and Delaware, and shows a total of 1,098,146 nonwhites. If we subtract these three areas the remaining states, the states of the Southeast and Southwest, contained only 10,400,000 of the 20,500,000 nonwhites in the United States. The "South" as defined in this more restricted sense had the following proportions of the nonwhite population:

1940	73%
1950	60
1960	51

Why the decreasing percentage? Although the factors responsible for the patterns of Negro migration are not completely known, some of the more important causes seem reasonably clear. The increased migration of Negroes to Northern areas around 1915 undoubtedly was caused by a combination of factors including: industrial expansion in the North, which increased the demand for unskilled labor; labor shortages resulting from the cessation of immigration during World War I; the lure of freedom and greater opportunities in the North as compared with the South; and the worsening of conditions in Southern agriculture due to the boll weevil, drought, soil depletion, and high birth rates.

The main trend in the shift of Negro population has been to the cities, and out of the South and into the Northeast and Midwest. Before World War II, very few Negroes lived in the West; as late as 1940 only 2.2 percent of the Negroes in the United States lived in Western states. In the North, Negroes migrated primarily to such cities as New York, Chicago, Philadelphia, Detroit, Cleveland, and Pittsburgh, which had about a third of the Northern Negro population in 1930 and about half of that population in 1940.

Most Northern Negroes have lived in cities and, although there has been an urban trend in the South, most Southern Negroes lived in rural areas until before World War II. About 64 percent of Northern Negroes lived in cities in 1860 as compared with 79 percent in 1910. Only 6.7 percent of Southern Negroes lived in urban areas in 1860, but this figure had increased to 22 percent by 1910. Negroes constituted 19.3 percent of the Southern urban population in 1860 and 24.5 percent in 1910. In 1960, 35 percent of American Negroes lived in Southern urban areas and 38 percent lived in Northern urban areas; only about a fourth of the nation's Negroes remained in Southern rural areas.

Not only were over three-quarters of all American Negroes still in the South on the eve of World War II, but Negroes were still concentrated primarily in the same areas as in 1860, namely the so-called "Black Belt" that forms a crescent of counties from the Potomac to Texas. Part of the explanation for the surprising continuity in the location of Negroes was the segregated occupational system which tended to restrict Negroes to agriculture and to only certain kinds of nonagricultural occupations. It is particularly significant that Negroes did not participate to an appreciable degree in the "New South's" nonagricultural industries, which grew up after the Civil War mainly outside the "Black Belt."

The Negro Work Force

Although most slaves were employed in agriculture, they also were trained for a variety of nonagricultural trades, especially those connected with the building crafts. Plantation owners frequently apprenticed their slaves to journeymen for training, and sometimes traveling teachers instructed them in various crafts. Planters rented their trained slaves to others during slack seasons on the home plantation, and white journeymen often augmented their incomes and supported themselves in retirement by buying and training slaves.[2]

Slaves were also used to frustrate the free workers' efforts to organize. In 1846, for instance, the superintendent of a South Carolina canal and railroad company recommended to his board of directors that slaves be bought to head off strikes, and other employers argued that a supply of slave mechanics was "our bulwark against extortion and our safeguard against the turbulence of white mechanics, as seen in the great strikes, both in England and in the North, and is the only protection we have in any possible struggle between capital and white labor."[3] The famed Tredegar Iron Company of Richmond used free labor almost exclusively until the 1840's, but in 1842 the company started employing slaves as a means of reducing labor costs. In 1847, when their white workers struck for higher wages and the removal of Negro workers, Tredegar broke the strike by expanding the use of slaves and by threatening to prosecute the strikers for criminal conspiracy. After the strike,[4] the company gradually filled almost all nonsupervisory jobs with slaves.

Pressure felt by white labor due to the presence of Negro workers was not restricted to the South. Spero and Harris tell us, "In the North, the presence of the free Negro workman was resented even more sharply than in the South."[5] It was even illegal for free Negroes to live in several Northern states and municipalities. In 1834, for example, a New Jersey newspaper called for the "rigid enforcement of the statute against the admission of blacks into our boundaries," when Negroes fleeing from a mob in Philadelphia sought refuge in that state.[6] Negroes had predominated in Philadelphia's nonagricultural work force before 1834, but subsequently were replaced by immigrants. White workers seriously objected to Negro competition in Cincinnati and New York, and in smaller cities in Illinois, Indiana, New Jersey, and Pennsylvania. Indeed, opposition to Negroes was so great that the Democratic party of New York City actually opposed the freeing of slaves for fear that it would lead to an influx of hordes of Negro workers from the South.

In spite of opposition from whites, Negroes were trained for many nonagricultural jobs before the Civil War; they seem to have predominated in many skilled crafts. Skilled immigrants, who made up an important part of the labor force of Northern cities, avoided the South. Although we have no good statistical evidence for the occupational distribution of Negroes before the Civil War, a survey made under the auspices of the Federal Government in 1865 indicates that Negroes constituted 80 percent of the South's skilled mechanics at that time, a proportion undoubtedly influenced by the fact that many white artisans had been drawn away by the war.[7]

Due to a variety of factors, the Negro's position in the Southern labor force changed markedly after 1865. The main occupations open to Negroes after Reconstruction were those which were regarded as "Negro" jobs (which were, by definition, hot, dirty, or otherwise disagreeable), those for which they were trained as slaves, or occupations which served the Negro communities. Racial job patterns had a strong caste element about them. Slavery and color marked the Negro as an inferior person; therefore whites considered it improper for Negroes to compete directly with them for the better jobs. It was especially unthinkable that Negroes should hold supervisory positions over whites.

Negro workers were to be found especially in the following industries: fertilizer, cigar and tobacco, slaughter and packing, lumber and furniture, turpentine and distillery, road and bridge construction and repair, steam railroad, water transportation, hotel and restaurant, laundry and cleaning, and dyeing and pressing.

Although, following the Civil War, Negroes were in many ways better off in the North than in the South they had better opportunities in the South in some professions and in some skilled trades. Frazier tells us that except where he had broken in as a strikebreaker, the Negro in the North was confined principally to domestic and personal service occupations.[8] After a careful study of conditions North and South, Myrdal concluded in 1944:

> Except during the war boom, Negroes realized that there were only a limited number of jobs in the North. Owners of Northern industry were not very willing to hire Negro workers except when orders were piling up, and European immigrant laborers could not be had because of the War or legal restrictions on immigration. Northern industrialists often believed in the stereotype of the lazy and inefficient Negro, and often their limited observations strengthened their belief. Some had the legitimate doubt whether Negroes, used to forced labor on farms, could be adapted to free labor in factories. Too, they did not wish to offend their white workers, who were in the majority. Most white unions, faced with Negroes coming into their industries, fought the Negroes; and white workers generally opposed black competition.[9]

The overall statistics on Negro employment in the South and the non-South indicate that racial employment patterns were only slightly more favorable to Negroes in the non-South. Table 2 shows the distribution of male employment in 1930.

TABLE 2

Occupation	South		Non-South	
Group	Negro	White	Negro	White
Total	100%	100%	100%	100%
Clerical or lower	95	79	95	82
Skilled or lower	93	60	91	64
Semiskilled or lower	86	38	83	41
Unskilled	71	20	66	21

SOURCE: *Socio-Economic Grouping of the Gainful Workers of the United States, 1930* (Washington, D.C.: Bureau of the Census, 1938), p. 36.

About 69 percent of nonwhite women were employed in domestic and personal services in 1940 and 60 percent remained in these occupation groups in 1962. About 41 percent of nonwhite males were farm workers in 1940 as compared with 14 percent in 1962.

The percentages of Negroes in some of the main building trades for various census years are shown in Table 3.

TABLE 3*

Craft	1940	1930	1920	1910	1900	1890
Bricklayers	6.0%	6.9%	8.1%	7.5%	9.0%	6.1%
Carpenters	3.9	3.5	3.9	4.3	3.7	3.6
Cement finishers	15.2	15.8	15.4	13.0	10.5	10.3
Electricians	.7	.7	.6	.6	—	—
Painters	3.8	3.6	3.2	2.9	2.1	2.0
Plumbers	2.2	2.0	1.7	1.7	1.2	1.1

*EDITOR'S NOTE: *These figures must not be confused with union membership.*

The Entrenchment of Segregation

Thus, emancipation and Reconstruction did very little to improve the economic condition of Negroes, in spite of high initial hopes and expectations. After the dream that the Yankee would furnish him forty acres and a mule had faded, the freed man was forced to turn to his old master and to the sharecropping system for subsistence. The low rate of economic growth in the South before 1880 made it difficult for Negroes to move into urban occupations, and Negroes thus tended to become frozen to agriculture. But even when he did move to town, the Negro was usually excluded from most of the new nonagricultural occupations except for disagreeable or low status "Negro" jobs. Except where the number of Negroes made it impossible, most unions either excluded or segregated Negroes. The main exceptions were the trowel trade unions, which had many Negro members, and the abortive attempts to form equalitarian unions made by the National Labor Union and Knights of Labor, discussed in the following chapter. Moreover, there were no longer slaveowners who could use their power to protect Negroes from the hostility of white workers. Indeed, the planters now took measures to restrict the Negro's movements in order to assure a continuous supply of labor for the plantations. These restrictive measures included the so-called "Black Codes," which were ostensibly vagrancy laws, and the use of a credit system which prevented Negroes from leaving the plantations until they cleared their debts with the planter.

Whites as well as Negroes suffered from the depressed condition of the Southern economy in the years following the Civil War. Because of credit shortages and the commercialization of agriculture, many planters were forced to leave the plantations or to remain as masters of declining estates. Poor whites and Negroes alike suffered from high birth rates, ignorance, depletion of the soil, high interest rates, and the disadvantages of the sharecropping system. However, although white sharecroppers were given no better employment terms than their Negro competitors after 1910 when segregation became firmly entrenched, they had greater freedom to move into nonagricultural jobs for which they could qualify, they had the right to vote, and they benefited from whatever comfort they derived from feelings of racial superiority.

These advantages were often more apparent than real, however, because it was very difficult for most Southern whites to overcome their environment and acquire good nonagricultural jobs. Moreover, white supremacy attitudes did harm in other areas, for the dominance of the race issue in Southern politics imposed a false unity of whites and prevented effective political solutions to many of the region's pressing economic problems. The South has defended its racial policies, which originated in the defense of slavery and were strengthened by the Civil War and Reconstruction, as necessary in order to keep the Negro from "taking over" as he is presumed to have done during Reconstruction, even though not many Negroes were elected to office at the time.[10]

This solid political tradition was not established immediately. For some time after 1877, following the withdrawal of Federal troops from the South, the Negro vote was coveted by conservatives and liberals alike. According to C. Vann Woodward, during the 1880's Southern Democrats and Republicans competed vigorously for the Negro vote. "The Negro voters were therefore courted, 'mistered,' and honored by Southern white politicians as never before."[11] It even appeared for a time that Southern Negroes and whites might be welded together politically and economically in such equalitarian labor federations as the National Labor Union, the Knights of Labor, and the Populist movement of the 1880's and 1890's. Ironically, however, the Populists were defeated by Negro votes that were controlled by conservative Democrats in the plantation belts. The Populists therefore became convinced that an economically oriented political movement required the disfranchisement of Negroes. Of course, many whites also favored disfranchisement because they feared that Negroes would become the balance of political power if whites split along economic lines. But once the Negro was in effect disfranchised through white primaries, poll taxes, and other restrictions, demagogues were able for many years to use the race issue to defeat the Republican party and to prevent Negroes from becoming significant politically. . . . [T]he Knights of Labor and the National Labor Union were also unable to overcome racial policy differences in their ranks.

Just as the disfranchisement of Negroes did not occur immediately after the withdrawal of Federal troops, the rigid form of legal racial segregation which became the pattern in the South took some time to develop. Whether from fear of a return of Yankee troops or recognition of the importance of the Negro vote, it was about a decade after the end of military occupation before the first segregation laws were passed.[12] By 1900, however, complete segregation became the accepted way of handling the race problem. A belief that most Northerners favored segregation and therefore would not send the troops back emboldened the South in this course. This conviction was supported by the segregation of the Negro in the Federal army; the prevalence of segregation in the North; the acquiescence of Northerners in the political compromise of 1877, which resulted in the withdrawal of Federal troops; and, finally, a series of United States Supreme Court decisions between 1873 and 1898 that established the legality of "separate but equal facilities" and denied the Negro Federal protection for acts committed against him by private individuals.

By 1900, therefore, Southern Negroes had become almost completely segregated by either law or custom. They rode in separate compartments or in the back of public conveyances, went to segregated public schools, could not marry whites, were buried in segregated cemeteries, and ate in separate restaurants. Employment, as we have seen, was also segregated. In the North, where unions were stronger and where there were fewer Negro craftsmen, resistance to Negroes was so strong that Negro leaders advised Negro workers to return to the South where the skilled crafts were still open to them.[13] In 1905, John R. Commons concluded that the plasterers, carpenters, masons, and painters admitted Negroes freely in the South, but that few Northern plasterers' unions and almost none of the other crafts accepted Negroes.[14]

REFERENCES

1. W. J. Cash, *The Mind of the South* (New York: Knopf, 1941), p. 107.
2. Marcus Jernigan, *Laboring and Dependent Classes in Colonial America* (Chicago: University of Chicago Press, 1931).
3. Quoted by Kenneth M. Stampp, *The Peculiar Institution* (New York: Knopf, 1956), p. 427.

4. R. B. Morris, "Labor Militancy in the Old South," *Labor and Nation,* vol. I, no. 5 (May-June 1948), p. 33.

5. Sterling D. Spero and Abram L. Harris, *The Black Worker* (New York: Columbia University Press, 1931), p. 11.

6. *Ibid.,* p. 11.

7. Gunnar Myrdal, with assistance of Richard Sterner and Arnold Rose, *An American Dilemma* (New York: Harper and Row, 1944), p. 1101.

8. E. Franklin Frazier, *The Negro Family in the United States* (Chicago: University of Chicago Press, 1939), p. 447.

9. Myrdal, *op. cit.,* p. 1965.

10. C. Van Woodward, *The Burden of Southern History* (New York: Random House, 1961), Chap. 5; John H. Franklin, *Reconstruction after the Civil War* (Chicago: University of Chicago Press, 1962; and Myrdal., *op. cit.,* p. 446.

11. C. Van Woodward, *Strange Career of Jim Crow* (New York: Oxford University Press, 1957), p. 40.

12. Vernon L. Wharton, *The Negro in Mississippi, 1877-1880* (Chapel Hill: University of North Carolina Press, 1947) and George B. Tendall, *South Carolina Negroes, 1877-1800* (Chapel Hill: University of North Carolina Press 1952).

13. Charles H. Wesley, *Negro Labor in the United States* (New York: Vanguard, 1927), p. 112.

14. John R. Commons, ed., *Trade Unionism and Labor Problems* (Boston: Ginn, 1905), p. 364.

II. Economic Conditions of Negro Workers

Ray Marshall

The pattern of segregation established in the South by 1900 extended to jobs as well as to other aspects of life. Since complete separation of the races obviously would have been very difficult in nonagricultural employment, job segregation was expressed more in terms of status than physical separation. In the building trades and on the railroads, where racism had its strongest manifestations, white engineers, electricians, and plumbers who barred negroes from their occupations and their unions nevertheless worked in close proximity with Negro firemen, laborers, helpers, and masons. In the shop crafts, Negroes were restricted to helper classifications, even when they taught the trade to white craftsmen.

Negroes held some skilled and supervisory positions, but these were either in all-Negro shops or in traditional "Negro" jobs; when jobs became mechanized, they were defined as white jobs. For example, when the locomotive firemen's job consisted of the hard, dirty work of shoveling coal into engines, it was regarded as "Negro" work, but when the automatic stoker made this job cleaner and easier, whites tried to displace Negroes. There also was an apparent tendency for whites to displace Negroes from certain low-status jobs, for example, as bellboys in hotels, during recessions. In factories, Negroes were rarely hired except in laborer and janitorial classifications. Although this system undoubtedly was more rigid in the South, the same basic pattern existed in the North. Indeed, in some trades Negroes actually had greater opportunities in the South than elsewhere.

These job patterns obviously tended both to reflect and to perpetuate the racial caste system. Restricting Negroes to inferior jobs strengthened the image

Reprinted with omissions from Ray Marshall, *The Negro Worker* (New York: Random House, 1967), by permission of the publisher. © 1967 by Random House, Inc.

of them as "inferior" people, and the low incomes associated with these jobs made it difficult for them to acquire the education, housing, and physical means necessary for participation in the mainstream of American life. Those Negroes who became educated and skilled were restricted to work in Negro neighborhoods, where work requirements and facilities were limited, even for the professions. Negro doctors were not permitted the advantages of practicing in the best hospitals or participating in local medical societies. Negro craftsmen could not fill the better jobs, and Negro teachers taught in inferior schools. This occupational caste system not only made it difficult for Negroes to work and develop to the limit of their capacities, but also cost the economy billions of dollars in lost productivity and wasted human resources. There is no way of knowing exactly how much the nation has lost from this system, but the President's Council of Economic Advisors has estimated that in 1962 the cost of discrimination was perhaps $13 billion.[1]

The statistical data available demonstrate some changes in racial employment patterns, but they also show remarkable rigidity through time.

The Patterns of Racial Employment

That nonwhites are gradually being upgraded into the white-collar and skilled-labor categories is shown in Table 4, but that they are still concentrated disproportionately in the less skilled and service occupations is also evident. In 1962, 47.2 percent of whites in the labor force were in the white-collar categories, compared with only 16.7 percent of nonwhites, and 14.7 percent of nonwhites and only 2.1 percent of whites were in the private household category.

In many ways, nonwhite females have better job opportunities than nonwhite males. In the professional and technical category, for example, nonwhite females were 4.6 percent of employed women in 1940 and 6.8 percent in 1962; the comparable figures for nonwhite males were 3.1 percent and 3.5 percent. Table 5 shows that nonwhite males increased their proportion relative to total male employment in every category between 1940 and 1944, but declined in every category except craftsmen, foremen, and kindred workers when the war was over. Although nonwhite males have never regained their wartime proportion of total male employment, they had regained their proportions of the craftsmen and white-collar categories by 1962.

* * *

Income and Labor Force Participation Rates

The evidence suggests that much of the improvement in nonwhite occupational levels in the postwar period has been caused by migration from rural areas

TABLE 4. *Occupational Distribution of the Civilian Labor Force by Color, 1957, 1962, and Projections for 1972*

Occupation Group	1957		1962		1972	
	White	Nonwhite	White	Nonwhite	White	Nonwhite
White-collar workers	43.9%	13.3%	47.2%	16.7%	53.4%	24.2%
Professional, technical	10.7	4.0	12.6	5.3	17.0	8.7
Managerial, props.	11.2	2.4	11.9	2.6	12.1	2.9
Clerical	15.1	5.5	15.8	7.2	16.8	10.4
Sales	6.9	1.4	6.9	1.6	7.5	2.2
Blue-collar workers	37.9	41.1	35.3	39.5	31.0	35.7
Craftsmen, foremen	14.3	5.4	13.6	6.0	12.9	7.3
Operatives	19.0	20.5	17.4	19.9	14.9	19.2
Laborers	4.6	15.2	4.3	13.6	3.2	9.2
Service workers	9.3	32.1	10.7	32.8	11.1	32.5
Private household	1.9	14.8	2.1	14.7	1.8	13.0
Other	7.4	17.3	8.6	18.1	9.3	19.5
Farmers	8.9	13.5	6.8	11.0	4.5	7.6
Total	100.0	100.0	100.0	100.0	100.0	100.0

SOURCE: Statement by Sidney Sonenblum of the Department of Labor to Senate Subcommittee on Manpower and Employment, *Hearings*, Part 5 (September 1963), p. 1400.

TABLE 5. *Proportion of Nonwhite to Total Males in Each Occupational Group, 1940-1962* *

Occupation Group	1962	1959	1952	1950	1948	1944	1940
Total employed men	9.2%	9.2%	8.9%	8.3%	8.4%	9.8%	9.0%
Professional, technical, and kindred workers	3.5	3.0	2.5	2.6	2.6	3.3	3.1
Managers, officials and proprietors, except farm	2.5	1.5	1.6	1.9	1.8	2.1	1.5
Clerical, and kindred workers	8.1	6.5	3.4†	2.8†	2.3†	2.8†	1.6
Sales workers	2.5	1.8					1.4
Craftsmen, foremen, and kindred workers	4.4	4.2	4.0	3.9	3.7	3.6	2.7
Operatives and kindred workers	11.4	10.7	10.4	8.5	10.1	10.1	6.1
Private household	—	37.7	31.6	51.3	53.7	75.2	61.8
Service, except private household	20.7	20.6	21.7	21.4	20.7	21.9	17.4
Laborers, except farm and mine	27.6	29.5	26.9	21.4	23.6	27.6	21.2
Farmers and farm managers	8.5	8.2	10.7	10.5	9.8	11.0	13.1
Farm laborers and foremen	24.9	24.0	16.2	19.8	15.8	21.1	22.5

* April of selected years.   † Includes sales 1944–1952.

SOURCE: Bureau of the Census, as reported by Department of Labor, Bureau of Labor Statistics, *Negroes in the United States: Their Employment and Economic Status*, Bulletin No. 1119, 1952 and *The Economic Situation of Negroes in the United States*, Bulletin S–3, 1962.

in the South and by other forces which also affect whites, and not because of significant changes in the factors influencing the Negro's job patterns themselves. Indeed, although there has been considerable improvement in the Negroes' relative family income position since 1939, their position relative to whites deteriorated in the 1950's and 1960's. The median nonwhite family income relative to whites reached a postwar high of 56.8 percent in 1952 but declined to 51.2 percent in 1958 and was only 53 percent in 1962. There has at the same time, however, been a rather steady improvement in the absolute income of nonwhites. In 1960, 49 percent of the nation's 4.3 million nonwhite families had annual incomes of $3,000 or less; in 1964, 39 percent of the 4.8 million nonwhite families remained in this category. The median wage or salary income of nonwhite males fourteen years of age or older who were employed full time increased from $639 a year in 1939 to $2,831 in 1955 and $3,799 in 1962. Relative to white males, these nonwhite incomes were 45 percent of whites in 1939, 64 percent in 1955, 67 percent at the relative postwar high in 1960, and 63 percent in 1962. The percentages of nonwhite to white males ranged from 61 percent to 67 percent in the 1955-62 period.

Not all of the factors responsible for these changes in relative income positions, however, are known. Clearly, the major causes of improvement in the Negroes' income have been their migration out of the rural South, declining racial barriers, better training, and improved education. The forces causing the deterioration in nonwhite incomes relative to whites during the 1950's and 1960's included the declining relative participation rates of nonwhite males (who have higher incomes than nonwhite women) and the nonwhite's higher rates of unemployment (again, with a worsening of the nonwhite male's relative position).

The civilian labor force participation rates in 1962 were 60 percent for nonwhites and 56.1 percent for whites, but the nonwhite male participation rate (76.4 percent) was *lower* than the white male rate (78.5 percent), while the nonwhite female rate (45.6 percent) was much higher than the white female rate (35.6 percent). The participation rates for both nonwhite males and females was higher in 1948 (84.8 percent and 44.4 percent) than the rates for whites (84.2 percent and 30.6 percent). Although the nonwhite and white female participation rates do not seem to follow this pattern, the disparity between the male participation rates seems to increase during periods of unemployment. The deterioration of the participation rate of nonwhite males relative to white males and nonwhite females undoubtedly is due in part to declining employment opportunities in many unskilled and semiskilled jobs where Negro males traditionally have been employed. There has at the same time been an increase in the demand for service workers, where nonwhite females have been employed. Nonwhite females and white males and females have had higher levels of education than nonwhite males, which is probably another important reason why nonwhite males have not been upgraded as rapidly as other groups.

In 1964, in spite of over twenty years of sustained agitation by civil rights groups, nearly half of all Negro men still worked in such service jobs as laborers, janitors, and busboys. Although they had made more progress than men, about 40 percent of Negro women were employed in domestic service. There was nevertheless a striking increase in the number of nonwhite women employed in the professional, clerical, and managerial sales categories; between 1960 and 1965, the proportion of nonwhite females in these categories rose from 18 to 24 percent.

The Problem of Unemployment

The deterioration in the nonwhite employment picture after 1953 is indicated by the following unemployment rates:

Year	White	Nonwhite
1947	3.3%	5.4%
1951	2.8	4.8
1952	2.4	4.6
1953	2.3	4.1
1954	4.5	8.9
1955	3.6	7.9
1956	3.3	7.5
1957	3.9	8.0
1958	6.1	12.6
1959	4.9	10.7
1960	5.0	10.2
1961	6.0	12.5
1962	4.9	11.0
1963	5.1	10.9
1964	4.6	9.8
1965	4.1	8.3

SOURCE: *Manpower Report of the President, 1966* (Washington, D.C.: Government Printing Office), p. 127.

Table 6 shows that unemployment rates for nonwhites were generally over twice those of whites but that the rates varied with occupations for both racial categories. Table 7 shows considerable variation in white and nonwhite unemployment rates between the various age groups.

Although unemployment rates of nonwhites are about twice those of whites, and have increased markedly since 1953, between 1956 and 1963 nonwhite unemployment did not increase relative to total unemployment or as a proportion of total unemployment, as indicated by the data in Table 8. Actually, these statistics, which are selected for years which minimize the importance of the business cycle, show that nonwhite unemployment rates *improved*

TABLE 6. *Unemployment Rates of Experienced Workers* by Color and Major Occupation Group, 1955 and 1962*

Major Occupation Group	White		Nonwhite		Nonwhite as Percentage of White	
	1962	1955	1962	1955	1962	1955
All occupation groups†	4.9%	3.5%	11.0%	7.7%	224%	208%
Clerical and sales workers	3.8	3.2	7.7	7.0	203	219
Craftsmen and foremen	4.8	3.9	9.7	8.8	202	226
Operatives	6.9	5.5	12.0	8.4	174	153
Private household workers	3.1	3.0	7.1	5.6	229	187
Other service workers	5.3	5.2	10.8	8.8	204	169
Laborers, except farm and mine	3.9	3.0	5.8	6.3	149	210
Farm laborers and foremen	11.0	9.8	15.8	12.1	144	123

*The base for the unemployment rate includes the employed, classified according to their current jobs, and the unemployed, classified according to their latest civilian job, if any; and excludes the unemployed persons who never held a full-time civilian job.
†Includes the following groups not shown separately: professional and technical workers; managers, officials, and proprietors; and farmers and farm managers.

SOURCE: Mathew A. Kessler, "Economic Status of Nonwhite Workers, 1955–62," Department of Labor, *Monthly Labor Review* (July 1963).

TABLE 7.   *Unemployment Rates by Color, Age and Sex, 1962*

	Unemployment Rates			
	Males		Females	
Age	*White*	*Nonwhite*	*White*	*Nonwhite*
14 years and over	4.6%	11.9%	5.5%	11.1%
14-19 years	12.3	20.7	11.5	28.2
20-24 years	8.0	14.6	7.7	18.2
25-34 years	3.8	10.5	5.4	11.5
35-44 years	3.1	8.6	4.5	8.9
45-54 years	3.5	8.3	3.7	7.1
55 years and over	4.1	10.1	3.5	3.6

SOURCE: Mathew A. Kessler, "Economic Status of Nonwhite Workers, 1955–1962," Department of Labor, *Monthly Labor Review* (July 1963), 3.

slightly relative to the totals between 1956 and 1963, suggesting that the *increases* in Negro unemployment rates are more cyclical than structural. This does not mean, of course, that the higher rates in 1956 and 1963 were not due to structural factors, or that significant structural changes did not occur before 1956.

Negro Employment and Economic Growth

In recent years, Negro unemployment rates seem to have changed at about twice the rate of total unemployment, whether the latter has been rising or falling. With respect to longer trends, a recent study of Negro and white employment patterns found no relationship between changes in Negro female and total employment, but concluded:

> In expanding fields Negro male employment has tended to grow at a faster rate than white male or total employment. . . . Even in slowly growing fields the em-

TABLE 8

	Ratio of Unemployment in Each Group to National Unemployment Rate		Percentage of Total National Unemployment in Each Group	
	White	*Nonwhite*	*White*	*Nonwhite*
1956	.87	1.98	78.5%	21.5%
1959	.88	1.95	78.8	21.2
1962	.87	1.97	78.1	21.9
1963	.89	1.91	78.8	21.2

SOURCE: Adapted from R. A. Gordon, "Has Structural Unemployment Worsened?" *Industrial Relations* (May 1964), 71.

ployment of Negro men has nevertheless tended to increase at a faster rate than total employment or that of white men. . . . In rapidly declining fields, however, employment of Negro men has tended to decline more rapidly than that of white men both nationally and in the South.[2]

This suggests that Negroes would gain relatively from sustained growth as well as full employment. As the general unemployment rate is reduced, the nonwhite rate will decline, and if a rate of below 4 percent could be sustained while the rate of economic growth is increased and measures are taken to upgrade nonwhites, the income and employment gap between whites and nonwhites could be narrowed still further. The trends suggest, however, that extraordinary efforts will be required to bring Negro unemployment rates into line with those of whites. The 1966 *Report of the National Commission on Technology, Automation and the American Economy* concluded:

> If nonwhites continue to hold the same proportion of jobs in each occupation as in 1964, the nonwhite unemployment rate in 1975 will be more than five times that for the labor force as a whole. . . . If trends in the upgrading of nonwhites continue at the same rate as in recent years, the nonwhite unemployment rate in 1975 will be about 2½ times that for the labor force as a whole.

Factors Responsible for Racial Employment Patterns

The factors responsible for these Negro employment patterns are complex and interrelated, making it very difficult to determine the contribution to the total pattern made by each of them. It is, however, possible to discern the main factors responsible for these patterns. These are the heritages of the past, and the Negro's self-image and lack of education and training.

The most important impediment to the Negro's ability to improve his occupational position undoubtedly derives from the disadvantages he has suffered because of slavery, segregation, and discrimination. Not having worked in a variety of skilled, technical operations, Negroes have become stereotyped for certain jobs by employers, white workers, and even by themselves. Since the Negro has been regarded as inferior by many whites, those who would perpetuate a feeling of superiority for their crafts or occupations have tried to exclude Negroes.

Negroes also are restricted in their employment opportunities by a host of cultural and social factors. Since Negroes usually live in segregated neighborhoods, they rarely learn about jobs with few or no Negroes in them, and they apply for the kinds of jobs they know they can get. Since aspirations are conditioned by one's associates, few Negroes are motivated to apply for jobs from which they have been excluded.

Education

Negroes also are inadequately prepared through education and training to compete on an equal basis with whites. While the educational level of nonwhites is improving, the median is still below that of whites. Since education is related to income, the Negro's position is in some sense self-perpetuating. The median incomes of heads of families and their educational attainments in 1961 are shown in Table 9. These data indicate that as a general rule the ratio of nonwhite to white income increases with the level of education.

TABLE 9

Education	White	Nonwhite	Nonwhite as a Percentage of White
Elementary	$4,378	$2,539	58.0%
Less than 8 years	3,656	2,294	62.7
8 years	4,911	3,338	68.0
High School	6,186	3,863	64.2
1 to 3 years	5,882	3,449	58.6
4 years	6,390	4,559	71.3
College	8,288	6,444	77.8
1 to 3 years	7,344	5,525	74.2
4 years or more	9,315	7,875	84.5

SOURCE: Bureau of the Census, *Current Population Reports,* "Income of Families and Persons in the United States: 1961," Series P-60, No. 39.

The percentage educational distributions of whites and nonwhites for various years are seen in Table 10. Only 25 percent of whites but 46 percent of nonwhites in the 18-24 age bracket had not completed high school in 1962, but there was a significant decline in the proportion of nonwhites who had less than five years of education and a marked increase in the proportion attending high school. Median nonwhite education lagged 3.8 years behind whites in 1952, 2.6 years in 1962, and 1.8 years in 1965.

These statistics do not tell the whole story, however, because it is well-known that Negro education has been inferior to that of whites in the South and, according to the 1964 *Manpower Report of the President,* "although Negro students in the North receive a better education generally than Negroes (and many whites) in the South, their education still tends to be inferior to that of the northern white students with whom they will later compete for jobs."[3]

Negroes also are disadvantaged because at the same level of education they have much more difficulty being absorbed into the labor force. Of the white high school graduates who last attended school in 1959, for instance, only 5.3 percent remained out of work 2.5 years after graduation as compared with 14.5 percent of nonwhite high school graduates. Of the 1959 dropouts, 10.2 percent of the whites and 18 percent of the nonwhites were unemployed two years later.[4] Thus nonwhite high school graduates had more trouble being absorbed by the labor force than white dropouts.

148

TABLE 10

Education	White					Nonwhite				
	1952	1957	1959	1962	1965	1952	1957	1959	1962	1965
Elementary										
Less than 5 years	5.2%	4.3%	3.7%	3.3%	2.7%	26.7%	21.2%	17.9%	15.5%	11.8%
5 to 8 years	29.3	25.8	23.6	21.4	18.9	38.7	34.9	34.3	29.8	25.7
High school										
1 to 3 years	18.7	19.0	19.4	18.8	18.4	15.9	19.3	20.6	23.2	24.9
4 years	28.3	30.8	32.0	33.5	36.8	10.8	14.8	15.8	21.0	24.4
College										
1 to 3 years	8.8	9.0	9.7	11.3	11.0	3.7	3.9	4.5	5.7	6.1
4 years or more	8.5	9.7	10.2	11.8	12.2	2.6	3.4	3.9	4.8	7.0
Median years completed	11.4	12.1	12.1	12.2	12.3	7.6	8.4	8.7	9.6	10.5

SOURCE: *Manpower Report of the President* (Washington, D.C.: Government Printing Office), p. 189.

The Influence of Unions

Employers are directly responsible for the racial employment patterns in most manufacturing jobs, but unions have been more responsible for racial employment patterns on the railroads and in the construction and printing trades, since unions are often strong enough in these occupations to control the supply of labor and maintain *de facto* closed shop conditions; they have thus been able to deny Negroes employment in the skilled trades by barring them from union membership. While they are not primarily responsible for industrial racial employment patterns, unions have perpetuated those patterns by maintaining segregated seniority rosters. Moreover, job segregation was often formalized by having different unions in each craft, as is true, for instance, among longshoremen and on the railroads.

Negroes have greater employment opportunities in the nonunion sectors of some building trades crafts, such as electricians and plumbers, but there is no evidence that nonunion manufacturing establishments have hired or upgraded more Negroes. Indeed, the virtually unorganized southern textile industry has had very few Negro employees and yet has maintained rigid racial segregation. Almost without exception, moreover, those firms which have desegregated their lines of progression in the South are unionized. The union can be accused of discrimination, however, where it fails to apply contracts equally and permits "informal" discriminatory practices to continue in violation of the contract.

Even though most of its efforts in this direction have been more for trade union than for racial reasons, organized labor has done many positive things to improve Negro job opportunities. For one thing, unions have introduced the principle of seniority, which has made it possible for Negroes to hold their jobs when those jobs become more attractive to whites during recessions or when employers are induced to displace Negroes with whites because wages are equalized. The principle of seniority also has been used to make it possible for Negroes to advance occupationally within many unionized firms. This is not to argue, of course, that all labor organizations have done what they should to protect the Negro's seniority rights. But the fact that discrimination *tended* to weaken seniority was a factor *undermining* discrimination by unions.

At the national level, the labor movement has contributed decisively to fights for civil rights, improved education, and other social legislation. Unions also have used their collective bargaining power to negotiate nondiscrimination agreements, which existed in about one-fifth of all major collective bargaining contracts in 1961.[5] Especially important nondiscrimination agreements were reached between the United Auto Workers and the Ford, General Motors, Chrysler, and American Motors companies in 1961 and between the Steelworkers and eleven major steel companies in 1964 (Armco, Bethlehem, Colorado Fuel and Iron, Great Lakes Steel, Inland, Jones and Laughlin, Pittsburgh Steel, Republic, United States Steel, Wheeling, and Youngstown Sheet and Tube).

In addition, the mere presence of a union in the plant has given Negro workers rights they would not otherwise have had. Not only can Negroes sue for the abrogation of specific contract rights, but the union is required by the courts, and more recently by the National Labor Relations Board, to follow nondiscrimination policies with respect to all workers in the bargaining unit.

Finally, unions have promoted Negro interests as a part of the basic equalitarian rationale of trade unionism. Union leaders fully realize that their organizations are weakened if they fail to promote equal seniority, wage, and other benefits for all workers regardless of race. Fringe benefits and the elimination of occupational wage differentials also help Negroes, who have been concentrated in lower job categories.

REFERENCES

1. 88th Congress, 2nd Session, Joint Economic Committee, *Joint Economic Report* (1964), Senate Report No. 931, p. 61.
2. DALE E. HIESTAND, *Economic Growth and Employment Opportunities of Minorities* (New York: Columbia University Press, 1964), pp. 110-111.
3. *Manpower Report of the President* (1964), p. 99.
4. Statement of SAMUEL GANZ, Assistant Director for Manpower and Automation Research, Office of Manpower, Automation and Training, U.S. Department of Labor, to the U.S. Senate Subcommittee on Employment and Manpower of the Committee on Labor and Public Welfare (September 10, 1963).
5. LEON E. LUNDEN, "Antidiscrimination Provisions in Major Contracts, 1961," *Monthly Labor Review,* vol. 86, no. 6 (June 1963), p. 643.

CHAPTER 11

Negro Workers in the Mississippi Delta: Problems of Displacement and Adjustment

Michael J. Piore

I.

In many respects, the racial dimension of Southern economic activity is better characterized by the term "white supremacy" than "segregation." Segregation describes the economic structure of many Northern cities where Negroes are confined to a ghetto area that has little import for white economic life. Were these ghettos to suddenly disappear, the white economy would continue, relatively unaffected. In the South, Negroes and whites have been part and parcel of a single economic entity. The racial distinction defines a division of labor. That division relegates to Negroes the menial, unskilled jobs; in the Delta of Mississippi, these jobs have been the picking and the chopping of cotton. But, however menial and unskilled, the jobs have been critical to the productive process upon which the society depends for its livelihood.

The plight of Negroes in the Delta today is the result of changes in that economic system. Suddenly, in the space of two years, the Negro part of the economy has been eliminated. In the spring of 1960, seasonal employment in the Mississippi Delta totaled 30,510; in the spring of 1965, it was 32,328. Last year spring seasonal employment was cut almost in half, from 32,328 to 16,571. This spring it fell by over half again to 7,225. Seasonal employment in the fall exhibits a comparable trend. The decline in seasonal employment is superimposed upon a long term decline in the number of farm operators; last year, it was slightly moderated by an increase in nonseasonal employment; this year, even that component of employment has declined. Incomes of

Reprinted, with omission of footnotes, from Industrial Relations Research Association, *Proceedings of the 20th Annual Winter Meeting,* 1967 by permission of the author and publisher. © 1968 by Industrial Relations Research Association.

Negroes in the Delta have always been among the lowest in the nation, but today, numbers of families have no income at all. What was once malnutrition and accumulated diseases has become virtual starvation. Even in the summer months, many families were begging from door to door.

Immediately responsible for the agricultural displacements is the shift from cotton to less labor intensive crops and, in cotton, to less labor intensive technologies of production. Cotton acreage has been cut back and converted to soybeans and, on some plantations, to cattle. In cotton itself, the spring labor once required to weed the crop has been replaced by chemicals sprayed from airplanes; harvest labor, by mechanical cotton pickers.

The causes of these changes are a matter of some dispute. Cutbacks in federal cotton acreage allotments are, in part, responsible for the crop diversification. Exogenous technological developments, spurred by federally subsidized research and high wages elsewhere in the country, may also be responsible. The introduction of the agriculture minimum wage last February which raised the wage for Negro workers from three dollars a day to one dollar an hour probably hastened the diffusion of the new technology.

But these are not the factors emphasized by Negro leaders in the Delta. They see the displacements as a white conspiracy to avoid, through forced outmigration, the threat of integration and Negro political power. The threat is real. The Civil Rights Act of 1965 created a potential Negro voting majority in most of the Delta counties. Federal pressure from without and the civil rights movement within are gradually curbing the physical and psychological repression which have kept the Negroes "in their place."

Circumstances within the state lend credence to the conspiracy theory. In private, the whites speak freely of outmigration as the only solution to the race problem. Individual planters are clearly hurt by and resentful of the response of the Negro community to the civil rights movement. They view that response as a lack of gratitude for previous paternalistic acts, and agricultural displacements have therefore been accompanied by the withdrawal of paternal protection. The practice of intervening with police officials in behalf of their own workers has sharply declined. This once moderated, albeit in an erratic and not always equitable manner, the harshness of Southern justice. The infinite series of small "loans" that whites were once willing to grant favored Negroes has come to an end. Institutionalized aid appears to reflect the hardening of private attitudes. The surplus food program, for example, shifted this year from commodity distribution to a food stamp system requiring minimal cash payments that many Negro families could not afford.

In the desperate climate of Mississippi, the prevalence of a conspiracy theory is not altogether surprising. But the theory retains a certain plausibility even at a distance. The beginnings of the agricultural displacement follow upon the Civil Rights Summer of 1964 and coincide with the passage of the Voting Rights Act and the shift in tactics of the white community from outright violence to reliance upon economic retaliation. The extension of minimum wage coverage required the acquiescence of the Mississippi congressional delegation, one of whose members chairs the House Agricultural Committee.

Since the agricultural displacements are now probably irreversible, the issue of their cause is largely academic. But the plausibility of the conspiracy theory is indicative of the social and political context in which the displacements have occurred. That context highly colors the character of the solutions which are being sought.

II.

Current efforts to solve the economic problems of Negroes in the Delta are confined, almost exclusively, to training. Present programs in the Delta are geared to train 7550 people a year. A new proposal for a training program to be run at the Greenville Air Force Base would add at least 1000, and possibly as many as 6000, places to current training capacity. The racial composition of these programs is not clear, but the Negro share appears to run somewhere between 50 and 80 percent.

The major problem with the training programs is that there are no jobs available for the graduates. Growth in Delta manufacturing employment in the May 1960-May 1967 period averaged about 10% a year. Were past trends to continue over the next four years, annual growth would average under 3000 jobs, considerably less than half of existing training capacity.

These figures do not include employment in the nonmanufacturing sectors. But in Mississippi, jobs in those sectors are almost totally barred to Negroes. In the public sector, Negroes are confined to janitorial and maid work and to the colored school system. Construction, in contrast to the North, is relatively open: in several Delta countries, there are even Negro construction contractors. Negro contractors, however, are heavily dependent upon the construction of white housing, and since 1964, the white market has been closed to them in retaliation for civil rights activities.

Even the manufacturing figures may exaggerate the employment opportunities available to Negroes. The 1960 census shows Negroes in Mississippi holding only 53 percent of the manufacturing jobs to which their share of the employed labor force entitles them. Federal antidiscrimination regulations — Executive Orders 10925 and 11246 and Title VII of the 1964 Civil Rights Act — should have improved this showing, yet the regulations may have had an adverse impact. Many employers have moved to evade equal opportunity requirements by imposing tests for hiring and promotion, and the effect of these tests is to deny Negroes jobs previously open to them.

Moreover, it is not at all clear that past rates of manufacturing growth can be sustained in the future. Last year (May 1966-May 1967) Delta manufacturing employment declined by six percent. This decline no doubt reflects the slowdown in national economic activity. But the magnitude is surprising. Even in the 1960-61 recession, manufacturing employment in the Delta managed to grow by 1.5 percent.

Given the lack of job opportunities, the training programs tend to degenerate into welfare programs, valued primarily for the stipend they provide to the trainee, and the trainee has no incentive to learn. The administrators have seen the symptom, but they have misunderstood the underlying problem. The new Concentrated Employment Program just getting underway, and the proposed training center at the Greenville Air Force base, are both open - ended, permitting the trainee to remain until he reaches a given level of competence. In such programs, the trainee has an incentive *not* to learn.

Moreover, because the programs are essentially welfare programs distributing income to a limited number of people in a context in which vastly larger numbers are living on the verge of starvation, the programs are open to all sorts of abuses. Places in the programs are distributed to reward and punish people for political activity. Neighborhood Youth Corps and work experience trainees are used for projects of exclusive benefit to the white community or, occasionally, to private individuals. Negro trainees are assigned to menial and humiliating jobs, and instructors are abusive and tyrannical.

III.

For Negroes, a viable, long-run solution to the Delta problem requires their transfer to productive, nonagricultural employment. The critical question is whether it is possible to speed the processes of economic development and of transition from agricultural to industrial work that, in most nations and for foreign immigrants to the United States, took, at least, a generation. This question might have been answered by the Federal training programs in the Delta, but the corruption inherent in the programs and in the environment in which they have operated makes that experience suspect.

Other potentially relevant experience is that of manufacturing firms in the Delta who have attempted to absorb Negro workers. These experiences are discouraging. In the face of the tremendous agricultural displacements, there is widespread talk of a shortage of labor willing to accept industrial discipline and able to learn relatively unskilled jobs. One manufacturer characterized his attendance, discipline and turnover problems in the past year as the worst since World War II.

Trends in manufacturing employment, however, make these comments difficult to understand. Labor shortages would not have been surprising the year before last when manufacturing employment jumped 22 percent. But last year there was a 6 percent decline in employment. One would have expected an easing of shortages, particularly in comparison with earlier years. The most likely explanation of this paradox is the development of an interaction between the exclusively white first-line supervision and young Negro employees. Supervisory techniques in Delta industry remain primitive. The supervision shares the racial prejudices of the white community; they have little managerial training, and rely heavily on abusive and dictatorial techniques to enforce the work pace. Negro youth are increasingly less willing to respond to such supervision. Those now reaching working age have grown up in the atmosphere created by the civil rights movement. They no longer accept the subservient role which the white community demands of them in personal relationships and are particularly resentful of abusive treatment from whites. If this explanation is indeed correct, it does not bode well for the autonomous development of solutions to Delta problems. But it does point to the importance of sympathetic supervision and instruction in any effort to speed the transition to industrial work.

Here the experience of the civil rights movement, whose efforts have been infused with a sympathy and understanding lacking in industry, is germane. When I first came to Mississippi as a civil rights worker in 1964, the Negro community was virtually devoid of organization and leadership. The thrust of the movement that summer was to organize. But although a great effort was made to generate indigenous leaders, local leadership was largely nominal; projects were originated and directed by outsiders. By the time I returned in 1967, most of the outside civil rights workers had left. The organizations were managed and controlled by local people and the nominal leaders of '64 had developed into sophisticated organizers and administrators. If such leadership can be developed in a period of three years, certainly a productive industrial labor force can be developed as well.

On the whole, moreover, the civil rights movement in Mississippi was built by the poorer and least qualified people in the Negro community. Access to the better educated and more resourceful individuals was barred by their dependence upon the white power structure. Negro teachers, who form the educated elite of the society, have scrupulously avoided civil rights activity for fear of jeopardizing their contracts with white school boards. Negro businessmen, fearing to jeopardize their credit, municipal permits, and lines of supply, have also shunned the movement. Most Negro businesses are trivial, but each of the larger counties has several families who have amassed substantial wealth. The variety of enterprises which such families manage simultaneously and their ability to prosper in a hostile environment imply a store of entrepreneural talent as well as capital.

There is also a group of skilled blue-collar workers attached more or less closely to the Delta which the movement has, to now, been unable to tap. The relationship between the Northern cities and the Delta communities is far closer than their geographic distance would suggest. Almost every Delta family has relatives in the North and there is a continual flow of traffic in both directions. Northern workers send their children South to live with their grandparents; some return home themselves for prolonged periods. In cities with a heavy population of in-migrants, there are clubs of workers from the larger Delta counties. The Delta is the permanent residence of a group of itinerant construction workers who live there between periods on the road. Many of these people claim to prefer life in the Delta to that elsewhere in the country and might be willing to return permanently were stable, high wage employment available.

Black Mississippians, no less than whites, recognized that the destruction of white supremacy would mean the destruction of the Delta economic structure as well. They had visions of building a new structure in its stead. And it was upon these resources that their visions were based. I do not believe that the visions were utopian. Despite relatively rapid growth in recent years, much of the Delta's industrial potential remains unexploited. There are opportunities for expansion in textiles, leather tanning and leather products, woodworking and paper. The Negro business community could mobilize a part of the capital and the managerial skill required for such ventures. Skilled blue-collar workers in the North might be attracted to provide the supervision and training. Common humanity commands a vast extension of social welfare services in the Delta, and many of these services would also permit the expansion of Negro job opportunities. The food stamp program alone would provide the base for the expansion of Negro commercial enterprises were the community to believe that white administrators would certify Negro owned stores. A program of housing construction and municipal improvement would revive the Negro construction industry. The provision of adequate medical care could open jobs for an army of paramedical personnel.

This is not to argue that such developments can be easily accomplished. In many respects, however, the feasibility of economic development within the Negro community appears to be greater today than it was in the early stages of the civil rights movement. The attitudes of the Negro middle class are changing. As the natural leaders of the Negro community, they have found themselves blamed by white society for civil rights activities irrespective of their actual role. They are beginning to accept the new climate as permanent, and to search for opportunities within it. In at least two counties, in fact, they have begun to plan cooperative industrial undertakings. The combined effect of civil rights progress in the South and racial violence in the ghettos may have reduced the relative attractiveness of Northern life and enhanced the ability of the Delta to recover its lost manpower. Title VI of the Civil Rights Act of 1964 promises that federal programs for business development, housing, farm improvement and the like, previously barred to Mississippi Negroes, will now be open. And press releases from Washington indicate new funds in all of these areas.

I think that the potential is present. But I have little hope that it will be realized. For despite the changing climate in the State and in the Nation, the only really tangible product of the past four years of intense civil rights activity is a dedicated and sophisticated leadership. The leadership has tried almost every form of constructive action: nonviolent demonstrations, intensive political organization and voter education, lobbying in Washington. Very little of that activity has paid off. The collapse of the Negro end of the Delta economy may be the final blow. In the climate of narrowing economic opportunity, the white community has become increasingly successful in deterring political support and dividing the leadership through the distribution of jobs and welfare. Most of the new federal programs in the state have been turned to this purpose. The funding of CDGM (a headstart program in a number of Delta counties) is the only Negro victory in the battle for programs free of white control, and these funds are now again in jeopardy. The November elections, the first major local elections since the Voting Rights Act, produced but a handful of victories, not enough to contribute to a solution of the economic problems.

The promises of Washington have proved empty. The Concentrated Employment Program, originally planned for a new agency with Negro participation and control, and the subject of intensive civil rights lobbying efforts, was finally funded through a consortium of the same state agencies that control other training in the Delta. The Clark committee hearings on starvation in Mississippi produced the Stennis Bill promising new funds for food and medical aid, but that Bill has apparently died in the House. The Delta was originally announced as one of the five pilot areas in the White House Test Program of subsidies for industrial development in poverty areas; upon inquiries, the movement was informed that the announced areas were only five *examples* of the five which would ultimately be designated, and the Delta was not included on the final list. The model cities proposals for the Delta were rejected and with them much of the hope for a housing program.

Many of the roots of the radical black power movement can be traced to Mississippi. The bitterness of its leaders is, in a large part, the product of the beatings and jailings to which they were subject as civil rights workers in the state. But violent and anarchistic radicalism have never found a home in black Mississippi. The radicals which the state spawned have departed to preach in the North. The leadership which remains continues to hold the visions of the early civil rights movement. They are committed to constructive action. But constructive action has worn them out. They are tired and disappointed; each new effort seems to compound frustration. Their exhortations to the community ring increasingly less true; however unintentionally, they inevitably convey their own disappointments and frustrations to their constituency. To the white community, they are reduced to threatening riots. Riots are not a prospect which the black leaders of Mississippi welcome. But they are not an idle threat. As the current leadership continues to lose its own confidence and that of the community; as the number of people exposed to the civil rights movement when they were young enough to believe in its promise and partake of its freedom from psychological subservience grows, riots become more and more likely. In its own way, white Mississippi understands this. By that time, it hopes, the black people will have gone North.

Part 5

The Tax System as a Means of Redistributing Income

Editor's Survey

In this chapter we shall be concerned with one means of redistributing incomes after they have been earned: through the relatively impersonal mechanism of the tax system. This approach has a number of virtues, an important one being the impersonality of the process. The selection from Pigou gives the classic case for shifting the distribution of income through progressive taxation. At the same time, it should be noted that, like all forms of taxation, use of this technique imposes burdens on the workings of the economy. If the rich save and the poor consume, taxation for any purpose including the transfer of purchasing power to the poor will reduce savings and thereby diminish the rate of economic growth. Thus, future GNP levels will not be as high. The reader is invited to examine the assumptions (for example, about the number and kind of investment projects which exist) which lie behind this conclusion. Further he should compare the social and economic costs of poverty and maldistribution of income with the costs of doing something about those problems.

Turning to the factual side of the matter, it can be seen from the calculations of Goode that the redistributive impact of U.S. federal income taxation in the United States must be considered modest by most standards. The redistribution of income effected through taxation is even further reduced when the impact of regressive state and local taxes (and federal excise taxes) is added to the picture.

Even if the scope of income reshuffling through the tax system were considerably greater, it is clear that the current arrangements would have very little effect upon poverty. Present tax mechanisms might take little or nothing *from* the poor if redesigned to do so, but still do nothing about directly transferring income *to* the poor. The idea that "taxation could become a two-way street" lies behind the development of proposals for negative income taxation. The non-poor would continue to make payments to the government, while the poor would receive payments from the government. When the pro's and con's of various negative taxation schemes are presented, the reader should pay particular attention to the formulation of criteria by which such alternative plans can be evaluated.

CHAPTER 12

The Effect on the National Dividend of the Expectations of Transferences from the Relatively Rich

A. C. Pigou

. . . . Pure public spirit often leads wealthy persons voluntarily to provide, partly in their lifetime and partly by legacies at death, large sums for the service of the poor. Often, too, public spirit is reinforced by the craving, strong in some men, for that sense of power which the fact of giving conveys.

The normal motives prompting men to these and other forms of voluntary transference of resources to public ends are already of considerable force, and it is open to us to stimulate them still further. "No doubt," Marshall writes, "men are capable of much more unselfish service than they generally render; and the supreme aim of the economist is to discover how this latent social asset can be developed more quickly and turned to account more wisely." Not much has yet been accomplished in this direction. It is well understood, however, that Government, if it so chooses, has power to harness to the nobler motives for generosity others of a lower order. Much will be done for the sake of fame and praise, and fame of a sort may be offered as a reward for private munificence. Thus the transference of resources from the rich can be purchased, in a delicately veiled manner, by honours and decorations that cost nobody anything. These things are at once symbols and conveyers of reputation; for, when a worthless man is decorated, those who feel, or pretend to feel, respect for the decorator, offer a vicarious respect to the decorated also. No doubt, in some degree, the issue of fresh decorations may diminish

Reprinted with omissions from A. C. Pigou, *The Economics of Welfare*, Part IV, Chapter IX (London: Macmillan and Company, Ltd., 1960), 4th ed. by permission of the publisher. Also reprinted by permission of Saint Martin's Press. This book is copyrighted in all countries which are signatories of the Berne Convention.

the value to their possessors of those already issued. To confer the Order of Merit broadcast among excellent bricklayers would annihilate its attractive power for the class in whose behoof it was originally designed. This difficulty can, however, be overcome to a great extent by the creation of new orders, instead of the extension of old ones. It is not impossible, therefore, that, along these lines, inducements might be provided adequate to secure the transference of a good deal of income from rich people, without the expectation of the transference involving any diminution, but, rather, some appreciable increase, in the waiting and effort furnished by them towards the upbuilding of the national dividend.

Unfortunately it is quite certain that, in present conditions, voluntary transferences will fall very much below the aggregate of transferences from relatively well-to-do people which the general sense of the community demands. A considerable amount of coercive transference is, therefore, also necessary. This means, in one form or another, taxes, and probably, in the main, direct taxes graduated against the owners of large incomes and properties. The taxes, to which resort is in practice most likely to be had, are taxes on incomes and taxes on property passing at death. In what follows attention will be confined to these taxes. It is proposed to examine the kind of reactions on the national dividend to which the imposition of the one or the other kind is likely to lead.

Let us consider first an income tax in which there is no differentiation against saving.* As I have shown elsewhere, this means, broadly speaking, an income tax under which either savings themselves or the incomes subsequently yielded by these savings are exempted. When such an income tax is graduated so as to yield a substantial contribution from the relatively well-to-do, in what way will the expectation of the levies to be made under it react on the size of the national dividend? Three possible lines of reaction may be distinguished. First, the knowledge that this tax is there might drive men capable of earning large incomes by their work to live and work abroad rather than in the taxing country. Secondly, it might drive men with large powers of saving to make their investments abroad rather than in the taxing country. Thirdly, it might cause men capable of earning large incomes by their work, while continuing to reside in England, to work less (or conceivably, as will be argued in a moment, to work more) than they would have done had there been no tax. These three lines of reaction will now be considered in turn.

If one country has a much higher income tax on large incomes than others, this fact will certainly constitute some inducement to men capable of earning large incomes to go and live abroad. There is reason to believe, however, that residence in their native land means so much to many rich men — particularly since the advantage of wealth is largely social advantage — that it would need a very large excess of tax to affect many of them in this way. Moreover, the

---

* EDITOR's NOTE. An income tax which falls on savings will reduce the flow of savings and consequently the future level of Pigou's "National Dividend." In the arguments which follow, Pigou assumes that this problem has been avoided.

movement towards high income tax on large incomes has a wide sweep, and the man who contemplates leaving his home to escape taxes there must reflect that similar taxes may before long be imposed in the country to which he goes. Along these lines, therefore, the reaction on the national dividend is not likely to be very important.

At first sight it might seem that the second line of reaction is, on the other hand, almost certain to be very important. For, whereas a rich man will dislike moving himself abroad, he will not, it would seem, as a rule object to sending his capital abroad. The fear, however, that high income taxes will, in this way, drive capital abroad in large quantities, arises, at all events so far as the United Kingdom is concerned, from an imperfect knowledge of the exact scope of the British income-tax law. It is, no doubt, true that a tax striking the fruits of capital, insofar as it impinges on the investments of foreigners in England, lessens the advantage to foreigners of investment here, and, *pro tanto,* stimulates foreign individuals to withdraw their capital, and foreign corporations with plant abroad to withdraw their head offices. This, however, is a minor matter, for foreign investment here is admittedly small in amount. The substantial fear is that high income tax will drive British-owned capital to foreign fields. This fear is not well grounded. Since the English income tax, unlike the income taxes of the colonies, is levied on incomes *received* in England, and not merely upon those *earned or built up there,* high income tax here, in general, constitutes no inducement to an Englishman resident in England to send his capital abroad for investment.

There remains the third line of reaction — that, namely, on the amount of work which those persons who are subjected to a high income tax will do. This is a more complicated matter. At first sight it might seem that the expectation of having to pay any tax upon the fruit of work *must* in some degree discourage the performance of work. This, however, is not so, because, if a man's income is reduced by taxation, the addition of a £ to his income will satisfy a more urgent want than it would have done had his income not been reduced, and, consequently, though extra work will yield a less net return of money, it may, under certain types of tax, yield a greater return of satisfaction. Proceeding on this line of thought, we observe that if an income-tax scale is so drawn as to impose equal sacrifice on all taxpayers (of similar temperament) whatever their incomes, the amount of work which they elect to do will not be altered at all by the expectation of it. As Professor Carver writes: "The minimum of repression (on industry and enterprise) is secured by so distributing taxes that an equal sacrifice is required of all. No one is discouraged from the acquisition of wealth or a large income, or from entering this or that occupation, if there is equal sacrifice involved in either case." Now, we do not know enough about the relation between differences in the sizes of incomes and differences in the amounts of satisfaction yielded by them to be able to say what scale of income-tax graduation would conform to the canon of equal sacrifice. It would, however, be generally agreed that a proportionate income tax would involve a heavier sacrifice to poor people than to rich people, and that *some* degree of progression in the tax rate could be introduced without making the sacrifice imposed on the rich exceed that imposed on the poor. It is not an untenable view, therefore, that taxes on the better-to-do classes adequate to yield the revenue we require for transference to the poor could be contrived on equal sacrifice principles, and, therefore, in a way innocuous to the national dividend. In view of the fact that, when an able man is actually engaged in work, a large part of his aim is simply "success," and that that is not interfered with by any tax that hits his rivals equally with himself, it may well be that, in the upper part of the tax scale, a fairly steep rate of progression might be adopted without the limits set by the principle of equal sacrifice being overstepped. It will be easily understood, however, that the scale of progression which conforms to the principle of *equal sacrifice* is very much less steep than that required to bring about minimum aggregate sacrifice. Most people will agree, therefore, that a scale somewhat steeper than that yielding equal sacrifice is desirable. If such a scale is adopted, *some* repressive influence on the amount of work done and, therefore, on the size of the national dividend must be exercised. It is important to realise, however, that, contrary to common opinion, the extent of this repressive influence upon any particular taxpayer depends, not on the absolute amount, or the absolute percentage of his income that he is required to pay in taxes, but on the relation between this amount or percentage and the amount or percentage which he would be required to pay if his income were a little more or a little less.

When an income tax of a type that does not differentiate against savings cuts down the national dividend of the moment by checking work, it will also indirectly cut down the dividend of future years, because, with the smaller dividend of the moment, there will be less to invest as well as less to consume. An income tax, which is constructed on the same general plan and yields an equal revenue, but which *does* differentiate against saving, may be expected to have a larger effect. We need not suppose that it will affect the amount of work done and, therefore, the size of the dividend of the moment otherwise than the non-differential tax would have done. The non-differential tax lessens in a given degree the advantage that work yields, whatever is done with the fruit of work; the differential tax lessens in a smaller degree the advantage which the part of it devoted to spending yields, and in a larger degree the advantage which the part devoted to saving yields. The net effect on the quantity of work done is likely to be much the same in either case.* It may be expected, however, that the differential tax will discourage savings more seriously — in spite of the fact that it may cause the savings of certain persons to increase† — than the non-differential tax, and, therefore, to contract more seriously the dividend of future years. How far it will do this it is im-

---

* If the desire for income to save is decidely more elastic than the desire for income to spend, the differential tax can be shown to be more restrictive of work than the other; in the converse case it can be shown to be less restrictive. But we have no reason to suppose that the desire for one of these uses is, from a long-period standpoint, much more or much less elastic than that for the other.

possible, with our present knowledge, to determine. All that can be said is that, if we take the point of view of a fairly long period, the succession of national dividends spread over a series of years is likely to be damaged somewhat more by the expectation of an income tax which differentiates against saving than it would be by that of a non-differential income tax yielding the same revenue.

The second fiscal instrument, distinguished [above], through which substantial levies on the relatively well-to-do can be made, is the system of graduated taxes upon property passing at death. These duties, which are actuarially equivalent to deferred income tax on income derived from property, plainly differentiate against savings. The expectation of them will, therefore, check savings and so contract the national dividend of future years. Since, however, they do not as a rule hit savings till some years after they are made, this repressive effect need not be very great. For let us suppose that twenty million £'s a year are to be raised. This can be done either by collecting, say, £100 every year from each of a group of 200,000 people (income tax), or by collecting £2000 from each of them at death, say, on the average, once in twenty years (death duties). The choice between the two methods is indifferent to the State. But it is not indifferent to the persons concerned. Since these persons discount future taxes precisely as they discount all future events, and since their concern in any event is largely diminished if the event is known to fall due when they themselves are no longer alive, the expectation of taxes levied after the second method will have the smaller restrictive influence upon the quantity of capital created by them.

The general result of this analysis is, unfortunately, very nebulous. It is probable on the whole that, unlike the expectation of voluntary transferences from the rich, the expectation of coercive transferences from them by taxation will do harm to the dividend, particularly if the taxation imposed is heavy or steeply graduated. But we cannot determine the size of the adverse influence, even when the quantity of revenue to be raised and the scheme of taxation to be enforced are exactly set out.

† The possibility that, for some people, a tax on savings might cause more savings to be made is parallel to the possibility that, for some people, a tax on work might cause more work to be done. The maximum amount that could in any circumstances be added to savings or to work is an amount sufficient to discharge the whole tax, in such wise that the taxed persons would be left with the same amount of available income as they would have had if there had been no tax.

CHAPTER 13

The Income Tax: Effects on Distribution of Income and Wealth

Richard Goode

A basic source of support for a progressive income tax is the expectation that it will reduce economic inequality or check the growth of inequality. The influence of the income tax on the size distribution of income and wealth, therefore, is an important part of the evaluation of American experience with the tax.

There are varying beliefs concerning the actual influence of the income tax in the United States. A common opinion is that steeply progressive income tax rates have greatly narrowed economic inequality over the past thirty years. Although this view has been taken more often by journalists than by scholars, it has had adherents among well-informed economists. Schumpeter, for example, in discussing redistributive taxation in 1947, wrote, "To an extent which is not generally appreciated, the New Deal was able to expropriate the upper income brackets even before the war" and added that "irrespective of the war, a tremendous transfer of wealth has actually been effected, a transfer that quantitatively is comparable with that effected by Lenin."[1] Among specialists in income distribution, on the other hand, the tendency has been to regard the income tax as a relatively unimportant influence on distribution. For example, Kravis refers to statistical support for the "impression that an increase in the progressivity of the tax structure has played little if any part in making the income distribution more equal" after 1929.[2]

In view of these differences of opinion and the unavoidable complexity of the subject, readers will not be surprised by a warning that the facts concerning the influence of the income tax on the distribution of income and

Reprinted with omissions from Richard Goode, *The Individual Income Tax* (Washington: The Brookings Institution, 1964), by permission of the publisher. © 1964 by The Brookings Institution.

wealth, as on many other questions relating to the tax, are far from clear and that skeptics question the statistics that are available. The purpose of this chapter is to bring together some of the relevant information and to attempt to interpret it. Emphasis is placed on the shares of groups with high incomes or large estates since this is the area in which the direct impact of a progressive income tax can be most clearly observed.

The first step is to consider the simplest aspect of the influence of the income tax on economic inequality, that is, its impact on a given distribution of income before taxes. For this purpose, the before-tax and after-tax distributions of 1960 are compared with each other and with the after-tax distribution that would have obtained in that year with different income tax structures.

. . . the distribution of wealth is briefly surveyed because it may be affected by the income tax through changes in saving and accumulation and by division of property for the purpose of avoiding top income tax rates. Also, data on wealth holdings are helpful as a check on the completeness and reliability of the income statistics.

Finally, some concluding remarks are offered concerning the objective of greater economic equality and the contribution that the income tax and other measures can reasonably be expected to make to its attainment.

In order to isolate the influence of the income tax, government expenditures will be taken as given, and it will be assumed that the same public expenditures would be financed by other taxes if the income tax were not levied. Thus, the discussion abstracts from the possibility that the direct distributional effects of the income tax are offset by government expenditures that are made possible or induced by the levy of the tax. Although this simplifying assumption does not seem so unrealistic as to be seriously misleading, it cannot be denied that a radical change in the tax system would be likely to have some influence on public expenditures. For example, the substitution of regressive taxes for the income tax might stimulate additional welfare expenditures which would mitigate the distributional effects of the change. If more reliance were placed on indirect taxes, it is possible — but in my judgment unlikely — that political opposition to government spending would diminish and the budget would grow more rapidly.

Impact on a Given Before-Tax Distribution of Income

Ideally, the influence of the income tax on income concentration should be measured by reference to statistics based on a comprehensive definition of accrued or realized income. . . . Unfortunately, such data are not available. The best statistics covering a period of years on a comparable basis are those of the Office of Business Economics (OBE) of the Department of Commerce. These statistics relate to the size distribution of "family personal income," which is the portion of total personal income received by consumer units consisting of families and unattached individuals. Income received by members of the armed forces living on posts, persons in institutions, and nonprofit organizations is excluded. The series includes important items of imputed income such as the rental value of owner-occupied dwellings and the value of farm-produced-and-consumed food and fuel.[3] For present purposes, an important shortcoming is the omission of net capital gains and the income tax on them.

TABLE 1. *Distribution of Family Personal Income Among Consumer Units and Effective Rates of Federal Individual Income Tax, 1960*[a]

	Percent Distribution of Income			Mean Amount of Income		
Before-Tax Income	Before Tax	After Tax	Lower Limit, Before-Tax Income	Before Tax	After Tax	Effective Tax Rate (Percent)
Top 1 percent	7.6	6.3	$30,130	$51,969	$38,491	25.9
Next 4 percent	12.0	11.4	16,240	20,422	17,516	14.2
Remainder of top quintile	25.8	26.0	9,270	11,728	10,629	9.4
4th quintile	22.7	23.1	6,530	7,731	7,075	8.5
3rd quintile	16.4	16.8	4,660	5,574	5,159	7.4
2nd quintile	10.9	11.5	2,770	3,725	3,515	5.8
Lowest quintile	4.6	4.9	—	1,562	1,507	3.5
All units	100.0	100.0	—	$ 6,819	$ 6,132	10.1

[a] *Derived from U. S. Department of Commerce, Office of Business Economics, Survey of Current Business, April 1964, pp. 5-9. Units are ranked by family personal income before tax. Income after tax is family personal income net of federal individual income tax liability other than tax liability on net capital gains. The effective tax rate is the amount of federal individual income tax liability, other than liability on net capital gains, as a percentage of family personal income. Figures for the top 1 percent and next 4 percent are based on my interpolations.*

The OBE estimates of the 1960 distribution of family personal income before and after federal individual income tax are summarized in Table 1. The statistics show that the tax does reduce income concentration; however, the reaction of those who examine such estimates for the first time is often surprised that the effect is not greater. The percentage share of the top 1 percent of consumer units in after-tax income in 1960 is about one-sixth smaller than their share in before-tax income (6.3 percent compared with 7.6 percent). For the next 4 percent, comprising families and unattached individuals with before-tax incomes of about $16,000 to $30,000, the after-tax percentage share is only one-twentieth less than the before-tax share. The remaining members of the highest fifth and all lower groups have greater percentage shares in after-tax income than in before-tax income, but the differences are small.

There are three factors that may contribute to readers' surprise about the estimates. First, the income tax is less progressive than commonly believed. The tax extends far down the scale. While effective rates rise with income, the slope of the rate curve is less steep than might be expected.

Second, it may not be generally appreciated that the degree to which percentage shares in disposable income are equalized depends on differences between effective tax rates on high, middle, and low incomes, rather than the average height of the rates. A proportional tax, no matter how high, would not bring about any redistribution of income — provided the before-tax distribution remained constant, as is assumed in this part of the analysis. With progressive rates, groups whose effective tax rates are above the average for the whole population will have smaller percentage shares in after-tax income than in before-tax income, while the reverse will be true for groups whose effective rates are below the average. This explains why, of the groups shown in Table 1, only the top 1 percent and the next 4 percent of units have smaller shares in after-tax income than in before-tax income. Furthermore, there is little difference between the before-tax and after-tax shares of the middle groups because their effective tax rates are not far from the average effective rate.

Third, some readers may think of equalization in terms of the absolute differences between high, middle, and low incomes rather than relative differences or income shares. As can be seen from Table 1, the federal income tax in 1960 sharply reduced the difference between the average income of the top 1 percent of consumer units and of all units, from about $45,000 before tax to about $32,000 after tax. While such figures are of interest, they do not distinguish between the weight of taxation and its redistributive effect. Estimates of percentage shares isolate the redistributive effect. These estimates can be readily compared over periods of change in income levels and tax rates and between countries. Finally, and more fundamentally, inequality is a relative concept and hence better measured by income shares or differences in relative size of income than by absolute income differences.

The effects of applying different income tax structures to the 1960 distribution of income are illustrated in Table 2. The whole population is divided into two groups, the 5 percent of consumer units with the highest incomes and the remaining 95 percent of units. While this procedure sacrifices some information, particularly with respect to the very top of the income pyramid, it greatly simplifies the estimates and thereby minimizes errors and the need for arbitrary assumptions.

The table refers to "tax structures" rather than tax rates, because an effort has been made to take account of personal exemptions, deductions, and other relevant provisions as well as statutory rate schedules. This is done, however, in only a rough way. The figures for the 1935-36 structure, for example, show the effect of applying in 1960 an income tax with the relative yield and progressivity of the 1935-36 tax (yield being measured as a fraction of family personal income and progressivity by the division of liability between the top 5 percent and lower 95 percent of consumer units). The other figures are similar.

As pointed out above, income shares are affected by differences of tax rates between income classes. These differences reflect both the progressivity of the tax, as measured by the ratio of high-bracket rates to low-bracket rates, and its relative yield, as measured by the ratio of total tax to total income. The two elements can be seen by comparing the 1960 distribution with the estimates based on the 1929 tax structure. The 1929 tax structure was more progressive than that of 1960; in fact, the whole federal income tax was borne by the top 5 percent in 1929. But the relative yield of the 1929 income

TABLE 2. *Effects of Applying Different Income Tax Structures to 1960 Income Distribution, Top 5 Percent and Lower 95 Percent of Consumer Units*[a] (In Percent)

Tax Structure and Item	Consumer Units (Ranked by Income Before Tax)		
	All	*Top 5 Percent*	*Lower 95 Percent*
A. 1960 actual			
1. Before-tax income	100.0	19.6	80.4
2. Income tax	100.0	36.1	63.9
3. Effective tax rate	10.1	18.6	8.0
4. After-tax income	100.0	17.7	82.2
B. 1929 income tax structure			
5. Income tax	100.0	100.0	—
6. Effective tax rate	0.7	3.6	—
7. After-tax income	100.0	19.0	81.0
C. 1935-36 income tax structure			
8. Income tax	100.0	96.3	3.7
9. Effective tax rate	1.4	7.0	0.1
10. After-tax income	100.0	18.5	81.5
D. 1960 income tax yield, maximum progressivity			
11. Income tax	100.0	100.0	—
12. Effective tax rate	10.1	51.4	—
13. After-tax income	100.0	10.6	89.4
E. 1965 income tax structure			
14. Income tax	100.0	37.9	62.1
15. Effective tax rate	8.1	15.6	6.2
16. After-tax income	100.0	18.0	82.0

[a] *Before-tax income is family personal income; income tax is federal individual tax liability, excluding tax liability on net capital gains; effective tax rate is that liability as a percentage of family personal income; after-tax income is family personal income minus federal individual income tax liability. Lines 1 to 4 derived from U. S. Department of Commerce, Office of Business Economics, Survey of Current Business, April 1964, pp. 5-9. Lines 5 to 16 are my estimates.*

tax was so low that the absolute difference between the effective rate payable by the top 5 percent and the zero rate of the remaining units was much smaller than the difference between the 1960 rates of the two groups. Hence the 1929 tax would have only a small influence on income distribution.

Between 1929 and 1935-36, total income tax liability doubled in relation to income, and nearly all of the increase fell on high incomes. According to the rough test being employed here, the 1935-36 tax would do more than half as much equalizing as the 1960 tax.[4] (In 1960, the after-tax share of the top 5 percent was 1.9 percentage points smaller than their before-tax share; with the 1935-36 tax, the difference would be 1.1 percentage points.) When the 1935-36 and 1960 tax structures are compared, equalizing power is found to grow less rapidly than yield; this reflects the reduction of personal exemptions and the sharp increase in low-bracket rates.

Section D of Table 2 shows the maximum equalization that could have been accomplished in 1960 merely by changing the allocation of income tax liabilities. It is assumed that the total income tax yield would have been maintained at the actual 1960 level but that the whole tax would have been assessed against the top 5 percent of income recipients. The figures are included only to mark off an extreme, without any suggestion that it would have been desirable or feasible to have adopted such a tax structure. Even with maximum progressivity, the average disposable income of the top 5 percent of consumer units would still have been more than twice as great as the average for all other units (indicated by the estimate that 5 percent of the units would have received 10.6 percent of total after-tax income).

Table 2 also gives rough estimates of the impact of the income tax rates and other tax provisions that are scheduled to be in effect in 1965, according to the Revenue Act of 1964. The estimates given in Section E are intended to show the effect that the 1965 provisions would have had if they had been in force in 1960.[5] While the estimates are only rough, approximately, they should give fairly accurate indications of orders of magnitude.

The 1965 income tax structure will be somewhat less equalizing than the previous structure, as indicated by the small increase in the fraction of after-tax income left in the hands of the highest 5 percent of income recipients (18.0 percent compared with 17.7 percent). In this respect, the influence of the over-all tax reduction outweighs the fact that the cut in effective rates was proportionately somewhat greater for the lower 95 percent than for the top 5 percent. In order to maintain the equalizing power of the income tax while reducing yields, it would have been necessary to allocate a larger part of the tax reduction to low brackets.

These comments relate to the effect of applying different tax structures to a given before-tax distribution. A large tax cut, such as that made by the Revenue Act of 1964, could stimulate economic activity and reduce unemployment to such a degree that gains in before-tax income realized by lower income groups would more than offset the apparent loss in equalizing power.

However, there seems to be little basis for predicting such an outcome. The available statistics reveal no obvious effect on size distribution of fluctuations in the level of income and unemployment rates of the magnitude that have occurred since the end of World War II.

There are some data suggesting that, if judged solely by impact on the top 5 percent of income-receiving units, the federal income tax in the United States may have been less equalizing in the period 1948-52 than the income taxes of the United Kingdom, the Netherlands, Denmark, and Sweden.[6] The statistics, however, vary so greatly in concepts and coverage that a comparison cannot be confidently made.

Changes in Before-Tax Distribution of Income

Statistics of the kind examined in the preceding pages will understate or overstate the equalizing power of the income tax if its existence causes the before-tax distribution to be less concentrated or more concentrated than it otherwise would be. The income tax may lessen the inequality of before-tax income by reducing the saving, wealth accumulation, and property income of high-income families; by inducing high-income investors to shift toward assets with lower actual or nominal rates of yield; by encouraging the splitting of property and income among family members who are in separate income units or its dispersal through philanthropic contributions; and by deterring highly remunerated personal effort. On the other hand, inequality of before-tax income can be increased if the income tax causes compensating rises in profit rates, executive salaries and bonuses, and professional fees. The existence of the tax may stimulate the use of forms of compensation that do not enter into the income statistics and may thus impair their reliability as indicators of inequality. Of course, the income tax is only one of many factors affecting the before-tax distribution of income.

Distribution of Wealth

Statistics on wealth, like those on income, show less concentration in recent years than in the 1920's. Lampman's study,[7] based on estate tax data, finds that the share of top wealth-holders in total personal wealth fell sharply from 1929 to 1949. Thereafter, their share increased, but tentative estimates for 1961 indicate that only about half of the previous decline had been recovered up to that time Lampman's estimates are summarized [in part 2 of this book].

Lampman infers that the most important proximate cause of the change in the position of the richest group was that its share of personal saving was well below its share of personal wealth, particularly between 1939 and 1949. While the income tax probably was partly responsible, the hypothetical figures mentioned above suggest that its influence can easily be exaggerated.

A factor in the decline of wealth concentration is the increased importance of consumer durables and pension and retirement funds, which are more widely held than are securities and equities in unincorporated business.[8] Investment in durables and pension funds may have been encouraged by the favorable income tax treatment of the returns, but other social and economic forces probably were more important.

A second cause of decreased concentration of wealth, at least in the statistical sense, is changes in property-transfer practices, which placed a larger fraction of wealth in the hands of women and young persons after 1922. Lampman attributes to these changes the fact that the share of the top 1 percent of adults fell more than the share of the top 2 percent of families from 1922 to 1953.[9] Income tax considerations, as well as the desire to minimize estate taxes, may have encouraged the splitting up of fortunes. Income tax incentives for splitting with wives disappeared after the universalization of splitting privileges between spouses in 1948 but continued with respect to splits with children and other relatives.

Two other factors that Lampman identifies as contributing to the fall in the share of wealth held by the top group — changes in relative prices of assets and demographic changes — seem not to be directly related to the income tax. Although the share of the richest group was influenced by cyclical swings in the composition of estates, Lampman finds "remarkably little noncyclical change [in estate composition] over the decades."[10] It is interesting that the most significant cyclical shift was the reduction in the top group's concentration on price-sensitive assets, such as corporate stocks and real estate, in the boom period 1922-29, which held down the growth of its share of total wealth.[11] These were years of low income tax rates, and it seems unlikely that the tax was responsible for the shift.

How can the estimates showing a partial reversal, after 1949, of the previous decline in wealth concentration be reconciled with the income statistics, which show no tendency for the share of the top income group to increase during the 1950's? Although there is no formal inconsistency, trends toward increasing or decreasing concentration might be expected to be parallel with respect to wealth and income. An important part of the reconciliation may be found in the way capital gains influence the two sets of statistics. Capital gains, regardless of whether realized or not, are reflected in the wealth statistics but are included in the OBE income statistics, even if realized. A comparison of Lampman's current-price and constant-price estimates of the wealth share of the top 1 percent in 1949 and 1953 indicates that capital appreciation was largely responsible for the increase in concentration over that four-year period. In constant dollars, the increase in the share of the richest group was less than one-third as large as the increase in current dollars.[12] Lampman does not give constant-price estimates for years after 1953.

The data contradict the popular belief that the high income tax rates of the postwar period have prevented the creation of new private fortunes. According to Lampman's estimates, the number of millionaires, that is, persons with gross estates of $1 million and over, increased from 13,297 in 1944 to 27,502 in 1953. Even with allowance for the fall in the purchasing power of the dollar, the number of millionaires grew by one-third.[13] During this period, the population grew by only 15 percent and per capita personal income in constant prices by about 4½ percent.[14]

Concluding Remarks

This extended review of the statistics neither corroborates the opinion that the income tax is a Draconian measure for redistribution nor justifies writing off its equalizing effects as inconsequential. Although the difference between the before-tax and after-tax distributions of income in recent years is not striking, neither is it trivial.

There is no evidence that the redistributive impact of the income tax has been offset by changes in before-tax income shares. Income before tax has become less unequal, and there is reason for believeing that the tax has contributed to a minor extent to this change. Part of the apparent decline in the before-tax share of the highest income classes after 1929 probably is spurious, reflecting efforts to avoid taxes and other factors that changed measured personal income more than true income; however, it seems unlikely that the major part of the apparent change can be explained in this way. It appears, therefore, that although the individual income tax has contributed significantly to lessened inequality of disposable income over the past three decades, it has been considerably less important in this respect than other governmental actions and developments in the private economy.

If Congress were determined to bring about a drastic reduction in economic inequality, it could do much more by means of the income tax. But extreme equalization has not been accepted even as an ultimate goal. The primary popular and legislative support of progressive taxation seems to derive from ideas about ability to pay or sacrifice rather than an intention to equalize incomes. Among those who explicity advocate taxation to reduce inequality, most would concede that substantial differences in income are justifiable on the basis of needs as indicated by family size, age, and other personal circumstances and on the basis of contribution to production and the public good.[15] Another source of differences between after-tax earned incomes that seem fully justifiable on egalitarian premises is the amount of time invested in preparing for occupations. A person in a profession requiring many years of education should have a higher annual income than a clerk, if for no other reason, because his earnings begin later and are received over a shorter period of time. Relatively noncontroversial differences of these kinds can account for a considerable amount of inequality.

Progressive taxation, moreover, is not the only means of reducing economic inequality. The wider dissemination of education, improved programs for health and medical care, and the breaking down of racial discrimination are desirable in themselves and may make a lasting contribution to the reduction of economic inequality by raising the incomes of the poor.[16] Transfer payments, though directed to the satisfaction of particular social needs, also have a significant influence on the distribution of personal income. Further improvements in these programs can be expected to reduce inequality unless the expenditures are financed by regressive taxes.

Progressive taxation and government expenditures cannot deal with all kinds of inequality since differences in measured wealth and income are not the only sources of privilege and power. Extreme efforts to reduce economic inequality would be subject to the risk that they would merely transfer to government and corporate bureaucrats powers that were formerly exercised by property owners.

The best approach to income distribution — both as a subject of analysis and a field of social action — is to adopt what Dahl and Lindblom call an "incremental attitude."[17] This attitude directs attention toward small changes rather than drastic redistributions. It supports the belief that inequality can be moderately reduced or increased by changes in the effective progressivity of the income tax, without radically altering the economic and political system.

REFERENCES

1. JOSEPH A. SCHUMPETER, *Capitalism, Socialism and Democracy,* 3d ed. (New York: Harper & Row, 1962), p. 381. The passage cited was introduced in the second edition, originally published in 1947.

2. IRVING B. KRAVIS, *The Structure of Income* (Philadelphia: University of Pennsylvania, 1962), p. 220.

3. See U.S. Department of Commerce, Office of Business Economics, *Income Distribution in the United States,* Supplement to *Survey of Current Business* (1953).

4. A more refined measure can be derived from Gini concentration ratios. A comparison of Gini coefficients is affected by changes throughout the income distribution but gives ambiguous answers when the Lorenz curves of before-tax and after-tax income cross. For a treatment using both the Gini coefficient and the share technique, see SELMA F. GOLDSMITH, GEORGE JASZI, HYMAN KAITZ, and MAURICE LIEBENBERG. "Size Distribution of Income Since the Mid-Thirties," *Review of Economics and Statistics,* vol. 36 (February 1954), pp. 1–32.

5. Based on the OBE distribution for 1960 and estimates of tax liability under the 1964 net given in *Revenue Act of 1964,* Senate Finance Committee S. Rept. 830, 88 Cong. 2 sess. (1964), p. 28 et passim.

6. United Nations Economic Survey of Europe in 1956 (Geneva, 1956, Chapter IX; for further comparisons, see L. NEEDLEMAN, "The Burden of Taxation: An International Comparison," *National Institute Economic Review,* London), March 1961, pp. 55-61.

7. ROBERT J. LAMPMAN, *The Share of Top Wealth-Holders in National Wealth,* 1922–1956 (Princeton, N.J.: Princeton University Press for National Bureau Economic Research, 1962).

8. Cf. RAYMOND W. GOLDSMITH, *A Study of Saving in the United States* (Princeton, N.J.: Princeton University Press, 1955), vol. I, p. 161.

9. *Share of Top Wealth-Holders,* pp. 237–43.

10. *Ibid.,* p.21.

11. *Ibid.,* pp. 208–209, 244.

12. In constant (1922) dollars, the share of personal wealth held by the top 1 percent of adults increased from 21.2 percent in 1949 to 22.3 percent in 1953, while in current dollars the increase was from 20.8 percent to 24.2 percent (*ibid.,* pp. 227, 24).

13. *Ibid.,* p. 276. Lampman estimates that in 1953 there were 17,611 persons with estates equivalent to one million or more 1944 dollars. The deflator here is the consumer price index, whereas the constant-price estimates mentioned in the preceding paragraph were derived by applying asset price indexes to the principal components of wealth.

14. Derived from *Economic Report of the President, January 1962,* pp. 214, 226, 227; personal income converted to constant prices by application of the implicit price deflator for the personal consumption component of GNP.

15. On the implications of such factors, see George Garvy, "Comment," in *Studies in Income and Wealth,* Conference on Research in Income and Wealth, vol. 13 (New York: National Bureau of Economic Research, 1951), pp. 217–18. Garvy remarks that the standard of full equalization and departures from it, as measured by the Lorenz curve (and Gini coefficient), have "a mathematical rather than economic meaning."

16. For effective statements of this view, see two papers by ALLAN G. B. FISHER. " 'Full Employment' and Income Inequality," *Economic Journal,* vol. 56 (March 1946), pp. 18–26; and "Alternative Techniques for Promoting Equality in a Capitalist Society," *American Economic Review,* vol. 40, Papers and Proceedings (May 1950), pp. 356–68.

17. ROBERT A. DAHL AND CHARLES E. LINDBLOM, *Politics, Economics, and Welfare* (New York: Harper & Row, 1953), p. 148.

CHAPTER 14

The Alleviation of Poverty

Milton Friedman

The extraordinary economic growth experienced by Western countries during the past two centuries and the wide distribution of the benefits of free enterprise have enormously reduced the extent of poverty in any absolute sense in the capitalistic countries of the West. But poverty is in part a relative matter, and even in these countries, there are clearly many people living under conditions that the rest of us label as poverty.

One recourse, and in many ways the most desirable, is private charity. It is noteworthy that the heyday of laissez-faire, the middle and late nineteenth century in Britain and the United States, saw an extraordinary proliferation of private eleemosynary organizations and institutions. One of the major costs of the extension of governmental welfare activities has been the corresponding decline in private charitable activities.

It can be argued that private charity is insufficient because the benefits from it accrue to people other than those who make the gifts — again, a neighborhood effect. I am distressed by the sight of poverty; I am benefited by its alleviation; but I am benefited equally whether I or someone else pays for its alleviation; the benefits of other people's charity therefore partly accrue to me. To put it differently, we might all of us be willing to contribute to the relief of poverty, *provided* everyone else did. We might not be willing to contribute the same amount without such assurance. In small communities, public pressures can suffice to realize the proviso even with private charity. In the large impersonal communities that are increasingly coming to dominate our society, it is much more difficult for it to do so.

Reprinted from Milton Friedman, *Capitalism and Freedom* (Chicago: University of Chicago Press, 1963) by permission of the publisher and author. © 1962 by The University of Chicago.

Suppose one accepts, as I do, this line of reasoning as justifying governmental action to alleviate poverty; to set, as it were, a floor under the standard of life of every person in the community. There remain the questions, how much and how. I see no way of deciding "how much" except in terms of the amount of taxes we — by which I mean the great bulk of us — are willing to impose on ourselves for the purpose. The question, "how," affords more room for speculation.

Two things seem clear. First, if the objective is to alleviate poverty, we should have a program directed at helping the poor. There is every reason to help the poor man who happens to be a farmer, not because he is a farmer but because he is poor. The program, that is, should be designed to help people as people not as members of particular occupational groups or age groups or wage-rate groups or labor organizations or industries. This is a defect of farm programs, general old-age benefits, minimum-wage laws, pro-union legislation, tariffs, licensing provisions of crafts or professions, and so on in seemingly endless profusion. Second, so far as possible the program should, while operating through the market, not distort the market or impede its functioning. This is a defect of price supports, minimum-wage laws, tariffs and the like.

The arrangement that recommends itself on purely mechanical grounds is a negative income tax. We now have an exemption of $600 per person under the federal income tax (plus a minimum 10 percent flat deduction). If an individual receives $100 taxable income, i.e., an income of $100 in excess of the exemption and deductions, he pays tax. Under the proposal, if his taxable income [were] minus $100, i.e., $100 less than the exemption plus deductions, he would pay a negative tax, i.e., receive a subsidy. If the rate of subsidy were, say, 50 percent, he would receive $50. If he had no income at all and, for simplicity, no deductions, and the rate were constant, he would receive $300. He might receive more than this if he had deductions, for example, for medical expenses, so that his income less deductions, was negative even before subtracting the exemption. The rates of subsidy could, of course, be graduated just as the rates of tax above the exemption are. In this way, it would be possible to set a floor below which no man's net income (defined now to include the subsidy) could fall—in the simple example $300 per person. The precise floor set would depend on what the community could afford.

The advantages of this arrangement are clear. It is directed specifically at the problem of poverty. It gives help in the form most useful to the individual, namely, cash. It is general and could be substituted for the host of special measures now in effect. It makes explicit the cost borne by society. It operates outside the market. Like any other measures to alleviate poverty, it reduces the incentives of those helped to help themselves, but it does not eliminate that incentive entirely, as a system of supplementing incomes up to some fixed minimum would. An extra dollar earned always means more money available for expenditure.

No doubt there would be problems of administration, but these seem to me a minor disadvantage, if they be a disadvantage at all. The system would fit directly into our current income tax system and could be administered along with it. The present tax system covers the bulk of income recipients and the necessity of covering all would have the by-product of improving the operation of the present income tax. More important, if enacted as a substitute for the present rag bag of measures directed at the same end, the total administrative burden would surely be reduced.

A few brief calculations suggest also that this proposal could be far less costly in money, let alone in the degree of governmental intervention involved, than our present collection of welfare measures. Alternatively, these calculations can be regarded as showing how wasteful our present measures are, judged as measures for helping the poor.

In 1961, government [spending] amounted to something like $33 billion (federal, state, and local) on direct welfare payments and programs of all kinds: old age assistance, social security benefit payments, aid to dependent children, general assistance, farm price support programs, public housing, etc.* I have excluded veterans' benefits in making this calculation. I have also made no allowance for the direct and indirect costs of such measures as minimum-wage laws, tariffs, licensing provisions, and so on, or for the cost of public health activities, state and local expenditures on hospitals, mental institutions, and the like.

There are approximately 57 million consumer units (unattached individuals and families) in the United States. The 1961 expenditures of $33 billion would have financed outright cash grants of nearly $6,000 per consumer unit to the 10 percent with the lowest incomes. Such grants would have raised their incomes above the average for all units in the United States. Alternatively, these expenditures would have financed grants of nearly $3,000 per consumer unit to the 20 percent with the lowest incomes. Even if one went so far as that one-third whom New Dealers were fond of calling ill-fed, ill-housed, and ill-clothed, 1961 expenditures would have financed grants of nearly $2,000 per consumer unit, roughly the sum which, after allowing for the change in the level of prices, was the income which separated the lower one-third in the middle 1930's from the upper two-thirds. Today, fewer than one-eighth of consumer units have an income, adjusted for the change in the level of prices, as low as that of the lowest third in the middle 1930's.

---

*This figure is equal to government transfer payments ($31.1 billion) less veterans' benefits ($4.8 billion), both from the Department of Commerce national income accounts, plus federal expenditures on the agricultural program ($5.5 billion) plus federal expenditures on public housing and other aids to housing ($0.5 billion), both for year ending June 30, 1961 from Treasury accounts, plus a rough allowance of $0.7 billion to raise it to even billions and to allow for administrative costs of federal programs, omitted state and local programs, and miscellaneous items. My guess is that this figure is a subtantial underestimate.

Clearly, these are all far more extravagant programs than can be justified to "alleviate poverty" even by a rather generous interpretation of that term. A program which *supplemented* the incomes of the 20 percent of the consumer units with the lowest incomes so as to raise them to the lowest income of the rest would cost less than half of what we are now spending.

The major disadvantage of the proposed negative income tax is its political implications. It establishes a system under which taxes are imposed on some to pay subsidies to others. And presumably, these others have a vote. There is always the danger that instead of being an arrangement under which the great majority tax themselves willingly to help an unfortunate minority, it will be converted into one under which a majority imposes taxes for its own benefit on an unwilling minority. Because this proposal makes the process so explicit, the danger is perhaps greater than with other measures. I see no solution to this problem except to rely on the self-restraint and good will of the electorate.

CHAPTER 15

Schemes for Transferring Income to the Poor

Christopher Green and Robert J. Lampman

This article is about various schemes for transferring additional income to poor people: the "negative income tax," modification of public assistance and social insurance, family allowances, and tax credits. Nine particular methods are evaluated and a selection is made by the authors of the one which seems to them to be most hopeful of a good result per dollar of expenditure.

A Description of Negative Income Taxation

Negative income taxation would use the individual income tax system as a vehicle for closing a portion of the poverty-income gap, i.e., the difference between the actual income of poor families and the income they would need in order not to be poor. It would pay money from the federal treasury to families according to a schedule based on actual income received and family size. For example, a family of four persons with an income of $2,000 might be said to have a poverty-income gap of $1,000. That is, their income is $1,000 below a "poverty line" of $3,000. Similarly, it is $1,000 below their total of personal exemptions and minimum standard deductions under the income tax law. Hence, the $1,000 is that family's unused exemptions and deductions and it can be called their "negative taxable income." To this negative base one could apply a tax rate to compute a "negative tax" or allowance. Thus, a 50 percent tax rate would yield an allowance of $500 in the example given. The scheme described above is one variant of negative income taxation. In this paper it is later referred to as negative rates taxation.

Reprinted with omissions from *Industrial Relations*, Vol. 6, No. 2, February 1967, by permission of the authors. © 1967 by Regents of the University of California, Berkeley.

One could achieve the same result by paying a standard allowance to all families and then taxing pre-allowance income in such a way that the tax is less than the allowance for poor families but more than the allowance for non-poor families. This is illustrative of the guaranteed minimum income[1] or social dividend[2] approach to negative income taxation.

The similarity between social dividend taxation and negative rates taxation can be understood by noting that each employs the same three basic variables. These basic variables are (1) an income guarantee; (2) a tax rate applied against a tax base; and (3) a break-even level of income where the tax liability equals the allowance guarantee. Any two of these three basic variables determine the third. In negative rates taxation, the income guarantee is the level of negative tax allowances that is received when income other than the allowance or guarantee is zero. In social dividend taxation, the guarantee is the level of gross payments or entitlement for which a family or individual is eligible. The tax base in negative rates taxation is the gap between some standard, such as the value of exemptions and deductions allowed a family or the family's poverty line, and the level of family income. In social dividend taxation the tax base is the family's income before allowance.

Table 1 indicates that a negative rates plan which fills 50 percent of a family's poverty gap would provide the same level of allowances as a social dividend plan which guarantees a minimum income equal to 50 percent of a poverty line and, at the same time, taxes family income up to the break-even

TABLE 1. *Net Allowance Received by a Family of Four Under a Negative Rates Plan and a Social Dividend Plan*

Negative rates plan			Social dividend plan		
(1)	*(2)*	*(3)*	*(4)*	*(5)*	*(6)*
Family income before allowance	*Poverty-income gap $3,000-(1)*	*Net allowance based on 50 percent of poverty gap*	*Basic allowance guarantee equal to $1,500 (equal to 50 percent of poverty line)*	*Tax liability with 50 percent rate (50% x (1))*	*Net allowance (4)-(5)*
$ 0	$3,000	$1,500	$1,500	$ 0	$1,500
500	2,500	1,250	1,500	250	1,250
1,000	2,000	1,000	1,500	500	1,000
1,500	1,500	750	1,500	750	750
2,000	1,000	500	1,500	1,000	500
3,000	0	0	1,500	1,500	0

line at a 50 percent rate. Columns (3) and (6) show that for any given level of before-allowance income the net allowance (gross allowance minus tax liability) is the same under each type of plan. Therefore, it is useful to think of negative rates and social dividend taxation as two types of what might be called "transfer-by-taxation."

Transfer-by-taxation differs from other modes of income maintenance in that income and family size are the leading factors which condition benefits. Most, if not all, the eligibility considerations which are used in public assistance or social insurance programs — assets, ability to work, relatives' responsibility, age, retirement status, employment record, previous taxes paid, and so forth — are left to one side. Hence, all families with incomes below some specified level — not just certain categories of families — would receive allowances. Moreover, every family would be assured a minimum (this may or may not be a "high minimum") level of income.

Ideally, the administration of transfer-by-taxation would be, like social insurance, so impersonal as to avoid most of the stigma generally associated with being "on relief." It could be administered in connection with the present income tax system and would require only that a beneficiary file tax forms at the beginning and end of a stated accounting period. The set of allowances or negative tax rates can be designed to induce work effort and thrift on the part of actual and prospective beneficiaries. In this regard, transfer-by-taxation may be more constructive than an extension of public assistance to the "working poor," since the latter typically involves a dollar-for-dollar substitution of benefits for other income foregone and vice versa. In other words, public assistance uses a 100 percent marginal tax rate, but transfer-by-taxation opens up the possibility of using lower tax rates and thereby supplementing low earned incomes without discouraging all work effort by recipients of such supplements.

A Comparison of Negative Income Tax Plans

Transfer-by-taxation is a flexible technique. In designing a plan, one may vary the level of the basic guarantee, the tax rate, and the break-even level of income. By changing the definitions of such key terms as "income" and "family" and by varying eligibility conditions one may alter the specific way in which a plan relates to the concepts and parameters of the present individual income tax system, as well as to public assistance and other social welfare systems.

Before designing and choosing among transfer-by-taxation plans, the following key questions need to be explored:

1. What portion of the poverty-income gap is closed by the plan?
2. Would any of those presently poor be made worse off by adoption of the plan? Are the poor and near-poor treated equitably in the sense that their rankings are the same before and after allowances are paid?
3. What effects will the plan have on work, saving and investment, family size, and family composition?
4. What is the budgetary cost of the plan and who will pay it?
5. How much of the total expenditure under the plan goes to poor families?

6. How would the plan relate to present provisions in taxation, public assistance, and other social welfare programs?

With these key questions in mind, we turn to an outline of five different transfer-by-taxation plans: tax-equity negative rates, social dividend, welfare-oriented negative rates, child's entitlement, and earned income supplement plans.

The Tax-Equity Negative Rates Plan

The simplest negative rates plan would refund to nontaxable income tax filers some percentage of their unused personal exemptions and minimum standard deductions (afterwards referred to as "unused EX + MSD).* Such a plan would produce greater equity in the income tax system. The taxpayer with unused EX + MSD is not now getting the full use of these provisions, nor does he benefit from tax rate reductions or increases in personal exemptions and allowable deductions. This results in an inequity whereby families of different size and the same income pay the same tax, namely, a tax of zero dollars. Applying even a modest negative tax rate, say 14 percent (presently the lowest bracket rate), to unused EX + MSD would allow the poor of differing family sizes to utilize the EX + MSD allowed them under the income tax system. A high tax rate, say 50 percent, would meet a substantial portion of the needs of the poor.

The cost of the Tax-Equity Negative Rates Plan with a 14 percent rate would have been about $2.8 billion in 1964; the cost with a 50 percent rate would have been approximately $10 billion.† The appeal of the plan is its simplicity, i.e., the relative ease with which it could be administered alongside the existing (positive) income tax system. The present tax return indicates whether the filer has unused EX + MSD and whether therefore he would be eligible for, and in what amounts he may receive, negative tax allowances. It would, of course, be necessary to make sure that persons not now filing tax returns (because they are not presently required to do so), but who would be eligible to receive allowances if they did so file, are encouraged to file and are aided in filing an income tax return.

The simplicity of the plan is also its major shortcoming. It ignores the fact that the present definition of income for positive income tax purposes excludes

---

* For simplicity the minimum standard deduction is used. It is a known amount varying with family size. An income tax filer receives a $200 MSD, and $100 for each dependent (including himself). Thus a family of four has $600 in MSD. Most low income families can be expected to use the MSD unless itemizing heavy medical expenses will increase their deductions.

† The cost figures are rough guesses since the aggregate amount of unused EX+MSD, calculated by the tax system's income concept of adjusted gross income, is not readily available. However, the Treasury has estimated that there was $22 billion in unused EX+MSD in 1961. By 1964 this figure can be supposed to have fallen slightly to about $20 billion. Part of this would be offset by savings on public assistance.

important forms of income such as transfer income. Because of this, some non-poor people would get negative tax allowances. Moreover, it does not take account of the fact that the welfare unit is "the family," whereas the tax unit is any income earner and his "dependents." Some families might have several tax filers under present law.

Another difficulty with the Tax-Equity Negative Rates Plan is that the use of unused EX + MSD as a standard in determining eligibility for allowances has the effect of shortchanging small families. The poverty-line incomes set by the Social Security Administration are well in excess of EX + MSD for families of one, two, or three persons. The problem, however, is offset some-what by the fact that the aged are presently allowed double EX + MSD. In 1964 over 50 percent of the one-, two-, and three-member families with money income below the poverty lines were headed by an aged person.[3] On the other hand, very large families are favored by the use of EX + MSD rather than poverty lines as a basis for calculating the negative tax base. Moreover, as Table 2 shows, the use of EX + MSD rather than poverty lines results in major variations in the proportion by which the poverty gap is closed for

TABLE 2. *Percentage of Poverty-Income Gap Filled for Different Size Families When 50 Percent Negative Tax Is Applied to Unused Exemptions and Deductions*

Income before allowance as percentage of poverty-line income	Size of family unit						
	Net allowance as percentage of poverty income gap						
	1	2	3	4	5	6	7
0	30	40	46	50	53	55	57
10	28	39	45	50	53	55	57
20	25	37	45	50	54	56	58
30	21	36	44	50	54	57	59
40	17	33	43	50	55	58	61
50	10	30	42	50	56	60	63
60	0	25	40	50	57	62	67
70	a	17	37	50	59	67	72
80	a	0	30	50	64	75	83
90	a	a	10	50	79	100	116

a No unused EX-MSD. Will pay a positive tax if adjusted gross income equals total money income.

different families. These variations are associated with differences in family size and income as a percentage of the family's poverty line. This variation in the treatment of poor families may be difficult to justify.

The Social Dividend Plan

The Social Dividend Plan is modeled after plans suggested by Lady Rhys-Williams, Robert Shutz, and D. B. Smith.[4] It would make periodic payments to every citizen (or family) sufficient to guarantee an annual "poverty-free" income. Using currently accepted poverty lines, the total or "gross" cost of such a guaranteed minimum income plan in 1964 would have been $155 billion. This enormous cost would be financed by a special tax on each family's money income before allowances. The level of the tax rate(s) will determine the plan's "net cost," or the amount of redistribution of income from families with before-allowance income above the break-even level to families with income below that level. In 1964 a single tax rate of 33⅓ percent applied against $465 billion of family money income would have raised $155 billion and would have redistributed out of that amount about $51 billion. Under such a plan a four-person family with a $3,000 guarantee would have a $9,000 break-even income level. That is, this family would not begin to pay "net" for the cost of the plan until its income before allowances rose above $9,000.

The important cost figure is the plan's net rather than its gross cost, because the former indicates the amount of income actually redistributed from those with above to those with below break-even incomes. For families with income above the break-even level of income, the guarantee would be a credit against the taxes they must pay to finance the plan. Families with expected income above the break-even level might sensibly forego receiving "allowances" and paying "social dividend taxes" on that portion of their income which equals their break-even income levels.

Still, a net cost of $51 billion reduces the attractiveness of the plan — at least to those who have to pay for it. Moreover, many families obviously not in any real need for income maintenance would receive allowances. In 1964, 68 percent of all families and unrelated individuals would have been eligible to receive net allowances under the plan just described. In that year, only 19 percent were adjudged to have been poor. Of the $51 billion paid out in net allowances, $28 billion would have gone to non-poor families. (However, some of the $28 billion would be income in excess of poverty-line income received by families who were poor before allowances.)

An alternative set of tax rates could reduce the net cost of the Social Dividend Plan and the percentage of families eligible for net allowances. If the tax rate on income before allowance was 50 percent rather than 33⅓ percent up to the break-even level of income — i.e., now twice the guarantee — the net cost of the plan in 1964 would have been about $30 billion.* This $30 billion "net cost" could have been financed by a 14 percent tax on all income (not only presently taxable income) above the break-even levels. There is a major reduction in the tax rate on "net" taxpayers from 33⅓ percent, when a single rate on all income is used, to 14 percent, when a 50 percent rate is

---

* The $30 billion is based on no adjustment for under-reporting of income in the Census survey. It assumes that no social welfare programs are reduced in scale. If public assistance were cut, the $30 billion figure would rise by half the amount of the cut. It also assumes no one does any less work because of the tax.

applied to income below the break-even level. This is due to (1) limiting the number of families eligible for net allowances and hence increasing the income base out of which the net cost of the plan is financed, and (2) a more rapid reduction in net allowances for each dollar of pre-allowance income received by a family.

The advantage of the Social Dividend Plan is that it guarantees a poverty-free minimum income. In other words, it would completely fill the poverty-income gap. It would make possible the elimination of public assistance, except in unusual cases, and perhaps reductions in some other social welfare programs. Aside from the heavy cost of the plan and its "inefficiency" (in the sense that most of the net allowances go to non-poor families), the plan has another disadvantage in that it fails to fit neatly into the existing income tax framework. This failure is due to two factors: (1) break-even levels of income are far in excess of the value of $EX - MSD$ presently allowed a taxpayer, and (2) the definition of "income" would need to differ from that for general tax purposes. High break-even levels mean that many "positive" taxpayers will be net allowance recipients.

The figure below illustrates the relationship between the different tax schedules. Schedule ABC is the social dividend tax schedule and DE is the present positive tax schedule. The "combined" tax schedule shows the allowance received or tax paid when both tax schedules are taken into considera-

A SOCIAL DIVIDEND PLAN (FAMILY OF FOUR)

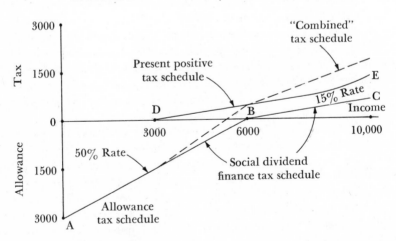

tion. Note that the combined schedule assumes that similar definitions of income are used for positive and social dividend tax purposes. The heavy cost of the plan will necessitate a broad definition of income for social dividend purposes — a definition of taxable income quite different from the present "taxable income" base.

Welfare-Oriented Negative Rates Plan

This plan is a refinement of the Tax-Equity Negative Rates Plan discussed above. It would recognize the following:

1. A family's poverty-income gap is a better guide to eligibility for allowances than is unused EX—MSD. Therefore, poverty lines are substituted for the value of EX—MSD used in the Tax-Equity Negative Rates Plan.

2. The present income tax unit often is not the same as the family unit which pools its income in order to meet its major items of expense. Thus the Welfare-Oriented Plan adopts a "basic" family tax unit consisting of spouses, all children under 19 years of age, and students under 22 years of age. The present income tax rules establishing dependency status would apply to persons outside the basic family unit.

3. The present definition of income for income tax purposes is an inadequate guide to a family's welfare. Therefore, as a step in the direction of a more complete evaluation of a family's economic position, family money income would replace adjusted gross income in determining eligibility for allowances.

The Welfare-Oriented Negative Rates Plan presumes that social insurance programs are to be continued and that the money income from these programs is to be included in the definition of income for negative tax purposes. Thus the negative rates allowances are designed to supplement the earnings and social insurance income of poor families. Public assistance would be treated otherwise. That is to say, public assistance (P.A.) would be excluded from the definition of income for the purposes of determining eligibility for and the level of negative rates allowances. There are two reasons for this differential treatment of public assistance. One is that P.A., unlike social insurance benefits, is conditioned upon a family's present resources — of which income is an important component. Thus the level of public assistance would depend, in part, upon the level of negative tax allowances a family received. But if P.A. were included in the definition of income, negative tax allowances would depend, in part, on the level of P.A. It would be very difficult for welfare officials to determine what P.A. payments to make if the level of negative tax allowances depended on the level of P.A., and vice versa.

There is a second reason for excluding P.A. from the definition of income for negative tax purposes. The objectives of transfer-by-taxation are to provide an income floor for all, to pay allowances to families only according to the family's income and size, to reduce the disincentives created by 100 percent tax rates, and to eliminate the stigma presently associated with being on relief. The objectives would be enhanced if P.A. were reduced to supplemental payments after negative tax allowances have been calculated. This would maximize the negative allowances paid to a family on P.A. and minimize its P.A. receipts.

The cost to the federal government of the Welfare-Oriented Plan, using the definitions stated above and a 50 percent tax rate, would have been $6.3 billion in 1964. This figure is a combination of $8 billion in negative tax allowances and an estimated $1.7 billion reduction in federally financed public assistance payments.

This plan, like the others, has shortcomings. It does not tie neatly into the existing individual income tax system because at several points the plan departs from concepts used by the positive system. For example, the use of poverty lines rather than EX—MSD as break-even levels of income means that some small families (less than four members) would be both taxable and eligible for allowances. Moreover, the broader definition of income and the "basic" family tax unit utilized by the plan mean that there would be two different definitions of income and tax unit within the individual income tax system. These might create administrative problems.

One disappointing feature of the Welfare-Oriented Negative Rates Plan is that it would require some supplementation by public assistance if none of the present poor are to be made worse off. If the tax rates to be paid by the working poor are to be kept at low levels, then, given the low break-even level of income, the guaranteed minimum income would be lower than the benefits public assistance provides in some of the states.

The Incentives Question

It will be apparent to the reader that the tax rate used in a plan is critical to its outcome. Given a low break-even point, a tax rate lower than 50 percent would not do much to fill the poverty-income gap. But why not apply a higher than 50 percent rate to the pre-allowance incomes of the poor? Indeed, why not apply a 100 percent rate? The basis for not doing so is that such a high rate would have undesirable side effects. It seems reasonable to assume that a 100 percent tax rate would reduce the supply of work effort at given wage rates, although it must be admitted that there is not an overwhelming amount of empirical evidence leading to this conclusion. On the other hand, we are not aware of evidence to the contrary.

Today the only instance of a 100 percent tax rate is found in relief programs. The retirement test in Old Age, Survivors, and Disability Insurance has effective rates of 50 percent, followed by 100 percent, over a short range of earnings. The rate at which unemployment compensation benefits are reduced is generally lower than 50 percent of added wages. Reducing the rewards for extra work effort by more than 50 percent of wages is relatively rare. A few very high income earners are currently earning enough to fall into a 50 percent or higher tax bracket on part of their earnings. Studies of such earners have shown that high marginal rates appear to have a negligible effect on the amount of work effort supplied.[5] However, what is true of highly paid executives and professionals may not be true of very low income, generally unskilled, workers. Status, power, and the demands of business associates and clients may be as important as net compensation rates in determining the amount of work effort an executive or professional supplies. This is not so likely to be the case in occupations providing low pay.

High tax rates within a given income range might not be the only factor to dampen work incentives. Another factor could be the guaranteed minimum income itself.[6] Some of the poor might find that the guaranteed minimum is as high or higher than their present earnings. While it is not likely that many poor families are satisfied with their present income level, it is possible that some (probably only a few) families might be content to stop work and simply substitute the guarantee for present earnings. A similarly unknowable number of persons might, because of the guarantee, be less pressured to seek an end to unemployment or to undertake an arduous training or retraining program. Moreover, a negative tax rate would tend to reduce the dollar value of training allowances; a 100 percent tax rate would, in many cases, reduce it to zero.

What about disincentives to work, save, and invest resulting from higher taxes on the non-poor who would, of course, have to bear the net cost of the several plans reviewed above? Only the Social Dividend Plan would require a notable increase in tax rates for the non-poor. As Figure 1 suggests, a 14 percent social dividend tax on all income above the break-even level combined with the present income tax rates would make for relatively high marginal rates on taxable income for upper income families. Under such a plan, 50 percent tax rates would apply at the lowest and the upper income levels. Persons subject to such a rate would find not only wages but also property incomes, social security benefits, and private pensions significantly altered.

Would transfer-by-taxation provide an inducement to have more children? An additional child in a poor family means a $500 increase in the poverty gap and a $700 increase in unused EX-MSD. With a 50 percent negative tax rate an additional child could mean as much as $250 to $350 more in net allowance. A higher tax rate would, of course, mean higher allowances. The possible effect on the incentive to have children is even less clear than in the case of the incentive to work. Additional children in an already poor family only increases the family's poverty. The negative tax allowances do not fully offset this increase in poverty if the tax rate is less than 100 percent.

Some account must also be taken of the possible effects a transfer-by-taxation plan would have on marriage and separation rates. Simply for getting married to a person with no income, a single person who earned a break-even or lower level of income would receive a $250 increase in income if the tax rate were 50 percent or $500 if the rate were 100 percent. A more significant social problem might derive from the tax penalty which would be placed on a marriage between two single persons with disparate incomes. In some cases their combined incomes and negative tax allowances after marriage would be much lower than before. Fathers with above break-even levels of income might find that a negative rates plan so well defends their families financial well-being that they are more likely because of the plan to desert their families.

All these possible incentive effects are no doubt enhanced by a higher tax rate. Moreover, there are a number of equity problems, e.g., the urban-rural comparison, which are intensified by a higher rate. The effects are hard to appraise, but they restrain us from going beyond a 50 percent rate. In addition to provoking socially undesirable behavior, a 100 percent rate would materially alter the cost estimates. We calculate that the Welfare-Oriented Negative Rates Plan would cost $6.3 billion with a 50 percent rate and about $25 billion with a 100 percent rate.

The three plans discussed so far are designed to cover all the population. However, it could be possible to restrict benefits to some selected parts of the population. Two such categorically limited plans are discussed below.

The Child's Entitlement Plan

The Welfare-Oriented Negative Rates Plan could be modified to confine eligibility for negative tax allowances to a specific demographic group, namely, families with children. This approach could be rationalized on the basis that the present income maintenance system does less for children than other groups among the poor, that 60 percent of the members of poor families are children,[7] and that income channeled in the direction of children would represent an investment in the future. The cost of the child's entitlement, using 50 percent rates, would have been $3.5 billion in 1964.

This plan would have all the shortcomings of the welfare-oriented plan. In addition, a problem of equity between the poor with and without children would be created. Using the poverty lines and tax rates discussed above, a family's maximum allowance would jump from zero with no children, to $1,250 with one child, to $1,500 with two children. Clearly, a new schedule of allowances would be called for, and it would, unfortunately, have to be one which filled less of the poverty-income gap for families with one or two children.

The Earned-Income Supplement Plan

Public assistance, as presently designed and administered, is generally not available to families headed by an able-bodied male. Why not, then, tailor transfer-by-taxation to cover only the "working poor," who, with their families, were 24 million of the nation's 32 million poor persons in 1964 and leave the "categorical poor" to public assistance? A plan for this group would, presumably, need to pay careful attention to the problem of incentives and not so much attention to the level of the guarantee since the idea is to supplement earnings. Hence, the plan tailored for this group would provide a family of four with an allowance of $750 so long as its income was less than $1,500. In other words, a zero tax rate would apply for non-assistance income levels up to $1,500. Once the family's pre-allowance income goes above $1,500, a 50 percent rate would apply, i.e., the allowance would be reduced 50 cents for each extra dollar earned and would fall to zero net allowance when the family's pre-allowance income reaches $3,000. Eligibility for earned-income supplements would be confined to those who are not receiving P.A. In 1964, the plan would have cost about $4 billion.

The shortcomings of this plan are associated with its categorical nature. Equally poor families may be treated differently by P.A. and by the earned-income supplement. Some of the present poor might be poorer after the plan is adopted if state and local P.A. policymakers modified their eligibility requirements because of the new plan.

Alternatives to Transfer-by-Taxation

What alternatives, short of negative taxation, are there that would provide substantially improved income maintenance for the poor? On the one hand, there is expansion of and changes in the present public assistance and social insurance programs. On the other hand, new programs could be adopted, such as family allowances and a cash credit tax credit.

Public assistance. Public assistance programs are designed to meet partially the needs of certain categories of the poor.* Although the number of families receiving P.A. has grown, only about a third of poor families and a quarter of poor persons received P.A. in 1965. Many of the poor do not receive P.A. because they fail to pass the means test (which compares a budget plan of expenditures with potential resources), fail to meet residence qualifications, do not know of their possible eligibility, or are frightened off by the stigma they feel is attached to receipt of relief payments. But many more of the poor receive no P.A. simply because they do not fall into any one of the prescribed categories.

There are two general ways to increase payments to the poor by public assistance. One is to improve benefits for the established categories. The other is to open up new categories. It is not hard to imagine constructive use of $3 billion of federal funds to raise minimum benefits, make them uniform in all states, and get rid of residence requirements. It takes considerably more

---

* Old Age Assistance, Aid to the Permanently and Totally Disabled, Aid to the Blind, and Aid to Families with Dependent Children. In addition, there is the General Assistance program. At any one time about eight million persons are receiving P.A.

imagination to see how the opening of new categories would work, since one confronts the problem of what to do with the working poor. For reasons reviewed above, the reduction of benefits by an amount equal to each incre- ment of earnings cannot lightly be extended to the working poor. Hence, it would be desirable to introduce a category of P.A. recipients for whom a lower than 100 percent tax rate is applied. This would not produce equity in the sense that equally poor families before assistance are equally poor after assistance. The equity problem can only be handled by putting all categories under one plan. Pursuit of an incentive system would lead to an earned- income supplement, and a search for equity would lead to the welfare-oriented negative rates plan.

If P.A. programs were reformed along the lines suggested above, it would be difficult to distinguish the reformed P.A. program from transfer-by- taxation. True, the administration of the programs might differ somewhat, but the fundamentals would be the same. Eligibility for payments would be income-conditioned and payments more or less standardized throughout the country. An income floor would be provided for the poor and additions to earnings would not be wholly offset by reduction in P.A. payments. This suggests that reform of P.A. may be one way of achieving the goals that a negative tax plan is designed to achieve. However, it may not be the best or shortest route and would necessitate a major break with P.A. traditions.

Social insurance. Although coverage by our social insurance programs is broad, eligibility for receiving benefits is restricted to those who are aged, disabled, survivors of insured workers, or unemployed. This means that only a fraction of the poor (and the non-poor) are eligible at any given time to receive income from the social insurance programs. This is not to under- estimate the importance of the social insurances, which in 1961 were respon- sible for keeping nearly four million families out of poverty. But, like public assistance, the present social insurance approach is categorical in nature and thus of limited usefulness as a measure to reduce poverty *further*. It is, of course, possible to add new categories of insured. For example, society could insure children against the possibility of being born into a poor family. How- ever, it is difficult to insure against all the eventualities that may lead to poverty.

Some steps toward reducing the number of poor persons and families could be taken without adding to the number of present social insurance programs. For example, the level of OASDI and unemployment compensation (U.C.) payments could be raised, all aged persons and survivors could be "blanketed in," U.C. could be extended to all workers, and the period during which an unemployed person is eligible for benefits could be extended. These efforts could bring as many as seven million persons out of poverty.[8] The difficulty with this approach is that it would be extremely costly. The benefits paid could not be confined to the poor. Raising benefit levels would mean raising them for all or most OASDI and U.C. beneficiaries. It would have cost, in 1964, $11 billion in the form of a 50 percent increase in OASDI benefits to get 2.5 million aged persons out of poverty. Only about $3 billion of that amount would have been received by the poor. Thus the social insurance approach must be termed rather inefficient.

Family allowances. Some thirty nations, mostly European, have adopted systems of family allowances or payments to families with children, the purpose of which is to promote the welfare of dependent children. The rationale for family allowances is that the modern industrial system fails to accommodate for differences in family size.[9] The difficulty with the family allowance as an antipoverty weapon is similar to the difficulty with the social insurance approach. It is inefficient because payments would be made to both the poor and non-poor. The poverty gap of families with children is estimated to have been $7 billion in 1964; the gap per poor child was $470.* However, if all children under 18 (not just poor children) had received $235 a year, the cost of the family allowance plan would have been $16.1 billion, only $3.5 billion of which would have gone to those who were poor.†

Family allowances could be income-conditioned, as they are in Denmark. That is, the level of family allowance payments could be varied both with number of children and with family income, reaching zero at some specified level of family income. If such an approach were adopted it is hard to see how it would differ in substance from the Child's Entitlement Plan discussed above.

Tax credit. Suppose, instead of concentrating on transfers, we were to refund the taxes, direct and indirect, that the poor pay. Some analysts have estimated that the poor pay nearly 30 percent of their income in taxes of one form or another.[10] If the poor, in 1961, received cash payments equal to 30 percent of their incomes, 3.3 million families would have been lifted out of poverty at a total cost of $4.5 billion.[11]

The difficulty with such a tax credit plan is that it is perverse in the sense that the level of payments varies directly rather than inversely with the level of the family's pre-tax credit income. The tax credit does most for the "best-off" poor and least for the "worst-off" poor. This is so because the tax credit is a percentage of the family's income. The cash tax credit also creates a "notch" problem. If only families with income below their poverty line are eligible to receive credit, families with income just above the poverty line could increase their money income by reducing their before tax credit income to a level which made them eligible to receive a tax credit.

If the tax credit were revised to avoid perversity and to get away from the notch problem, it would be a negative rates tax plan.

* $7 billion divided by 14.8 million poor children. This means filling the poverty gap of the parents as well as that of the children.
† In 1964 there were approximately 69 million children under 18 years of age.

Conclusion

We have reviewed nine different schemes for adding to the incomes of the poor. On close examination, the number shrinks to six which are really different from one another. The tax equity and tax credit plans are only crude variants of the welfare-oriented plan; and the family allowance, if it is income-conditioned, is similar to the child's entitlement plan.

Which of the six would make "best" use of the nation's resources depends on the priority one accords each of several questions. If one asks, Which scheme will close the poverty-income gap at the least cost? then the answer is, the social dividend plan at a cost of $30 billion. If, on the other hand, one asks, Which plan does the most to close the gap per dollar spent? then the answer is not the social dividend (which pays only $12 out of $30 billion to the poor), but an expanded, still categorical P.A. or any one of three negative rates plans. Note that social insurance falls out of the running on both counts.

If we give priority to the second question, the choice is cut down to one noncategorical plan — the welfare-oriented plan — and three categorical plans, namely, improvements in P.A. which exclude the working poor, the earned-income supplement, and the child's entitlement. The noncategorical plan would cost about $6 billion and each of the others would cost between $3 and $4 billion. The choice is not necessarily an exclusive one. For example, P.A. improvements could be combined with the earned-income supplement.

A way to make the choice as set out is to ask the question, Which of the four plans causes the least deviation from an equity standard? To that question the answer is clear; it is the welfare-oriented negative rates plan. Therefore, while there is a case to be made for each of the several plans reviewed, we conclude that the strongest case is that for the noncategorical plan which would fill half the remaining poverty-income gap. The adoption of this plan, along with evolutionary improvements in existing public and private transfer programs, would constitute one important aspect of a broad-ranging war on poverty.

REFERENCES

1. See ROBERT THEOBALD, *Free Man and Free Markets* (New York: C. N. Potter, 1963), pp. 192–197, and EDWARD E. SCHWARTZ, "A Way to End the Means Test," *Social Work*, IX (July 9, 1964), 3–12.
2. See LADY RHYS-WILLIAMS, *Something to Look Forward To* (London: MacDonald, 1943), and *Taxation and Incentive* (New York: Oxford University Press, 1953), pp. 121–137.
3. Derived from *Current Population Reports*, U.S. Bureau of Census. Series P-60, No. 47 (Washington, D.C., September, 1965), Tables 3 and 4, pp. 24–25.
4. RHYS-WILLIAMS, *op. cit.;* ROBERT R. SHUTZ, *Transfer Payments and Income Inequity* (Ph.D. dissertation, University of California, 1952); D. B. SMITH, "A

Simplified Approach to Social Welfare," *Canadian Tax Journal,* XII (May–June 1965), 260–265.

5. THOMAS SANDERS, *Effects of Taxation on Executives* (Boston: Graduate School of Business Administration, Harvard University, 1951); GEORGE F. BREAK, "Income Taxes and Incentives to Work: An Empirical Study," *American Economic Review,* XLVII (September 1957) 529–549; JAMES N. MORGAN, ROBIN BARLOW, and HARVEY E. BRAZER, "A Survey of Investment Management and Working Behavior Among High Income Individuals," American Economic Association, *Papers and Proceedings,* LV (May 1965), 252–264.

6. See the study by C. T. BREHM and T. R. SAVING on "The Demand for General Assistance Payments," *American Economic Review,* LIV (December 1964), 1017–18.

7. MOLLIE ORSHANSKY, "Who's Who Among the Poor: A Demographic View of Poverty," *Social Security Bulletin, XXVIII* (July 1965), 14. "Families" exclude unrelated individuals.

8. In 1963, there were 5.2 million aged poor and 1.9 million poor persons living in families headed by an unemployed worker. ORSHANSKY, *op. cit.,* pp. 12–18, 28.

9. JAMES VADAKIN, *Family Allowances* (Miami: University of Miami Press 1958) pp. 1–4.

10. RICHARD MUSGRAVE, "The Incidence of the Tax Structure and Its Effects on Consumption," in *Federal Tax Policy for Economic Growth and Stability,* Joint Economic Committee, Subcommittee on Tax Policy, 84th Cong., 1st sess. (Washington, D.C.: 1956), Table 2, 98.

11. The estimates are derived by the authors from Subproject B of a special tabulation of the Bureau of Labor Statistics' *Survey of Consumer Expenditure, 1960–61,* made for the U.S. Treasury Department, Office of Tax Aanaylsis.

CHAPTER 16

Second Thoughts on a Negative Income Tax

George H. Hildebrand

I readily admit to finding the negative income tax a highly attractive idea. It offers a method of doing something prompt and substantial about poverty, while taking a long step toward tax equality at the same time. Nonetheless, the more I reflect on the practical implications of the scheme, the more skeptical I become. In my judgment, these emerging doubts are serious, not fanciful or trivial. Unless they can be resolved by the proponents of the plan, I hold that we should concentrate our attention on less ambitious ways to improve the present system of income maintenance and supplementation.

Variants of the Tax

By "negative income tax" I mean any form of income maintenance and supplementation based on the mechanism of the personal income tax. In essence this requires the introduction of Treasury subsidies, payable to low income households, as the counterpart of taxes paid to the Treasury by households that are better off. Technically, these subsidies are a form of transfer from government to persons. On the same definition, taxes paid are a negative transfer, as Lampman has pointed out.

The logic of the idea is unassailable and is one of the main reasons for its attractiveness. By means of exemptions, deductions, and excludable forms of income now allowed at law, Congress in effect has established a structure of minimum earned incomes, geared to family size and composition, that are exempt from income tax. However, the income must be earned by the house-

Reprinted from *Industrial Relations,* Vol. 6, No. 2, February 1967, by permission of the author. © 1967 by Regents of the University of California, Berkeley.

hold in the first place — from its labor and its property holdings. Above this no-tax limit — presently $3,000 for a family of four, with both parents under 65 and not blind — the Treasury now claims the right to share in household income, by levying taxes.[1] But as the law now stands, the Treasury has no collateral obligation to supplement incomes below that line, that is, to share its revenues by payment of subsidies. Thus, the system is both incomplete and inconsistent. The negative income tax, or better, supplementation through subsidy based on the income tax, would cure these defects. At the same time, it would reduce the present inequality of incomes among persons by using subsidies to alter distribution at the lower end, just as taxes now result in altered income distribution at the middle and upper levels.

Among the proposals now in circulation, there are two main alternative methods for determining income deficiency, both to be self-administered by the reporting family or unit.[2] One of them, originally suggested by Milton Friedman, is to find the amount by which the total value of exemptions and deductions exceeds income and then to fix the subsidy at some percentage of this excess, after deducting 50 percent of income. The other method — proposed by Lampman, Tobin, Schwartz and Theobald — is to assign every reporting unit an initial fixed allowance or credit (varied by family size and perhaps composition), to reduce the initial value of the credit by some percentage applied to income received, and then to pay out the net value (if any) as subsidy.[3] In essence, this technique substitutes an allowance for the present exemptions and deductions.

Distinction must also be made between full and fractional guaranteed income plans. With a full guarantee, if there is no other income, the subsidy is fixed at 100 percent of the designated upper limit to the range of poverty incomes, i.e., any short-fall of income relative to those limits is wholly made up. For a family of four, this amounts to $3,000 in Schwartz's proposal and $3,200 in Theobald's. By contrast, in a fractional guarantee, again asuming no other income, only part of the deficiency is covered by subsidy. For Friedman, the minimum for this size of family is set at $1,500. For Lampman, it ranges from $420 to $2,000, according to the particular variant. Tobin's minimum is fixed at $1,600.[4] Table 1 presents a systematic comparison of these proposed minimum guarantees.

It must be conceded that any version of the negative income tax involves a fiscal innovation of the first magnitude, simply because it proposes to pay out transfers in cash as an integral part of the income tax itself, rather than as social insurance benefits, public assistance payments, or subsidies of a less obvious kind (low-rent public housing, farm price supports, and so on). But from the standpoint of American socio-economic thought and policy, what is really revolutionary about the proposal are its broader implications: namely, that government should now guarantee minimum incomes and that this guarantee should be available to all poor households filing a tax return, regardless of the reasons for their poverty.

TABLE 1.   *Guaranteed Minimum Incomes Payable to a Four-Person House-hold Under Various Negative Income Tax Plans*[5]

Type of plan	Total subsidy payable	Per capita subsidy
Full guarantee:		
Schwartz	$3,000	$750
Theobald	3,200	800
Fractional guarantee:		
Friedman	1,500	375
Lampman[b]		
I	420	105
II-A	1,500	375
II-B	1,500	375
II-C	750	188
II-D	2,000	500
Tobin[c]	1,600	400

SOURCES: *Milton Friedman,* Capitalism and Freedom *(Chicago: University of Chicago Press and Phoenix Books, 1963), pp. 190-192; Robert J. Lampman, "Negative Rates Income Taxation", prepared for the Office of Economic Opportunity (unpublished, 1965), "The Guaranteed Minimum Income: Is It Worth What It Would Cost?" delivered at a conference on the Guaranteed Minimum Income, Univrsity of Chicago (unpublished, 1965), James Tobin, "Memorandum on Basic Income Allowances" (unpublished), and "On Improving the Economic Status of the Negro,"* Daedalus *(Fall, 1695), pp. 878-898; Edward E. Schwartz, "A Way to End the Means Test,"* Social Work, *IX (July, 1964), 3-12, 97; and Robert Theobald, "Free Men and Free Markets" (New York: Potter, 1963), pp. 165-201.*

EDITOR's NOTE: *Green and Lampman's article in the present symposium classifies plans somewhat differently from the method of classification used in papers cited by Hildebrand. The "tax equity negative rates plan" described by Green and Lampman in the present symposium is equivalent to Plan I in Hildebrand's table. Plans II-A to II-D are all versions of "welfare-oriented negative rates plans," while the "social dividend plan" does not correspond to any of the plans discussed in Hildebrand's paper.*

[a] *Assumes no other income received and that family files as a unit.*

[b] *Version I is based on 14 percent of excess of total exemptions and deductions over other income (none in this case). II-A through II-D are based on fractional allowances rather than deduction and exemptions.*

[c] *Based on $400 allowance for each member of reporting unit.*

To undertake such a guarantee and to make it universally available would require a decisive break with some deeply ingrained traditions: first, because at these low levels it would effect a divorce of the receipt of income from the correlative performance of labor or ownership of property; and, second, because it would make the guarantee dependent solely on the fact of income deficiency, regardless of cause. This latter element represents an innovation of singular importance. No longer would the right to assistance depend on a showing of handicaps to earning a living — such as old age, disability, or a broken home — the so-called "categorical" approach now followed, under which the able-bodied adult poor and their families are largely excluded from income maintenance.

But there is more to the formal side of the negative income tax. Any version of the idea must face up to the double nemesis of disincentive to work and total fiscal cost. What shall be done about the other income of most poor families? Shall it be offset against the guarantee, as all plans except Lady Rhys-Williams' propose? If so, what should be the rate of offset? If there is to be one, shall benefits from OASDHI or unemployment compensation, or payments from public assistance, be included within other income? And if the guarantee is to be based on existing exemptions and deductions, shall the double exemption privilege for certain persons be retained or dropped?

Any minimum income guarantee must accommodate three mutually interdependent elements: the level of guarantee itself, the rate at which income is to be offset against the initial guarantee, and the total cost of the plan. With a full guarantee, the rate of offset must be made extremely high. Otherwise leakages to those who are not poor will be substantial, and the already huge cost of the plan will become truly astronomical. To constrain cost, Schwartz adopts an average rate of offset of 70 percent of the first $3,000 of earned income, while Theobald actually proposes a 90 percent rate. But to get around awkward problems in the income range immediately above $3,000, Schwartz chooses to exempt from tax all incomes up to $4,500. In other words, to avoid resort to an even higher rate of offset, he must open up extensive array of non-poor incomes to leakages.

Furthermore, what these inordinately high offset rates would actually mean is punitive "taxes" on the labor of the some seven million who make up the working poor. In turn, this would invoke a serious disincentive effect: they would be encouraged to get out or to stay out of the labor market because the terms of trade between income from work and income from the subsidy have been made so unfavorable to remunerative labor. To the extent that these workers withdraw from the labor market, other income falls and the cost of the plan is inflated all the more.

By contrast, a fractional guarantee offers considerable relief from these difficulties, but only at the expense of providing a much smaller contribution to arising poverty incomes. The rate of offset can be made lower — for example, 50 percent of other income for Friedman, 33⅓ percent for Tobin, and variable rates of between 25 and 75 percent, according to the particular variant, for Lampman.[5] In turn, these much more modest rates of "tax" on the labor of the poor would involve much smaller disincentive effects. For this reason, as well as the much lower level of basic guarantee, the total cost of the plan can be sharply reduced. Instead of the roughly $25-30 billion required for Schwartz's or Theobald's 100 percent plan, Tobin's fractional guarantee would cost around $14 billion, Friedman's about $10 billion, if double exemptions are retained, and Lampman's various versions somewhere between $2 billion and $11 billion as estimated on the basis of 1963 data.[6]

A final consideration concerns the "step" or discontinuity problem, which emerges in the income range where transition occurs from supplementation to taxes payable. To illustrate, suppose that Friedman's plan were adopted: a family of four without other income could establish an income deficit of $3,000, against which $1,500 could be claimed as subsidy on a 50 percent basis. If, instead, the head earned $1,500, the subsidy falls to $750, and final disposable income becomes $2,250. By reason of a 50 percent rate of offset, a 2:1 relationship holds right up to $3,000 of other income, at which no net transfer is payable. Below $3,000, then, earnings from work are "taxed" at 50 percent. By contrast, each added dollar of income earned within the $3-$4,000 bracket is subject to direct income tax at 14 percent. From the standpoint of equity, therefore, the poorer worker pays a much stiffer rate of "tax" than the one who is somewhat better off. For the same reason, the distinctive effect would be greater in the low income group.

The situation might be corrected by fixing the offset rate at 14 percent which would greatly curtail the contribution of the subsidies to poverty incomes. Or the positive tax rate in the first bracket could be raised to the punitive level of 50 percent, with unacceptable consequences for incentive for those who are self-supporting and not poor. Alternatively, the offset rate could be graduated downward as income rises, to reach 14 percent on the last increment of income, or the lower end of the present tax schedule could be abolished. But descending graduation reduces the value of the transfers, while raising the level of minimum income subject to tax would mean severe losses of revenue together with substantial direct leakages to those who are not poor by official standards.[7]

Advantages of the Tax

There seems to me to be four basic reasons for the interest that the negative income tax now commands. The most obvious one of them, of course, is the rediscovery of poverty under the impetus of the civil rights movement. Another is that, compared with techniques for demand management and for increasing the productivity of the working poor, the device provides a quick and universal method for raising poverty incomes to any level desired. A third is that it seems to offer a unitary solution to the problem of income maintenance. The tax supposedly would permit us (1) to get rid of categorical public assistance and its means test, and (2) to extend and improve income maintenance, while simplifying and rationalizing it. Finally, as already noted, the proposal carries considerable technical appeal for the economist because it would complete the logical symmetry of the income tax, while achieving greater equality at the same time.

So far as our new-found impatience with large-scale poverty is concerned, it may be remarked that this sentiment began to become manifest early in the sixties, when the growth-gap problem was also paramount. It seemed easy at that time to contemplate a major new program of transfer payments, both as a means for relieving poverty and as a way to combat the depressive effects of fiscal drag on total demand.

Turning to the second factor, there is no doubt that the negative income tax is a speedy and all-inclusive method of getting cash into the hands of those who need it, one that has incidental advantages as a new form of automatic income stabilizer as well. True, a direct and perhaps even universal scheme of children's or family allowances, quite separate from the income tax, would be another method for using the transfer technique in a large way. As for demand management and efforts to improve the earning power of the working poor by vocational preparation and training and by breaking down discriminatory barriers to better jobs, we are dealing here with much slower and much less dramatic methods. But they do go to causes, rather than to the effects of poverty, for they attack one of the roots of the low income problem, that is, low earning power. By contrast, transfer approaches deal primarily with relieving the consequences of poverty. Only indirectly do these techniques promote attainment of the valuable ideal of adequate self-support, i.e., by helping the children of the poor to obtain more education.

But what about the negative income tax as a transfer device? The urge for a unitary solution to the "welfare problem" and perhaps even for all income maintenance is perfectly understandable on the part of those who are impatient with the scope and nature of present arrangements and who are profoundly dissatisfied with the results. The tax helps convert the receipt of public assistance from a matter of stigma to a matter of right and speeds the transition from status to contract.

These motives led Lady Rhys-Williams, a member of the Liberal Party in Britain, to propose universal allowances, financed through the income tax, as a total substitute for the traditional social insurances, with all their apparatus of payroll taxes and complex benefit schedules, and for payments under "national" (public) assistance. For somewhat different reasons, Friedman seems to take a similar view in his suggestions that the subsidies under his plan could replace the whole "rag bag" of existing measures. And even if one stops short of the sweeping Rhys-Williams proposal, as Lampman and Tobin do, surely there is ample room for concern about public assistance today.

For one thing, both in intent and in effect the categorical programs exclude perhaps fifteen million adults and children in families which are mostly headed by the able-bodied working poor.[8] In the main, only the small ADC — Unemployed-Parent program or locally controlled general assistance (G.A.) are available to this large group, and then only in parsimonious amounts.[9] Some grave criticisms have been made of the federal-state Aid to Families with Dependent Children (ADC) program, which covered 3.4 million children and 1.1 million adults in January 1966.[10] Monthly benefits vary greatly, ranging from $8.36 per recipient in Mississippi to $51.39 in New Jersey (national average: $34.97), mainly because they are determined by the states.[11] In 1961, two-thirds of the cases involved families with an absent father (desertion, divorce, separation, or as what May calls an "itinerant lover"). Precisely because 29 states tie eligibility to absence of the male head, the program does provide incentive to desert, although the scale of this effect is another question.[12] More serious, primitive "suitable home" policies have allowed some administrators to refuse eligibility where illegitimate children are involved — a curious example of punishing the offspring for the sins of the parents. Still worse, strict application of the means test frequently has the effect of imposing a 100 percent "tax" on earnings from work. As a result, the mother and her older children are given an incentive either not to work or to conceal such income. On another count, there is enormous community pressure to hold down costs, which restricts the admission of eligible families. There is also a legitimate interest in policing the more egregious forms of "chiseling" and outright fraud; this task has so burdened the social workers that little opportunity exists for remedial case work.[13] Clearly, no further demonstration is needed to justify careful consideration of the need to improve existing welfare policies.

Finally, the negative income tax offers some tangible advantages. If it really could be a full substitute for categorical assistance, it could replace the present 100 percent "tax" on work, although it can do so only with a fractional guarantee. It also could do much to expand badly needed rehabilitative case work. It would involve an approach to income maintenance that would enlarge the freedom of choice of the poor, because the subsidies would be paid in cash and not in kind. If the scheme is carefully designed to preserve the incentive to work, it would represent a market-oriented solution to the welfare problem. This, in turn, would be consonant with the country's traditions. However, because it proposes to make assistance generally available — a real advantage from the standpoint of relieving poverty — the plan must encompass the families of the able-bodied, whether they are employed, unemployed, or idle. At this point, a sharp conflict emerges with the popular and tenaciously held belief that the able-bodied should be required to support themselves.

This conviction comprises a central element of the individualistic system of values by which our work- and property-oriented society has been organized from its very beginnings. It is the basic reason why income maintenance in the United States rests on social insurance arrangements, in which benefits are so largely tied to past earnings and contributions, and on the categorical approach to public assistance. The linkage between earnings, contributions, and benefits is a way of recognizing alike the ideals of self-reliance and payment according to productive contributions. By its very nature, categorical assistance is an indirect means of paying deference to self-reliance, while at the same time giving acknowledgement to our Judao-Christian tradition of charity toward the unfortunate, the handicapped, and the helpless.

Obviously there is a running conflict between these two principles, which is the reason why public assistance is so often characterized by niggardliness, hostile and punitive attitudes, and spasmodic Draconian attempts to cut welfare costs. Thus it has been relatively easy to obtain pensions, tax privileges, and assistance for the aged; they can no longer work and are viewed as having already earned such provisions in the past. It has also been relatively easy to get appropriations for training and retraining projects for poor youngsters and displaced adults; such efforts are directly linked to improving personal earning power. But until the ideal of a deliberate strengthening of family solidarity can gain the same degree of social acceptance as that of self-reliance, any scheme of universal income maintenance and supplementation for the poor — be it children's or family allowances or transfers through the negative income tax — seems likely to be wrecked on the shoals of popular politics.

Disadvantages of the Tax

No feasible version would obviate the need for public assistance. Given the traditional American attitude toward public assistance and the extremely tight fiscal circumstances now prevailing and likely to prevail for some time to come, a 100 percent guarantee plan is simply out of the question. This is to say nothing of the dubious social wisdom of having the federal government, to paraphrase Lampman, make the following declaration to every poor household: "We will pay you $3,000 a year if you promise not to work; and if you insist on working anyway, we will tax your earnings at a rate even higher than that applied to a multimillionaire." This is not the way to strengthen the position of the father in the family, nor to foster the still socially valuable ideal of self-support. But it is a way to establish politically a large dependent class, readily identifiable, fully subject to stigma, and well isolated from the rest of the community.

We are left, then, with an array of proposals for a fractional guarantee. Would any of them improve on payment levels now available under OASDHI and the categorical programs and serve as a more humane substitute? Table 2 below suggests the answer, and it is largely negative.

With the sole exceptions of a single person or a couple at the minimum under OASDHI, Friedman's plan would do nothing for those now receiving some form of income maintenance and would seriously lower the positions of most of them. Tobin's version would also fall far short of present payments under assistance, except for G. A. Lampman's Version (see Table 1) would be of real help to those at the OASDHI minima, but otherwise lies well below present levels. If substituted, his Versions II-A through II-D would injure those now on Old Age Assistance, Medical Aid to the Aged, Aid to the Permanently and Totally Disabled, and Aid to the Blind; II-D would distinctly benefit families on Aid to Dependent Children and General Assistance, but II-A through II-C would not, All of these plans would aid poor households now excluded from any public income maintenance and supplementation — clearly a major gain on its own terms.

TABLE 2. Per Capita Benefits Under Existing Income Maintenance Programs Compared With Those Payable Under Various Fractional Guarantee Plans^a (Annual Value)

| Existing programs | Current average per head | Payment per head under negative income tax for those with no other income | | | | | | |
| | | Friedman^b | Tobin^c | Lampman^d | | | | |
				I	II-A	II-B	II-C	II-D
Old Age Assistance (OAA)^e	$ 941	$ 800	$ 400	$ 224	$ 375	$ 375	$ 188	$ 500
Medical Aid to the Aged (MAA)^e	2,175							
Aid to the Permanently and Totally Disabled (APTD)	1,012	450-800	400	126	375	375	188	500
Aid to the Blind (AB)	1,105	450-800	400	126	375	375	188	500
Aid to Families with Dependent Children (ADC)	420	375	400	105	375	375	188	500
General Assistance (GA)	364	375	400	105	375	375	188	500
OASDHI:^f								
Single person, minimum	528	800	528	752	528	528	528	528
Single person, maximum	2,016	800	2,016	2,240	2,016	2,016	2,016	2,016
Couple, minimum	396	750	400	606	396	396	396	396
Couple, maximum	1,512	750	1,542	1,712	1,512	1,512	1,512	1,512

SOURCES: Figures for payments under assistance programs from Welfare in Review, U.S. Department of Health, Education, and Welfare, Vol. IV (April 1966); figures for OASDHI benefits from Social Security Bulletin, Annual Statistical Supplement, XXVIII (December 1964), 25; values for subsidies estimated by the author.

a For OAA and MAA, subsidy under negative income tax assumes a single-person reporting unit. For ADC and G.A., subsidy is based on a four-person family reporting as a unit. All cases assume no other income besides subsidy, except, where applicable, OASDHI benefits. All assistance figures based on national averages.

b Assumes double exemption privilege is retained; OASDHI benefits excluded. Range shown for APTD and A.B. reflects possibility that recipient is under 65 or 65 and over.

c Tobin would exempt OASDHI beneficiaries from his plan, save that where such benefits fall below $400 the latter figure would become the minimum.

d Lampman would retain all OASDHI benefits; his Plan I retains

Assuming that any form of the negative income tax should make no poor household worse off than it is already, two conclusions became obvious. First, none of the plans can serve as an overall substitute for the existing categorical assistance program. And second, none of them would be an overall substitute for the present social insurances. In fact, all but Friedman's plan explicitly assume the retention of OASDHI and unemployment compensation. In consequence, these feasible versions of the negative income tax do not represent a unitary solution to the problem of income maintenance, either as a whole or for public assistance alone. Indeed, both Tobin and Lampman expect assistance to survive in some form. What we actually have proposed here, then, is one more addition to the present pluralistic system, an addition whose basic merit is that it would extend transfer payments at once to many millions now excluded from the system.

It is true that subsidies under these plans would be larger in some states than those now paid under the various assistance programs — in some instances much larger. But in the richer states the converse holds. The primary problem is how to make sure that supplementation by Treasury subsidies would be effective, not just *substitutes* for existing rates of payment under assistance. Since some form of assistance will continue to be needed even if the negative income tax were adopted, it is equally important to reform the old programs.

The negative income tax would not displace the means test. There are two reasons for this contention. The first is that public assistance will have to be retained. Since this is so, it will continue to be necessary to audit the income and assets of claimants, both to fix net payment rates according to schedules and to police cases of gross fraud. Local communities would accept no less.[14]

Second, if it could be a full substitute for existing public assistance, the negative income tax would still not displace the means test. Even in this optimal situation the most the device could do would be to introduce a self-administered means test, since every return must require a declaration of income. The returns filed by those claiming the subsidies would have to be checked, sampled, and audited — what else is this but a form of means test? In extreme cases, there would have to be prosecutions for fraud. And if the old principle of taxation still holds, that the higher the tax the greater the

---

double exemptions, meaning that subsidies would be added to OASDHI benefits, which are now excluded from other income. For versions II-A through II-D, his figures all apply to a family of four, converted here to per head equivalent.
e Present payments under these programs, assuming the same person was a recipient for a full year. Subsidies for both are calculated solely on the basis of income deficit. Actually, under the OAA and MAA programs, there is some possibility of overlap and a recipient may obtain payments from both programs.
f Assumes worker retires at 65 and that if there is a spouse, she, too, is 65 or over. Minimum and maximum are based on top and bottom monthly brackets under 1965 amendments, converted to annual values. Figures for couples are on a per capita basis. Figures for Lampman's plans II-A through II-D are for OASDHI benefits only. Subsidies may increase these, but the amounts could not be calculated.

frequency of evasion, then surely the higher the prospective subsidy the greater will be the incidence of fraud — another, less welcome aspect of the symmetry concept.

It would be difficult to provide adequate, regular, and frequent assistance. The basic principle of all modern public assistance is that transfer payments should be provided to help fill the unmet needs of poor households. To do this properly the degree of need must somehow be measured; payments must bear a reasonable relationship to need as determined; payments must continue to be made available in adequate amounts so long as the need lasts. How well would the negative income tax meet these criteria?

The use of some set of minimum income standards, with built-in adjustment for family size, is a simple and objective way to measure "need."[15] The difficulties begin when one considers timing. If the subsidy is to be paid after the final return is filed, then the sum forthcoming will reflect "other" income already received and the size of the family at the time of filing. Under present practice, any qualified taxpayer can claim a lump-sum refund at this point. Is the subsidy to be treated in the same way? Is it to be paid over to the filer (say the male head), perhaps to be dissipated quickly, even though the household's need is a continuing one? If not, on what legal basis can the amount be parcelled out over the next 52 weeks? Suppose, further, that the household's capacity to earn other income or to get assistance payments is reduced in the year ahead, or that it suffers heavy medical expenses or acquires twins or an aged grandmother as new dependents. Any of these events will increase current need under the means test. But if the subsidy has been fixed on an ex post basis, it will have no reasonable relationship to actual need.

Suppose, instead, that income deficiency is calculated on an ex ante basis for the year ahead or, better, by quarterly declarations. I will pass over entirely the question of how to instruct perhaps ten million inexperienced prospective filers in the delicate art of preparing a tax return. I simply say that poor households will be no more able to avoid errors of optimism and pessimism in predicting other income than anyone else. If the family overstates its expected other income, it will receive a lump sum at the end of the period rather than at the time the money was needed. If it understates income, it will have overdrawn the subsidy; it will have to settle up with the Treasury at that point — or accept a lower rate of payment for the next period. In either case, the consequence is the same: the subsidy ceases to bear any relationship to continuing current need. This difficulty seems inherent in any proposal to tie transfer payments to the mechanism of the income tax. I know of no way to get around it.[16]

Double exemptions and excludable income would disrupt the equity of the subsidies. The premise of the negative income tax is that income deficiency is the best way to measure need — a proposition that I accept. As we have seen, there are two ways to calculate the deficiency: (1) fix a flat allowance per capita and set off other income at some rate, as Tobin and Schwartz would do, or (2) gauge deficiency by the value of unused deductions and exemptions (net of other income), as Friedman does and also Lampman in his Plan I. If this second method is used and if the subsidies are actually to reflect need as so measured, a major reconstruction of present tax law becomes necessary, as Lampman recognizes but Friedman does not. Otherwise, the amounts payable will depend on critical variables other than family size, i.e., the age of family members and the type of "other" income received. In other words, it will pay to be 65 years or over and it will pay to have income deriving from OASDHI benefits and tax-exempt bond interest. The reason is that double exemptions are now awarded to the elderly (and to the blind), while OASDHI benefits (for retirement, widowhood, or disability) and interest on certain securities need not now be counted in adjusted gross income for purposes of taxation.

Consider, for example, a pair of two-person families composed of man and wife. In the first, the couple is under 65; the husband earns $1,570 as an unskilled laborer; there is no other income. Exemptions and deductions total $1,600. Deducting "other" income, their deficiency is $30. Under Friedman's 50 percent plan, their subsidy is a niggardly $15. Under Lampman's Plan I at 14 percent, it is a microscopic $4.20.

Now take the second couple, both over 65 and receiving $1,570 from OASDHI, without other income.[17] Double exemptions make their total exemptions and deductions worth $3,000. Retirement benefits need not be included as income. On Friedman's proposal, their subsidy would be $1,500, as against Lampman's $420. On the basis of final disposable income after subsidy, the first couple has only $1,585 under Friedman's plan, while the second gets $3,070, although household size and initial income are the same. The reason is that as the law now stands the subsidy would yield the elderly pair a 100:1 advantage over the working couple. Can it be seriously argued that their actual need is 100 times as great, especially with Medicare and MAA?

Looking at the matter in another way, under present law each child is "worth" $700 in exempt income, if one has the income in the first place, while each elderly person is worth either $1,500 or $1,600, depending on whether he or she files the return. Indeed, through the exclusion privilege, receipt of OASDHI benefits makes the aged person worth considerably more from the tax standpoint.

Justification for this differential treatment is not convincing, but to assault the tax privileges of the aged, many of whom are not poor on any standard, is no easier than an attack on motherhood. Yet, if equitable treatment is to be had under the negative income tax and the subsidies are to conform to the purposes of the proposal, then neither age nor type of other income should influence the size of the transfer. The problem is easily solved in principle. The real difficulty is political. It can be evaded simply by leaving tax privileges intact, as the price to be paid for getting more income into the hands of those poor who are now excluded from public assistance. However, this choice involves other encumbrances: the total cost of the new transfers might rise as much as 40 percent, there would be substantial leakages to those who are not poor in terms of "all other income," benefits would not be geared strictly to number of dependents, and the self-supporting poor would receive grossly inequitable treatment.

Partly for these reasons, Tobin would exclude OASDHI beneficiaries and abolish single or double exemptions for those who are covered by his plan. Lampman, in all versions of his Plan II, would count OASDHI benefits as income and use a flat allowance in place of deductions and double or single exemptions for determining income deficiency. Obviously this is the preferred course if the intent of the negative income tax is to be served with full integrity. But to undertake it is to open up a political hornet's nest, sufficient probably to defeat the proposal itself.

Conclusion

The weaknesses of the negative income tax fall into two classes: those that are technical and those that turn on questions of cost and ideology. Some of the technical problems probably could be overcome. The level of minimum guarantee and the rate of offset could be high enough to replace most forms of public assistance. The means test feature cannot be eliminated and will continue as long as we have public assistance. Problems concerning the timing, adequacy, and frequency of payments will be much harder to resolve. Finally, it is theoretically possible to remove the tax privileges of the aged; to set up new controls to forestall induced splitting up of non-poor reporting units and to redefine the status of dependents; and to achieve a more general reform of the law, which now permits so many non-poor taxpayers to escape so much income taxation.

Questions of cost and ideology are quite another matter. Putting the poverty-income gap at about $12 billion in 1963, a new transfer program of at least $5 billion net would be required to accomplish anything significant, with OASDHI and assistance payments unchanged. Ignoring the question of whether the country can now afford even this much, the basic difficulty is to make sure that an adequate and equitable version could be had within this limit. With removal of double exemptions and excludable income, Friedman's plan would cost roughly $5 billion, *if* there were no disincentive efforts.[18] Lampman's II-D, to me his most attractive formulation, implies a minimum guarantee of $500 per head, and could involve a net cost of anything between $2 and $11 billion depending on the extent of disincentive effects and reductions in public assistance. Thus neither Friedman's nor Lampman's plan assures a firm cost ceiling. Tobin's scheme is the most carefully drafted of all and has many attractive features. But on his estimate, it would cost at least $14 billion on 1962 data. As for the Schwartz and Theobald proposals, they would involve a net cost of over $25 billion and therefore are out of the question on this count alone.

I submit that the federal budget today cannot supply even $5 billion without substantial curtailment of other forms of expendiure. The one possibility would be to capture the needed revenue by all-out reform of the income tax law, including introduction of an equitable form of the negative income tax. I doubt that the needed reforms can be had, however, because they require the consent of the middle and upper income groups. The plea that the proceeds could be used to finance massive transfers to all of the poor, including the able-bodied, is likely to fall on deaf ears. Assistance by category is still a "categorical" imperative in our system of values. Although I prefer children's or family allowances — on a universal basis as a matter of right — to income maintenance through the income tax, I admit that they too suffer from the same political and fiscal handicaps.

If the above assessment stands up, then those of us who want to raise low incomes will have to settle for more modest immediate gains, deferring larger schemes for later and more appropriate times. This means we should concern ourselves now with reconstruction of public assistance.

Because of limited space, I venture into this subject only briefly, and even then somewhat timorously, because it is so complex. As a starting point, I take it for granted that some form of public assistance will always be needed, to fill out the interstices among the social insurances and also to supplement such benefits where they are too low. For the long term, it seems to me desirable to make need the sole criterion for eligibility, and where need is proved on clear standards, to make provision a matter of right.[19] Incidentally, this is the most that the negative income tax itself would do. Both are simply alternative ways to provide universal transfer payments to the poor.

To put public assistance on these new foundations means that the categories must go and that all the onerous existing restrictions based on age, residence, length of residence, suitable home requirements, unemployability of either parent, total and permanent incapacitation, and relatives' responsibility must eventually be supplanted. It also means a greatly increased role for the federal government in setting standards and providing grants-in-aid.

These changes cannot be accomplished overnight. For one thing, they will cost a great deal of money — out of a population of 34 million poor persons in 1965, only 7.4 million were receiving public assistance, mostly at levels below those now being recommended.[20] For another, these proposals would arouse militant opposition in Congress, whose members are responsible to local constituencies in which the traditional "Poor Law" approach finds expression in these very restrictions. Nonetheless, these objectives seem sound to me as long-term goals.

In the meantime, some practical changes can be made even in a regimen of tight budgets. The 2.1 million aged poor now on OAA might be transferred to OASDHI at corresponding benefit levels. It also may well be possible to drop MAA as Medicare and complain state programs under Title XIX get under way. The main candidate for practical reform would be ADC, and I do not underrate the obstacles here. I estimate that it would cost about $500 million to raise the *minimum* payment rate per recipient to $50 monthly (the national average is now $35). If new federal standards could be imposed, desertion or divorce as a condition for eligibility could be ended (now imposed in 29 states). It would also be desirable to allow each ADC family to earn some minimum amount of other income — initially, say, $500 — without deducting it from assistance payments. Coupling these changes to existing subventions to poor youngsters enrolled in the various job corps and training programs would achieve a substantial advance, at a net added cost of well less than $5 billion.

In counseling caution and delay regarding the negative income tax, I am not saying that it should be rejected out of hand. But I do contend that it is not demonstrably superior to a different kind of allowance system, entirely divorced from the income tax, or even to a major overhaul of public assistance. I also hold that it is a serious mistake to believe that all that the poor really need is a large-scale infusion of new money. They also require far more skilled social work as well as increased provision of other services in kind rather than in cash, for instance, education and vocational training.

REFERENCES

1. Each member of the reporting unit now has a $600 exemption. The person filing gets a $200 minimum deduction, plus $100 additional for his own exemption and a $100 deduction for each additional exemption. For those who are 65 and over or who are blind, double exemptions are awarded.

2. MILTON FRIEDMAN, *Capitalism and Freedom* (Chicago: University of Chicago Press and Phoenix Books, 1963), pp. 190–192; ROBERT J. LAMPMAN, *Negative Rates Income Taxation*, prepared for the Office of Economic Opportunity (unpublished, 1965), and *The Guaranteed Minimum Income: Is It Worth What It Would Cost?* delivered at a Conference on the Guaranteed Minimum Income, University of Chicago (unpublished, 1966); JAMES TOBIN, *Memorandum on Basic Income Allowances* (unpublished), and "On Improving the Economic Status of the Negro," *Daedalus* (Fall 1965), pp. 878–898; EDWARD E. SCHWARTZ, "A Way to End the Means Test," *Social Work, IX* (July 1964), 3–12, 97; and ROBERT THEOBALD, *Free Men and Free Markets* (New York: Potter, 1963), pp. 165–201.

3. The allowance approach was initiated by Lady Rhys-Williams in England in her pamphlet, *Something to Look Forward To* (London: MacDonald, 1942). As originally formulated, her scheme proposed a weekly national dividend in cash for everyone except those unemployed who refused suitable employment. See also, LADY RHYS-WILLIAMS, *Taxation and Incentive* (New York: Oxford University Press, 1953), pp. 120–149.

4. LAMPMAN also considers a full guarantee at $3,000 or $3,130, but has objections to going this far.
5. Lampman's Plan II-A calls for a 50 percent rate; II-B, for 75, 50, and 25 percent on successive increments of $1,000 of other income; II-C, for a zero rate on first $1,500 and 50 percent on second $1,500; and II-D for 75 percent on first $1,500 and 33 perecnt on next $1,500. The high initial rates in II-B and II-D are intended to discourage small amounts of work by the very poor and their children, while much lower rates in the higher brackets are aimed at encouraging incentive among the adult working poor who are already partially or fully self-supporting.
6. Based on 1962 or 1963 income and poverty data.
7. Tobin's flat allowance with a uniform 33 1/3 percent rate of direct tax on all amounts of other income in the lower and middle brackets is the nearest solution. But observe the consequences: for a family of four, net subsidies would be paid all the way up to $4,800 of other income, and taxes due on the present schedule would be reduced on all incomes between $4,800 and $6,289 by using the allowance as a tax credit. Furthermore, Tobin estimates total leakage to the non-poor at $3.2 billion.
8. There are three competing hypotheses to account for the low incomes of the able-bodied poor: (1) by reason of monopsony—monoply, they do not get full marginal products; (2) by reason of a network of imperfections in the labor and capital markets, they do not get a fair chance for an education and to compete for better jobs; or (3) they are at the low end of a Gaussian distribution of native endowments. The main explanation probably lies in (2) and (3). If (3) is significant, it follows that increased income maintenance must be the basic approach. For the same reason, unionization and higher minimum wages are irrelevant, as well as down-right harmful, to the poor on economic grounds.
9. Incomplete figures for January 1966 show only 715,000 recipients of G.A., with per capita payments of only $30.36 monthly on the average. Averages by state range from $3.94 monthly in Arkansas to $68.74 in Maryland. *Welfare in Review,* IV (April 1966), 38.
10. Many of these charges have been reviewed and appraised by EVELINE M. BURNS, *Social Security and Public Policy* (New York: McGraw-Hill, 1956), pp. 86–89; EDGAR MAY, *The Wasted Americans: Cost of Our Welfare Dilemma* (New York: Signet, 1965), pp. 47–66; and MAURINE MCKEANY, *The Absent Father and Public Policy in the Program of Aid to Dependent Children* (Berkeley: University of California Press, I, 32–40.
11. *Welfare in Review,* IV (April 1966), 35. ADC now includes a small "unemployed parents segment" and a foster-care program. It began in 1935 as a successor to earlier measures to aid widowed mothers.
12. Whether the program fosters illegitimacy is also another matter. May contends that about 25 percent of the children involved are illegitimate, but this is not necessarily the effect of the program itself. As he suggests, the begetting of illegitimate children is about the worst example of the profit motive in action in the world, since it "pays" an average rate of return of only $35 a month.
13. The profession is badly unpaid, overburdened by case loads, and usually not adequately trained—all evidence of its low social esteem.

14. In my judgment the case against the means test has been seriously overdone, identified as the test is with the parsimonious "Overseer of the Poor" of earlier times, and with the British dole under "supplemental alowances" to the permanently unemployed of 1931. In fact, the test can be made no more obnoxious than a credit application. Federal standards could be introduced or improved to insure a more humane use of the test, mainly by reducing the discretion of the investigator and the traditional tie to relatives' responsibility. Granted, it would be ideal if we could eschew the whole distasteful business. But this is just not in the cards until American society is ready to accept some kind of universal allowance system, "as a matter of right."

15. Except that need depends also on differences in living costs. The Social Security Administration calculated its poverty income minimum at $3,130 for an urban family of four (1964 prices) and at $2,190 for a farm family of the same size. Under the negative income tax, both families would get the same cash grant, given the same amount of other income.

16. On some of these points, see THOMAS K. HITCH, "Why The Negative Income Tax Won't Work," *Challenge* (July–August 1966), pp. 13–15.

17. Average retirement benefit in 1964 for worker and his wife at age 62 or over. *Social Security Bulletin, Annual Statistical Supplement,* XXVIII (December 1964), 29.

18. This calculation is for 1963 data, assuming deductions and exemptions of $750 each for 35 million poor people, and accepting Lampman's figures of $4 billion in OASDHI benefits paid to the poor only. Total deductions and exemptions then amount to $26.2 billion; "other income" is $16.4 billion ($12.4 billion in earnings, on Internal Revenue data, plus $4 billion OASDHI); total deficiency is $9.8 billion, and half this becomes subsidy at the 50 percent rate.

19. See *Having the Power, We Have the Duty,* Report of the Advisory Council on Public Welfare to the Secretary, U.S. Department of Health, Education, and Welfare (Washington, D.C.: 1966). See also, ELIZABETH WICKENDEN and WINIFRED BELL, *Public Welfare: Time For a Change* (New York: New York School of Social Work, Columbia University, 1961).

20. *Having the Power* . . . p. 8. This report provides an eloquent and cogent statement of long-run principles for rebuilding public assistance. However, I can find no estimate of total costs. On a rough estimate, about 15 million out of 34 million poor persons in 1965 received neither public assistance payments nor social insurance benefits, nor both together. To provide this large, excluded group with $500 each in yearly assistance would require $7.5 billion, assuming no disincentive effects and allowing nothing for increased payments to those now on assistance. The omission of cost figures may have been deliberate. To supply them on the basis of an ultimately desired minimum income standard would have crippled the report's practical appeal. To base them on what is feasible for the budget would imply endorsement of a much lower standard, which also would be undesirable.

Part 6

Aiding the Poor Through the
Labor Market: Minimum Wages
and Manpower Programs

Editor's Survey

This chapter focuses on two different ways of affecting poverty through the impact upon the lower range of labor incomes (or the complete lack of such incomes) that emerge from the workings of our economy. The selection by Kaufman and Foran examines the role of minimum wage legislation in anti-poverty strategy. It is clear that raising the minimum wage without instituting other policies to create new jobs or upgrade skills can do nothing for the income levels of the unemployed. Indeed, such action may reduce some workers' incomes by eliminating jobs. Only those workers who remain employed (and for about the same number of hours per year) will register unambiguous gains from hikes in the minimum wage.*

Thus, just as when Alfred Marshall wrote on the same subject, a key issue in evaluating changes in the minimum wage revolves around the amount of unemployment which will thereby be created. Kaufman and Foran deal with a number of studies which have been addressed to the question of the wage and employment effects of minimum wage legislation. Yet few of the studies have utilized modern statistical techniques for dealing with economic data. One such study, carried out several years ago at the International Labor Office, confirmed Kaufman and Foran's conclusion from their survey of the literature, but found substantial differences in the way minimum wage changes were absorbed by different industries. Since industries differ in the elasticity of demand for their products, one of the large areas of diversity was in the price and output response to changes in minimum wages. For those industries where prices could be raised with only modest impacts upon demand for the goods produced by that industry, then the impacts upon employment (and

* This may not be the whole story. If wage differentials between skilled and unskilled workers (the bottom range of whom are directly affected by minimum wage) tend to be re-established over time, then workers far above the minimum wage level may also gain. This is again subject to the proviso that their jobs and hours are not adversely affected.

hence the industry's wage bill) would be less severe. In other industries with more elastic demand, the total wage bill might even be reduced. Perhaps, even when all the economic evidence is in, the level of the minimum wage remains a largely moral issue: are there some jobs that pay so badly that a wealthy society can live without them? If so, should we be prepared to support those who previously relied upon them for their livelihood, meagre as it may have been?

The manpower programs of the sixties antedate the general anti-poverty campaign. In a sense, this nation has always had manpower programs of one sort or another, usually focused on the supply of skills viewed as critical to national strength (i.e., military officers, skilled craftsmen, or Bachelors of Arts). The earliest programs of the last decade centered upon a different group — those threatened by unemployment due to technological or economic change. Only as they evolved did these programs come to have the "disadvantaged" as their major concern. By the end of the decade, some progress had been made toward the integration of manpower programs (particularly training programs) into the broad stream of poverty programs. Simultaneously, there was a move toward greater involvement of the private sector in the provision of training and the creation of new jobs for the disadvantaged.

Some idea of the growth of Federal involvement in manpower programs is obtained by comparing 1969's funding level of $2.5 billion with the figure for 1961, which was roughly one-tenth as large. The lessons to be learned from this decade of experience are summarized in the paper by the National Manpower Policy Task Force. There are in the literature any number of articles evaluating the success or failure of particular programs; the Task Force's significant contribution is to identify the economic conditions required for manpower programs to succeed.

CHAPTER 17

The Minimum Wage and Poverty

Jacob J. Kaufman and Terry G. Foran

Introduction

This paper examines the relationship between legislated wage minima and poverty. This is certainly not a novel context in which to view minimum wages since the Fair Labor Standards Act of 1938 stated that:

> It is hereby declared to be the policy of this Act, . . . to correct and as rapidly as practicable to eliminate . . . labor conditions detrimental to the maintenance of the minimum standard of living necessary for health, efficiency, and general well-being of workers.[1]

In 1966, 28 years after the original Federal legislation, Congress amended the original Act for the fourth time by raising the minimum wage and extending its coverage. Its objective, as stated by the Congressman who brought the House bill from committee to the floor of the House, was: "this new reason for this legislation [is] the living power of our working people."[2]

From its inception up to the present the federal legislation in this field has been concerned primarily with the elimination of poverty. If raising the minimum wage would eliminate poverty, then the only argument remaining would be that of values. It is interesting to note that, according to one survey, 61 percent of university economists opposed the amendments to the minimum wage law even though 88 percent favored the so-called "War on Poverty."[3] Apparently, the majority thinks that minimum wage legislation is an inadequate tool for the elimination of poverty.

The primary concern of this chapter is the investigation of the role of a minimum wage law as a vehicle for the elimination of poverty. No attempt is made to compare the efficacy of such legislation with other measures which

Reprinted with omissions from Sar A. Levitan, Wilbur J. Cohen and Robert J. Lampman, editors, *Towards Freedom from Want,* (Wisconsin: Industrial Relations Research Association, 1967), by permission of the publisher and authors.

are, or might be, employed to fight poverty. Such an undertaking is beyond the scope of the present paper.

The poverty group includes persons 65 years of age or older; residents in rural-farm areas; nonwhites; families headed by females; families headed by persons with limited education; and, the unemployed. To the extent that a minimum wage affects the individuals in these categories, it will have an impact on the structure of poverty. This paper, therefore, investigates the impact of minimum wages on unemployment in general and, where possible, on unemployment of the disadvantaged groups. The ability of minimum wage legislation to raise wages and affect income distribution is also examined. As background to these problems a brief description of the legislation in this area is in order.

The Objectives and Theoretical Considerations of Minimum Wage Legislation

Federal Legislation

Minimum wage legislation has a long history, both foreign and domestic. Although the Fair Labor Standards Act of 1938 (FLSA) contained statutory minima, the administrator was allowed some discretion, reflecting, in part, a concern over the adverse employment effects of such legislation and an interest in spreading available work. The latter objective is revealed in the overtime provisions of the law.

It is important to point out that the coverage of the Act, even with its most recent amendments, is not universal and excludes certain industries engaged in interstate commerce and all industries engaged in intrastate commerce. There are about 41.4 million workers presently covered by the FLSA. Those covered are primarily nonsupervisory employees. The excluded nonsupervisory employees fall into the following categories: outside salesmen, domestics, agriculture, retail trade and services. Others not covered by the Act are: self-employed; governmental workers; unpaid family workers; and executive, administrative, and professional employees.

The minimum wage was originally set at 25¢ an hour in 1938. It was increased to 75¢ in 1949. The 1956 amendment raised it to $1.00. The 1961 amendments raised the wage of previously covered workers to $1.15 in 1961 and to $1.25 in 1963. The timing of the increases for newly covered employees was more gradual. The same is true of the timing provided for by the 1966 amendments. For the previously covered workers the legislated floor was raised to $1.40 in 1967 and will be increased to $1.60 by February of 1968.

The purpose of including this brief wage chronology is twofold. First, it provides a benchmark for later discussion, and, second, it demonstrates the concern on the part of advocates of the minimum wage over the possible unemployment effects of raising wages. The planned gradual wage increases attest to the fairly well grounded belief that too large an increase in the minimum wage might have serious unemployment repercussions.

State Legislation

Complementing the federal minimum wage legislation — in fact antedating it — is the minimum wage legislation in the individual states. Today, 38 states, the District of Columbia, and Puerto Rico have such laws. At first blush, it would seem that the state laws possess certain desirable qualities which are superior to the federal law. First, the federal law cannot consider the particular economic status of every state. Any given state may be justified in setting a minimum above that set by the federal government because of a better than average "economic condition." Second, a state may legislate a minimum for workers not covered under federal law. Third, more than one-third of the states set minima utilizing the wage board system, rather than setting a statutory minimum. This permits greater flexibility, particularly with respect to "area" conditions, than is provided for by the Fair Labor Standards Act. State minimum wage laws are capable, if properly formulated and conscientiously executed, of far greater flexibility than the federal law.

Unfortunately, the apparently superior avenues open to the states have been inadequately realized.

of the 40 jurisdictions with laws: 14 jurisdictions apply only to women and/or minors and do not cover men.
15 do not set a statutory rate.
3 states do not have minimum rates in effect for any occupation.
15 jurisdictions have statutory rates lower than $1.25 an hour.[4]

For example, New York which has one of the most enlightened minimum wage programs requires approximately 18 months to bring to fruition a wage order once it has been conceived.[5]

The New York law does, however, complement the federal law by covering employees outside the stipulations of the latter. The wage board system also enables the New York minima to account for "zone differentials," so that different wage floors exist in different areas in accordance with the different economic environments.

Theoretical Considerations

The standard argument of minimum wage proponents is that it raises the wages of the poorly paid and, therefore, boosts their incomes. Opponents retort that "It's better to receive a low wage than no wage at all," suggesting that a legislated minimum wage eliminates jobs. Although the arguments as stated in this fashion appear rather simple, they do, however, succinctly summarize the major area of conflict. This has been the primary issue in the literature to date. But it is not the only pertinent question. One question which does not appear to have received adequate attention is: What is the combined effect of the wage change and the employment change? That is, what is the effect on labor's share? This question is probably most relevant to the poverty problem.

Under competitive conditions each worker is paid the value of his marginal product. Therefore, given a normally downward sloping demand curve for labor, a minimum wage will cause the least efficient workers to be laid off, unless certain conditions hold. Although these conditions will be discussed below, at present, assume the competitive state.

Minimum wage regulation is not universal. Its coverage applies to specific industries within the economy, although it is likely that part of its effect is similar to that which would be generated from a general regulatory wage. The effect of the minimum wage as a specific regulatory device is the same as that which occurs from a decline in demand for labor in particular sectors:

> In this case, it is not the unemployment which is economically speaking, the most significant effect of regulation (in an extreme case, where the affected firms are abnormally prosperous, and the rise in wages is only just sufficient to prevent their expanding employment or to diminish their expansion, there may be no net unemployment due to the regulation); the important effect is the redistribution of labor — the fact that some men are prevented from securing employment in a trade where they would be better off than they are otherwise condemned to be.[6]

However, if there are no industries available or suitable to absorb the unemployed, then the unemployment created will not be of a temporary nature. This unemployment "must go on until the artificial wages are relaxed, or until competitive wages have risen to the artificial level."[7] Realistically, the former alternative may be discounted.

It is probably more realistic to assume, in light of the type of regulation provided for in the Fair Labor Standards Act and its evolution, that, if competitive conditions hold, there will be some redistribution of labor; but more predominantly there will be unemployment which will be eliminated only with the restoration of preexisting wage differentials. This is due to the imperfect mobility of labor, and the trend toward greater coverage under the federal minimum wage law.

Given the present assumptions, then, one can expect a certain amount of lengthy unemployment as a result of an increase in the minimum wage. The question thus becomes "how much unemployment?" This question really breaks down into two questions: (1) What percentage of workers lose their jobs? and (2) How does the increased unemployment compare to the increase in wages? The first is the traditional query; the second is relevant to the total wage bill, or labor's share.[8]

In the short-run, both answers are given by the elasticities of the relevant demand curves for labor. The relevant demand curves are the industry demand curves, because of the assumption of competitive conditions and, more realistically, because of the manner of coverage stipulated in the Fair Labor

Standards Act and its amendments. The elasticity of the short-run demand curve for labor will depend on the technique of production, the demand for the product, and the supply curves of other (non-fixed) factors. The two pertinent factors for discussion are output market elasticity and percentage of labor cost to total cost, because they are the only factors amenable to empirical investigation. The more elastic the demand curve for labor the greater the unemployment which will result from any given wage increase. The demand curve for labor will be more elastic the greater the percentage of labor cost to total cost and the more elastic the demand for the product sold by the industry.

The evidence seems to indicate that those industries primarily affected by minimum wages have both a relatively high percentage of labor cost to total cost and have relatively elastic product demand curves. Four out of the five industries surveyed by the U.S. Department of Labor after the increase in the minimum wage in 1950 possessed a degree of monopoly power well below the average for manufacturing. As a general rule, the lesser the degree of monopoly the more elastic the product demand curve. A comparison of the lowest paying industries in 1954 showed that five out of the six had below average degrees of monopoly, and above average relative labor costs.

In general, the labor demand curves in those industries affected by minimum wage legislation will be more elastic than in other industries. This statement is made on the basis of the only observable parameters affecting these curves. The implications for employment changes and labor's share in the short-run are clear. Adverse employment changes will be relatively large and labor's absolute share will decline. These changes will be accentuated, the higher the minimum is above the old wage in any particular industry. If these assumptions are valid, the long-run results are the same. First, the increased ability to substitute factors increases the elasticity of the demand for labor. Thus, machinery may be used to replace labor. Second, certain types of product lines may be dropped because they are no longer profitable. Third, the least efficient firms in the industry may find their demise hastened by the added burden imposed by the minimum wage rate.

To what extent are these conclusions modified by relaxing the implicit assumptions of the above analysis? If the relevant laborers were not operating at peak efficiency before the establishment of the minimum wage, it is possible that they may subsequently do so, thus increasing their productivity and preventing unemployment. The only plausible reason for this occurrence is the spur of theatening unemployment. This particular influence, however, will probably not be great enough to save many jobs.

The second assumption to be dropped is that of the maximizing firm. This calls for the introduction of the standard textbook "shock effect." The basic premise underlying the shock effect is that management is too lazy and content to bother maximizing. The minimum wage thus "shocks" management out of its lethargy with the higher costs. It begins to alter its technique of production in an effort to cut costs, thus increasing worker productivity and preventing unemployment. However, as pointed out by Stigler,[9] and as argued above, the industries primarily affected by minimum wage legislation are, by and large, competitive and have a higher percentage of labor cost to total cost. Thus, it is unlikely that the managements in these industries have overlooked opportunities to minimize labor costs.[10]

In this same context, it might be noted that if one accepts Hicks' theory, then any sort of "shock" received by management as the result of a wage increase will result in "induced" innovation, as the result of the change in relative factor prices. "Its effect on the marginal productivity of capital is bound to be much more favorable than its effect on the marginal productivity of labour."[11] In other words, the types of inventions adopted because of higher minimum wages can be expected to be of a labor-saving type and, as such, they will have the least effect upon mitigating unemployment. The impact of this type of innovation would be to reduce labor's share.

A second factor which might mitigate against the unemployment effects of higher minima is the existence of monopsony in the labor market. When an employer has monopsony power he finds it necessary to increase wages to hire additional workers. If he cannot discriminate among his employees he must not only pay the new higher wage to the worker just hired, but also raise the wage of his other workers. Because of this, his additional labor cost of hiring one more worker is greater than the wage paid to that new worker. This will constrain the employer from hiring further workers. The effect of a minimum wage set above the old wage will, within a certain range, eliminate this constraint because now the cost of a new worker is simply the wage rate he gets paid. The result of this may be that a minimum wage will cause no unemployment and may even cause more workers to be hired.

However, it is unlikely that the monopsony element exists to any degree in the low-wage areas covered under the Wage-Hour Act, and if it does, it is unlikely that a nationally set minimum will fall within the relevant range in many cases.

The primary emphasis of empirical studies on the effects of minimum wage legislation has been on the relevant labor market variables. A brief analysis of the possible effects of such legislation on non-labor market variables is in order.

It has already been pointed out, or implied, that the effects on the firms in the economy will be, in the absence of technological change, higher costs, higher prices, lower profits, and the possible elimination of some of the more inefficient firms.

It is also argued by some that minimum wage legislation may contribute to inflation (1) via the cost-push mechanism and (2) via an increase in demand, on the assumption of a redistributed income. One study has pointed out, however, that "The wholesale price index remained stable through the last two increases in the minimum, and only recently has started to rise, at a time when there was no increase in the minimum. . . . The slight upward trend in the index of consumer prices, which may largely reflect an upward bias in the index, has shown no jump following increases in the minimum in the past. Increases in the past year certainly cannot be attributed to higher minima in 1961 and 1963."[12]

If the inflation argument is eliminated, so is the argument that an increase in the minimum wage is injurious to our balance of payments. If it does aggravate the problem, the damage is minor. Given the more powerful tools available to combat this problem, it is difficult to envisage the use of "not-passing-a-higher-minimum-wage" as a policy instrument to correct the balance of payments.

It is, of course, possible that increases in the minimum wage do contribute to, rather than cause, inflation. This, however, would be difficult to verify empirically. Even if this is the case the question to be considered is whether this cost — undoubtedly slight — offsets the benefits derived from legislated wage floors.

Impact Studies on Minimum Wages

There is no question that the immediate impact of raising minimum wages is to increase the wage of covered workers. There is also little question that given a once-and-for-all increase, pre-existing differentials eventually will be reestablished. There may also be an almost immediate increase of the wages of non-covered workers due to personnel policies and a worker efficiency rationale. From the preceding discussion it has been shown that there will be some unemployment under a static situation. This unemployment will be greater, if entire firms are forced out of business, to the extent that they themselves are not dissolved by merger, and to the extent to which their shares of the market are lost to the industry. Further, this unemployment may either be accentuated or alleviated by technological changes introduced by the affected firms. The questions with regard to unemployment, therefore, are how much and for how long.

Naturally, the economy is not as static as is the theory. The difficulty of isolating the effects of minimum wages in a dynamic economy is obvious. Nonetheless, scholars, after stating this, proceed to do the best that is possible under existing conditions. It is to this research that we now turn.[13]

The first minima were the 25¢ and the 30¢ hourly rates, and finally the 40¢ hourly rate. In this early period there were not many special studies conducted to determine the impact of the legislation. "Of the 690,000 workers estimated to be receiving less than 30¢ an hour in the spring of 1939, 54 percent were in the South."[14] At the time, in the southern fertilizer industry, 17 percent of common labor was receiving less than the minimum. About 55 percent of the common labor in the cottonseed crushing industry was also below the minimum. The increase in average hourly earnings in this industry between 1937-38 and 1939-40 was 30 percent. The wages of the unskilled workers rose more than the skilled. Despite a period of rising prosperity, employment decreased 19 percent. The indications were that, after the imposition of the minimum wage, labor-saving machinery was adopted in the industry.

The seamless hosiery industry was also rather severely affected by the initial minimum. Comparing employment in the industry for the first 9 months of 1938 with the employment for the first 9 months of 1939, it was found that employment was 10.1 percent higher in the later years for the industry as a whole but 7.4 percent less for those establishments which were paying an average hourly wage below 25¢ before the minimum was set. Most of the plants which suffered the greatest declines were in the South. "Over the two-year period (1938-1940) employment in northern plants increased by 4.9 percent but decreased 5.5 percent in Southern plants."[15]

The firms in the industry made the predictable adjustments, following the legislation, of introducing labor-saving machinery and altering existing equipment to produce new lines of products.

The U.S. Department of Labor planned a rather extensive study as a follow-up on the 1950 increase to 75 cents per hour. This study was focused primarily on five low-wage industries: southern sawmilling, fertilizer, men's dress shirts and nightwear, men's seamless hosiery, and wood furniture. Unfortunately the Korean War intervened, disrupting the economic forces then at work in the United States. "As a result, only the more immediate, short-run effects of the 75-cent rate — those occurring during the comparatively stable economic climate of first half of 1950 — are determinable with any degree of clarity."[16]

The results of the 1950 increase as presented by the U.S. Department of Labor are essentially of a standard nature. The wage impact was greatest in those industries with the lowest average hourly earnings at the beginning of the period. For example, in the short period covered by the study the increase in average hourly earnings was 16 percent in southern sawmilling, as opposed to a very small increase in wood furniture. Wage increases were also correlated with low wage regions — primarily the South.

There was, in addition, an indirect impact on the wages of workers getting paid above the minimum but this was quite small. This would indicate that a personnel policy of maintaining an internal equilibrium wage structure was not in effect in industries affected by minimum wage legislation. In three of the industries surveyed, no unemployment declines due to the higher minimum were apparent.

Peterson, using the 1950 survey and supplementary data and utilizing more sophisticated techniques, did not arrive at the same conclusions. In men's seamless hoisery he obtained a correlation coefficient of — .476 (significant at the 1 percent level) between percentage changes in average hourly earnings and percentage changes in manhours. "This relation does not appear to be explainable in terms of prior seasonal or cyclical patterns."[17] In men's cotton garments Peterson also found a negative correlation between the two variables, although it was not significant. There is a definite indication that low-wage plants suffered less favorable employment changes than high-wage plants. By disaggregating the Southern sawmill industry by type of mill and by state, Peterson again found a relationship between wage increases and adverse employment effects.

The 1950 study of the U.S. Department of Labor also noted a plant mortality of about two percent in men's dress shirts and southern sawmills. It is not at all clear whether or not these events were caused by the minimum wage or by other influences.

The next set of studies undertaken by the Department of Labor was designed to determine the impact of the $1.00 minimum wage. The major part of the survey program was directed toward 12 manufacturing industries which were known to come under the impact of the new increase.

In all of the industries studied there was an increase in the average hourly earnings immediately following the wage increase. These increases ranged from 5.3 percent to 21.7 percent. The wage structures in the industries were compressed, and the immediate indirect impact on the wages of non-affected workers was small. The re-establishment of pre-existing differentials was not particularly in evidence in the short-run. The evidence indicates that employers began to re-establish the differentials in the second payroll period following the increase in the statutory wage; this was continued into the third payroll period. In other words, the restoration of an equilibrium wage differential following the impact of a legislated disequilibrium is a slow process.

There did not appear to be any effect on workers in non-covered industries as a result of the wage increase in other industries.

The employment effects were adverse in all but one of the twelve industries, with employment declines ranging from 3.2 percent to 15 percent in the year following the increase in the minimum. A very small percentage of plants interviewed stated that the discharges were the result of the higher minimum wage, nonetheless the evidence is fairly convincing that this was the case. Certainly declining demand, inefficiency, substitution of machinery, or whatever reasons might have been offered by those interviewed, would not negate this conclusion.

The survey found that there were various degrees of non-wage adjustments by plants in eight affected industries and it is probable that some of these were precipitated by the minimum wage increase. It would be impossible to determine how many.

Richard Lester disagrees with the interpretation given above of the results of the B.L.S. study on the $1.00 minimum wage. Lester bases his disagreement primarily upon two tables which he has constructed. The first table presents the employment changes in the "high-impact" establishments as a percentage of the employment in all establishments in the study. "Thus, employment changes in high-impact establishments are being compared with employment

changes in lower-impact establishments in the same sections of an industry."[18]
Looking at Lester's table the employment changes are negative in 9 out of 13
observations. Admittedly a few of these declines are small. However, it would
seem that the table, if anything, supports the conclusion of adverse employment changes created by increased minimum wages.

Lester's second table compares percentage changes in employment with
percentage changes in earnings among high-impact, middle-impact, and low-
impact industries. With 24 observations (using overlapping time periods)
employment changes are negative in all but two instances. While it is true that
the data "do not lend much support to the notion that a forced increase in
the minimum wage will soon lead to a reduction in a firm's employment *in
proportion to the relative size of the wage increase,*"[19] they do, nonetheless,
add strong support to the hypothesis that an increase in the minimum wage
will create unemployment.

Utilizing traditional data sources, such as the census of manufacturers,
Kaun has conducted a study covering the post-war period from 1947 to 1958,
which included the increases to 75¢ and $1.00.[20] On the assumption that the
low-wage industries would be most significantly affected by the statutory
increases, Kaun found that there were greater increases in the capital-labor
ratio over the period in those industries assumed to be primarily affected by
minimum wages. Minimum wages cause a decline in labor intensity as a result
of the substitution of capital for labor. Kaun also found that there were
definite adverse effects on the number of establishments in five low-wage
paying manufacturing industries.

The latest studies conducted by the U.S. Department of Labor are significant in that they, for the first time, due to the extension of coverage of the
1961 amendments, deal with the impact of minimum wage legislation on
non-manufacturing industries (specifically retail and wholesale trade). They
also, for the first time, attempt to assess the degree of influence of the maximum hours or overtime provisions of the Act.[21]

The 1961 amendments required the payment of time and one-half for
hours in excess of 44 per week effective in September 1963 and after 42 hours
the following September. The study cited covers only the first of these. The
minimum wage of $1.25 was made effective in the newly covered establish-
ments in 1961.

In the aggregate, there was no decline in employment in retail trade as a
result of the 1961 increase. In fact, there was an increase in employment.
Nevertheless, within certain categories and within certain regions (particularly non-metropolitan areas of the South), there were declines in employment.

There appeared to be a general shortening of the work week in retail trade,
despite being newly covered under F.L.S.A. and with, as yet, no overtime
coverage. This result, as well as the increasing employment, is neither consistent with the conclusions derived from static theory nor is it consistent with

previous studies on manufacturing. It is possible that the decline in the length of the work week may have been due to an anticipation of the impending overtime coverage so that a number of these establishments may already have begun adjusting their work procedures and recruiting the necessary additional work-force. This would also partially explain the growth of employment. This latter is probably better explained in terms of the generally favorable economic environment surrounding retail trade at the time of the increase.

The effect of the overtime provision would necessarily be small when finally instituted in 1963. In a matched sample study, in 1962 only 12 percent of employees were working beyond 44 hours a week. This percentage then decreased to 10 percent in 1964. The greatest declines were in the South and in non-metropolitan areas, which also had the greatest proportions of persons working overtime.

Minimum Wage Legislation and Its Impact
Upon Disadvantaged Groups

Existing evidence indicates that younger and older workers, women, workers with little education, and nonwhite workers are "disadvantaged" in today's labor market. These people carry the burden of unemployment and poverty. The concern over poverty in recent years has drawn attention to these particular groups. Since minimum wage legislation is considered a tool to combat poverty, it is not unusual that attention has been drawn to its possible impact on the disadvantaged.

If minimum wage legislation causes adverse employment effects, then it seems to follow intuitively that these disadvantaged groups of workers will be most harmed by legislated wage floors. A number of economists have recently attempted to bolster their intuition with evidence. These include Arthur F. Burns, Milton Friedman and Yale Brozen.[22]

It is the contention of Friedman and Brozen that a disequilibrium wage differential has been created by the minimum wage law and its subsequent amendments, thus creating unemployment of covered workers.

> The damage that has been done by the minimum wage has been caused, in large part, because the minimum has risen faster than the average manufacturing wage. The significant period is the last decade, 1955-1965, in which the minimum wage went up 67 percent while the average manufacturing wage went up only 40 percent.[23]

This is the first stage in the argument. The second stage is to single out the disadvantaged groups who are primarily affected by the disequilibrium in the wage structure created by the increased minima.

Friedman asserts that "The fact is — it can be demonstrated statistically — the minimum wage rate is a major cause of Negro teenage unemployment." This statement is supported with a chart graphing the unemployment rates for white male teenagers and non-white male teenagers. "It leaves out girls — and girls as we know always raise special problems." The chart shows "how a small gap opened up between unemployment rates for Negro and white boys in 1949-50, when the minimum wage was being increased from 40 cents to 75 cents. It closed temporarily during the Korean War emergency — so that in 1951-54 unemployment rates were about the same for both groups. But, at the end of the emergency, this small gap opened again. And then a much larger gap emerged. Today the unemployment rate is over 22 percent for nonwhite boys and under 12 percent for white boys." "This difference emerged all at once in 1956 and '57 — with the 1956 increase in the minimum wage rate from 75¢ to $1.00 an hour."[24] Following this demonstration another graph is presented showing that a similar gap was created after 1956 between unemployment of adult males and teen-age males.

It may very well be that a disequilibrium wage differential is created by minimum wages and that this disequilibrium is the cause of teen-age unemployment, and more specifically, Negro teen-age unemployment. However, if such a disequilibrium exists, it is argued that it is overstated by the authors cited; and if it increases the rate of unemployment of disadvantaged workers, a better demonstration will be required as proof than that which has been offered.

The measure of wage differential disequilibrium employed by Friedman and Brozen is the relationship between the minimum wage and the average wage in manufacturing. They examine wage rates rather than wage costs. In other words, the argument should be the relationship of the minimum wage to total employee compensation. It is probably the case that those people being paid the minimum wage do not receive as much in additional benefits as the more highly paid workers. Whereas the average manufacturing wage increased by 40 percent over the period 1955-1965, annual employee compensation per employee increased by 53 percent over the period. If this latter figure is employed then the differential disequilibrium postulated is not as drastic as it appears: the minimum wage increased 67 percent during the period. The figure of 53 percent is undoubtedly exaggerated for two reasons: (1) it is a yearly total and (2) it includes salaried workers as well as wage earners. The greater increase in this figure is not due completely to the salary component, however, because the wage and salary category increase was substantially less over the period. As for the fact that the figure is not an hourly figure, it appears that the total number of hours worked in manufacturing did not increase significantly over the period. The relevant figure probably lies somewhere between 40 percent and 53 percent.

Accepting the statement that the minimum wage has risen faster than the average hourly labor cost in manufacturing, it remains to be determined whether or not this disequilibrium has generated the results described by Friedman and Brozen.

In the period covered by Friedman and Brozen (1948-1965) there occurred four separate increases in the minimum wage — in 1950, 1956, 1961 and 1963. After the increases in 1949 and 1956 a gap widened between the rates of unemployment of white and nonwhite teenagers (male). The increases in 1961 and 1963 did not widen the already existing gap. With regard to the comparison of teenagers and adults (males) the gap was widened in 1956: it was not adversely affected by the two subsequent increases. With the increase in 1949, the unemployment gap between the two narrowed rather than widened. In summary, with 4 observations, Friedman's contention shows up statistically 2 out of 4 times in one comparison; 1 out of 4 times in the second, and appears to be repudiated in at least one instance.

The bulk of the case presented by Friedman and Brozen relies on the minimum wage increase of 1956. Therefore, the following discussion is concerned with this period.

One must, of course, grant the fact that women have "special characteristics," but which one of these "special characteristics" is that it makes them immune to an increase in unemployment due to an increase in the minimum wage? For it is only on this basis that one has a rationale for excluding them from a study of this type. From 1956 to 1957 female white teenage unemployment rose from 8.9 percent to 9.4 percent whereas for nonwhites in the same category the unemployment rate fell from 21.6 percent to 18.9 percent. The adult female unemployment rate rose from 3.7 percent to 3.8 percent over the 1 year period and the teenage female unemployment rate rose from 10.2 percent to 10.5 percent. These data indicate that the increase in the minimum wage in 1956 created no significant widening of the unemployment gap in Friedman's categories among the female members.

Turning now to the juxtaposition of white vs. nonwhite teen-age unemployment among males (W.T.M. vs. N.T.M.) it might be pointed out that the type of statistic cited lends itself to a particular type of distortion. The finer the categories are drawn in this type of analysis, the greater the impact of the absolute change on the percentage change. From 1956 to 1957 unemployment of N.T.M. increased by 8,000 and by 28,000 in the category of W.T.M. In terms of percentages this translates into an increased unemployment of about 3 percent for N.T.M. and only about 1 percent for W.T.M. Even though the absolute unemployment created over the relevant period was distributed between the two groups in almost precisely the same proportion as it had been distributed before the increase in the minimum was put into effect, the unemployment *rates* indicate a worsening of the N.T.M. employment status relative to the W.T.M.

The point of this discussion has been to suggest that the use of unemployment rates in this case obscures the relative movements of absolute unemployment. When both comparisons are made, the minimum wage argument of Friedman is somewhat weakened.

Turning now to the second comparison made by Friedman and Brozen, that between adult males (A.M.) and teenage males (T.M.), one finds the gap between the two unemployment rates widening by about 1½ percentage points from 1956 to 1957 and by almost 3 percentage points from 1956 to 1958. This divergence, as a matter of course, is attributed to the implementation of the minimum wage increase of 1956. From 1948 to 1954 the labor force population of T.M. was declining but in the period 1955 to 1957 there was an increase of 5.7 percent. In contrast, throughout the early period, the labor force of A.M. increased steadily and in the 2 year period from 1955 to 1957 it increased by only 1.6 percent. Thus, the widening of the unemployment gap between the A.M. group and the T.M. group may well have occurred in the absence of a minimum wage increase after 1956 because of the greater number of teen-age males who began to seek work during this period, relative to the increase in the number of adult males looking for work.

One might counter this argument by proferring the possibility that the increased number of teen-agers might still have been able to find employment if the barrier of the new minimum wage increase had not existed. However, one study shows not only an increase in the number of teen-agers in the labor force not hired in 1956 but also a decline in the number of job vacancies.[25] Further, it cannot possibly be argued that the decline in job vacancies was caused by the new minimum wage increase because the decrease occurred in the professional and managerial category and the skilled category, and subsequent to 1957 in all categories but the professional and managerial. Something other than the increase in the minimum wage was affecting employment adversely in 1956 and the years immediately following.

From the second quarter of 1956, the economy was following the road to recession: the inventory-sales ratio was increasing, investment in inventories was declining, and total output had leveled off. These changes would certainly dictate a degree of unemployment independent of a minimum wage increase.

The major changes in unemployment in Friedman's charts occur during the recession itself. The widened gap between N.T.M. and W.T.M. which occurred in 1949 and 1950 also took place during a downturn in the economy. In addition, this widening gap occurred *before* the minimum increase became effective, and began to narrow once it had become effective. It is not a new proposition that unemployment rates for the disadvantaged workers are the most greatly affected by downturns in economic activity. As pointed out before, one of the major reasons for this is difference in population size.

The major point is that out of 8 possible instances and with 4 increases in the minimum, Friedman and Brozen can cite only 3 of these instances to support their contention that Negroes and teenagers are the ones who suffer most from such increases. Of these three cited instances, one is not valid (1949-50) because the gap between the two groups compared actually narrowed after the increase. The two instances left are for the years 1956-58, a period of recession or almost recession. The general economic conditions existing in 1956 were such as to create the unemployment which resulted.

It may very well be, however, that the increase in the minimum wage in 1956 did add to the relative unemployment changes. If this is the case, it still remains to be demonstrated. The only instance where the minimum can possibly have had a definite adverse influence on the disadvantaged segments of the labor force under discussion was in the years 1956-58. The changes in these years are explainable without recourse to a change in the minimum wage; and this phenomenon of the effect of recession on disadvantaged workers is in evidence throughout post-war cycles. If the minimum wage does have the independent impact claimed, why then is this impact not in evidence with every increase? It is not only that the supposed impact occurs only in recession, it does not even occur in *every* recession. There appears to be nothing in the data to substantiate the claims of Friedman and Brozen.

In support of the above argument a recent study paper on "Employment Gains and the Determinants of the Occupational Distribution of Negroes" found, using multiple regression analysis, that "Given the coverage that existed until 1967, minimum wages have played no part in the deteriorating employment picture for teen-age vis-à-vis adults or Negro teen-agers vis-à-vis white teen-agers. While the minimum wage variable is significant for adult Negro males, the size of the effect is small. . . . The income effects obviously outweigh the employment effects although the individuals who receive the income gains are not the ones who lose their jobs."[26]

The Minimum Wage and Income Distribution

It has been asserted that "The manipulation of individual prices is neither an efficient nor an equitable device for changing the distribution of personal income."[27] It is of course true that a higher wage rate does not necessarily yield an adequate income. Nevertheless, it is one of the primary ingredients. In fact, wage income is the primary source of income of low-wage families. In 1955, 63.4 percent of the income of non-farm multi-person families with incomes under $4,000 was derived from wages and salaries. In 1964, of the 47.5 million families with incomes under $3,000, about 50 percent had one family member employed and 20 percent had 2 family members employed. In other words, a good deal of the poverty which exists today is wage related.

Therefore, if minimum wage legislation is a factor in redistributing factor shares in favor of labor, one possible inference might be that it is effective in redistributing the personal distribution of income toward the low income classes. A redisribution of income in favor of the low income classes is usually defined as alleviating poverty. If it can be shown that minimum wages do alter the personal distribution of income through its influence on factor shares in the manner suggested then it must be considered an effective weapon to combat poverty.

One major difficulty with this simple proposition is that the necessary data are not available to test it empirically. The least aggregative data available on labor's share is on the S.I.C. 2 digit classification level. The Labor's Share data utilized below are from Schultz and Tryon.[28] One caveat with respect to the data is that the employee compensation figures used to derive the estimates include both wages and salaries, so that a change in "labor's share" can be attributed to an increase in the salary component. The earnings and employment statistics are those presented in the B.L.S. series.

The basic assumption made for purposes of this analysis is that those industries which in 1947 had the lowest average hourly earnings would be the industries most affected by minimum wage increases. In other words, it is assumed that the dispersion of wages about the average is the same in all industries. It might be noted also that the B.L.S. average hourly earnings data include overtime hours, so that the changes in earnings figures used in the correlations below may be affected by this factor. There appears to be no relationship between amount of overtime and basic rates in the data, however, so that any bias which might exist is indeterminate.

Rank correlations were used because of the smallness of sample and the historical nature of the data. The value for the correlation of levels of earnings in 1947 (lowest to highest) against changes in labor's share for the period cited (highest to lowest) was +.691 which is significant at the 1 percent level. The relative increases in wages for the period correlated against wage levels was not significant (+.196). If anything the sign of the coefficient would indicate that the higher paying industries experienced greater relative wage increases. Despite this, however, the low paying industries seemed to experience the smallest increases in employment: the rank correlation between wage levels and employment changes was +.327 (significant at the 5 percent level), indicating that the higher paying industries had the greatest increases in employment, or that the low wage industries experienced the least amount of increased employment over the period.

The conclusion must be then that the increase in labor's share in the low wage industries was not the result of increased labor productivity or product demand pulling up wages. The evidence of small employment changes indicates, to the contrary, that the relative wage increases, although not necessarily the highest in manufacturing were the result of a cost-push factor.

The villain most commonly sought in the case of a wage-push mechanism is unionism. Correlating wage levels in 1947 with degrees of unionism yields a coefficient of +.503, which is significant at the 1 percent level, and indicates that the higher paying industries have the greatest degree of unionism; or, conversely, that the low paying industries had the least amount of unionism. Such a correlation detracts considerably from unionism being the explanation of the cost-push factor in the low wage industries. Another possible, and traditional explanation is the contagious nature of union increases; i.e., the "sympathetic pressure" which transmits wage increases in the organized sector to the unorganized sector. This factor, however, is to be doubted as an explanatory variable in the present case. If union wage increases in the high paying firms were transmitted to the low paying firms, then the percentage increases in the latters' wages would be greater. The evidence indicates that this is not the case for the period under study in which the low wage industries did not have greater relative wage increases.

A third possibility is that minimum wage legislation was a causal factor in the wage-push in the low wage industries in the post-war period, and that the result of this wage-push was a greater increase in labor's share than occurred in other, less affected industries.

One might ask at this point why did labor's share show the greatest increases in those industries with the lowest wage increases and the greatest amount of unemployment. In the short-run, a wage increase will result in an increase in labor's share. The more elastic the labor demand curve, the greater will be the resulting unemployment. As was argued earlier the more concentrated (monopolistic) industries will have the more inelastic demand curves. The high paying industries are the more monopolistic industries and, during this period, granted the greatest wage increases. The rank correlation between 1954 levels of concentration and wage changes for the period under consideration was $+.450$ and significant at the 1 percent level. Relative elasticities of labor demand, in the face of wage increases, easily explain the antithetical movement of employment and labor's share. In other words, the more elastic labor demand curves in the low wage industries would necessarily create more unemployment than in the high wage industries (with inelastic demand curves) for the same relative wage increase, and might very well do the same for differing relative wage increases.

In the long-run it can be argued that (assuming monopoly and size are synonymous) : (1) there is more scope for the utilization of machinery in the larger firms; (2) large firms are able to purchase machinery at lower prices than smaller firms, because of a better bargaining position; (3) small firms are limited in their access to capital, whereas large firms are not.[29] In light of these considerations, one might expect that the larger firms are more readily able to innovate. Granting Hicks' argument that these induced innovations tend to be of a labor saving nature, they will provide for the employment of more labor.

Thus, both in the short-run and the long-run, the low-wage industries of the economy appear suited to the translation of minimum wage increases into a higher labor share and it is possible that they have done just that.

The connection between this increased labor's share in the low wage industries of the economy and the personal distribution of income is at best tenuous. In fact from 1947 to 1961 the percentage of total family income accruing to the bottom 2/5 of consumer units fell from 16 percent to 15.6 percent, a slight movement toward greater inequality. If minimum wages have been effective in the manner postulated a movement toward greater equality in the distribution of income would be expected.

One explanation offered for the relative stability of the post-war personal distribution of income is that an increase in the wage and salary component tending to create more equality was offset by an increased share of wages and salaries going to the top 10 percent of consumer units. This latter development being primarily due to the increased number of high income salaried managers and professionals.[30]

Thus, the possibility presents itself that the increased labor share evidenced in low wage industries may be due primarily to an increase in the salary component. However, it is equally possible that this increased labor share is at the lower end of the distribution, but is not reflected in the personal distribution because it has been outweighed by the factors creating inequality.

This brief study of labor's share is far from adequate. In large part this is due to the paucity of appropriate data. The correlations above do not unequivocally demonstrate that minimum wage legislation has increased labor's share. However, they do hold out a fairly strong possibility that this may have been the case, and further that, even though this may not have created an increased equality in the distribution of income, it may have helped prevent a movement toward greater inequality.

Conclusion

The nexus between minimum wages and the problem of poverty is not easily demonstrated. The connection runs from increased wages through changes in employment to the aggregate effect of both on labor's share, and the effect of this on the personal distribution of income. Also important is the consideration of who the individuals are who are most affected by these changes.

The conclusions of this paper — which, it must be stressed, are not all conclusive — are:

(1) minimum wages raise the wages of workers;

(2) minimum wages create adverse employment effects, but there is no strong evidence that this unemployment is unequally distributed toward the "disadvantaged" groups in society;

(3) minimum wages may very well have the effect of redistributing income in favor of labor, thus creating a tendency toward less inequality in the personal distribution of income.

Many argue that the number of "poverty" families affected by minimum wage hikes is a small proportion of the total "poverty" category. This, however, is not a relevant argument. Granted, there are more efficacious means to eliminate poverty, but no comprehensive program is available. Social security goes *part* of the way; unemployment compensation goes *part* of the way; all welfare measures go *part* of the way; and minimum wage legislation goes *part* of the way.

Of all these means of eliminating poverty, the minimum wage is the only one which does not impair worker incentives. In fact, it will increase the

the incentive to work in most instances in a way that a negative income tax cannot be expected to do.

As with any other measure designed to reduce poverty, the benefits to society which result from a rise in the minimum wage must be weighed against the costs to society. This paper has attempted to point out these benefits and costs.

REFERENCES

1. Sections 2 (a) and 2 (b) Fair Labor Standards Act.
2. John H. Dent (D-Pa.), *Congressional Record,* vol. 112, No. 85, p. 10740.
3. *Business in Brief,* no. 68, June 1966, issued by the Chase Manhattan Bank. 79 percent of Business Economists opposed the legislation.
4. State Minimum Wage Legislation: *A Weapon in the War on Poverty,* U.S. Department of Labor, Women's Bureau (Washington: June 1966), p. 6.
5. I. Lubin and C. A. Pearce, "New York's Minimum Wage Law: The First Twenty Years," *Industrial Labor Relations Review,* January 1958, p. 206.
6. J. Hicks, *The Theory of Wages,* 2nd ed., (London: Macmillan & Co., 1964), p. 180.
7. *Ibid.,* p. 181.
8. This discussion has ignored the question of a minimum wage setting a barrier to the expansion of further employment. This is, of course, an important aspect of the impact of a minimum wage. To the degree that a minimum wage causes workers to lose jobs, it must *a fortiori* be a barrier to further employment.
9. G. Stigler, "The Economics of Minimum-Wage Legislation," *American Economic Review,* June 1946, pp. 358–363. Reprinted in W. Bowen, *Labor and the National Economy* (New York: Norton & Co., 1965), p. 43.
10. For a point of view different from this see the argument of R. Lester, *Economics of Labor,* 2nd Edition (New York: Macmillan, 1964), pp. 516–518.
11. J. Hicks, *op. cit.,* p. 204.
12. *Legislative Analysis,* American Enterprise Institute (Washington, 1966) p. 10.
13. At the outset of this discussion, it should be stated that much of the writing on the impact of minimum wages is in the nature of summarizing the studies that have been done. This discussion is in part a summary of summaries. For the sake of expediency the following borrows heavily the summaries printed in:
    (1) Peck, *Economic Factors in Statutory Minimum Wages* (Washington: The Legis. Ref. Ser., L. of C. 1948).
    (2) J. F. Maloney, "Some Effects of the Federal Fair Labor Standards and upon Southern Industry." *Southern Economic Journal,* July 1942, pp. 15–21.
    (3) H. Weiss, "Economic Effects of a Nationwide Minimum Wage," *Industrial Relations Research Asociation, Proceedings,* 1956, pp. 154–166.
    (4) H. M. Douty, "Some Effects of the $1.00 Minimum Wage in the United States," *Economica,* May 1960, pp. 137–147.
14. Maloney, *op. cit.,* p. 17.
15. See H. M. Douty, "Minimum Wage Regulation in the Seamless Hosiery Industry," *Southern Economic Journal,* Oct. 1941, p. 184.

16. *Results of the Minimum-Wage Increase of 1950,* U.S. Department of Labor, Wage and Hour and Public Contracts Divisions (Washington: 1954), p. 2.

17. J. PETERSON, "Employment Effects of Minimum Wages 1938–1950," *Journal of Political Economy,* October 1957, p. 429.

18. R. LESTER, *op. cit.,* p. 520.

19. *Ibid.,* pp. 523–524. Emphasis added.

20. D. KAUN, "Minimum Wages, Factor Substitution and the Marginal Producer," *Quarterly Journal of Economics,* 1965, pp. 478–486.

21. *An Evaluation of the Minimum Wage and Maximum Hours Standards of the Fair Labor Standards Act,* U.S. Department of Labor (Washington: 1965) and "Report Submitted to the Congress in Accordance with the Requirements of Section 4 (d) of the Fair Labor Standard Act," U.S. Department of Labor (Washington: 1963).

22. Burns' discussion appears in ARTHUR F. BURNS, *The Management of Prosperity,* Columbia University Press, New York, 1966, pp. 46–48. Burns' arguments echo those of Friedman and Brozen explored below.

23. YALE BROZEN AND MILTON FRIEDMAN, *The Minimum Wage Rate* (Washington: The Free Society Association, Inc., April 1966), pp. 46–47.

24. *Ibid.,* pp. 11 and 13.

25. See ELEANOR A. GILPATRICK, *Structural Unemployment and Aggregate Demand* (Baltimore, Maryland: The Johns Hopkins Press, 1966), Table 46, p. 158.

26. L. THUROW, paper presented in Madison, Wisconsin, May 12, 1967.

27. G. STIGLER, *op. cit.,* p. 44.

28. U. S. Congress Joint Economic Committee, *Prices and Costs in Manufacturing Industries,* Study Paper No. 17 (Washington: GPO, 1960).

29. TIBOR SCITOVSKY, "Economic Theory and the Measurement of Concentration": *Business Concentration and Price Policy,* National Bureau of Economic Research (Princeton, N.J.: Princeton University Press, 1955), p. 130.

30. W. AVRIL, *The Size Distribution of Income in the U.S.: 1947 to 1961.* An unpublished Master's Thesis at The Pennsylvania State University, 1965.

CHAPTER 18

The Nation's Manpower Programs

National Manpower Policy Task Force

I. The Status of Manpower Policy

Manpower policy is aimed at developing and using the capacities of human beings as actual or potential members of the labor force. Although its central operational field is the labor market, manpower policy also has a bearing upon economic, education, and military policies, not to mention programs in welfare, antipoverty, and urban development. In fact, there is a manpower dimension of almost every aspect of economic, social, and political policy.

In most of these policy areas, manpower problems are but one aspect— albeit important—of the decisions our society must reach. Education, for example, has many purposes beyond preparing people to be workers. Learning enriches human life, shapes attitudes and values, extends knowledge, makes better citizens, and prepares man for leisure. Yet all would agree that education also helps develop the skill, knowledge, and motivation that enable individuals to participate in the labor force. Thus, manpower considerations are a crucial element of education policy.

Economic policy likewise has concerns broader than the employment or utilization of workers. Yet, as the Employment Act of 1946 declares, the United States is committed to maintaining high employment levels. Today there is broad consensus that manpower considerations must play an important part in economic decisions. As an example, the 1964 tax reduction was initiated primarily to stimulate economic expansion and reduce unemployment.

Reprinted from "The Nation's Manpower Programs," a position paper of the National Manpower Policy Task Force, Washington, D.C., January 7, 1969.

Insofar as poverty may be alleviated and diminished by creating jobs and educating, training, or upgrading the members of poor families, manpower policy is centrally implicated. It is also involved in programs to provide people on welfare incentives to seek and hold jobs.

Likewise, a viable science policy requires selection, training, motivation, and effective utilization of high-level professional manpower. The military, too, is centrally concerned with manpower. As the nation's largest employer, it is a major participant in the building of the nation's manpower policy. The armed forces draw upon the country's pool of manpower and operate a massive training organization which has a far-reaching impact on the nation's labor force.

As the scope of manpower policy is broad, so the policy-makers are many and diverse—including employers, unions, school boards, local, state, and federal agencies, colleges, and voluntary organizations. As a result, no single, consistent, or cohesive strategy has emerged—or perhaps can emerge—for developing and utilizing human resources in the United States. Manpower policy comes in pieces, and pieces do not fit easily into a neat pattern.

Most experts agree that our manpower policy should be directed at the full range of problems. They differ not over the broad objectives of manpower policy, but over methods of implementation, the amount of effort which can be mounted to attain the desired goals, and the most effective instruments for coordinating and integrating a wide array of efforts. The 1969 manpower policy agenda for the new Administration and Congress centers on the above issues.

A successful manpower policy requires the recognition of several basic principles:

1. A high level of effective demand, maintained through appropriate monetary and fiscal policies, is the single most important condition for a succesful manpower policy.

2. Education, housing, health, transportation, welfare, and manpower policies are interdependent, yet we know little about the trade-offs among them. In some respects these policy areas are competitive and in others complementary. Careful judgment is required in allocating funds among them.

3. The interdependence of rural areas and cities must also be recognized. Economic development of rural areas, for example, can reduce in-migration to already congested urban areas. Moreover, the manpower policies of one area affect, and in turn are affected by labor patterns in other localities.

The change in Administration offers new opportunities and challenges based on the experiences of the past years. It is our conviction that the three highest priority manpower problems are:

1. Providing adequate jobs for the competitively disadvantaged.*

* EDITOR'S NOTE: Only that part of the Task Force statement dealing with the disadvantaged is reproduced here, although one should be aware of the relationships between these problem areas. Some military programs, for example, have trained the disadvantaged.

2. Developing the talents and abilities of the entire labor force, but with emphasis on longer-term professional, technical and skilled personnel; and

3. The manpower aspects of military requirements.

Though these problems will confront the new President as soon as he assumes office, his freedom of action will be sharply restrained by the realities of the current political and economic scene. Therefore, we set forth only those recommendations which we consider to be of highest priority. Some are immediately actionable. Some can be implemented only over a longer period of time. Some are aimed at improving the efficiency of current spending. Others would require a realignment of spending priorities at existing expenditure levels; still others would require increased expenditures.

II. Programs for the Disadvantaged

Even with the high level of employment since 1965 and with 96.5 percent of the labor force working,* there still remain serious unemployment and related manpower problems:

1. Unemployment levels of nonwhites remain approximately twice the average rate:

2. Unemployment of youth about three times this average;

3. Unemployment of nonwhite youth double the rate for white youngsters;

4. High incidence of unemployment in central cities and in depressed rural regions;

5. High incidence of unemployment among the undereducated, particularly undereducated youth; and

6. Several million persons living in poverty despite their demonstrated commitment to self-support because they hold low-paying jobs which, even at full-time, full-year employment, pay too little to raise them above the poverty threshold.

Excessive unemployment among the disadvantaged during a period of continuing prosperity is itself a serious social problem which may have grievous consequences. The Kerner Commission on Civil Disorders reported that, in the 20 riot-torn cities it studied, unemployment and underemployment were among the deepest and most intense grievances in Negro communities — second only to police practices as a source of bitterness. Full employment in the ghetto would not completely solve this nation's urban problems, but no solution which neglects the consequences of unemployment will be efficacious.

It would be a serious mistake, however, to consider hard-core unemployment as an exclusively Negro problem. Even in the poverty areas of the larger cities, there are almost as many unemployed whites as Negroes; and nationally, among the long-term unemployed (15 weeks or longer) there are about four times as many whites as Negroes. Unemployment also contributes

*EDITOR'S NOTE: January 1969.

significantly to poverty, although most poor families are headed by persons who are unable to work because of age, disability, or home responsibilities.

In the 1930s, when one of four workers was without work, it was obvious that the fault lay with the economy rather than the individual; now, with widespread talk of labor shortages and unfilled jobs, the public tends to believe that anybody who is unemployed doesn't want to work. Yet high unemployment among certain groups suggests strongly that these present-day unemployed, like the masses of workers in the 1930s, are largely the victims of labor market forces over which they have little control.

Looking ahead to the next four years, we must take account of the effects of the Vietnam war on employment and unemployment. Since mid-1965, the size of our armed forces has grown by 700,000 men, most of whom were taken from the civilian labor force or would have joined it if the war had not intervened. Careful estimates indicate that the growth of defense expenditures since mid-1965 has directly increased civilian employment by about one million. Nearly 60 percent of this increase has occurred in blue-collar occupations, although in 1965 only a little more than 40 percent of total employment was in such occupations. Unless appropriate measures are taken, the employment prospects of the disadvantaged may become more severe when the demands generated by the war decline. Returning war veterans and released war production workers may not experience excessive difficulty in obtaining jobs, but they will make it even more difficult for disadvantaged groups to find employment. If, as all of us hope, the Vietnam war is phased out, the labor market outlook is for rising competition for available lower-level jobs and increasing hardships for those who, in a peacetime economy, are among the last-hired and the first-fired. Communities concentrating on military production will also face substantial problems of adjustment.

A Review of Current Programs

Jobs for the disadvantaged must continue to be a high-priority manpower objective. Because substantial experience in these matters has accumulated during the 1960s, it is well to review and evaluate that experience for the lessons it holds for the future.

The Manpower Development and Training, Economic Opportunity, Vocational Education, Vocational Rehabilitation, and Social Security Acts have spawned a variety of programs which are more valuable as experiments than as permanent administrative structures. The Manpower Development and Training Act is the most effective and most popular. It has proved the ability of remedial basic education and skill training to enhance the employability of ambitious but under-prepared people. The skill centers developed under MDTA represent a new concept in remedial institutions.

The Neighborhood Youth Corps in-school program enables poor youth to earn money and stay in school. The summer program may provide a measure of "riot insurance" by keeping these young people off the street in the absence of anything better to do. The NYC out-of-school program offers needed income but adds little to employability, a fact which suggests that a substantial training component should be added to the program. The Job Corps has developed better ways of training extremely disadvantaged youth, but it has not proven that the high expense of residential facilities was necessary, other than for those from areas of sparse population.

The Work Experience and Training Program, designed to provide training or useful work experience to welfare recipients and other adult poor, left much to be desired. Yet it demonstrated the potential contribution of a public employment program in depressed rural areas — where older, immobile, illiterate workers with obsolete skills have no alternative earning opportunities, and where community services and facilities are largely lacking. Operation Mainstream capitalized effectively on this experience by providing useful public service jobs for older workers. The New Careers program has opened a limited number of subprofessional jobs to the most able of the poor. Its progress has been slow, administration complex, and resistance considerable. Its potential is uncertain but should be further explored. Special Impact, designed to promote job development in areas with concentrations of low-income people, has been implemented in only a few pilot projects, and returns from these isolated efforts are not in yet.

The Job Opportunities in the Business Sector program, sponsored by the National Alliance of Businessmen, is also new. Difficulties notwithstanding, the impressive commitment of many businessmen and their companies in hiring and training the disadvantaged lend promise to the program. Interest has grown out of a sensitive combination of social concern, publicity, subsidy, and labor shortage; maintaining it may prove somewhat arduous. The Administration should be aware that any substantial rise in unemployment will make participation untenable for companies with regular employees laid off.

The more successful of these programs have been seriously under-financed. Of far more value than launching new, untried efforts would be the identification of such successful existing manpower services and the commitment to bring their budgets more closely in line with needs.

The 1967 amendments to the Social Security Act may be viewed as a new departure in Congressional support of manpower policy. Through these amendments, Congress expressed its belief that persons on welfare should be encouraged to accept training and employment.* To this end, Congress approved a new incentive system whereby people who accepted training or employment while receiving assistance could retain part of their additional income. Moreover, Congress acted to expand daycare centers to encourage mothers with young children to accept training or employment. While the

---

*EDITOR'S NOTE: This trend has been continued by President Nixon's Family Assistance proposal, given in Chapter 2.

primary motivation was the hope of arresting the rapid increase of people on public assistance, Congress, for the first time since the passage of the Employment Act of 1946, took cognizance of the choice which society should make: either people should be offered the chance to work or they should be supported out of public funds.

We recommend that the experience of the newly-instituted Work Incentive Program (including the associated supportive services) be carefully monitored and evaluated, because it provides the first large-scale effort to relate part- and full-time work to income supplements.

While the magnitude of the manpower programs during the 1960s was modest, these efforts have enhanced the employability and improved the employment of enough persons so that the potentialities of concerted efforts cannot be questioned. And the necessity of governmental participation is conceded. In this short time, new problems have been identified, the needs of previously neglected groups have finally been recognized, and the Employment Act's commitment of "maximum employment, production and purchasing power" has been interpreted to embrace job access for persons able and willing (even if not seeking) to work.

Much of the legislative foundation for a wide-ranging manpower policy already exists, and constitutes a major resource for the future. In the relevant House and Senate committees, legislators and staff members of both political parties have developed great interest and considerable expertise in manpower policy issues. Among such knowledgeable members, sophisticated discussion and critical evaluation of programs can now take place.

A single Manpower Administration in the Labor Department has gradually been forged during these years. While many manpower activities are handled by other agencies, and while relations with state and local officials need improvement, the essential mechanism for the administration of manpower policies has emerged. Some necessary changes in the Employment Service have also occurred. While the Manpower Administration still needs much improvement, progress to date is a triumph of patience and leadership.

Financial incentives and community interest have combined to enlist the active involvement of many major business enterprises in recruiting and training of disadvantaged workers. A number of non-profit organizations — such as the community action agencies, Opportunities Industrialization Centers, Workers Defense League, and the Urban League, and such business enterprises as Mind, Inc. — have meanwhile appeared on the scene with specialized personnel, capability, and interest in training and other manpower activities. A number of labor organizations have expanded their interest and capacity for training. The supply of university manpower specialists has grown considerably, forming a vital contribution to improvement of public and private manpower programs.

Many problems have yet to be overcome. Short-term, crisis responses to perceived needs have tended to crowd out the longer-range fashioning of coordinated policies, programs, administrative mechanisms, personnel, and relationships among levels of government. Because specific services are tied to discrete programs, applicants have often been forced to fit program molds rather than receiving a variety of services tailored to their individual needs. Nor have the great diversities in local conditions been sufficiently recognized in formulating or implementing programs. Administration and agency publicity have all too often generated expectations which outran the allocated resources. Also, too little attention has been directed, for example, to developing a system of data collection and interpretation which would provide a sound basis for program design and evaluation.

Lessons from the Experience

For all of these problems, those involved need offer no apologies. Hindsight shows that all the programs could have been improved, but who could have done better by foresight? The present challenge is to apply the lessons of these years to develop a coherent manpower policy, not just for the moment but for the 1970s and beyond.

The first lesson is that at the local level, where people are located and must be served, available manpower services should be provided on the basis of need, not impeded by diverse eligibility requirements, varying administrative practices, or competing agencies. The separate programs must be fused into a single comprehensive federal manpower program — providing a variety of services in varying mixes depending upon national conditions and local need, preferably funded by a single federal source.

This means that each community should have a single contact point within reach of each individual, to dispense all services, or refer the individual to places where needed employability services can be obtained. A one-to-one relationship is frequently required between the individual and a skilled counselor, so that an effective plan can be worked out, attuned to the individual's needs and preferences as well as the realities of the labor market. The counselor must be able to furnish or obtain the necessary services, whether remedial basic education, training, a sheltered job, a pair of eyeglasses, or day care for young children. Such counselors, and other staff, will not appear by chance, and their recruitment and development must be an integral part of the manpower program. Evaluation must be continuous and thorough, assuring that successful programs expand and that mediocre or substandard efforts are quickly terminated.

In the past decade of experimentation, federal initiative stimulated programs, and problems were approached nationally. National objectives and policies, reflecting the aggregate of individual and community needs, are important; but unique problems occur within states, communities and job markets whose conditions differ widely. We must now build upon trends already under way to strengthen the capabilities of communities and states to plan their own manpower programs to implement national objectives with the financial support and technical assistance of the federal government.

Because state governments have traditionally been rurally dominated and unfamiliar with urban problems — and because many urban problems were new to everyone — the rush for action has tended to bypass the states in favor of direct federal-community relations. A new modesty born of experience admits the limits of federal administrative capability, while mayors and governors are increasingly asserting themselves and demanding a more direct role in the planning and delivery of services. Many of the urban areas flow across state lines in a vast, formless interdependency. These city-states need a new federal-metropolis relationship. But these are relatively few and there are simply too many cities, towns, hamlets, and rural areas for the federal government to seek a direct local relationship.

The federal government needs the states and the states need it, and both need and are needed by the cities. The Cooperative Area Manpower Planning Systems (CAMPS) represents the first halting steps toward a comprehensive planning system merging the interests, powers, and resources of federal, state, and local governments. Needed is an administrative system whereby the federal government identifies national priorities and issues guidelines for states (and perhaps for major metropolitan areas). The states, in turn, should do likewise for cities and other local jurisdictions. The goal is a three- or five-year plan, updated annually, to meet local needs and objectives in harmony with those of the state and nation. The delivery of services then becomes a local and state responsibility with federal monitoring. For those jurisdictions which fail, whether for apathy or prejudice, to pursue their objectives aggressively, funds withheld from state allocations for use at federal discretion would provide ample insurance that the needy could be served.

The emphasis of manpower programs in the past decade has been strongly remedial. Given the backlog of problems caused by years of neglect in our schools and public institutions and years of rapid change in our society and economy, that backlog has not significantly declined and it must. Remedial efforts are bound to be unsatisfactory as long as the flood of underprepared new entrants remains uncurtailed. Herein lies the task of compensatory early childhood education to make up for the deficits of home and neighborhood environments; improved elementary and secondary education, particularly in urban slums and rural backwaters; effective and modernized vocational and technical education; and assurance that all these, and college as well, are available to all who are or can be qualified, regardless of finances, race, or ethnic origin.

Some Alternative Approaches

Current programs designed to remedy the deficiencies of people in the job market serve perhaps one million people per year — only a fraction of those who experience serious difficulty in finding and keeping steady employment. Yet we must seriously consider the possibility that the nation will choose to do no more — or even less — than it now does to help the disadvantaged to overcome their labor market difficulties. Such a choice might flow from a desire to control inflation more rigorously through restrictive monetary and fiscal policies. What are the likely consequences of such a choice? Almost certainly the national unemployment rate would rise, with disproportionate increases in unemployment among the less-skilled and less-educated members of the labor force and among those who are heavily concentrated in the central cores of the big cities. Continued or accelerated growth in the numbers of welfare clients and an increased potential for civil disorders in the cities might be further consequences. And the nation as a whole would lose the goods and services that might otherwise be produced by those who are rejected by the "normal" labor market.

Another alternative which is receiving current attention is some form of "guaranteed annual income" for the rejects of the labor market. This approach raises some fundamental policy questions that cannot be discussed adequately in a relatively brief statement focused on manpower. We express serious doubts concerning the desirability or political acceptability of any guaranteed income program offered as a substitute for employment or for the provisions of services to the needy. We strongly favor national minimum standards of income maintenance at an edequate level for all those who cannot or should not work.

But we believe it is far better to provide the able-bodied with useful work. Income maintenance for the latter group would involve such large expenditures that remedial services — such as education and job training — would almost certainly be precluded, relegating a large portion of these people to a permanent state of idle dependency. According to public opinion surveys, in our work-oriented society, overwhelming majorities reject a universal "guaranteed income" program, but equally large majorities support a "guaranteed employment" program. We believe that this preference has a reasonable basis and that national policy should be shaped accordingly. Not even a country as wealthy as ours can afford the waste of human resources which would flow from a program of permanently subsidized idleness.

As a third alternative stratagem, many have advocated large expansion of on-the-job training through a system of tax credits. This device has been quite successful in stimulating investment in new equipment, and it is argued that the device might be equally effective in promoting private investment in human beings. Some even suggest that this approach would be "costless." This latter claim is an illusion: tax credits obviously reduce tax revenues below what they would otherwise be, and others would have to pay higher taxes or forego tax reductions that might otherwise be possible. Although administrative simplicity is another virtue claimed for this device, it would be essential to draw up and enforce detailed rules to prevent subsidization of training that would have been undertaken even in the absence of the tax credit, to insure that opportunities are opened for the disadvantaged, and to prevent other possible abuses. We must find ways of determining the true costs of such a program and evaluating its results in comparison with other possible uses of the funds. We urge continuing study of these matters and believe that endorsement of this approach prior to the completion of such a study would be premature.

A fourth approach, which we strongly favor, is provision for a wide range of manpower services, out of which programs for particular localities or individuals can be adapted to meet the specific needs and opportunities as described in the foregoing review.

Part 7

The Welfare System and Its Reformation

Editor's Survey

The selections at the end of the preceding part were concerned with ways to take a look at the dimensions of social welfare programs in the United States, some of the apparent social and economic factors affecting their size and evolution, and some of their drawbacks. This may seem to be a backward to help America's needy in more efficient and satisfactory ways. It is now time procedure — to look at reforms first, and then at the problem — but it allows us to lead naturally into presentation of President Nixon's welfare reform proposal of 1969, which appears as the result of the whole debate.

The selection by Skolnick and Dales gives us a broad picture of the shape of American welfare programs and some idea of their rates of growth. Using data of this sort, Lora Collins has attempted to sort out the statistical regularities which lie behind the superficial incoherence and possible inequities which characterize a system which is largely run by the individual states. We then look behind the cold numbers at two brief insights into the life of mothers receiving the most controversial type of welfare payment: Aid to Families with Dependent Children. The vignette from the Manpower report of 1968 is more discouraging than the summary of Professor Podell's work. In the latter case, one is particularly struck by the attitude responses given by the recipients. One might well ask how these responses might look today (some four years later) after a protracted period of organization and agitation by various groups, such as the National Welfare Rights Organization.

The proposal summarized in the article by Schorr represents an alternative route to welfare reform from the negative tax plans presented in Part 5. Many of the developed countries have one form or other of family or children's allowances, which are either payments to the child's mother (as in Canada) or are part of the pay-packet, received by the worker (as in France). It may come as a surprise to most American students that the popular slogan "equal pay for equal work" is not accepted abroad as the obvious social goal which

251

Americans would consider it. In fact, two men standing at adjacent machines might take home very different pay, depending on the number of their dependents. Yet, so foreign is this concept to our history and ideology, that only variants of children's allowances on the Canadian pattern were seriously considered in the debate on welfare reform.

The culmination of many years of argument and growing disenchantment with the costs and effectiveness of the current welfare arrangements is to be found in President Nixon's message. The level of income guarantee embodied in his proposal is relatively low ($1600 for a family of four). This guarantee lies below current welfare payment levels in many states and large cities, and even below the recommendations of the President's Commission on Income Maintenance ($2400 per year, family of four). Despite the low level of allowances, the proposal is somewhat revolutionary by standard American thinking about efforts and rewards. The bow to the work ethic is certainly there (in the form of day-care centers and required training), but so is the principle of a basic (if qualified) right to a minimum income. If this principle were to be accepted, then future increases in benefit levels would be matters of quibbling over numbers and not fundamental struggles over principles. The example of 35 years' growth and extension of the Social Security System may provide a relevant parallel.

Several other features of Nixon's proposal deserve mention. With its exclusion of the first $720 per year of earned income before benefit offsets are begun the plan embodies a primitive period of "progressive" negative income tax — the rate of reduction of benefits is 0% at first, and then rises to 50%. One implication of this exemption feature is that, for a given base level of income, the break-even point and the total costs of the program will be higher than under a plan which starts reducing benefits with the first dollar of earnings. Thus, although the base income and the marginal tax rate as one approaches the poverty level are the same for Nixon's plan and Friedman's proposal (Chapter 5), Nixon's proposal would transfer more income to its recipients (which is the exact converse of "costing more"). Beyond this, the student should explore the implicit assumptions about the responsiveness of the very poor to work incentives which lie behind the choice of a progressive negative tax principle instead of a regressive one (where benefits would fall rapidly at first, and then more slowly as one approached the point where positive income taxation began).

A bill incorporating the President's proposal (sponsored by Representatives Mills and Byrnes) passed the House in early 1970, but ran into trouble in the Senate. One of the objections was that, as the nation moved into a recession, the plan would cost perhaps one-quarter more than anticipated. It would seem that the impending hardships of a recession would increase the urgency of an income maintenance plan, but the student should think through the broader question of how public and private unemployment compensation should be related to an anti-poverty program of this nature.

A second major line of objections had its source in the complexity of current Federal welfare programs. One of the objects in designing negative tax plans has been to avoid gaps or discontinuities; many welfare programs have not circumvented this problem. Thus, under a hypothetical program, you might be guaranteed $1000 if your earnings were under $2000 per year. With earnings of $1900, your total income would be $2900; with earnings of $2000, your total income would fall to that same level due to complete loss of your allowance. A number of programs (notable examples, food stamps, public housing) operate with these all-or-nothing cutoff lines. Disincentives to work could hardly be more obvious. Critics of the Nixon proposal found (in their presentations to the Senate committee) that when the various existing programs were pulled together and combined with the program under consideration, something very similar to our simple example would occur. As the earned income of a typical welfare unit approached $5000, total income would begin to fall, and would continue to fall up to a level of earnings around $6000. Work disincentives and pressures to break up the family unit would be perpetuated under the new program, although at a higher level of income than at present. These objections were sufficient to shelve the proposal for the time being.

CHAPTER 19

Social Welfare Expenditures, 1968-1969

Alfred M. Skolnik and Sophie R. Dales

The second half of the 1960's has been characterized by strong upward movement in social welfare expenditures under public programs in the United States. At $127 billion, in fiscal year 1969 these expenditures continued to display annual increases of about the same magnitude as those in each of the past 4 years — about 13 percent.

Social welfare expenditures include cash benefits services and administrative costs of all programs operating under public law that are of direct benefit to individuals and families. These programs include those for income maintenance through social insurance and public assistance, and the public provision of health, education, housing, and other welfare services.

Each of the major social welfare categories contributed to the general expansion, but the largest advances continue to be recorded in the cash benefit and Medicare programs of old-age, survivors, disability, and health insurance (OASDHI), in education, and in the medical assistance program for the medically indigent (Medicaid).

Rising social welfare expenditures are accounting for an ever-larger proportion of the gross national product (GNP): the ratio was more than 14 percent in 1969. They also continue to grow as a proportion of total government expenditures and reached almost 45 percent in 1969. Even after discounting for population growth and for inflation, social, welfare programs registered a real expansion of 8 percent in fiscal year 1969 and of 41 percent since fiscal year 1965.

With private social welfare spending included, the grand total for social welfare expenditures reached $181.6 billion in fiscal year 1969, and the proportion of GNP devoted to these purposes rose to 20 percent. Public spending accounted for nearly 70 percent of all social welfare expenditures and con-

Reprinted with omissions from the *Social Security Bulletin,* December 1969.

tinued to dominate the areas of education and income maintenance and welfare. The Federal Government continued to be the major source of this spending — supplying 54 percent of all social welfare expenditures from public funds. The latest year in which State and local funds were the dominant source was the fiscal year 1965.

Expenditures Under Public Programs in 1968–69

Nearly seven-eighths of the $15 billion rise in fiscal year 1969 occurred in three social welfare categories: social insurance, with a $6.0 billion increase, accounted for 40 percent of the total growth; education expenditures, which

SOCIAL WELFARE EXPENDITURES UNDER PUBLIC PROGRAM: AS A PERCENTAGE OF THE GROSS NATIONAL PRODUCT, FISCAL YEARS 1950-1969.

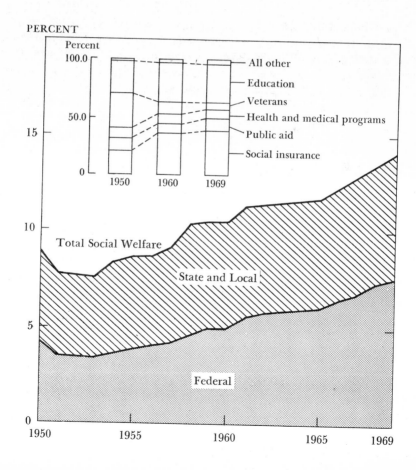

rose $4.3 billion in fiscal year 1969, provided nearly 30 percent of the total; and public aid — mainly public assistance — which was $2.4 billion higher, accounted for 16 percent. The remainder was contributed by other groups of social welfare programs in amounts ranging from $754 million in the "other social welfare" programs to $128 million for housing.

About $4.7 billion of the total increase in social insurance expenditures was accounted for by the OASDHI program, a 16-percent rise that was fractionally smaller than the preceding year's increase. The monthly benefits rose by $3.4 billion as the effects of the 1967 amendments continued to make themselves felt. Expenditures for health insurance for the aged (Medicare) increased 23 percent or $1.3 billion to a total of $6.6 billion.

The other social insurances together accounted for the remaining $1.3 billion of the group increase, with the bulk ($896 million) attributable to the public employee retirement system. Expenditures for unemployment insurance and public employment service operations remained nearly stationary at about $3.0 billion, although the small program for railroad workers declined somewhat.

Of the $4.3 billion expansion in education outlays, $3.7 billion was provided by elementary and secondary schooling, not counting vocational education. The bulk of the $34 billion spent for elementary and secondary education was furnished by the States and — mainly — the localities, with the Federal Government's $2.5 billion representing only 7 percent of the total.

The $2.4 billion growth in public aid expenditures in 1969 was accounted for very largely by the 21-percent rise in public assistance payments, services, and administration. More than two-fifths of the public assistance increase, in turn, resulted from increased spending for the Medicaid program for the medically indigent. The "other public aid" programs increased at exactly the 21-percent rate of the public assistance programs, to $1.5 billion. These "other" programs include the job-training programs of the Economic Opportunity Act, food stamps, surplus food, and repatriate and refugee assistance.

Growth in each of the other four social welfare expenditure categories, totaling $2.1 billion, made up the remaining portion of the annual increase of $15 billion. Relatively, the largest of these increases, although it totaled only $128 million, was the 30-percent rise in the annual rate of public spending for housing that carried the housing total for the year to well above the half billion mark.

A 22-percent rise in the miscellany of "other social welfare" programs took that group to a $4.2 billion total. About two-thirds of the increase is attributable to the $483 million growth in institutional care, almost exclusively at the State and local level.

Veterans' program expenditures increased 9 percent in the fiscal year 1969 to a new high of more than $8 billion. About half of the increase was caused by a raise in veterans' pensions and compensation, with a somewhat smaller rise in expenditures under the education programs for veterans and their children. Although the education benefits rose by but $205 million, the increase represented a 44-percent growth of the education program from 1968 and a 126-percent increase from 1967, as returning Viet Nam veterans begin to take up their educational benefit options.

The smallest increase, 7 percent, was registered by those health and medical programs concerned exclusively with health. (Health services that are part of other social welfare programs are reported with those programs, although later in this article all public expenditures for health are drawn together.) Health expenditures in fiscal 1969 totaled $8.8 billion. Increases of varying proportion were made in all aspects of health and medical care except for medical research where the $1.5 billion spent in fiscal year 1969 represented a 5-percent drop from the 1968 total.

In the fiscal year 1969, for the first time in several years, state and local social welfare expenditures increased at the same pace as Federal social welfare expenditures — about 13 percent. In 1966 Federal expenditures had risen 20 percent, while State and local expenditures rose only 8 percent. Since then the rate of increase in Federal expenditures has been fluctuating between 13 and 17 percent and that of State and local expenditures has been steadily accelerating: 9 percent in 1967, 11 percent in 1968, and 13 percent in 1969. A major factor in this acceleration has been the growith in expenditure for public assistance and education.

As a result of this trend, the proportion of Federal spending has remained about the same during each of the last two completed fiscal years for most of the seven social welfare categories and, in the case of education, has even dropped. From an all-time high of 14.8 percent of all education expenditures in fiscal year 1967, the Federal proportion has dropped to 13.2 percent in 1968 and to 11.8 percent in 1969.

Measures of Growth

Since 1960, public social welfare expenditures have increased by $75 billion. About one-third of this increase took place in the first 5 years of the decade; two-thirds in the past 4 years. This acceleration of the national commitment to social welfare is further highlighted by a comparsion.of expenditures with some of the more important economic indicators. In fiscal year 1969 the American people devoted 14.1 percent of the GNP to public programs of social welfare. From 1961 to 1965 the proportion of the GNP spent for social welfare rose only 0.3 percentage points (11.5 percent of the 1961 GNP to 11.8 percent in 1965), but the next 4 years produced an increase of 2.3 percentage points to the 1969 level (chart 1). Table 3 indicates that all but two of the social welfare expenditure categories played a role in this growth. Health and medical programs have remained at a static 1 percent of the GNP since 1965 and the veterans' programs have stayed at 0.9 percent for the same period.

TABLE 1. *Social Welfare Expenditures Under Public Programs as Percent of Gross National Product, Selected Fiscal Years, 1889-90 Through 1968-69*

| Fiscal year | Gross national product (in billions) | Social welfare expenditures as percent of gross national product | | | | | | | Total health and medical expenditures as percent of GNP[2] |
		Total[1]	Social insurance	Public aid	Health and medical programs	Veterans' programs	Education	Other social welfare	
1889-90	$ 13.0	2.4	(3)	(4)0.3	0.1	0.9	1.1	(4)	(5)
1912-13	39.0	2.5	(3)	(4) .3	.4	.5	1.3	(4)	(5)
1928-29	101.0	3.9	0.3	.1	.3	.7	2.4	0.1	0.5
1939-40	95.1	9.2	1.3	3.8	.6	.7	2.7	.1	.8
1949-50	263.4	8.9	1.9	.9	.8	2.6	2.5	.2	1.2
1954-55	379.7	8.6	2.6	.8	.8	1.3	2.9	.2	1.2
1959-60	495.6	10.6	3.9	.8	.9	1.1	3.6	.2	1.3
1964-65	655.6	11.8	4.3	1.0	1.0	.9	4.3	.3	1.5
1965-66	718.5	12.2	4.4	1.0	1.0	.9	4.6	.3	1.5
1966-67	771.1	12.9	4.8	1.1	1.0	.9	4.6	.4	2.1
1967-68	827.6	13.5	5.2	1.3	1.0	.9	4.7	.4	2.4
1968-69[6]	900.6	14.1	5.4	1.5	1.0	.9	4.8	.5	2.5

[1] *Includes housing, not shown separately.*
[2] *Combines "health and medical programs" with medical services provided in connection with social insurance, public aid, veterans' programs, vocational rehabilitation, and antipoverty programs.*
[3] *Less than 0.05 percent.*
[4] *"Other social welfare" included with "public aid."*
[5] *Not available.*
[6] *Preliminary estimates.*

TABLE 2. *Per Capital Social Welfare Expenditures Under Public Programs in the United States, Territories, and Possessions, in Actual and 1967-68 Prices, Selected Fiscal Years, 1928-29 Through 1968-69*

Fiscal year	Per capita social welfare expenditures in current prices[1]							Constant 1968-69		Implicit price deflators (1968-69=100)
	Total[2]	Social insurance	Public aid	Health and medical programs	Veterans' programs	Education	Other social welfare	Total social welfare expenditures[1]		
								Amt. (in millions)	Per capita	
1928-29	$31.80	$ 2.78	$ 0.49	$ 2.85	$ 5.31	$ 19.75	$ 0.62	$ 8,572.6	$ 69.58	45.7
1939-40	65.56	9.49	26.84	4.59	4.61	19.11	.87	23,425.1	174.83	37.5
1949-50	152.59	32.20	16.26	13.44	44.20	43.47	2.92	34,807.3	226.73	67.3
1954-55	194.50	58.72	17.98	18.58	28.29	66.68	3.71	42,464.7	254.25	76.5
1959-60	286.46	105.74	22.54	24.54	29.64	96.76	6.26	61,674.4	339.01	84.5
1964-65	391.60	142.42	32.00	31.82	30.40	142.82	10.52	86,000.0	438.03	89.4
1965-66	441.06	159.59	36.73	34.91	31.64	164.85	11.65	96,338.7	484.68	91.0
1966-67	494.37	184.55	43.82	38.84	33.81	177.16	14.32	106,318.7	528.73	93.5
1967-68	549.78	209.21	54.57	40.70	35.78	190.48	16.94	116,034.4	570.90	96.3
1968-69	616.01	236.33	65.48	42.95	38.67	209.43	20.44	126,465.0	616.01	100.0
Percentage change for 1968-69 expenditures[3] (1968-69 prices) from —										
1928-29	+785	+3,787	+5,120	+588	+233	+385	+1,403	+1,375	+785	
1939-40	+252	+834	−9	+251	+215	+311	+781	+440	+252	
1949-50	+172	+394	+171	+115	−41	+224	+371	+263	+172	
1959-60	+82	+89	+146	+48	+10	+83	+176	+105	+82	
1964-65	+41	+48	+83	+21	+14	+31	+74	+47	+41	
1965-66	+27	+35	+62	+12	+11	+16	+60	+31	+27	
1966-67	+17	+20	+40	+3	+7	+11	+33	+19	+17	
1967-68	+8	+9	+16	+2	+4	+6	+16	+9	+8	

[1] Excludes expenditures within foreign countries for education, veterans' payments, and OASDHI benefits; see Table 1 for data including such expenditures.
[2] Includes housing, not shown separately.
[3] Preliminary estimates.

SOURCE: *Per capita figures based on January 1 data from the Bureau of the Census for total U.S. population, including Armed Forces overseas and the civilian population of territories and possessions. Deflators based on implicit price deflators for personal consumption expenditures prepared by National Income Division, Office of Business Economics, Department of Commerce.*

To determine what part, if any of the relatively sizable increases in social welfare expenditures is the result of genuine program expansion, one must remove the effects of population growth and of the progressive erosion of purchasing power. Elimination of the effect of these two.factors will show the "real" development of program expenditures. For example, the 13-percent hike in the current-dollar social welfare expenditures during fiscal year 1969 is reduced to 8 percent when adjusted for population growth and price changes. Similarly, the 64-percent rise in total social welfare spending that occurred from fiscal year 1965 to 1969 is reduced to 41-percent increase. Table 2 shows social welfare expenditures for each part of the public series in terms of the amount spent per person and thus clears out all effects of population change. The table also presents the data for these expenditures in terms of constant value (1968-69 dollars) and thereby discounts the effect of upward or downward movement of purchasing power.

Another indicator of the importance with which social welfare is viewed in our economy is the proportion of government expenditures that is allocated for these programs (see figure). In fiscal year 1969, social welfare spending accounted for almost 45 percent of the outlays of governments at all levels; it represented 38 percent of all Federal spending and 57 percent of all State and local expenditures. The overall proportion devoted to social welfare purposes has been growing in small steps during the sixties with fractional annual fluctuations, but the increase has not been shared equally by all levels of government. The proportion of all Federal spending that went for social welfare was 28 percent in fiscal year 1960; by 1969 it had reached 38 percent. State and local spending for social welfare rose from 58 percent of total expenditires in 1960 to 62 percent in 1965 but declined each year since then—to 57 percent in 1969.

As with all government outlays, social welfare expenditures from public funds can be divided into two groups—those from trust-fund and non-trust-fund sources. Trust funds generally represent fixed obligations; as their popular designation implies, "earmarked" money can be spent only for the purpose for which a trust fund was established. Non-trust-fund expenditures, therefore, demark areas of greatest "discretionary" authority in legislative budget-making.

Since fiscal year 1965 there has been relatively little change in the ratio of non-trust-fund social welfare outlays to all non-trust-fund government expenditures: about 34 percent. But here, too, the proportion for social welfare has been increasing at the Federal level (from 19 percent in 1965 to 22 percent currently) and declining at State and local level (from 58 percent in 1965 to 55 percent in 1969, about the 1960 level of expenditure). Nevertheless, discretionary spending of State and local governments for social welfare purposes continues to claim a far larger proportion of their total annual non-trust-fund expenditures than such spending by the Federal Government with its continuing national defense commitments.

At both the Federal and State-local levels, virtually all trust fund expenditures are social welfare expenditures, and virtually all of those are for the social insurances. In fiscal year 1969, 16 percent of government expenditures for all purposes were expended from social welfare trust funds — an increase of 2-3 percentage points since the early 1960's. Federal trust fund expenditures for social welfare rose from 15 percent of all Federal expenditures in fiscal year 1960 to 18 percent in 1965. By fiscal year 1969 these trust funds, with

SOCIAL WELFARE EXPENDITURES IN RELATION TO GOVERNMENT SPENDING FOR ALL PURPOSES, FISCAL YEARS 1950-1969

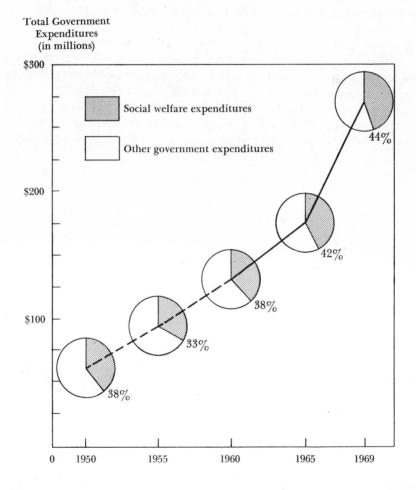

expenditures of $38 billion, were financing more than 21 percent of Federal spending, chiefly because of expansion in the OASDHI program. State and local trust fund expenditures have remained at the $4-6 billion level all during the sixties. Consequently, as a proportion of total State and local government spending, these expenditures have fallen from 9 percent in 1960 to 6 percent in 1969. Their pinnacle was reached in 1950 when they provided nearly one-eighth of all State and local expenditures for all purposes.

Private and Public Expenditures

When public and private expenditures for social welfare are combined, their differing roles in each of the main areas — health, education, welfare — come in sharp focus. For many years private spending has provided approximately a third of combined public and private spending for these purposes. Despite major increases in public expenditures for health, private spending continues to dominate this field; five-eighths of the Nation's health bill was met through private resources in 1969. Private expenditures for education and for welfare play a far smaller role — only about one-sixth to one-fifth of the total outlay in these areas through most of the last two decades.

Private expenditures, as used here, represent direct consumer expenditures for medical care and education, expenditures of private employee-benefit plans (including group health and life insurance for government employees), industrial in-plant health services, private health insurance benefits and the cost of providing this protection and philanthropic spending for health and welfare.

Health

Continuation of the 1968 accelerated rate of increase (12 percent) during fiscal year 1969 brought this Nation's public and private health bill to $60.3 billion, or 6.7 percent of the gross national product. Health outlays are currently more than one and one-half times the expenditures of 1965 and nearly five times those of 1950.

The main spurt occurred in fiscal year 1967 when a $5.9 billion increase effected a 14-percent rise in total health expenditures. Playing no small role was the introduction of Medicare benefits, which accounted for $3.3 billion or 56 percent of the increase, and growth of medical vendor payments under public assistance, which contributed $0.7 billion to the increase; together they provided two-thirds of the 1967 increase in total public and private health expenditures.

In the perspective of overall economic growth, 4.0 percent of the 1940 GNP was spent for health purposes. Two decades later the ratio had increased by only 1.3 percentage points. It took just 9 years to add another 1.4 percentage points to bring the proportion of the Nation's output devoted to health purposes to 6.7 percent.

Part of this growth in the proportion of the GNP stems from a higher rise in prices for medical care than for all other items. The Bureau of Labor

Statistics consumer price index (CPI) for all items rose 21.3 percent from the fiscal year 1960 to the fiscal year 1969. During these 9 years the index of medical care prices rose 41.0 percent, about double the rise for all items. In fiscal year 1969 the all-item CPI increased 4.8 percent, the medical component 6.5 percent.

Along with the increased spending for health care and the rising costs of this care has come a shift in the sector of the economy footing the bill. Through the fifties and the sixties to the end of fiscal year 1966, about three-fourths of all health expenditures came from the private sector, with public funds financing only one-fourth. In fiscal year 1967 the swing began, as public expenditures for health rose to one-third ($15.9 billion) of the year's total health costs and private expenditures dropped to two-thirds ($32.3 billion). By 1969, public funds amounting to $22.6 billion provided 37.5 percent of all health care, and $37.7 billion in private money provided 62.5 percent.

In less than two decades, 1950-69, public spending for health grew to seven and one-half times the amount spent at the beginning of the period. More than four-fifths of the increase took place in the sixties, notably from 1966 on. A doubling of public spending for health over the entire fifties was matched by the doubling of expenditures in just the last 3 years of this decade, which saw annual increases of 47 percent, 24 percent, and 15 percent, respectively.

Until the middle sixties the States and localities had traditionally been the providers of the bulk of public expenditures for health and medical care. Federal health expenditures had been increasing steadily even before Medicare, however, and by fiscal year 1966 they were providing exactly one-half of the total ($10.8 billion) spent in the public sector for health. By 1969, the ratio had risen to two-thirds of the $22.6 billion total.

Private expenditures still dominate the Nation's health outlays, however, and they are continuing to rise. The pace of the rise has again picked up after a noticeable deceleration in fiscal year 1967. Private health spending stood at $29.4 billion in fiscal year 1965. The next year the increase was 7 percent, then a dip to 3 percent in 1967 was followed by successive increases of 6 percent and 10 percent to the 1969 level of $37.7 billion.

A large proportion — about seven-eighths — of all public and private health and medical care expenditures are for personal health care. Through 1966, public expenditures had financed only about one-fifth of all personal health care. This ratio had been stable for at least 15 years. In 1967 the ratio of public financing jumped to 30 percent of all personal health care expenditures, and in 1969 it went to 36 percent.

The major factor, as might be expected, was the introduction of the Medicare and Medicaid programs. The Medicare program, itself, has raised the proportion of personal health care expenditures in the public sector that are financed according to insurance principles from less than one-tenth in both 1960 and 1965 to almost two-fifths in 1969.

In the private sector, the role of insurance benefits has also been growing.

These benefits provided about one-fourth of all private personal care expenditures in 1960, compared with more than one-third in 1969. Because of the impact of Medicare and Medicaid, however, the proportion of total personal health care expenditures being met through private insurance has dropped from one-fourth in 1965 and 1966 to 22 percent in each of the succeeding years. Combining private insurance benefits with public outlays for personal health care and other third-party payments currently leaves only 41 percent of the Nation's personal health bill to be paid by the consumer directly. In 1965, the out-of-pocket costs by the consumer came to more than half (52.5 percent of total personal health care expenditures).

Education

At $52 billion, the 1969 education bill met from combined public and private sources is about one and one-half times larger than the 1960 costs of education, and nearly four times larger than they were in 1950. Since the early fifties the public has provided 83 percent of all education expenditures. Part of the steady rise in the rate of public spending in recent years is undoubtedly attributable to the intensification of Federal aid to education in the late 1960's. The new Federal programs more than made up for the decline in Federal veterans' education benefits. State and local governments continue to bear most of the burden of educational costs, however. Their education bill has increased nearly fivefold from 1950 to 1969 and at an accelerating pace in the past several years.

Since State and, particularly, local governments have been very largely the paymasters for elementary and secondary education in this country for most of the twentieth century, private spending for education has had its biggest impact at the level of higher education. With burgeoning college attendance and rapidly rising costs of such attendance, private expenditures — both personal and philanthropic — rose from $0.8 billion in 1950 to $5.5 billion in 1969. In 1969 expenditures for private provision of higher education were 11 percent higher than they were in 1968, although private spending for all education increased only 8 percent. Combined private and public education expenditures — and total public education expenditures as well — rose 11 percent during 1969.

Income-Maintenance Programs

The public sector continued in fiscal year 1969 to account for all but about 15 percent of income-maintenance payments to the non-self-sustaining part of the population, as it has through most of the sixties. In fiscal year 1969, cash payments under public programs of social insurance, public assistance, and veterans' benefits provided $51 billion and private employee-benefit plans almost $9 billion for a total that was 12 percent higher than 1968 expenditures. During 1969 the public programs paid out 13 percent more than they paid in 1968, but the private plans just about maintained their relative proportion of all income-maintenance programs with a 10-percent increase in payments.

The social insurance programs have led the expansion in the public sector. These programs were paying out $35.2 billion more in 1969 than in 1950 — an eightfold rise. All other public income-maintenance programs increased their benefit expenditures one and one-half times during this period. Paralleling the popularity in the public sector of the insurance principle to provide cash transfer payments, private employee-benefit plans also enjoyed a tremendous growth. By 1969, payments for private pensions, life insurance, and cash sickness and accident insurance had also shown an eightfold rise over their 1950 levels.

Some small part of philanthropic expenditures for welfare purposes, estimated at about $1.9 billion in fiscal year 1969, goes for cash payments to needy persons. The estimate itself is so rough that a break-out of an amount for cash transfers has not been attempted. The major part of philanthropic welfare expenditures in recent years has been for institutional care, family counseling, day care, and other social services.

Combining Expenditures for Major Areas

Combining the dollar figures shown in tables [in the original text] produces a total figure on private and public expenditures for social welfare, distributed by the three major functions — health, education, and income maintenance and welfare. The total figure thus obtained is adjusted to eliminate the overlap that occurs because small parts of private expenditures for health and education represent the spending of cash benefits received under public programs and, to a lesser extent, under private employee-benefit plans.

Total unduplicated expenditures for health, education, and income maintenance and welfare in the public and the private sectors of the economy amounted to $181.6 billion in fiscal year 1969. This sum represents an annual increase of $19.6 billion, and a $50.0 billion increase since 1966. With the 1969 increase the proportion of the gross national product represented by all social welfare expenditures passed the 20-percent mark, from which it has been separated only fractionally for the 2 preceding years.

Public social welfare expenditures continue to dominate the total, as well as the education and income-maintenance and welfare groups. For the past two decades the public sector has provided about two-thirds of the total, and the proportion now verges on seven-tenths. Public spending has provided about 85 percent of all education and income-maintenance and welfare programs during this period. In the health field, the proportion provided through public funds was one-fourth in 1950 and by 1969 was approaching two-fifths.

Despite the decreasing proportion of total health expenditures provided through private means, the largest share of private spending is still for

DISTRIBUTION OF PUBLIC AND PRIVATE SOCIAL WELFARE EXPEND-
ITURES BY THE MAJOR FUNCTIONS OF HEALTH, EDUCATION, AND
INCOME MAINTENANCE AND WELFARE, FISCAL YEARS 1950, 1960,
AND 1969.

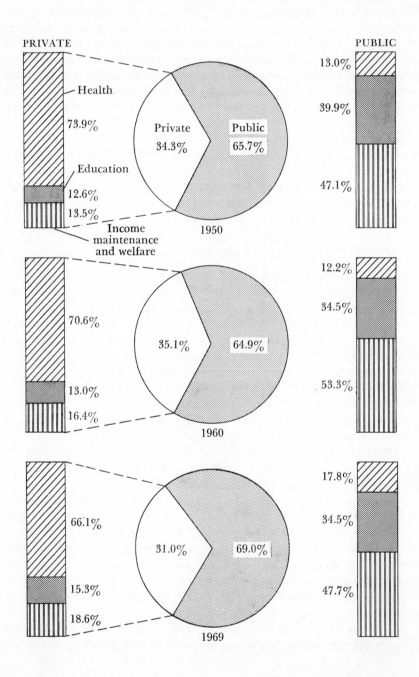

health — 66 percent in fiscal year 1969 (see figure). Education accounted for 15 percent of all private social welfare expenditures and income maintenance and welfare for 19 percent. In fiscal year 1960, the respective shares were 71, 13, and 16 percent.

This distribution may be contrasted with the 1969 distribution in the public sector, where health expenditures accounted for only 18 percent of the total. Income-maintenance and welfare programs had the greatest share with 48 percent, and education had 34 percent of the total.

CHAPTER 20

Public Assistance Expenditures in the United States

Lora S. Collins

Public Assistance is the general term for a group of federally assisted programs which provide aid to needy persons in certain categories: Old Age Assistance (OAA) for those aged sixty-five and over; Aid to Dependent Children (ADC)[1] for children under eighteen deprived of one or both parents and, when necessary, for a needy adult relative; Aid to the Blind (AB) with age limits varying among the states; and Aid to the Permanently and Totally Disabled (APTD) for persons aged eighteen and over. Federal aid for public assistance originated with the Social Security Act of 1935, which authorized federal grants-in-aid based on state and local government expenditures for the programs. The establishment of the programs depends on state implementation.[2]

The States' Discretion in Matters of Policy

Each state has a great deal of control over the number of recipients and virtually total control over the size of payments to recipients in its public assistance programs. Federal standards relate largely to procedure, not to the content or adequacy of the programs. Thus, in determining who is needy and how much assistance is to be paid to those so classified, the states do not operate their public assistance programs under national standards. The Social Security Act also allows the states considerable latitude in setting and inter-

Reprinted from Otto Eckstein, editor, *Studies in the Economic of Income Maintenance* (Washington: The Brookings Institution, 1967), by permission of the publisher. © 1967 by The Brookings Institution.

preting the definitions of "dependent child," "blindness," and "permanent and total disability."

Given this decentralized structure, the possibility exists that a substantial part of the interstate variation in public assistance expenditures results from nonsystematic (and certainly nonquantifiable) factors, particularly the attitudes and policies of states. The more important such influences, the less successful will be any attempt to quantify the determinants of assistance expenditures. Such influences apparently do have important effects on the assistance programs, but significant quantitative relationships are nevertheless to be found.

Table 1 summarizes the extent of interstate variation of public assistance expenditures, recipient rates, and average payments in 1960. For each program, the table shows the highest and lowest state values for these variables and the average values for the nation as a whole.

Summary of the Empirical Results*

Recipient rates vary inversely with income level in all of the public assistance programs. There is a strong statistical relationship; interstate variation in income level can account for over 50 percent of the interstate variation in the proportion of the total population that receives some type of public assistance.

The extent of social insurance coverage can be an important determinant of assistance outlays. The results clearly show that the larger the number of aged persons receiving OASI, the smaller is the need for OAA. Social insurance coverage may also have an influence on AB (since blindness is especially common among the aged) but this does not show clearly in the results. There is a mild indication of negative correlation between the APTD recipient rate and the Disability Insurance beneficiary rate. No direct evidence is found of a relationship between social insurance and ADC.

The unemployment rate appears to be a significant determinant of the OAA and ADC recipient rates, but not of those for AB and APTD. This seems reasonable, for recipients in the latter two groups are presumably much more definitely out of the labor market.

The greater the urbanization of the population, the more likely it would seem that care of the needy will be a social rather than a family function, and urbanization is, in fact, generally associated with higher recipient rates. This is true even when income, which is highly correlated with urbanization, is held constant. However, as might well be expected, urbanization is really significant only with respect to the ADC recipient rate.

Racial composition also has a bearing on public assistance recipient rates; the recipient rates in the programs are positively associated with the non-

*EDITOR'S NOTE: A detailed discussion of procedures and results for each public assistance program is found in the original manuscript.

TABLE 1. *National Averages and Range of Interstate Variations in Assistance Program Variables in 1960*

Program	Per Capita Expenditure (In Dollars)			Recipient Rate (Varies; see note)			Average Payment (In Dollars)		
	Low State	U.S. Average	High State	Low State	U.S. Average	High State	Low State	U.S. Average	High State
Old Age Assistance	1.74 (Del.)	10.69	37.08 (Okla.)	34 (N.J.)	140	518 (La.)	32.20 (Miss.)	69.31	110.26 (Conn.)
Aid to Dependent Children	1.80 (Tex.)	5.83	12.33 (W.Va.)	14.3 (N.H.)	36.2	88.2 (W.Va.)	38.07 (Ala.)	110.84	170.84 (N.Y.)
Aid to the Blind	0.11 (Haw., Md.)	0.52	1.39 (Pa.)	.118 (Conn.)	.602	2.912 (Miss.)	38.55 (Miss.)	72.57	118.32 (Mass.)
Aid to the Permanently and Totally Disabled	0.43 (Tex.)	1.64	4.39 (Okla.)	1.05 (Cal.)	3.82	10.75 (Miss.)	32.54 (Miss.)	65.57	128.19 (Conn.)
Combined Public Assistance Programs	5.71 (Va.)	18.63	52.80 (Okla.)	12.8 (N.J.)	32.4	80.3 (Miss.)	—	—	—
General Assistance Programs	0.01 (Ala.)	2.39	6.56 (Ill.)	0.04 (Ala.)	3.96	7.92 (Ill.)	12.99 (Ala.)	68.75	96.66 (Mich.)

SOURCE: *U. S. Bureau of the Census and U. S. Social Security Administration.*
Recipient rates are expressed as follows:
OAA: Recipients per 1,000 persons aged 65 and over.
ADC: Child recipient per 1,000 persons under age 18.

AB: Recipients per 1,000 persons aged 18 to 64.
APTD: Recipients per 1,000 persons aged 18 to 64.
Four public assistance programs combined: Total recipients, including adults in ADC, per 1,000 total population.
General assistance: Cases (not persons) per 1,000 persons aged 18 to 64.

white proportion of the population. However, this relationship is not as strong as one might expect and, somewhat surprisingly, it does not hold at all for ADC.

Recipient rates also tend to be higher in the states that have had the relatively slowest rates of population growth; this relationship is strongest for OAA and APTD.

In contrast to the public assistance programs, the general assistance recipient rate apparently varies less with need than with the ability of state-local governments to support general assistance programs, since the recipient rate is positively correlated with income level.

The poorer states are doubly burdened in the matter of relief, for it appears that blindness, serious disability, and childhood dependency are more prevalent at lower income levels. Relatively larger proportions of the populations of poorer states are potentially eligible for public assistance — by virtue of being blind, disabled, and so forth — and, because of generally lower incomes, relatively larger proportions of these potential recipients in poorer states actually receive public assistance.

Average Payments per Recipient

There are high positive correlations between income level and average monthly payments to assistance recipients. This presumably means that higher-income states have higher assistance standards in terms of items considered in evaluating needs and the dollar values established for them; in addition, recipients in higher-income states may face higher prices.

With the state income level given, there is some tendency for average payments to vary positively with the degree of urbanization of the recipients of assistance. There is also a tendency for the average payment to be smaller the greater the proportion of nonwhite recipients, which may reflect some element of discrimination. Also, nonwhite recipients apparently have lower living standards and therefore smaller evaluated dollar "needs" to be met by assistance payments. In general, state assistance standards do not operate to bring all recipients up to some defined standard of living, but only provide guidelines for putting dollar values on food, shelter, and other requirements. Evaluation of "need" is conducted on an individual basis for each recipient and takes into account his own particular circumstances.

Competition Among Programs

There may well be competition among assistance programs — specifically, competition for a limited total amount of state-local funds available for "relief" in each state, and for the goodwill of legislators — but the empirical evidence of the present study is not suited to identifying it.

Interprogram competition might result in a more restrictive assistance standard of need in one program than in others, thus making the average payment or the recipient rate in that program "unexpectedly" low relative to the other programs. However, at any point in time, if a state has a large number of recipients in one program by comparison with numbers of recipients in other states, it tends to have a relatively large number in other programs as well; thus, in a cross section of states, any effects of possible intrastate discrimination among programs are obscured. Similarly, if a state's average payment in one program is relatively low by comparison with other states' payments, its average payments in other programs also tend to be relatively low. Thus, the question of interprogram competition cannot be answered by looking, for example, at the correlation between per capita expenditure for one program and that for another (or all others,) because these correlations are all positive and quite high. The question of competition is much better suited to institutional rather than statistical treatment — that is, to an investigation into the manner in which states do, in fact, treat the several programs relative to one another. On that basis, it has generally been observed that ADC is unpopular and operates at a disadvantage in relation to the others.[3]

REFERENCES

1. [EDITOR's NOTE: Elsewhere referred to as AFDC.]
2. The 1935 legislation authorized the first three programs; APTD was added in 1950. Because it is not dealt with in this study, Medical Assistance for the Aged (MAA) is omitted from the list. MAA, which became operative in October, 1960, differs in purpose and content from the older programs; its sole object is to pay medical costs for "medically indigent" but otherwise self-sufficient persons aged sixty-five and over. MAA is commonly called the Kerr-Mills program. Another recent development not treated in this study is the "unemployed parent" component of ADC. Since May 1961, states have been permitted to establish a subprogram within ADC for families in need due to the unemployment (rather than the death, disability, or absence) of a parent.
3. See, for instance: U.S. Advisory Council on Public Assistance, *Report,* Senate Doc. No. 93, 86 Cong. 2 Sess. (1960), especially pp. 18–19; ELIZABETH WICKENDEN and WINIFRED BELL, *Public Welfare: Time for a Change* (1961), especially Chap. 2.

CHAPTER 21

The Irregular Economy and the AFDC Mother

Manpower Report of the President (1968)

The Irregular Economy of Poverty Areas

The barriers which separate sub-employed slum residents, nonwhite or white, from the mainstream of economic and social life have resulted in the creation of a separate economic world, which differs vitally, and in many ways, from the middle-class world surrounding the slums. This world has its own special values, own strategies for survival, its own moral standards, its own criteria of success or failure.

The sources of income of the poor and dependent — those at the bottom one-fifth of the income distribution — are varied, and public policy is directed at altering them in many ways. When income from employment is low, unstable, and unpredictable, the traditional distinctions between employment and unemployment, work and welfare become blurred, and extra-legal sources of income may be sought.

The contrasts between this irregular economy of the slums and the country's regular economy are sharp. In the regular economy, work offers ópportunities for vertical mobility, a reasonably predictable pattern of wage improvement with increasing seniority and skill, and the possibility of stable employment. Jobs can be classified in terms of status, skill requirements, and level and stability of earnings — as white- or blue-collar, skilled or unskilled, salaried or paying an hourly wage. By contrast, the irregular economy is characterized by horizontal mobility, erratic wage fluctuations, and overlap between the

Reprinted from U. S. Department of Labor "The Irregular Economy and the AFDC Mother," *Manpower Report of the President* (1968).

welfare and the wage systems. Jobs are better described as dead end, low wage, sporadic, extra-legal, and so forth.

The size, characteristics, and fluctuations of the irregular economy are not well known nor understood. How does this economy work? How does it overlap with the regular economy? What are its implications for public policy?

The irregular economy has many different income streams, which blend into economic sustenance for slumdwellers. Many people work in low-wage, part-time, marginal jobs that provide no ladder to better opportunities. The work may be physically exacting, job security low, and employment offered only on a short-time basis. In some jobs, the employer pays so little that employees have great temptation to steal from him in order to supplement their earnings. Occasionally, a criminal activity may be the source of income, but the situation is seldom so clear-cut. A man may have his own type of "hustle" — an easy way to money, sometimes legitimate, sometimes partly not, that puts him in a quasi-entrepreneurial role. For example, he may discover where he can get a watch cheap — a "hot" watch — and then sell it to someone on his block. A woman may be on welfare for some months of the year and work in other months;* or she may receive welfare and at the same time work covertly; or a man may be living with a woman receiving welfare. As another alternative, a man may enroll in one of the training programs which pay stipends, in order to get funds to tide him over a lean period. Or he may borrow money, to be repaid when he gets a job or a hustle. Or he may decide to retire temporarily from the "scuffle" for a livelihood, and so swell the ranks of the jobless. However, many ghetto residents show high motivation and unusual resourcefulness and persistence in efforts to earn a living.

A possible basis of life for marginal workers is thus provided by the irregular economy. The variations of this world, its occasional excitement and flexibility, may have more appeal to many such workers than do low-paid, demanding, regular jobs. According to a recent study:

> . . . the streetcorner man . . . knows the social value of the job by the amount of money the employer is willing to pay him for doing it. . . . every pay day, he counts . . . the value placed on the job by society at large. . . . Nor does the low-wage job offer prestige, respect, interesting work, opportunity for learning or advancement, or any other compensation . . . [The low-wage job in the regular economy is] hard, dirty, uninteresting and underpaid. The rest of society . . . holds the job of the dishwasher or janitor or unskilled laborer in low esteem if not outright contempt. So does the streetcorner man. He cannot do otherwise. He cannot draw from a job those social values which other people do not put into it.[1]

The marginal economy develops a social psychology appropriate to its work world. As the streetcorner man views his future:

---

* In 1966 about 12 percent of the case closings on AFDC were attributable to employment or increased earnings of the mother.

It is a future in which everything is uncertain except the ultimate destruction of his hopes and the eventual realization of his fears. . . . Thus, when Richard squanders a week's pay in two days it is not because . . . he is . . . unaware of or unconcerned with his future. He does so precisely because he is aware of the future and the hopelessness of it all.[2]

Since the jobs typically available to slum residents have no attraction in terms either of income or of the nature of the work, it is not surprising that many of these jobs are rejected or held for only short periods. A taxing regular job must offer higher income than the economic activities of the irregular economy to appear preferable to them. And it must offer compensation also for the strain of regular hours of work day-in and day-out, often in physically demanding or boring work, and of accommodating to supervisors.

There is evidence that many from poverty areas do not stay, even on better jobs. They may not know how to behave on such jobs or find it difficult to maintain the routine; or too much may be expected of them too soon; or their off-job situation may make it difficult to keep the job. For such workers, placement in jobs in the mainstream economy may not be enough; they will need assistance in handling and adjusting to the new jobs.

Employers and supervisors need to develop increased understanding of these workers' problems and to learn how they can be handled. When jobs are opened up for the disadvantaged, changes in the customary work patterns and in supervisory relationships are likely to be essential if the workers are to succeed in, and stay on, the job.

Furthermore, manpower and social policy must be concerned with the ways in which work-training and welfare programs influence the irregular economy. The more differentiated and partial the benefit system, the more opportunities for integration of this system with the irregular economy's other income sources. Programs which provide only marginal increases in an individual's income tend to reinforce this economy.

To challenge it effectively, more attractive alternatives must be provided. This can be done by helping private employers open reasonably well-paying jobs in the regular economy to sub-employed workers. Many individuals who live in the irregular economy are eager to leave it, provided they have a chance to really advance their position in a society strongly oriented toward consumption. They would welcome an opportunity to move from a dead end job to a career opportunity, such as the New Careers Program is designed to offer.

The AFDC Mother — A Case Study of Sub-Employment

Mothers receiving assistance through the Federal program of Aid to Families with Dependent Children (AFDC) provide an illustrative case study of one group of sub-employed in the irregular economy — their problems, their difficulties in meeting these problems, and the way in which they react not only to their individual situations but also to the economic opportunities available to them.

Many theories have been evolved, and myths created, about this relatively small group of the underprivileged. Recipients of AFDC have been widely regarded as caught in a chronic, static condition of dependency, handed down from one generation to the next. Welfare has been viewed as an alternative to work, increasingly unrelated to such economic factors as the general level of unemployment or the participation of women in the labor force. This discussion looks at some of these theories in the light of available evidence. Obviously, there are families whose members have been brought up with welfare support and then have gone on to raise their own families with such support. But there are also many families whose members are on welfare rolls for very short periods of time and never sever their connection with the labor force, even when they are on welfare.

AFDC recipients are encouraged by welfare agencies to find work. Their earnings are included in the total family income that is considered when the amount of welfare payment is determined. States may, however, disregard some part of the earnings of mothers in order to conserve them for the future needs of children[3].

Each state sets its own cost standards for living requirements under AFDC. But many states also set arbitrary ceilings on the amount of assistance that will actually be paid — often well below the amount of determined need.

Data for the analysis that follows are drawn largely from the only two available national studies of AFDC caseloads. A study sponsored by the American Public Welfare Association was based on a 1-in-3 sample of cases closed during the first 3 months of 1961;[4] a study sponsored by the Department of Health, Education, and Welfare (HEW) covered a 1-percent sample of the cases currently active during the last 2 months of 1961.[5] The situation has undergone changes since that time — one of the most notable being the continuing increase in the AFDC caseload, despite the marked reduction in the overall rate of unemployment. The increased caseload is the result of many factors, including an increase in the numbers of young children, of female-headed households, and of children in such households; a relaxation in eligibility requirements in many States; and wider knowledge of the existence of the AFDC program. However, more recent evidence, including several studies of local situations, in general bears out the conclusions reached in the two nationwide surveys.

Length of Time on Welfare

One way of the exploring whether welfare is in fact a way of life, passed on from one generation to another, is to examine the length of time individual recipients remain on welfare. In 1961, the median length of time on AFDC was 27 months for currently active cases and 18 months for closed cases. But the length of time on assistance varied widely with both race and residence. For closed cases, the median time spent on assistance was higher for Negroes (22 months) than for whites (15 months) and lower in urban areas (16 months) than in rural areas (20 months). Periods of dependency tended to be longer in medium-sized cities (50,000 to 500,000) than in the largest cities. In general, however, the mothers in rural farm and nonfarm areas were those who spent the longest continuous periods of time on assistance.[6]

These figures on "continuous time" on assistance obscure the great turnover in the AFDC rolls. A recent analysis of case turnover showed that 584,000 cases were authorized and 508,000 cases were closed in calendar year 1966, while slightly more than 1 million were carried over from the preceding year. Averaged over the year, about 45,000 new families were added to the rolls each month, while 41,000 left. Certain families have repeated periods on relief; of the cases added in 1966, about 34 percent had received assistance previously.[7]

Since individuals do go on and off welfare, cumulative data showing the total time spent on welfare by an AFDC mother and her children are important in determining how welfare fits into their life cycle. According to the study of cases closed in 1961, 10 percent of the Negro and 7 percent of the white mothers had spent 9 or more years on welfare. Nevertheless, in absolute terms, white families outnumbered Negro families among the very small minority of AFDC cases on assistance for as long as this.[8]

The proportion of their adult life that women spend on AFDC is another significant measure of their dependence on this assistance. A study based on a 1-percent random sample of AFDC cases in Philadelphia (drawn in 1959, and followed through to 1962) showed that the majority (60 percent) had spent slightly less than half (47 percent) of their adult life on welfare.[9] In at least one city, then, welfare was not a permanent or exclusive style of life for all of the women on AFDC during the time they raised their children.

Finally, intergenerational dependency on welfare can also be measured. In the cases closed during early 1961, less than a third both of the white and of the Negro mothers had grown up in families in which their parents had also been on assistance.[10] However, a study in the State of Washington in 1964 yielded a substantially higher figure. About 43 percent of the AFDC mothers in the sample reported that their parents had been on assistance — 3 percent said their parents had been dependent for as long as they could remember; 27 percent said that they had been dependent for several years; and 13 percent said that they had received assistance for a brief period[11]

Altogether, the generalization that welfare becomes a permanent style of life for all or most AFDC recipients is not supported by the available evidence. The people on welfare are a varied group. Many of the families are not involved in long-term or intergenerational dependency. It must be recognized, however, that significant proportions of AFDC families do represent a second generation on welfare. This is one of the problems to which the program changes provided for by the 1967 amendments to the Social Security Act are addressed.

Welfare and Work

Welfare and employment are widely regarded as alternative rather than complementary or overlapping sources of income. The AFDC caseload is generally seen as made up of nonworking mothers. This is consistent with the theory of public assistance embodied in the original Social Security Act of 1935, which assumed that social insurance protected members of the labor force when their income was interrupted, while federally financed social assistance was for the unemployable. The 1967 amendments to the Social Security Act are directed at promoting economic independence — a permanent or long-term break from the irregular economy — through a program of social services, job training, and cash incentives.

The recent amendments are based on the assumption that AFDC mothers have been entirely outside the labor force and that, if adequate child-care facilities are made available, they can, through training and other services, be enabled to care for themselves and their families. But, in fact, AFDC mothers have frequently been active members of the sub-employed labor force — the underemployed and low-wage workers. Public assistance often served as a form of wage supplementation for the low-paid, partially employed worker. Welfare status did not necessarily represent a sharp break with the labor force, as the theory of assistance would imply.

The study of AFDC cases closed in 1961 showed that about 26 percent of the white and 41 percent of the Negro children were in families where the mothers had maintained some degree of attachment to the labor force during the periods on AFDC. (See Table 1.) About half of the mothers had been regularly employed before receiving welfare and continued to be regularly employed after receipt of AFDC payments.[12]

The HEW study of AFDC cases active in late 1961 showed the mother's employment status at a given point in time, rather than over a longer period. Of all AFDC mothers on the rolls at the time of the study, 14 percent were employed — including 11 percent of the white and 19 percent of the Negro mothers.[13]

The study of the AFDC caseload in Philadelphia in 1962 classified the work history of AFDC mothers in terms of their level of skill and job stability, based on information on their first job, their longest job, and their most recent job. About 40 percent of the women had a stable work history, and 47 percent an unstable one. Only 13 percent had no history of work. Of those with a work history, 40 percent had been employed in skilled or semi-skilled jobs.

Thus, AFDC mothers can hardly be described as a group made up predominantly of "work-shy women" who inherited their welfare status. However, there appears to be a generational difference in these women's work histories. The older ones had the more stable work history but lower levels of

TABLE 1. *Percent Distribution of AFDC Children by Color and by Employment Status of Homemaker During Period on AFDC*[1]

Employment Status of Homemaker	White	Negro
Total: Number	9,629	4,245
Percent	100.0	100.0
Employed	26.4	40.6
Full-time throughout period	3.0	5.4
Full-time most of period	4.5	4.4
Part-time throughout period	4.8	11.0
Part-time most of period	7.2	12.6
Other employment history	6.9	7.2
Not employed	73.2	58.8
Employment status unknown	.4	.6

[1] *Based on a sample of cases closed in first 3 months of 1961; includes children born in wedlock only.*
SOURCE: *M. Elaine Burgess and Daniel O. Price, "An American Dependency Challenge" (Chicago: American Public Welfare Association, 1963), based on table on p. 268.*

skill, while the reverse was true for the younger women. These different work habits may have resulted from the nature of the job market at the time the women entered it. Older women had apparently been able to develop a pattern of stability in a job world which accepted their low level of skill, but younger women with higher education and somewhat more skill appeared unable to develop a pattern of work stability in the present, more demanding job market. In general, the women who were unskilled workers had spent less of their adult lives on assistance than had the more skilled.

In view of the generally higher overall rates of unemployment among unskilled than higher skilled workers, this is a rather significant finding. It underlines the special circumstances — social and psychological as well as economic — which affect the work situation of these sub-employed women and other groups in the irregular economy.

The type of locality in which these mothers lived also had a marked effect on their pattern of employment. According to the study of cases closed in early 1961, the proportion of mothers who had been employed was lowest in large cities. This was true of both white and Negro mothers, but geographic location had a greater effect on the employment pattern of Negro women than on that of whites. Only about one-fourth of the Negro women in cities of over half a million had worked while on welfare, as compared with nearly 3 out of every 4 of those on farms. (See Table 2.)

TABLE 2. *Place of Residence and Employment Status of Homemaker During Period on AFDC, by Color[1]*

Place of residence	All AFDC families[2] (percent distribution)	Percent with homemaker employed	
		White	Negro
Total	100.0	26.4	40.6
METROPOLITAN COUNTIES			
City of 500,000 or more	25.3	16.4	23.5
City of 50,000 to 499,999	21.1	25.9	45.8
City of 2,500 to 49,999	7.5	25.8	44.4
Rural nonfarm	4.4	25.6	56.5
NONMETROPOLITAN COUNTIES			
City of 2,500 to 49,999	19.4	33.2	57.6
Rural nonfarm	18.4	26.7	56.5
Farm	3.9	20.8	72.9

[1] Based on a sample of cases closed during first 3 months of 1961.
[2] A few families, 0.3 percent, were in farm areas of metropolitan counties.
SOURCE: M. Elaine Burgess and Daniel O. Price, "An American Dependency Challenge" (Chicago: American Public Welfare Association, 1963), based on tables on pp. 264, 265, and 268.

Some Implications and Program Developments

These findings cast some doubt on two of the dominant ideas which color much of the discussion about the public assistance program — that being on welfare generally becomes a permanent style of life and that the benefits it provides are an alternative to work. Employment and welfare are systems which mesh in complex ways. Welfare is a form of social provision when income is absent, interrupted, or inadequate, and not simply a cash transfer system operating outside the world of work.

Much more information is needed, however, about the interrelationships between work and welfare and, in particular, about why many AFDC mothers work. At present, there is no definitive information on this latter point. One can do little more than speculate regarding the factors that enter into the situation and even about how many mothers do and do not increase their total income through their work.

To throw light on these basic questions will require extensive study of the circumstances surrounding these women's employment, as well as analysis of their budgets. The need for such research is the more urgent because of the possible implications of the findings for current programs aimed at increasing employment of AFDC mothers.

It seems probable that, in many cases, monetary incentives may not be the crucial factor in the mothers' decisions to work. At the same time, it is likely to take more than minimum earnings to effect a real change in the status of AFDC recipients; this requires income adequate for upward mobility — for a takeoff from dependency to economic self-sufficiency. Thus, programs of income incentives and work training may not reverse the upward trend in the welfare rolls, unless the training is designed to move clients to permanent employment at adequate wages. The new Work Incentive Program established under the 1967 Social Security Act amendments is aimed at precisely this objective.

An expansion of child-care facilities is also provided for by these amendments, on the assumption that lack of such facilities has been one of the factors which prevent AFDC mothers from seeking employment. The total capacity of licensed child-care facilities in the United States is placed presently at only 310,000 to 350,000. So the proportion of working women using such facilities is necessarily small. According to a 1965 study, only about 5 percent of all working mothers placed their children in group care. Of those with low incomes (under $3,000), only 3 percent used such facilities.

In view of these findings, it is not clear how expansion of child-care facilities will affect the AFDC mother's entry into the labor force. But whether or not the number of such mothers who become economically self-sufficient increases markedly, the provision of more good facilities for child care should help both the mothers and the children who use them. It may reasonably be expected that such services will ease the tensions of work for these women and reduce their absences from the job. They will also improve the situation of the children, who will benefit socially and educationally from organized programs of care.

REFERENCES

1. ELLIOT LIEBOW, *Tally's Corner* (Boston: Little, Brown and Co., 1967), pp. 57–59. This study describes the job and other experiences of the Negro marginal worker in a big city.
2. LIEBOW, op. cit., p. 66.
3. The 1967 amendments liberalize somewhat the amount of income which may be excluded in determining AFDC assistance. See *Summary of Social Security Amendments of 1967* (Washington: 90th Cong., 1st sess., Committee on Finance of the U.S. Senate and Committee on Ways and Means of the U.S. House of Representatives, December 1967), p. 17.
4. M. ELAINE BURGESS AND DANIEL O. PRICE, *An American Dependency Challenge* (Chicago: American Public Welfare Association, 1963).
5. *Study of Recipients of Aid to Families with Dependent Children, November–December 1961: National Cross-Tabulations* (Washington: U.S. Department of Health, Education, and Welfare, Welfare Administration, August 1965).
6. BURGESS AND PRICE, op. cit., p. 50.

7. WILBUR COHEN, testifying as Undersecretary of HEW said that it would be a great mistake to think of the caseload as being static, with the same families continuing to receive assistance for long periods of time. *Social Security Amendments of 1967,* Hearings Before the Committee on Finance (Washington: 90th Cong., 1st sess., U.S. Senate, Committee on Finance, 1967), H.R. 12080, pt. I, pp. 254 and 730.
8. BURGESS AND PRICE, op. cit., p. 49.
9. JANE C. KRONICK, "Family Life and Economic Dependency, A Report to the Welfare Administration," October 27, 1965 (mimeo.). In addition, a special analysis of the relationship between welfare and work experience of AFDC families in Philadelphia was made for this report.

    The age of the mothers is important since a high proportion of adult life can mean a short period of time in the case of young mothers. In the Philadelphia study, the average age of the mothers was 35, and as only a small proportion of young mothers was included, age bias does not appear important in this case.
10. BURGESS AND PRICE, op. cit., based on tables on pp. 258, 259, and 280.
11. *Public Welfare, Poverty—Prevention or Perpetuation* (New York: Greenleigh Associates, December 1964), p. 32.
12. BURGESS AND PRICE, op. cit., pp. 28 and 250.
13. *Study of Recipients of Aid to Families with Dependent Children, November–December 1961: National Cross-Tabulations,* table 25.

CHAPTER 22

Families on Welfare in New York City

Irene Cox

What are families like who receive welfare assistance? What are their attitudes, preferences and expectations for the future? How many are able to work? How long have they lived in the community? What are the circumstances of their early lives? How many are second generation recipients of assistance? These and many other questions are the concern of welfare administrators, legislators, program planners and a wide cross section of the community. More definitive answers are needed for a better understanding of the nature and effects of welfare programs, and of the problems facing families receiving public assistance in order to develop programs to attack dependency.

In recognition of this need, the Center for Social Research of the City University of New York has prepared a series of Preliminary Reports on welfare families in New York who were receiving assistance in April 1966. Data for the Reports were obtained in the course of conducting a research project dealing with the utilization of health services by welfare recipients. Selected characteristics of these families are presented without extensive analysis and with the recognition that they represent "social bookkeeping" more than "social research."

Among the characteristics reported were the family's welfare experience, living conditions, education and employment of the mothers, presence or absence of the husband, and nativity and immigration to New York. Tables included in the Reports provide detailed information on welfare families by age, ethnicity, marital status, community of rearing and other relevant variables.

Reprinted from Department of Health, Education and Welfare, *Welfare in Review* (March/April 1968). This selection summarizes the results of unpublished research directed by Professor Lawrence Podell for H.E.W.

Data in the Reports are based on interviews with a stratified sample of 2,179 families receiving Aid to Families with Dependent Children; Temporary Aid to Dependent Children (families with an unemployed father); and Home Relief (families receiving supplementation of low earnings of an employed father). The latter two categories were overrepresented in order to insure enough two-parent families for analysis, but when generalizing findings to the total welfare population as of April 1966 a weighting procedure was used.

The results of the investigation included in this review are descriptive of the total caseload of families on welfare in New York City in April 1966, as projected from information obtained from the sample. However, the Reports contain a note of caution that findings do not necessarily describe the present caseload as there has been a considerable increase in the number of families receiving assistance in New York City since the time the survey was conducted.

Some Major Findings

Fifty percent of the families on welfare in New York City in April 1966 were Negro, 40 percent were Puerto Rican and 10 percent were white. Husbands were present in more than one-fourth of the households. Ten percent of the mothers were either divorced or widowed and nearly 20 percent were unmarried. Mothers were without husbands due to separation or desertion in over 40 percent of the families. It is noted that the high rate of desertion as a cause of dependency is given little attention and that research has been lacking in recent years on separation and desertion in low-income families.

A finding of interest was that most deserted mothers reported that the separation from the husband occurred following the family's first receipt of assistance rather than before. The author comments that this sequence of events is contrary to customary expectation and may indicate an opportunity for prevention of family breakdown when the family is known to the welfare department before the separation occurs.

Nearly 40 percent of the mothers were under 30 years of age, 40 percent were in their thirties and the remaining 20 percent were 40 years of age or older. Two-thirds of the families had three or more children in the home under 19 years of age, and two-thirds had preschool age children. Nearly all of the mothers in the sample who were in their teens and twenties had preschool children; over 40 percent of Negro and Puerto Rican women in this age range either had very young infants or were pregnant at the time of the survey.

Only 11 percent of the welfare families lived in public housing. Respondents reported rat infestation in one-third of the buildings in which they lived. Most recipients owned a clock, a television set and/or a radio, but only one in four had a telephone. The latter situation, the author points out, was related to Departmental policy limiting possession of a telephone by welfare families.

Continuous time on assistance was not reported. More than half of the families first received assistance in 1960 or thereafter. One-third first received assistance within two years prior to the time of the survey. Families without fathers in the home were more likely to have received assistance before 1960.

Women with husbands in the household were more likely to have been reared by both parents in rural communities and to have had less schooling. Unmarried women in their teens and twenties were more likely than married women of the same age to have grown up in New York City, to have graduated from high school, to have been reared by their mothers only and to have fewer children.

When those women who were separated from their husbands were asked how they felt, more than half replied that they were not at all concerned about being separated. Two-thirds of the unmarried mothers expressed some concern about not being married.

Concern about not being married	*Separated mothers* %	*Unmarried mothers* %
Very concerned	18	36
Moderately concerned	9	13
A little concerned	14	19
Not at all concerned	53	29
Don't know or no answer	6	1
Total	100	100

Family and Community Origins

About a fifth of the mothers on welfare were born in New York City, about a third in the South, and over a third in Puerto Rico. Three out of 10 mothers grew up in New York City; three in 10 came to the city before they were 19 years of age; another three in 10 arrived as young adults. Only 10 percent came to the city when they were over 30 years of age. Half of the mothers were reared in small town or rural areas. (Table 1)

Half of the mothers on welfare were brought up by both parents. A fourth were raised by mothers only and a fourth by other relatives or in foster homes or institutions. Half of the mothers had four or more siblings.

Among the mothers in the sample, those under 30 years of age and those who grew up in an urban community were less likely to have been reared by both parents. Those born and/or reared in New York City were most likely to have been brought up by their mother only and to have had fewer siblings.

TABLE 1. *Community of Rearing by Ethnicity*

Community of Rearing	White	Negro	Puerto Rican
	%	%	%
New York City	78	32	8
Another city	12	21	30
Small town	6	21	33
Farm	3	26	38
Total	100	100	100
Number	(208)	(1017)	(954)

Fifteen percent of all mothers on welfare reported that their parents had received public assistance. Negroes reported that 21 percent of their parents had received assistance, whites, 16 percent and Puerto Ricans, 9 percent.

The Reports discuss some of the problems involved in defining inter-generational dependency and determining how extensive it is. Concern, it is pointed out, is usually focused only on those families receiving public support continuously for decades, overlooking the many siblings who are fully self-supporting. However, it is noted that families might receive assistance for a few weeks or months during periods of unemployment or illness, or for a few years until their children are in school. This raises a question as to whether such short-term assistance recipients are to be considered "dependent" along with the more chronic cases. Another factor to be considered is the variation in past and present State and local assistance programs. It is noted that such programs in the rural South and in Puerto Rico differ considerably from programs in the urban North. This helps to explain why respondents born and/or reared in New York City showed a greater tendency to indicate that their parents were on welfare than did those reared elsewhere and why Puerto Rican mothers were least likely to indicate that their parents were ever on welfare.

Education and Work Experience

Fifty-seven percent of the mothers on welfare had attended high school and one out of six were graduated. Another one out of six had not gone beyond the fourth grade of elementary school. Mothers with higher educational attainment were younger, more likely to be unmarried or separated and more likely to have been reared in New York City. Most mothers stated they did not get as much education as they wanted.

Eighty percent of the mothers had some employment experience. Usually this was prior to the birth of the first child but almost one-half of the mothers worked afterward. Three out of 10 had worked three years or less but almost one-half had worked six years or more. Three out of 10 were employed for more than 10 years. White mothers were more likely to have been employed as clerical workers, Negro mothers as operatives or service workers, and Puerto Ricans as operatives.

The Reports comment on the implications of findings for planning work training and employment programs for welfare recipients. If the target population is to be younger women who have more education, an extensive day care program would be needed since these women are more likely to have preschool children. Overall planning must also take into account that training and employment of this group of women might be interrupted by pregnancy and care of the infant. More older women are probably available for employment since they are less likely to have preschool children. However, since their level of education is lower, basic education courses as well as vocational training would be required to enable them to improve earning capacity.

In terms of programs to upgrade recipients' skills and incomes, the observation is made that men should not be overlooked. Although employed and employable men constitute only about 5 percent of the recipients, their continued dependency directly affects probably 20 and possibly 25 percent of New York City's welfare population.

Attitude Toward Welfare and Work

More than half of the mothers said they "felt bothered" about being on welfare and agreed with the statements on the questionnaire that "Getting money from welfare makes a person feel ashamed" and "People should be grateful for the money they get from welfare." The majority of respondents believed that many undeserving people were assisted by welfare and that the Department has the right to question the spending of money received. (Table 2)

Seven out of 10 mothers said they would prefer to work rather than stay at home. Child care was the major reason given for wanting to stay at home. However, six out of 10 mothers with preschool children said they would prefer to work if appropriate day care facilities were available. (Table 3) The author cautions that a "stated preference on a survey should neither be equated with a decision to act accordingly nor a readiness to do so, although it may involve both."

Two-thirds of the mothers planned to work in the future although six in 10 said they still expected to be receiving public assistance the next year. Younger women, those with more schooling, and those with fewer children, were less likely to expect to remain publicly assisted. Eight out of 10 mothers on welfare believed that their children would not become dependent adults. Only 3 percent felt that their children surely or probably would require welfare assistance as adults.

TABLE 2. *Selected Attitudes of (a) all Mothers on Welfare and (b) Respondent Mothers, by Ethnicity*

	All mothers*	Respondent mothers		
		White	Negro	Puerto Rican
	%	%	%	%
Felt bothered by being on welfare	58	63	66	45
Agreed that people on welfare feel ashamed	56	61	55	53
Strongly agreed that people should be grateful for welfare money	61	50	52	76
Agreed that many undeserving people get welfare money	71	56	70	76
Agreed that the Department of Welfare has no right to question spending	44	42	44	44
Agreed that welfare workers made her feel that she should not bother them	36	32	41	29
Number		(208)	(1017)	(954)

* Weighted projections from stratified sample.

The Preliminary Reports illustrate the usefulness of data about conditions and characteristics relative to receipt of public assistance. Even though the survey was not directly concerned with causes and solutions to the problems of dependency, the information obtained from recipients does broaden understanding of variations among welfare families and has implications for flexible program and policy planning.

TABLE 3. *Preference for Working or Homemaking, Assuming Appropriate Child Day Care Arrangements, of Mothers with Preschool Children, by Ethnicity*

Preference	Mothers with Preschool Children		
	White	Negro	Puerto Rican
Prefer to work	38	69	54
Prefer to stay home	55	28	43
Don't know	6	2	2
No answer	1	2	2
Total	100	100	100
Number	(114)	(729)	(646)

CHAPTER 23

The Case for an Income Guarantee

James Tobin

In the national campaign to conquer poverty there are two basic strategies, which may be labelled concisely, if somewhat inaccurately, "structural" and "distributive." The structural strategy is to build up the capacities of the poorest fifth of the population to earn decent incomes. The distributive strategy is to assure every family a decent standard of living regardless of its earning capacity. In my opinion both strategies are essential; correctly designed, they are more complementary than competitive. To date the main emphasis of the Federal "war on poverty" has been the structural approach. I shall argue that the war will not be won without a new and imaginative distributive strategy as well.

General economic progress raises the earning capacities of the populations at large — even of the less educated, less skilled, less experienced, less motivated, and less healthy. Even without Federal programs (other than overall fiscal and monetary policies to keep the labor force fully employed and the economy growing), the incidence of poverty gradually declines. Measuring poverty by the government's official [1966] income standard ($3130 a year for 4-person nonfarm families, and amounts estimated to yield comparable standards of living for households of other sizes and circumstances), its incidence has fallen from 22 percent to 17 percent since 1959.

The "war on poverty" testifies that the decline has not been fast enough for the American conscience. But accelerating it by structural measures is bound to be a slow and expensive process. Adults must be trained or retrained; they must acquire work experience, good work habits, self-confidence, and motivation; they must be made medically fit for regular employment; they must

Reprinted from *The Public Interest*, No. 4, Summer 1966, by permission of the publisher and author, © 1966 by National Affairs, Inc.

be placed in jobs and often moved to new locations. What is required is almost a case-by-case approach. Leaving the aged aside, there are about 8 million poor households including 9½ million persons of ages 22-54 and 3 million in ages 16-21. The task of upgrading the earning capacities of the present generation of adults is staggering, a fact which in no way diminishes the importance of the effort or the value of each individual success.

The earning capacities of the next generation may be successfully raised by general structural measures — radical improvements in the education, health, and residential environment of the 14 million children of the poor. Again, the urgent importance of these efforts is in no way dimmed by recognizing the great difficulties they confront.

But the structural strategy will take many years, probably more than a generation. Even then its success will be incomplete; there will remain a hard core of families with inadequate earning capacity because of ineradicable physical, psychological, or circumstantial disabilities. And in the interim many more families, with disabilities remediable but not remedied, will fail to earn a decent living.

Today's Symptoms, Tomorrow's Causes

A distributive strategy is necessary, too, and the sooner the better. Families must have a minimally decent standard of living, whether or not they now have the ability to earn it in the job market. This can be provided by public assistance, and to withhold it from poor families is neither just (since their disabilities are, if not irremediable, the consequences of past discriminations and deficiencies in public services) nor necessary (since the upper four-fifths of the nation can surely afford the 2 percent of Gross National Product which would bring the lowest fifth across the poverty line).

Sometimes income assistance is scorned as treating the symptoms of poverty, in contrast to the structural strategy, which treats the causes. This reproach is not justified. For one thing, there is nothing intrinsically wrong with treating symptoms, and sometimes it is the best the doctors can do. More seriously, the symptoms of today's poverty may be the causes of tomorrow's. The conditions of life in which many children now grow up may predestine them to low earning capacity as adults.

However, many of those who distrust the distributive strategy have a more sophisticated point in mind. They are afraid that more generous income assistance to the poor will actually retard improvements in their earning capacities. If a decent standard of living is guaranteed, why should anyone work to get it or to acquire the ability to earn it on his own? For centuries this cynicism about human nature has been the excuse by which the affluent have relieved their individual and collective consciences and pocketbooks of the burden of their less fortunate brethren.

We cannot dismiss the question just because it has a shabby history. "Human nature" is not a reason to withhold public subsidies from people with low-earning capacity. But it definitely is a reason to give the subsidies in a way that does not destroy but indeed reinforces the incentives of the recipients to work and to increase the economic value of their work. The war on poverty needs a distributive strategy, but one that is carefully designed to support and strengthen its structural strategy.

Unfortunately our present congeries of public assistance programs — Federal, state, and local — has just the opposite effect. The incentives built in to our present subsidy programs are perverse. Unless public assistance is reformed and rationalized, it will seriously handicap the structural weapons deployed in the campaign against poverty. An improved public assistance program will not be cheap. It is designed to aid rather than retard the conquest of poverty, its cost will for some years be more than our present programs. But it offers the hope that the conditions giving rise to the need for public subsidies will gradually be remedied.

II.

What are the defects of public assistance today? First is its inadequacy. Our governments administer a bewildering variety of welfare and social insurance programs, from Federal Old Age, Survivors, and Disability Insurance (OASDI) to township relief. *Yet half of the poor benefit from none of these; and most of the public money spent to supplement personal incomes goes to families above the poverty line.*

These facts are shocking but not as surprising as they may at first appear. Eligibility to benefit from most government income supplements depends on circumstances quite remote from current economic need. For social insurance — OASDI and unemployment compensation — eligibility and size of benefits depend on past contributions by the individual or his employer. Many programs assist particular groups — veterans, farmers, retired railroad workers, the blind, etc.

Even in the main noncontributory general assistance programs, economic need is a necessary condition for benefits but not a sufficient one. The most important of these is Aid for Dependent Children (AFDC), administered under Federal supervision by the states and localities, and financed almost wholly by Federal funds. AFDC payments are based on need, but the several states define need with widely varying degrees of realism and seldom attempt to meet fully even their own calculations of need. A 1961 study showed that the Middle Atlantic states met all the income requirements they estimated. The East South Central States — Kentucky, Tennessee, Mississippi, and Alabama — estimated need at 20% less, met on average only 61% (Mississippi 38%) of the need so estimated, and met full need in only 3% of their cases. Federal law permits payments only to families with children, and of these only to families without an employed male adult — where, in effect, the father has died or deserted, or is disabled or unemployed. Most states restrict eligibility more than the Federal law requires.

There are also Federally financed programs of assistance to the aged and disabled which fill some of the gaps Social Security still leaves both in eligibility and in adequacy of benefits. For the indigent who qualify for nothing else there is old-fashioned local relief, but here the applicant may run afoul of local residence requirements and other defensive stratagems.

Incentives in Reverse

Second, public assistance is geared to need in a manner that provides perverse incentives to those dependent upon it. One major destructive incentive is the one which AFDC gives for the break-up or non-formation of families. *Too often a father can provide for his children only by leaving both them and their mother.* It is hard to imagine a social contrivance more surely designed to perpetuate dependence on "welfare" in one generation after the other. We know that the major problems of poor people of all colors are related, as both cause and effect, to unstable and chaotic family structures. We know that, for historical reasons, Negro families tend to be matriarchal. We know that crucial importance of home environment in education, and we know the dangers of depriving boys of male adult models. To accentuate all these difficulties by deliberate public policy is a piece of collective insanity which it would be hard to match.

The "means test" provides other disincentives — disincentives to work, to save, to gain skills. The "means test" seems innocent enough in appearance and intent. It says that the welfare payments shall be made only if, and only to the extent that, the family cannot meet its needs (as officially calculated) from its own resources. Thus if, in a given locality, the effective standard of need (which may be only a fraction of an estimated minimal budget for a mother and four children is $2500 a year, the family will receive $2500 from the state if its members earn nothing on their own, $1500 if they earn $1000, $500 if they earn $2000, and so on. This arrangement, under which your total take-home pay is the same no matter how much you earn, is obviously not designed to encourage work or training for future work. One way to describe it is to say that the marginal tax rate on earnings is (so long as earnings do not exceed $2500 in the example) 100%. The accuracy of this description, so far as incentive effects are concerned, is not impaired by the fact that the "tax" on additional earnings is not a literal payment to the government but a reduction in the government payment to the family.

The means test also discourages thrift. Consider two self-supporting families, one of whom saves while the other incurs debts. When and if misfortunes occur, the welfare authorities will give full help to the second but will generally force the thrifty family to use up its savings. Similarly, a man who has over a lifetime of work acquired his own home may be required to surrender title to it if he can't get by without public assistance in his old age.

It is true that there remains the incentive to escape public assistance entirely and, since the welfare standard of life is a meager one at best, this incentive may seem substantial. But to many welfare households, especially the broken homes, it is too big a jump to be a realistic aspiration. Unattainable goals may be demoralizing rather than motivating. Most welfare dependents cannot set their sights higher than part-time low-paid employment. Yet this may be extremely important, both to acquire work experience and rudimentary skill and to build up the family's morale and sense of achievement. The system is rigged against it; there is nothing in it for them.

The welfare system of the United States contains plenty of ironies. A nation which regards the integrity of the nuclear family as the very backbone of its social structure provides incentives for its dissolution. A society which views high marginal income tax rates as fatal to the incentives for effort and thrift essential to its economy imposes 100% rates on a large fraction of its population. The explanation of such bizarre behavior is probably that present welfare policies represent an uneasy compromise among several principles. Since the thirties our society has acknowledged its responsibility to assure through government a minimal standard of living for all citizens. But the corollary charge on the public purse has been accepted grudgingly, and the fear that the "privilege" of welfare might be abused has dominated policy.

A by-product of this dominant fear is that much of the considerable administrative effort in public welfare reduces to detective work, to make sure there are no "cheaters" on the rolls, and to close surveillance of the clients' sources and uses of funds, to make sure that tax money is not wasted in riotous living. Everything confirms welfare families in the demoralizing belief that they cannot manage their own affairs. This tendency is reenforced by the propensity of legislators to give assistance in kind — surplus foods, subsidized housing, medical care for the indigent or "medically indigent." Eligibility for these benefits is usually defined by a maximum income limit, awkward to administer and perverse in incentive effects.

CHAPTER 24

Against a Negative Income Tax

Alvin L. Schorr

One can only agree with the basic assumption of Professor Tobin's article. That is, the nation requires two complementary strategies to deal with poverty. One would educate and train our citizenry to earn as much income as they can. The other would assure income, by some system of government payments, to those who have not succeeded or cannot succeed in securing adequate income through work. Beyond that assumption, Professor Tobin's presentation of the negative income tax is thoughtful and enlightened.* It therefore offers an unusual opportunity — without necessity for detour into minutiae or underlying ideology — to identify serious limitations in the only type of plan for assuring income that has drawn public attention since the declaration of a war against poverty.

The Incentive Scale

Professor Tobin himself identifies one of the serious limitations of the negative income tax. There are, he says, "inexorable conflicts" among three objectives of such a program: providing a substantial payment to families that earn little; building in a strong incentive to earn more; and limiting the cost of the program by avoiding payments to those who do not need them. Until recently, for example, public assistance theoretically provided exactly the difference between a family's income and total needs. If their income rises, their payment falls — a painful balance that can only discourage voluntary

* Editor's Note: Tobin's proposal has been omitted from the preceding selection, but is summarized by Green and Lampman in Chapter 15.
Reprinted from *The Public Interest,* No. 5, Fall 1966 by permission of the publisher and author. © 1966 by National Affairs, Inc.

effort. The negative income tax incorporates a response to this problem: the family retains a percentage (two-thirds, in Professor Tobin's proposal) of any income they earn. Unfortunately, such an incentive scale gets caught between opposing pressures. Either the rate at which payments are made pushes downward and many people receive inadequate income, or it moves upward and people with comparatively decent incomes receive assistance.

The illustration that Professor Tobin uses of his proposed scheme — a married couple with three children — makes the opposing pressures clear. Under the scheme, such a family would receive an income allowance until its own income reached $6,000. That figure is very nearly the median family income in the United States, which is to say that nearly half of all couples with three children would receive some payment. At the same time, families with less than $2,500 of their own income would receive a government payment too small to bring them above the poverty line. As it happens, almost half of poor married couples with three children have less than $2,500 in income and, though perceptibly helped by the income allowance, would remain poor. Because for obvious reasons their earnings are less, families without a husband or father would fare even worse. Four out of five of those with three children would remain poor while receiving an income allowance under the plan.

One could do better for families at the bottom by pushing the whole scale upwards, but then families with even higher than median incomes would receive payments. One could avoid payments to families with average income, but then families at the bottom would receive even less. The difficulty is not an accident of Professor Tobin's particular plan or example; as he says, the conflict is intrinsic in the general concept. The nature of the anxiety that this conflict arouses should be made explicit. Payments that would push too far into the higher income brackets cost a good deal; they also undermine the credibility of a program said to be designed for poor people. Therefore, such a plan is not likely to be enacted. But payments that are too low at the bottom of the scale fail to assure income in terms appropriate to the third decade of affluence.

A Single Program

Simplicity and widespread coverage are among the chief attractions of the negative income tax; unfortunately, they constitute a second limitation. The notion of providing a decent income to men who might work calls forth passions in Americans that are never fully explained on rational grounds. One might think that we suffer from a buried desire not to work at all, so bitterly do we regard people who we think are bringing it off. We have avoided this problem in the past assuring income to identifiable groups that do not provoke us — old people, children without fathers, the blind. As for the others, we have invoked a variety of unwieldy devices more or less obnoxious to beneficiaries and reassuring to the citizenry. We have conducted medical examinations on applicants and required them to report for job referrals or rehabilitation. We have scrutinized their affairs and cut them off, willy nilly, after thirteen weeks or twenty-six.

The negative income tax promises, in a brilliant stroke, to pare away these unworthy practises. With an incentive scale, the individual could be trusted to work when he should and be spared the restraints of policy and investigation. In applying it to all, however, we give up for old people, children, and the disabled (who together constitute at least two-thirds of the poor population) the protection of separate treatment from the suspect employables. Separate status is an expensive nuisance if employable people are to be decently treated. But it is vital if — a possibility that must at least be entertained — the pressures on an incentive scale produce a desperately inadequate payment for those with the lowest earned incomes. Under the negative income tax proposal, for example, an old man who is not covered by social security and has no earnings would receive total income of $400 a year. The average payment to an old person under public assistance is more than twice that.

In short, a danger — not to say, irony — of the negative income tax is this: carefully engineered to the requirements of people who should work, the penalty of the lowest total incomes (including income allowances) will be suffered by families included, as it were, by courtesy — families without earners. Conceivably, the income of such families could be supplemented through public assistance. We should wind up then with a large public assistance program, raising the question whether the new departure had achieved anything of significance.

Income Testing

The third limitation of the negative income tax is that it is a conservative and even retrogressive movement in the development of income assurance. The case that is made *for* the negative income tax is, in some measure, simply the case *against* public assistance; yet the two programs are as much alike as different. Public assistance has been characterized by two offensive qualities. One is a detailed investigation of applicants' affairs; it is proposed that the negative income tax do away with this. The other is the provision of a government payment based on a demonstration, however simple, that income is lacking. Income testing, as we shall call this quality, is also fundamental to the negative income tax. Although the principle may seem the commonest of common sense, Americans have been plotting to do away with it for years. When we succeed, the plea will be justifiable homicide.

When a third of the nation was poor, by standards even more stringent than we use today, experts cast about for ways to provide income as a matter of right. As it has turned out, many rights would do — a history of work, contributions to a fund, payment of a government tax, old age, veteran status, and so forth. Social Security was, in this sense, a product of widespread revulsion against income testing. We sought for a way to provide income in old age (and, later, in case of death of a husband or father, and in case of disability) that would not require a demonstration of need, and the way was found. Much more recently, medicare represented a struggle on the same issue. The American Medical Association and others argued that medical care should be provided on the simplest demonstration of need. But old people did not want an income test, the Administration did not want it, and Congress was persuaded.

Need or want is the only quality that we have not by itself converted into a right or, on the receiving end, been able to feel as a right. It is not, in truth, for lack of trying. Our most embattled income assurance program was conceived in the 1930's in a deliberate attempt to protect children from the humiliation and inadequacy of general relief. If mothers' aid or children's aid could be singled out, experts reasoned, assistance would be rendered as a matter of right to those who could demonstrate need. The history of Aid to Families with Dependent Children provides a bitter rebuttal to that fond hope.

The reaction so far — or lack of reaction — of potential beneficiaries of the negative income tax is itself a bit of evidence about the meaning of income tests. The writer's impression is that poor people would, if they were consulted, reject the negative income tax. Civil rights leaders have shown less than spontaneous enthusiasm for the notion. It was conspicuously absent from the recommendations laid before the White House Conference "To Fulfill These Rights" last summer, although they dealt with guaranteeing income. Poor People would probably say that they want to make good as others have. They will be glad to take the fringe benefits that go with making good — including exemptions, pensions, benefits, allowances, and insurance payments — but are willing to be spared a new set of payments based on a demonstration that they are poor (read: are supplicants).

In strictly economic terms, the distinction between one type of government payment and another may be trivial. The medicare payment to a hospital for an old person not covered by social security is a transfer payment quite like his Old Age Assistance. Yet, obviously, such distinctions affect how people feel in receiving the payment; they also affect whether programs are administered with decent respect for them. In these terms, the negative income tax would continue and even extend the domain of the income test. If we try it, we may be tutored once again in a lesson we seem regularly to forget. We are brutal in the giving of money we define as relief; we are sweetly charitable only when we have succeeded in defining a payment as something else — a right based on age, on paid-up status, on some event (military service, death of a husband). It is rather the latter types of program we should seek to extend.

At least the first two limitations of the negative income tax — the difficulty of providing a *decent* payment to those who need it, without paying to many who do not, and the risk to those who cannot work of sharing the payment levels of those who can work — may ultimately be appraised against the actual payment levels that are proposed to Congress. The debate on these two points need not be carried on solely in the abstract. We have noted that Professor Tobin's illustrative plan provides inadequate income for many families. If payment levels should be enacted no lower than he proposes, and even indeed higher, it might be hoped that these two limitations were not serious after all. On the other hand, a plan with payment levels that are any lower cannot be regarded as a first step towards a program that will eventually become adequate. The effect of these two limitations is precisely that a small, inadequate program is likely to be attractive, while a plan with decent payment levels raises conflicts that cannot be resolved. The third limitation — that the negative income tax travels the income-test route rather than the income-by-right route — is an issue upon which citizens ought to reflect and be heard.

An Alternative Course

Presumably, a communication should not be longer than the article to which it responds. In the space that decently remains, an alternative course to take in assuring income will at least be indicated. In brief, we might accelerate the course we have been following since 1935, strengthening a series of programs based on established rights and devising programs to fill the gaps that will remain.

The Social Security system is our most successful mechanism for assuring income, and it can readily be strengthened. For example, almost two out of five people who receive retirement benefits are poor. The minimum benefit for an aged person is now $44.00; doubling the figure would be a long step towards wiping out poverty among old people. Benefits for those with higher than minimum earnings would also be raised, of course, but not as quickly at first. Such a strategy would provide an interesting international reversal. Great Britain and Sweden began their systems with a flat payment that was essentially an antipoverty device and held little attraction for those accustomed to good incomes. Recently, the two countries have added a benefit related to wages on top of the minimum. In effect, in establishing an antipoverty minimum, we should be moving toward a similar two-decker system from the opposite direction.

Apart from the question of payment, something over one million aged people are now quite uncovered by Social Security or similar public systems.

They may be provided status under Social Security, following the precedent of the 1965 amendment that "blanketed" people over 72 into Social Security. (Professor Tobin may agree with these proposals regarding the aged, as he writes that Social Security might handle all the income problems of the aged. However, he does not mention blanketting-in and seems to imply lower levels of Social Security.) Provision for other Social Security beneficiaries might also be strengthened. A widow with three or four children may receive as little as $66.00 a month under Social Security. Obviously, minimum payments levels in such cases require improvement. Appraised in terms of assuring a minimum income, the Social Security definition of who is gravely disabled probably needs to be liberalized. Nor should we be limited to perfecting existing provisions. For example, the man is his mid-fifties who is laid off from work may be a natural candidate for a new extension of retirement insurance; one day, we shall no doubt seriously consider such proposals.

It is probably not necessary to review in detail all the other income assurance programs that require strengthening — unemployment compensation, workman's compensation, medical care for the poor who are younger than 65. (Some other part of the task, of course, lies with assuring that decently paid jobs and the education or training necessary to perform them are made available.) The point may be clear: if we perfect and expand social security programs and others like them, we can assure proper income to a great many people who are now poor. The Commissioner of Social Security has estimated that in this manner a third to a half of poverty in the United States could be avoided.

A Program for Children

When we have visualized what might be achieved by improving existing mechanisms, we shall doubtless be struck by one major omission in the general plan. In so child-centered a nation as ours, it is a curious fact that the major omission is a program to assure income for children. Particularly at risk are children whose parents have separated or divorced — *socially* orphaned children — and children in large families. A single statistic may dramatize this point. Three out of four youth who are poor can make one or both of these statements: "I did not live with my father or even a man I could call father," and "my family has five or more children." Even full-time work may not exorcise poverty for a woman raising children alone (she earns little; she pays for day care) or a couple with five children or more (poverty level, $4,600 or more). Whether children face one problem or the other, their difficulty is not confronted by any income assurance program short of public assistance.

Probably the foremost nominee as a method of providing income to children by right would be a program of children's allowances. As an illustration, a program of children's allowances designed to cost about $12 billion* might work like this:

A benefit of $50 a month would be payable for each child under 6 years of age and $10 a month for each older child. Present income tax exemptions for all children would be eliminated, and the benefit itself would be taxable. The cost would be borne out of general revenue.

A family with *taxable* income between $4,000 and $8,000 that has only school-age children would about break even in comparison with our present taxing arrangement. (They would receive $120 per child in exchange for the tax benefit to them of a $600 exemption.) Families with only school-age children and higher taxable incomes would register a net loss — from only a few dollars a year to as much as a couple of hundred dollars in the highest brackets. All families with pre-school children and all low- and middle-income families would register a net gain. Over a period of several years, the program would probably be regarded with gratitude by families that started out with modest means and achieved a good income later on — a not uncommon pattern. In effect, some income would be moved forward for them from the years when they would have most to the years when they most need it.

The program would be quite as simple to operate as to describe. Everyone having care or custody of a child would receive a monthly check after he once provided a simple statement of the child's age and relationship.

As all Western industrialized nations have a program of children's allowances, their experience answers the questions that come to one's mind. Would the money really be spent on children? Yes. Would it lead to an increase in birth rates? Despite conventional wisdom on the subject, it would not. (One may look, for example, at neighboring Canada and at France, which makes the largest allowance payments in the world. The striking quality of birth rates in both countries in the last twenty years is that they closely resemble trends in the United States.) Would allowances tend to keep children in school? Probably, if enrollment was a condition for the payment. Would payments interfere with incentive to work? Not at all, for — contrary to the negative income tax — the allowance payment does not alter, whether income is little or very large indeed. The allowance payment is a right of childhood, a birthright, one might say.

The particular arrangement of benefits offered here — $50 and $10 — is unusual. It is designed as nearly as possible to wipe out poverty among families in the first few years of marriage or, to shift perspective, to wipe out

---

* Professor Tobin estimates that his illustrative scheme would cost $12 to $15 billion. It might be argued that the cost of the alternative being outlined here would be $12 billion for children's allowances *plus* the costs of improving social security. On the other hand, it might be argued that social security levels of payment and coverage are quite regularly improved — every two years or so. The social security improvements outlined here merely affect the allocation of funds that are going to be committed to income assurance in some fashion or other.

poverty for preschool children. These years are irrecoverably important to young parents. Considerable evidence suggests that they may falter in efforts at self-improvement (fail to take a better job in another city, drop out of school or a training program) because their income does not provide enough flexibility to gamble on their future. These years, which are also crucial to children's development, are the very years when we can barely reach them except through their parents. Finally, in these years the mother — not to say children — is least able to supplement what a husband can earn. All these factors fade in significance or urgency when children enter school; therefore, in this particular proposal, the largest share of money is funnelled to preschool children.

Conclusion

Major differences between the possible courses for assuring income might be put as follows. Professor Tobin proposes a general program that would become the core of income assurance. Other programs would not expand greatly and might even diminish. The core program would be income-tested. An incentive plan would be built into the program in order to assure that incentive to work was not eroded. The result would be a comparatively simple, rational system with every poor person getting something, but many families failing to escape above the currently defined poverty line.

The alternative that has been indicated here would improve and expand existing programs to create a pattern that assured income for virtually everyone. For such groups as needed it, new programs would be devised. Programs would be based on a variety of rights and income-testing would be used as little as possible. Because programs based on right do not in general reduce payments when there in other income, incentive plans would not be required. In systematic planning for a pattern that assures income, a more orderly plan should emerge than now exists. Nevertheless, the result would be less tidy than with Professor Tobin's proposal.

Although the issues may be clear, they are readily clouded with technical detail; the issue of income-testing versus income-by-right rests very much on how people feel; a part of the judgement that must be made requires some degree of prescience. Two considerations weigh heavily for the writer against the negative income tax and for an alternative course.

First, less than enough is not enough. Income assurance means that no one shall be poor. Professor Tobin's proposal does not achieve that. Moreover, there is reason to suspect that it *could not develop* into a program that would achieve that objective.

Second, almost as important as not *being* poor is not *feeling* poor. Only income-by-right achieves that.

CHAPTER 25

Proposals for Welfare Reform (August 11, 1969)

Richard M. Nixon

A measure of the greatness of a powerful nation is the character of the life it creates for those who are powerless to make ends meet.

If we do not find the way to become a working nation that properly cares for the dependent, we shall become a Welfare State that undermines the incentive of the working man.

The present welfare system has failed us — it has fostered family breakup, has provided very little help in many States and has even deepened dependency by all-too-often making it more attractive to go on welfare than to go to work.

I propose a new approach that will make it more attractive to go to work than to go on welfare, and will establish a nationwide minimum payment to dependent families with children.

I propose that the Federal government pay a basic income to those American families who cannot care for themselves in whichever State they live.

I propose that dependent families receiving such income be given good reason to go to work *by making the first sixty dollars a month they earn completely their own, with no deductions from their benefits.*

I propose that we *make available an addition to the incomes of the "working poor,"* to encourage them to go on working and to eliminate the possibility of making more from welfare than from wages.

I propose that these payments be made upon certification of income, with demeaning and costly investigations replaced by simplified reviews and spot

Reprinted from the 91st Congress, 1st Session, *House of Representatives Document No. 91-146,* August 1969.

checks and with *no eligibility requirement that the household be without a father.* That present requirement in many States has the effect of breaking up families and contributes to delinquency and violence.

I propose that all employable persons who choose to accept these payments be required to register for work or job training and *be required to accept that work or training,* provided suitable jobs are available either locally or if transportation is provided. Adequate and convenient day care would be provided children wherever necessary to enable a parent to train or work. The only exception to this work requirement would be mothers of preschool children.

I propose *a major expansion of job training and day care facilities,* so that current welfare recipients able to work can be set on the road to self-reliance.

I propose that we also *provide uniform Federal payment minimums for the present three categories of welfare aid to adults* — the aged, the blind and the disabled.

This would be total welfare reform — the transformation of a system frozen in failure and frustration into a system that would work and would encourage people to work.

Accordingly, we have stopped considering human welfare in isolation. The new plan is part of an overall approach which includes a comprehensive new Manpower Training Act, and a plan for a system of revenue sharing with the States to help provide all of them with necessary budget relief. Messages on manpower training and revenue sharing will follow this message tomorrow and the next day, and the three should be considered as parts of a whole approach to what is clearly a national problem.

Need for New Departures

A welfare system is a success when it takes care of people who cannot take care of themselves and when it helps employable people climb toward independence.

A welfare system is a failure when it takes care of those who *can* take care of themselves, then it drastically varies payments in different areas, when it breaks up families when it perpetuates a vicious cycle of dependency, when it strips human beings of their dignity.

America's welfare system is a failure that grows worse every day.

First, it fails the recipient: In many areas, benefits are so low that we have hardly begun to take care of the dependent. And there has been no light at the end of poverty's tunnel. After four years of inflation, the poor have generally become poorer.

Second, it fails the taxpayer: Since 1960, welfare costs have doubled and the number on the rolls has risen from 5.8 million to over 9 million, all in time when unemployment was low. The taxpayer is entitled to expect government to devise a system that will help people lift themselves out of poverty.

Finally, it fails American society: By breaking up homes, the present welfare system has added to social unrest and robbed millions of children of the joy of childhood; by widely varying payments among regions, it has helped to draw millions into the slums of our cities.

The situation has become intolerable. Let us examine the alternatives available:

— We could permit the welfare momentum to continue to gather speed by our inertia; by 1975 this would result in 4 million more Americans on welfare rolls at a cost of close to 11 billion dollars a year, with both recipients and taxpayers shortchanged.

— We could tinker with the system as it is, adding to the patchwork of modifications and exceptions. That has been the approach of the past, and it has failed.

— We could adopt a "guaranteed minimum income for everyone," which would appear to wipe out poverty overnight. It would also wipe out the basic economic motivation for work, and place an enormous strain on the industrious to pay for the leisure of the lazy.

— Or, we could adopt a totally new approach to welfare, designed to assist those left far behind the national norm, and provide all with the motivation to work and a fair share of the opportunity to train.

This Administration, after a careful analysis of all the alternatives, is committed to a new departure that will find a solution for the welfare problem. The time for denouncing the old is over; the time for devising the new is now.

Recognizing the Practicalities

People usually follow their self-interest.

This stark fact is distressing to many social planners who like to look at problems from the top down. Let us abandon the ivory tower and consider the real world in all we do.

In most States, welfare is provided only when there is no father at home to provide support. If a man's children would be better off on welfare than with the low wage he is able to bring home, wouldn't he be tempted to leave home?

If a person spent a great deal of time and effort to get on the welfare rolls, wouldn't he think twice about risking his eligibility by taking a job that might not last long?

In each case, welfare policy was intended to limit the spread of dependency; in practice, however, the effect has been to increase dependency and remove the incentive to work.

We fully expect people to follow their self-interest in their business dealings; why should we be surprised when people follow their self-interest in their welfare dealings? That is why we propose a plan in which it is in the interest of every employable person to do his fair share of work.

The Operation of the New Approach

1. *We would assure an income foundation throughout every section of America for all parents who cannot adequately support themselves and their children.* For a family of four with less than $1,000 income, this payment would be $1600 a year; for a family of four with $2,000 income, this payment would supplement that income by $960 a year.

Under the present welfare system, each State provides "Aid to Families with Dependent Children," a program we propose to replace. The Federal government shares the cost, but each State establishes key eligibility rules and determines how much income support will be provided to poor families. The result has been an uneven and unequal system. The 1969 benefits average for a family of four is $171 a month across the Nation, but individual State averages range from $263 down to $39 a month.

A new Federal minimum of $1600 a year cannot claim to provide comfort to a family of four, but the present low of $468 a year cannot claim to provide even the basic necessities.

The new system would do away with the inequity of very low benefit levels in some States, and of State-by-State variations in eligibility tests, by establishing a Federally-financed income floor with a national definition of basic eligibility.

States will continue to carry an important responsibility. In 30 States the Federal basic payment will be less than the present levels of combined Federal and State payments. These States will be required to maintain the current level of benefits, but in no case will a State be required to spend more than 90% of its present welfare cost. The Federal government will not only provide the "floor," but it will assume 10% of the benefits now being paid by the States as their part of welfare costs.

In 20 States, the new payment would exceed the present average benefit payments, in some cases by a wide margin. In these States, where benefits are lowest and poverty often the most severe, the payments will raise benefit levels substantially. For 5 years, every State will be required to continue to spend at least half of what they are now spending on welfare, to supplement the Federal base.

For the *typical "welfare family"* — a mother with dependent children and no outside income — the new system would provide a basic national minimum payment. A mother with three small children would be assured an annual income of at least $1600.

For the *family headed by an employed father or working mother,* the same basic benefits would be received, but $60 per month of earnings would be "disregarded" in order to make up the costs of working and provide a strong advantage in holding a job. The wage earner could also keep 50% of his benefits as his earnings rise above that $60 per month. A family of four, in which the father earns $2,000 in a year, would receive payments of $960, for a total income of $2,960.

For the *aged, the blind and the disabled,* the present system varies benefit levels from $40 per month for an aged person in one State to $145 per month for the blind in another. The new system would establish a minimum payment of $65 per month for all three of these adult categories, with the Federal government contributing the first $50 and sharing in payments above that amount. This will raise the share of the financial burden borne by the Federal government for payments to these adults who cannot support themselves, and should pave the way for benefit increases in many States.

For the *single adult* who is not handicapped or aged, or for the *married couple without children,* the new system would not apply. Food stamps would continue to be available up to $300 per year per person, according to the plan I outlined last May in my message to the Congress on the food and nutrition needs of the population in poverty. For dependent families there will be an orderly substitution of food stamps by the new direct monetary payment.

2. *The new approach would end the blatant unfairness of the welfare system.* In over half the States, families headed by unemployed men do not qualify for public assistance. In no State does a family headed by a father working full-time receive help in the current welfare system, no matter how little he earns. As we have seen, this approach to dependency has itself been a cause of dependency. It results in a policy that tends to force the father out of the house.

The new plan rejects a policy that undermines family life. It would end the substantial financial incentives to desertion. It would extend eligibility to *all* dependent families with children, without regard to whether the family is headed by a man or a woman. The effects of these changes upon human behavior would be an increased will to work, the survival of more marriages, the greater stability of families. We are determined to stop passing the cycle of dependency from generation to generation.

The most glaring inequity in the old welfare system is the exclusion of families who are working to pull themselves out of poverty. Families headed by a non-worker often receive more from welfare than families headed by a husband working full-time at very low wages. This has been rightly resented by the working poor, for the rewards are just the opposite of what they should be.

3. *The new plan would create a much stronger incentive to work.* For people now on the welfare rolls, the present system discourages the move from welfare to work by cutting benefits too fast and too much as earnings begin.

The new system would encourage work by allowing the new worker to retain the first $720 of his yearly earnings without any benefit reduction.

For people already working, but at poverty wages, the present system often encourages nothing but resentment and an incentive to quit and go on relief where that would pay more than work. The new plan, on the contrary, would provide a supplement that will help a low-wage worker — struggling to make ends meet — achieve a higher standard of living.

For an employable person who just chooses not to work, neither the present system nor the one we propose would support him, though both would continue to support other dependent members in his family.

However, a welfare mother with preschool children should not face benefit reductions if she decides to stay home. It is not our intent that mothers of preschool children must accept work. Those who can work and desire to do so, however, should have the opportunity for jobs and job training and access to day care centers for their children; this will enable them to support themselves after their children are grown.

A family with a member who gets a job would be permitted to retain all of the *first $60 monthly income,* amounting to $720 per year for a regular worker, *with no reduction of Federal payments.* The incentive to work in this provision is obvious. But there is another practical reason: Going to work costs money. Expenses such as clothes, transportation, personal care, Social Security taxes and loss of income from odd jobs amount to substantial costs for the average family. Since a family does not begin to *add* to its net income until it surpasses the cost of working, in fairness that amount should not be subtracted from the new payment.

After the first $720 of income, the *rest* of the earnings will result in a systematic reduction in payments.

I believe the vast majority of poor people in the United States prefer to work rather than have the government support their families. In 1968, 600,000 families left the welfare rolls out of an average caseload of 1,400,000 during the year, showing a considerable turnover, much of it voluntary.

However, there may be some who fail to seek or accept work, even with the strong incentives and training opportunities that will be provided. It would not be fair to those who willingly work, or to all taxpayers, to allow others to choose idleness when opportunity is available. Thus, they must accept training opportunities and jobs when offered, or give their right to the new payments for themselves. No ablebodied person will have a "free ride" in a nation that provides opportunity for training and work.

4. *The bridge from welfare to work should be buttressed by training and child care programs.* For many, the incentives to work in this plan would be all that is necessary. However, there are other situations where these incentives need to be supported by measures that will overcome other barriers to employment.

*I propose that funds be provided for expanded training and job develop-
ment programs* so that an additional 150,000 welfare recipients can become
jobworthy during the first year.

Manpower training is a basic bridge to work for poor people, especially
people with limited education, low skills and limited job experience. Manpower training programs can provide this bridge for many of our poor. In
the new Manpower Training proposal to be sent to the Congress this week,
the interrelationship with this approach to welfare will be apparent.

*I am also requesting authority, as a part of the new system, to provide child
care* for the 450,000 children of the 150,000 current welfare recipients to be
trained.

The child care I propose is more than custodial. This Administration is
committed to a new emphasis on child development in the first five years of
life. The day care that would be part of this plan would be of a quality that
will help in the development of the child and provide for its health and
safety, and would break the poverty cycle for this new generation.

The expanded child care program would bring new opportunities along
several lines: opportunities for the further involvement of private enterprise
in providing high quality child care service; opportunities for volunteers;
and opportunities for *training and employment in child care centers of many
of the welfare mothers themselves.*

I am requesting a total of $600 million additional to fund these expanded
training programs and child care centers.

5. *The new system will lessen welfare red tape and provide administrative
cost savings.* To cut out the costly investigations so bitterly resented as "welfare snooping," the Federal payment will be based upon a certification of income, with spot checks sufficient to prevent abuses. The program will be
administered on an automated basis, using the information and technical experience of the Social Security Administration, but, of course, will be entirely
separate from the administration of the Social Security trust fund.

The States would be given the option of having the Federal Government
handle the payment of the State supplemental benefits on a reimbursable
basis, so that they would be spared their present administrative burdens and
so a single check could be sent to the recipient. These simplifications will
save money and eliminate indignities; at the same time, welfare fraud will
be detected and lawbreakers prosecuted.

6. *This new departure would require a substantial initial investment, but
will yield future return to the Nation.* This transformation of the welfare
system will set in motion forces that will lessen dependency rather than perpetuate and enlarge it. A more productive population adds to real economic
growth without inflation. The initial investment is needed now to stop the
momentum of work-to-welfare, and to start a new momentum in the opposite direction.

The costs of welfare benefits for families with dependent children have been rising alarmingly the past several years, increasing from $1 billion in 1960 to an estimated $3.3 billion in 1969, of which $1.8 billion is paid by the Federal government, and $1.5 billion is paid by the States. Based on current population and income data, the proposals I am making today will increase Federal costs during the first year by an estimated $4 billion, which includes $600 million for job training and child care centers.

The "start-up costs" of lifting many people out of dependency will ultimately cost the taxpayers far less than the chronic costs—in dollars and in national values—of creating a permanent under-class in America.

From Welfare to Work

Since this Administration took office, members of the Urban Affairs Council, including officials of the Department of Health, Education, and Welfare, the Department of Labor, the Office of Economic Opportunity, the Bureau of the Budget, and other key advisers, have been working to develop a coherent, fresh approach to welfare, manpower training and revenue sharing.

I have outlined our conclusions about an important component of this approach in this message; the Secretary of HEW will transmit to the Congress the proposal legislation after the summer recess.

I urge the Congress to begin its study of these proposals promptly so that laws can be enacted and funds authorized to begin the new system as soon as possible. Sound budgetary policy must be maintained in order to put this plan into effect—especially the portion supplementing the wages of the working poor.

With the establishment of the new approach, the Office of Economic Opportunity will concentrate on the important task of finding new ways of opening economic opportunity for those who are able to work. Rather than focusing on income support activities, it must find means of providing opportunities for individuals to contribute to the full extent of their capabilities, and of developing and improving those capabilities.

This would be the effect of the transformation of welfare into "workfare," a new work-rewarding system:

For the first time, all dependent families with children in America, regardless of where they live, would be assured of minimum standard payments based upon uniform and single eligibility standards.

For the first time, the more than two million families who make up the "working poor" would be helped toward self-sufficiency and away from future welfare dependency.

For the first time, training and work opportunity with effective incentives would be given millions of families who would otherwise be locked in to a welfare system for generations.

For the first time, the Federal government would make a strong contribution toward relieving the financial burden of welfare payments from State governments.

For the first time, every dependent family in America would be encouraged to stay together, free from economic pressure to split apart.

These are far-reaching effects. They cannot be purchased cheaply, or by piecemeal efforts. This total reform looks in a new direction; it requires new thinking, a new spirit and a fresh dedication to reverse the downhill course of welfare. In its first year, more than half the families participating in the program will have one member working or training.

We have it in our power to raise the standard of living and the realizable hopes of millions of our fellow citizens. By providing an equal chance at the starting line, we can reinforce the traditional American spirit of self-reliance and self-respect.

Total income	New benefit	Earned income
0	$1,600	$1,600
$500	1,600	2,100
$1,000	1,460	2,460
$1,500	1,210	2,710
$2,000	960	2,960
$2,500	710	3,210
$3,000	460	3,460
$3,500	210	3,710
$4,000	0	4,000

Note: For a 4-person family with a basic payment standard of $1600 and an earned income disregard of $720.

Epilogue

The "War on Poverty" was a watchword of the last half of the 1960's, with public attention frequently focused on the plight of America's poor or on the development of programs in their behalf. Yet the very word *poverty* has vanished from the 1970 Economic Report. Are we to conclude from this that the problem has been solved, or that concern with poverty was simply a fad of unusual duration? We can be certain of the answer to the first question, but concerned students may find it unsettling to contemplate the second. Given a feeling of concern, this book reflects an attempt to provide some of the equipment and materials needed for the transition from a general concern with "the problem of poverty" to deeper understanding — perhaps even to effective action.

Aside from depicting some of the features and incidence of poverty, with particular emphasis on the issue of discrimination, we have addressed ourselves to two major areas. First is the development of criteria for evaluation of the various facets of any social welfare program or proposal for reform. Awareness of the differing costs and benefits of competing programs has been stressed by the selections' authors with hardly an exception. Second, one of the most important questions to be raised in assessing a program should be its efficiency: How much of the total expenditure on the program gets to the people it is supposed to help? In this regard, children's allowances as an anti-poverty measure are quite inefficient in comparison with negative income taxation. Unfortunately, the objective of efficiency may conflict (as with the two programs just cited) with another criterion — filling the largest portion of the poverty gap.

Efficiency and effectiveness in eliminating poverty are but two of the tests which appear in a full recapitulation. Beyond these, lie a series of questions which focus on the various welfare programs' impacts on the rest of the economy and on the surrounding society. The classical objection to all taxation — particularly to that which reduces the savings ability of the society — must be recognized, although the student may wish to contend that this objection is of less importance to a wealthy, developed nation than to England in 1800 or India today. Against the possible cost to the economy in terms of growth rate must be set the economic and social costs which may be incurred through unrest associated with poverty and extremes of inequality. Similarly, we must be certain to include all the potential benefits of the program in our evaluation — to consider, for example, that children's allowances might stimulate more investment in the education of one's offspring than would AFDC, thereby having more powerful future effects on the elimination of poverty.

In concluding this incomplete listing of criteria for evaluation, I would place particular stress on the following point, one often overlooked in the development of programs: Social programs establish, wittingly or not, a set of pressures or prices to which people respond. Great care must be taken to identify these hidden prices and to be sure that the predictable response serves the goals of the program. The most obvious example must be the incentives contained in AFDC for the dissolution or concealment of the normal family unit. Misplaced incentives in a program can easily lead to distortion of other decision-making processes in our society.

Finally, as we look toward the future, it is proper to raise some broader, more speculative questions about income maintenance, and indeed about the role of a market system of income distribution in an increasingly wealthy America. Even if transfers of income to the poor entail a lower level of average income for the future, how should our valuation of the elimination of poverty be changed as those average family incomes rise to $10,000 and beyond? How does the addition to society's well-being vary, depending on whether the average goes up another $1,000 per non-poor family or whether we spend this increment on the eradication of poverty? What are we to make of Galbraith's point that, dollar-for-dollar, increased consumption by the well-off in America is of less value than the provision of more basic social and individual needs? If we cannot have as much of everything as we want, where does the elimination of poverty stand relative to our concern with the environment, with economic assistance to developing countries, or with any other of the desirable improvements we could make in our society and world?

To conclude on the most speculative plane, what is the future of our system of income distribution, based largely on compensation for provision of labor services or the ownership of capital? The prophets at Santa Barbara expect that one of the basic elements of the system — inputs of labor — will be eroded by rapid automation and computerization of production processes, which will destroy a predominant source of family incomes. There is little evidence (in a burst of exceptionally high rates of productivity increase, for example) to suggest that such a change in the fundamental ground-rules of American income distribution has begun, but the possibility of such a change should be considered by thoughtful citizens. After all, our record as a society with regard to handling past and present cases of breakdown in the work-income nexus leads to only modest confidence in the adequacy or swiftness with which we might respond to a future crisis.